Happy Reading
to Laura
from Sharon
Christmas, 1984

A
VERY
PRIVATE
EYE

A
VERY
PRIVATE
EYE

*An Autobiography
in Diaries and Letters*

Barbara Pym

Edited by Hazel Holt
and Hilary Pym

E. P. DUTTON, INC.   NEW YORK

Published in the United States by E. P. Dutton, Inc.,
2 Park Avenue, New York, N.Y. 10016

Library of Congress Catalog Card Number: 84-70153
ISBN: 0-525-24234-1

Published simultaneously in Canada by Fitzhenry and Whiteside Limited,
Toronto.

10 9 8 7 6 5 4 3 2 1
First Edition

Contents

List of Illustrations

Acknowledgements

We wish to express our thanks to Philip Larkin and Bob Smith who have kindly allowed us to use the letters they received from Barbara, which form a major part of the third section of this book. We are deeply grateful for their help and encouragement in so many ways.

Our thanks are also due to Henry Harvey and to Elsie Harvey for permission to use their letters from Barbara, and we are very grateful indeed to the former for his meticulous annotations which helped us to keep straight the chronology of the letters and the geographical whereabouts of the recipients. We would also like to thank Richard Roberts, who so kindly sent us Barbara's letters to him as well as the photograph which we wished to include in this volume.

We are greatly indebted to Tim Rogers and Colin Harris of the Bodleian Library, Oxford, for their friendly help and efficiency. Our grateful thanks are also due to Robert Liddell for valuable information and comments; to Honor Ellidge (Wyatt) for her help and support; to Sylvia James and Molly Marshall for a great deal of practical help that was quite invaluable; and to Tom Holt for his help in the preparation of the manuscript and for giving us the title for the book.

We are very conscious of the stimulus we have received from the many admirers and students of Barbara's work, especially visitors from the United States, who convinced us of the need for this book.

Finally, we would like to thank especially Alan Maclean and James Wright for Macmillan and Paul De Angelis of Dutton, whose advice and friendship Barbara so greatly valued in her lifetime, and who have, by their help and enthusiasm, made this book possible.

Note

The index contains biographical information, with cross-references under Christian names and nicknames, identification of places and vocabulary definitions as well as references to Barbara Pym's novels. Where the reference to an incident or a character is implied (i.e. where no actual reference to the title of the novel is made in the text) the page number is given in italics.

Preface

It is now possible to describe a place, a situation or a person as 'very Barbara Pym'. She is one of that small band of writers who have created a self-contained world, within which her characters move freely. This she achieved through her own personal, idiosyncratic view of life, expressed in a unique style. The development of that view and that style can be seen in the diaries, letters and notebooks which she left behind her, an incidental and eloquent commentary.

After Barbara's death in 1980, her sister Hilary and I (as her literary executor) received many requests for biographical information from scholars, in Britain and the United States, who were engaged in critical studies of her work, and it became apparent that an account of her life would be of value not only to them but also to those of her readers who simply wanted to know what she was like. But a conventional biography could hardly give a complete picture of Barbara; her shyness and reticence concealed much of the variety and complexity of her personality, even from those who had known her for many years. It was with some excitement, then, that we realised, as we went through her papers, that there was ample material for Barbara to tell her own story.

From 1931, with occasional breaks, she kept full diaries, recording the events of her life and her reactions to them. These were written – and certainly preserved – to be read, and are, especially those written in 1943, finished pieces of writing. Everything she wrote was distinctively hers and it is delightful to watch her style develop. Nevertheless, we find in these writings the spontaneity which gives to all diaries their quality of immediacy.

After the war she gave up keeping a formal diary, writing instead in a series of small notebooks, from 1948 until her death in 1980. In them she recorded not only events but random thoughts and ideas for her novels, so that they are, in effect, working notebooks.

She was also an entertaining letter-writer and her correspondence fills in the gaps in the narrative and illuminates various aspects of her work. The zealous preservation of these letters, some written many years ago, by their recipients is some indication of their quality.

From this material, then, we have been able to produce a kind of autobiography, using Barbara's own words and simply cutting and arranging it to form a coherent and continuous narrative.

The material fell naturally into three parts; the early years, mostly in Oxford – extrovert, full of naive enthusiasms; the more sombre and unhappy war years; and, finally, her life as a novelist, her success, her years of rejection, and her eventual reinstatement. For reasons of space and to avoid repetition, we have only used just over half the material. It is, however, all lodged in the Bodleian Library, Oxford ('Wouldn't it be marvellous if you could give all your love letters to the Bodleian and then go and read them 30 years later!'), and with it the manuscripts of her published and unpublished novels.

There are many references in the letters and notebooks to the characters and situations in her novels and parallels with her own experiences as well as her observations upon them. These will, of course, be of interest to scholars; but our main purpose has been to give to all who read and enjoy her novels another book by Barbara Pym.

The diaries will, I believe, come as something of a surprise to those who knew her only in her later life. I myself discovered aspects of her character that I had not known of in nearly 30 years of close friendship. I joined the staff of the International African Institute in 1950 and worked with Barbara for 25 years, for much of that time sharing a small office with her, editing monographs, seminar studies and articles and reviews for the Institute's journal *Africa*. It was, in fact, Barbara who taught me the craft of editing.

Through her eyes I saw the whole richness of academic life – the extraordinary quirks and foibles of eccentric personalities and the bizarre quality of the jargon – while her comic extrapolations and inventions (the Indigent Anthropologists' Food and Wine Fund, for example) made the earnest world of the Africanists a vastly entertaining place to inhabit. She infected me, too, with the fascination of finding out about people, and lunchtimes were often spent in public libraries, searching for clues in Crockford's, Kelly's Directories or street maps.

In the endless afternoons of office life and in our free time, we talked about her books and the characters she had created (what happened *after* Mildred had married Everard, what the original of

Rocky had really been like) so that the world of the novels soon became as much a part of our lives as the real world.

In 1956, Barbara gave me the first draft of *A Glass of Blessings* to read and asked for my comments. I made some (largely technical) suggestions which she adopted and I read the proofs for her. I did the same for the rest of her novels, and she asked me to be her literary executor. When she realised that she would only just live long enough to complete *A Few Green Leaves,* she said that she knew that I, with Hilary's help, would see it through the press for her.

From 1963 until 1977, when her work was not published, we discussed endlessly the reasons for this rejection. Her confidence was shaken and she only partially accepted the reassurances of her friends that it was the times that were out of joint and not her talents. But she never stopped writing, and there are several drafts of novels from this period. Her natural curiosity, her detective work, her 'research into the lives of ordinary people' continued, to become (especially in the notebooks) what the keeping of field notes is to an anthropologist.

Throughout these years she had the comfort and stability of a happy life with her sister Hilary, with whom she shared a home for most of her life. The domestic routine of Harriet and Belinda in *Some Tame Gazelle* gives a foretaste of what life was to be like in Brooksville Avenue or Barn Cottage and the affection and amity of the two sisters in the novel is a loving mirror of their relationship.

Even though she could no longer call herself a published novelist, Barbara had evolved a pleasant life, with her work at the Institute, a life 'bounded by English literature and the Anglican church and small pleasures like sewing and choosing dress material for this uncertain summer'. But, as she had decided as far back as 1938, that was not enough. With no real hope that it would ever be published, she wrote *Quartet In Autumn* 'to please myself and a few friends'.

But, unlike so much of modern life and literature, there was to be a kind of happy ending. In 1977, both Lord David Cecil and Philip Larkin, writing in *The Times Literary Supplement,* chose her as one of the most underrated novelists of the century. Her literary reputation was restored, indeed enlarged. She was, and still is, sometimes compared with Jane Austen. Barbara herself regarded this as mildly blasphemous. Of a visit to Jane Austen's house she wrote in her diary:

"I put my hand down on Jane's desk and bring it up covered with dust. Oh that some of her genius might rub off on me!"

She lived long enough to publish three more books and to have the pleasure of being shortlisted for the Booker Prize.

In her later years, Barbara took up the making of patchwork. The analogy with her novels is striking: each patch or incident is not only the best, most representative piece of fabric, cut to precisely the right shape and fitted neatly into the whole, but it is also evocative of the source from which it is derived. Here then, in this book, are the original lengths of material from which she fashioned her novels.

Hazel Holt

A
VERY
PRIVATE
EYE

The Early Life

by

Hilary Pym

Barbara Mary Crampton Pym was born on 2 June 1913, the first child of Frederic Crampton Pym, solicitor, of Oswestry, Shropshire, and Irena Spenser Pym, who had been married at Oswestry Parish Church on 26 October 1911 when he was thirty-two and she was twenty-five.

Frederic Crampton Pym's father is stated on the marriage certificate to be Thomas Pym, farmer, deceased, but this is not in fact the case. Frederic was the illegitimate child of Phoebe Pym, Thomas Pym's daughter, a domestic servant, of Poundisford Park Lodge, Pitminster, Somerset, and no father's name is given on the birth certificate. (This information only came to light after Barbara's death in 1980, and, alas, she never knew about it.) The name Crampton, which he in turn gave to his two children, suggests to me that his father's name was Crampton. The following is a brief summary of my research and speculation up to date:

Poundisford Park, Somerset, was in 1879, the year of Frederic's birth, the home of Edmund Bourdillon and his family, and Phoebe Pym was presumably a servant in their employ. At Fosgrove House nearby lived the author A. W. Kinglake. He and his friend the Irish author Eliot Warburton, and members of the Bourdillon family, were all at Cambridge and were later called to the Bar. It is quite likely that at Cambridge they would have known members of the Crampton family, also from Ireland and also connected with the legal profession; and it seems not impossible that a Crampton could have been staying at Poundisford Park during the period in question. Phoebe Pym emigrated to Canada (information from her father Thomas Pym's will) some time before 1900; she had already left Poundisford by 1881 (census returns). Frederic was educated in Taunton and then articled to a firm of solicitors there, through the generosity, I imagine, of public men in Taunton, like the Badcocks and the Whites, who were also friends of the Bourdillon family. He met Irena Thomas on holiday at Ilfracombe in Devon about 1910.

Irena Spenser Thomas was the daughter of Edward Thomas of Oswestry, who founded an ironmongery business in the town in 1865. She was the youngest of ten children. The Thomas family were originally farmers in the border country round Llanrhaeadr-ym-Mochnant and traced their ancestry back to the early Welsh kings and beyond.

I imagine it was the fact that Irena Thomas came from Oswestry that made Frederic Pym decide to set up in practice there, once she had agreed to marry him – and he was already practising in Shropshire, in Wellington and Shrewsbury, when they met – but by a strange coincidence there is an Oswestry connection further back in the Crampton family: in 1857 George Ribton Crampton, barrister-at-law of Dublin, married Helen Roden Croxon, daughter of the banker John Croxon of Oswestry.

Their first home in Oswestry was 72 Willow Street, where Barbara was born on 2 June 1913. Then they moved to Welsh Walls where I was born in 1916; but the house which was to be our real childhood home was Morda Lodge, a substantial, square red-brick Edwardian house with a large garden on the outskirts of the town on the way to Morda. Next door to it was Scotswood, where the Thomas relations lived, grandmother and Aunts May and Janie. Visiting them (which was often) was just a question of climbing over the garden wall.

It was a happy, unclouded childhood. In those days there was domestic help, two maids who slept in a candle-lit room at the top of the house next to the 'box-room', with a picture of an apple-cheeked Victorian child; one of them took the role of Nanny. Our father was extremely good-tempered, undemanding and appreciative. He walked to his office every day in the middle of the town, and came home for lunch. Sometimes we would visit him there, at the Cross, up a narrow flight of stairs to the small book-lined rooms, where he had a clerk and a girl typist. He was not called up in the first world war because he had a stiff knee as a result of an injury while running (in his Somerset days). This didn't prevent him from becoming a very good golfer later on. Our mother was athletic too – she had been a keen hockey-player in her youth and rather regretted, I think, that neither Barbara nor I showed much enthusiasm for games or energetic things like cycling (though I did well at golf in my teens).

We had a small paddock in which we kept a pony called Mogus, not for riding but for driving in a governess cart. Morda Lodge had a stable (which later became a garage) with a harness room and a loft above it where we used to play games. We kept hens, too, somewhere in this region, so there were sacks of what used to be called 'Indian corn' and other things.

I can't remember when Barbara made up nicknames for our mother and father, or why, but they stuck and were soon taken for granted. She was 'Links' and he was 'Dor'. Our favourite Aunt Janie was 'Ack'. I suppose this could be taken as an early example of an original mind at work! I soon became part of her stories and scenes, perhaps as 'little fishy' or 'a fierce drowdle'. She had a very protective attitude towards me, and an early remark, often quoted later by our mother, was 'What are you doing to Hilary? Put her down.'

Church was a natural part of our lives because our mother was assistant organist at the parish church of St Oswald, and her family had always been on social terms with the vicar, curates and organists. Having curates to supper was a long-established tradition; and for Barbara and me there were children's parties at the vicarage. Our father, too, sang bass in the church choir. Barbara and I started our church-going with the children's service on Sunday afternoons for which our mother would be playing. One might sometimes sit on the organ-stool with her. Music and acting were important to both our parents: they were members of the Oswestry Operatic Society in the 1920s, the heyday of amateur productions of Gilbert and Sullivan, and they both took leading roles. I suppose it was this influence that was responsible for Barbara's first (publicly recognised) creative work, an operetta called *The Magic Diamond*, which was performed at Morda Lodge in April 1922. The 'Morda Lodge Operatic Society' consisted of us and our Selway cousins. Our mother's sister Nellie was married to C. J. Selway and lived at Hatch End in Middlesex. Their four children were our favourite cousins and used to come and spend Christmas and Easter with us. Family ceremonials evolved, rituals like the sugar mice on the Christmas cake and celluloid animals in our stockings (nowadays they would be considered too dangerous!).

Apart from Gilbert and Sullivan (which of course we knew by heart) our mother taught us songs like 'Oh Oh Antonio', 'Going to School' (both quoted in *Less than Angels*), 'The Poodledog' and the first-world-war song 'We're going to tax your butter, your sugar and your tea'. One of her favourite books which she would read to us was *The Adventures of a Donkey*, a translation of La Comtesse de Ségur's *Memoires d'un Ane*. We always liked animals better than dolls. There were also many family jokes and sayings: it was she who encouraged

3

Barbara to write and me to draw, and I'm sure it was her determination that sent us away to a boarding school rather than continue our education in Oswestry. Barbara was twelve when she went as a boarder to Liverpool College, Huyton. I missed her very much, just as I had missed her when she went to her first school and I had (apparently) spent the whole day waiting at the gate for her to come home!

I can't remember that we ever asked about our father's family in Somerset – we seemed to have plenty of relations and a very full life. There was a biography of John Pym in the house, with the name 'Harriet Pym' on the flyleaf (my father's grandmother, I think). The story we were told, regarding the name Pym, was that we were descended from the brother of John Pym the Parliamentarian – but I'm sure we never checked it. (I don't think there's any evidence that John Pym ever had a brother.) There was one Taunton connection that we did know about: Frank and Mildred White were great friends of our father and one gathered that he had been brought up in their house during part of his youth. Mildred White was my godmother.

At Huyton Barbara had an average career, not being particularly good at anything that counted; but she was chairman of the Literary Society. (The senior English mistress was Hélène Lejeune, sister of C. A. Lejeune, the film critic.) During this period she wrote poems and parodies. Huyton was a very disciplined school and there was a lot of local churchgoing – this was before the dedication of the School Chapel, recalled by Mildred and Dora in an episode in *Excellent Women* – and her friends remember her amusing observations and fantasies about the different clergy and other characters who appeared on the scene. During her school years too, influenced by our family interest in golf and the fact that our cousin N. C. Selway was a Cambridge blue, she started the Hartley Book, a detailed record of the achievements of the two famous golfing brothers, Lister and Rex of the jam-making firm. It goes up to 1931 and includes autograph letters from them both. Meanwhile, her early reading of Edgar Wallace and Kipling (both admired by our father) and a lesser-known sleuth from *The Scout*, Frank Darrell, 'the man of many faces', had given place, when she was sixteen, to poetry and the novels of Aldous Huxley.

In 1931 Barbara went to Oxford to read English at St Hilda's. From 1932 we have her own account of those days. I followed her there three years later (to Lady Margaret Hall to read classics). Being younger, I was rather in awe of her circle of friends at first, but we gradually began to have friends in common. It was never our

4

particular intention, in spite of the prophetic circumstances of *Some Tame Gazelle*, which she had started in 1934, to live together, but it somehow turned out that from about 1938 right up until the time of her death in 1980 we were never apart for more than a year or so at a time. In 1946, when I left my husband Sandy Walton, we started sharing a flat in London, then in 1961 we bought a house, and eventually, in 1972, a country cottage in Oxfordshire.

We didn't necessarily do everything together – our different jobs after the war (Barbara worked at the International African Institute and I was already in the BBC) gave us a variety of interests and friends and holidays – but the bond between us was strong enough to keep us always on good terms. As we both got older, our lives did come together more. There never seemed to be too much argument about who did what in our domestic round: we both genuinely liked housework, but Barbara was by nature better at cooking and planning meals (a fact borne out by the interest in food in her books). I never got the feeling that she shut herself away to write, as she always seemed to be available and enjoyed social life and entertaining. I suppose I was in some ways more practical and down-to-earth; I also earned more money, but this never caused difficulties or came between us. As our salaries were the only money we had, it was there to be used.

We had a saying that Barbara used to make things happen by writing about them. It seemed to become increasingly true, and could sometimes work in reverse. Or it might produce rather alarming results, as for example when a church that she had brought into a book might become redundant or be demolished. Not so with the shared life of 'Belinda and Harriet', which started well and ran a good course.

Part I

OXFORD

1932–1939

To a young girl coming straight from boarding school, Oxford in the early 1930s must have seemed like total freedom – a room of one's own, no more timetables, self-expression in one's clothes and the opportunity, after living in a one-sex community, to meet Men. The old chaperone rules had gone and the remaining restrictions (signing the book if you wanted to be out after 10.30 and never being allowed to entertain men in your room) seemed negligible. Barbara went up to Oxford in 1931 eager for a lively social life as well as for academic achievement.

She planned a whole new wardrobe of clothes (an abiding passion), many of which she made herself, and evolved a decorative scheme for her room at St Hilda's which featured checked gingham and a doll called Wellerina, of a kind then very fashionable.

Her cushions were embroidered SANDRA, which was the name she had given herself, and the name she often uses in her diaries to indicate the more dashing aspects of her character. This name may have been (as her friend Robert Liddell suggests) short for Cassandra, but it seems possible that it was simply a name she considered glamorous and sophisticated, being short for Alexandra and thus having overtones of Russian and Central European aristocracy.

She was a tall, good-looking girl, very extrovert and entertaining, and she had many admirers – the ratio of women undergraduates to men being quite disproportionate. These early diaries are written with a kind of breathless vivacity and a vibrant enjoyment of everything that Oxford had to offer, both intellectual (her love of 'our greater English poets' – a source of comfort as well as pleasure in later years – was born here) and social. There was an endless round of dinners, tea parties, sherry parties (a newly fashionable form of entertainment), theatres and, above all, the cinema, to which she went several times a week and even, amazingly, on Christmas Day.

All these activities she recorded with enthusiasm but also with style. There is no doubt that she was a born writer. The fluency of her writing, the vividness of her descriptions and the sharp observation of comic detail are all

9

present from the beginning. The style had to be polished and the craft learned, but the fundamentals were there, bright and true. Her first attempt at novel writing, Young Men in Fancy Dress *(1929), was dedicated to a perceptive friend 'who kindly informed me that I had the makings of a style of my own'.*

After her meeting with Henry Harvey (Lorenzo), a deeper, sadder theme develops and the writing becomes more mature and introverted.

She had always had a passion for 'finding out' about people who interested or attracted her. Tracking people down and looking them up were part of her absorbing interest (that continued all her life) in 'research into the lives of ordinary people'. Her researches ranged from looking people up in Who's Who, Crockford *or street directories to the actual 'tailing' of the object of her investigation. She was very resourceful at this and often said that she would have made a good detective. Her powers of observation and research were certainly of great benefit to her as a novelist.*

Barbara noticed Henry Harvey at lectures and in the Bodleian Library and had thoroughly investigated him (tracking him around Oxford and asking a friend to look at his pile of books in the Bodleian to find out his name) long before she actually got him to speak to her. Henry was two years older than she, and he and his friend Robert Liddell (Jock), who was then working on the staff of the Bodleian, seemed very much her intellectual superiors. 'I was inclined to be rather aggressive in my "lowness", talking about dance music etc. I think I did this because I felt intellectually inferior to them.'

In 1934 she went on a National Union of Students' tour of Germany and in Cologne she met Hanns Woischnick and Friedbert Gluck, who were officially entertaining the student party. Both young men were attracted to her and she and Friedbert had a love affair which continued for several years, both by letter and when Barbara visited Germany again in 1935 (when they went to Prague together) and in 1937. These were the early days of National Socialism but Barbara was far more concerned with the language, poetry and the general romanticism and Stimmung *of Germany than the politics, which interested her not at all. She was really rather naive:*

There was much merriment – shouting and singing too – English and German songs. We sang *God Save the King* and *Deutschland Uber Alles* – that rather worried Friedbert, although I couldn't understand why. He and Hanns had an animated talk about it in German.

She found Friedbert glamorous ('The Germans are glorious to flirt with') and good for her self-confidence ('The Germans appreciate me even if the English [i.e. Henry Harvey] don't').

In 1934 Henry Harvey took up an appointment at the University of Helsingfors and in 1937 he married a Finnish girl, Elsie Godenhjelm. Barbara was badly hurt, though characteristically, she wrote them lively,

satirical letters (some in the styles of Ivy Compton-Burnett and Stevie Smith)
and even some to 'My darling sister Elsie'.

She divided her time between Oswestry and Oxford, with occasional visits
to her relations at Hatch End, living on a very small allowance from her
family. 'I wrote home [from Oxford] for some books to try to sell them' and 'I
want so terribly to go to Germany again and I am 12/10d overdrawn.' At that
period there was no pressure on girls to take up any sort of job or career, many of
her social class simply remained at home until they married or as 'the daughter
at home' if they did not. Barbara already knew that she was going to be a
writer. In 1934 she wrote:

Sometime in July I began to write a story about Hilary and me as
spinsters of fiftyish. Henry and Jock and all of us appeared in it. I
sent it to them and they liked it very much. So I am going on with it
and one day it may become a book.

This was Some Tame Gazelle, *'my novel of real people'. It was, in fact,*
the only one of her novels whose characters were taken directly from life:
Belinda was Barbara herself, Harriet was Hilary, Henry was Henry
Harvey, Agatha was Alison West-Watson, Lady Clara Boulding was Julia
Pakenham, John Akenside was John Barnicot, Dr Nicholas Parnell was
Robert Liddell, Edith Liversidge was Honor Tracy and Ricardo Bianco was
Count Roberto Weiss.

She finished the novel, revised it and had it typed by November 1935 and
sent it to Chatto and to Gollancz, both of whom rejected it. She then sent it to
Cape. In August 1936 she had a letter from Jonathan Cape himself, saying
that if she would make certain minor alterations 'I may be able to offer to
publish it.' She made the alterations and returned the manuscript but in
September it was sent back to her with a letter from him.

It is with very great regret that I do not find myself in a position to
make you an offer to publish your novel. There is not here the
unanimity of appreciation of the book's chances that I feel is
essential for successful publication. Personally I like your novel, but
I fear that if I were to offer to publish it, we should be unable to give it
all the care and attention which I feel are necessary if it is to be
successfully launched.

This rejection distressed her very much, and she put the novel aside.

(After the war she revised it and sent it to Jonathan Cape again. This time
he 'read it with interest and pleasure'. It was accepted and published in
1950.)

Some Tame Gazelle, *even in its earliest form, was a considerable*
achievement. It was unusual enough for a girl of twenty-two to choose to make
her heroine fifty years of age, but to have created such a believable middle-aged

world was quite remarkable. The observation and language were already mature, the cadences of speech were idiosyncratic and the handling of character wholly assured.

In December 1937 she had a very consciously Romantic encounter in Oxford with a young undergraduate six years her junior. 'Oh how absurd and delicious it is to be in love with somebody younger than yourself! everybody should try it.'

This theme, the love of a woman for a younger man, occurred again later in her own life and she used the experiences with great delicacy in several of her novels, The Lumber Room *(an unfinished novel started in 1938),* The Sweet Dove Died *and* An Unsuitable Attachment.

In August 1938, realising she had to leave Oxford, she went to Poland to teach English to the daughter of Dr Michal Alberg in Katowice, but she had to return to England after only a few weeks because of the worsening political situation. She enjoyed the experience and noted, as always, the unusual:

Went into the town by myself. Saw a large animal like a wolf hanging up outside a provision shop. After supper a Polish cavalry officer and his wife came in. They were sitting drinking tea and eating *Kuchen*. A lovely picture.

Went to Czestochowa by car with Mme A. Forests and barefoot peasants. Saw a wonderful church – turquoise marble, pink, grey, white fawn, green crochet work around the pulpit and altars in green and puce. Virgin Mary portrait with doors sliding over it.

Went into a dark romantic forest (belonging to the Prince of Pless). Had tea at a deserted Beergarden – great *Stimmung*. Walked in the forest and visited a Golf Club. Very nice clubhouse, all notices written in English.

Back in England she and Hilary, who was now taking a secretarial course, moved into rooms in London in Upper Berkeley Street ('Hilary paid £1.5s.2d. for my rooms'). Hilary got a job as a secretary with the BBC and Barbara worked hard at her writing.

The war was coming nearer. There were 'territorials, with rifles but no uniforms, in the streets' and she met again Dr Alberg and his family, now refugees from Poland. 'One almost thinks how comforting to be in the obituaries . . . "in her 93rd year".'

In July she returned to Oswestry to make black-out curtains and help to prepare the house to receive six evacuees from Birkenhead.

H.H.

1932

15 January. A new term in a new year – a golden opportunity to get a peer's heir – a worthy theological student – or to change entirely! But Oxford really is intoxicating.

26 April. Today was an important day. I went to tea with Rupert Gleadow in George Steer's sitting room – it was littered with books and we had tea off a table covered with a skin – on his sofa were lovely leopard skins. We ate a large tea and talked much. We got on amazingly well – Rupert was far more human than I'd thought. It surprised me when he put his hand on mine – and when he asked me to kiss him I was even more amazed but I refused! Went to the Union in the evening too sleepy to realise the brilliance of Philip Guedalla's speech.

28 April. Was in the Bodleian with Mary Sharp – coming out at lunchtime we met Rupert at the corner of Catte St. Neither of us knew quite what to say – a bad sign – or good. In the afternoon I had a letter from him in green ink, which cheered me up, as I was in the middle of a foul Sidney–Spenser essay. I saw him just before tea and he came back into St Hilda's with me. After tea I returned to the Bod. – tried to finish my essay – but naturally I was thinking about Rupert the whole time.

29 April. I met Rupert at Carfax at 10.15. We went into Stewart's and had coffee – then we wandered down the Banbury Road and thereabouts in the pouring rain. When we were thoroughly wet we went to 47 and drank some sherry. I remember putting my arms round him and loving him, because he was very wet and shivering and looked at me so sweetly.

2 June. My 19th birthday. I worked – or rather tried to – in the Bod. till 12, when Rupert came for me. He was wearing his purple subfusc coat. We went out to Elliston's and he bought me a heavenly scarf. Royal blue and orange. We went into St Hilda's, sat on a seat, and because of the ever-present and watchful eyes, behaved very well. Dinner at Stewart's with Miles and Rupert. Then *Frankenstein* at the Super – Miles laughed so I couldn't be terrified. I loved stealing surreptitious glances at Rupert's profile – and was very thrilled by him.

5 June. A fine morning – I went with Rupert up to Boars Hill – we went into a wood and sheltered from the showers under trees. He was very Theocritean and loving. I got a wee bit sick of it – but tried to please him as I was determined to treat him as kindly as possible as he'd Schools on the 9th.

7 June. In the evening we had a last do before Schools – Miles came too and it was great fun. Dinner at Stewart's plus liqueurs, then *The Case of the Frightened Lady* at the Super. I felt sad but happy saying goodbye to Rupert. Sad because I thought I wasn't going to see him for ages – so I thought – happy because I liked him so much.

13 June. I had a note from Rupert and Miles asking me to go to the flicks. I dashed to Carfax at 7.30 and we went to *Goodnight Vienna* at the Queener. It was lovely, and somehow appropriate. We sat at the back in the corner and I had two arms around me for the first time in my history. The flick was over at 10, so we stopped at the coffee stall by Cowley Place on our way back. We drank to each other in chocolate Horlicks.

15 June. In the afternoon went on the river with Rupert and Miles. We had tea at the Cherwell tea gardens. Much semi-nakedness to be seen on the river. We landed at a bank and Rupert dropped his watch in the water. He had to undress and fish for it – but didn't get it.

16 June. Had my report in the morning, and a letter from R. on Air Squadron paper. The former amused me much – keen, etc. – I seem to give rather a good impression of myself! In the afternoon it was Rupert and Miles' Viva. In the evening I met R. at the corner of the Turl and he told me the joyous news that they'd both got Firsts, and gave me a letter which he was bringing, written in all different coloured inks and pencils. I was overjoyed!

19 June. In the morning Sharp and I went to the University sermon – Dr Alington. It was somewhat dull I thought and full of blaa and waffle. We prayed for Trinity a good deal – as he came from there. Went on the river in the afternoon. I found it thoroughly depressing, as it was crowded with townspeople, all of whom seemed to have gramophone records of 'Ain't it grand to be blooming well dead'.

20 June. Rupert and I drank chocolate at the Queener – and went on to 47. Oh blessed George Steer and his lovely leopard skins – I hope he gets a First! This kind of a *Private Lives* love scene was far better in reality than in anticipation. A somewhat hurried meal at Elliston's – for at 2.15 we were taking George Steer and Geoffrey Grimwood to Ramsden in R.'s car. Both men are very typical of the House – particularly G.G. – in voice and dress. R. and I were very staid and sober. After we'd dropped them we drove on all over the place – Great Tew – Charlbury, where we had tea at a pub. Then we went back into Oxford plus the two Christ Church men and met Miles at 47. After drinking sherry we went to Stewart's and the Super. I just got in for 10 o'clock.

21 June. Rupert came for me and we wandered about talking in broken English. We went into Trinity and Rupert telephoned Prof. Griffith. He kissed me in the telephone box, having heard that a man was progged for a similar offence!

22 June. We dined at Stewart's (upstairs) and I felt in a v. sentimental, sad mood – mainly because the radio (or whatever it is) played *'Auf Wiedersehen'*. Then we went to 47 – finished up George Steer's port. We all behaved rather appallingly and I was escorted back to St Hilda's by 10. I felt very lonely as all my friends had gone down – and I was sleeping in my new room – which seemed very large and infested with moths!

23 June. Rupert and I went to buy some things for lunch – as we intended to take it with us on the river. We then took Miles up to Boars Hill as he had to see Prof. Griffith. Rupert and I went to a pub to get some gin and then waited for Miles in the car. There it was that Rupert said to me Marvell's 'To his Coy Mistress' and 'Definition of Love'. And I had never heard them before. The more one talks with him the more one realises that he really *is* brilliant – in all sorts of ways. Then on to the river, from the Cherwell Arms, where we drove in the car. Getting into the punt I half fell in – and Miles got his trousers entirely wet trying to rescue me. We had an amusing time getting dry. I lay on my tummy in the middle of the punt – Rupert punted and Miles sat at the other end with his trousers on the end of a paddle. I rushed back to St Hilda's and changed, then we met at 131 Iffley Road and decided to dine out of Oxford. We went to the Spreadeagle at Thame – Lovely! Before dinner we wandered about in the charming garden – the flowers seem to grow at random but it is very well planned. Then we ate a marvellous dinner – at which everything ordinary (i.e. fish) tasted extraordinarily good. We finished with yellow Chartreuse – Rupert laughed at me because it made me cough.

24 June. Rupert and Miles came and we went off for lunch. In Stewart's they played *'Wien du Stadt meiner Träume'* – I heard it for the first time there. At the station I held Miles' and Rupert's hands tightly and gazed into their blue and brown eyes respectively. Then we said goodbye and I settled down to a sober journey home. A marvellous ending to a marvellous term.

July. The Long Vacation. Oswestry. At first I was bored but gradually settled down – letters from Rupert and Miles helped things considerably. On 8 July I went to Huyton for the weekend – it was fun seeing people again – but tiring having to look and be somewhat sophisticated and there was *rather* a lot of chapel. On 19 July Rupert sent me *The Weekend Book* most charmingly inscribed – and a long letter – one of the nicest I've ever had from him. He has bought an aeroplane.

15 September. On this day Rupert came. I went to meet him at 3.23, wearing a summer frock and a yellow jersey (it was a hot day) – feeling very excited. He arrived in his white shorts and not as disreputable as he said he'd be. I was pleased to find him about 20 times nicer looking than his photo.

16 September. We walked up to Llynclys Hill, and when up by Jacob's Ladder found a convenient resting place and had our lunch there. Rupert had some beer (which I tasted) and I had Dry Ginger. We walked up again to the hill and made ourselves comfortable in the sun. We lay half asleep with our faces close to each other for a long time. We laughed out of sheer happiness. Had supper alone, which was lovely, we were both feeling excited and happy. Went to the flicks and saw Marie Dressler in *Emma*.

17 September. Went out to Pant on the 2 bus and up on to the hill. Seeing me run down a hill Rupert gave me the name Atalanta. I think we managed to behave fairly well thro' supper, but I was still feeling ridiculous, and drank some beer out of a cup.

21 September. We talked a lot – or rather Rupert did and I listened – about his father and Trinity and lots of things. Before we went out he had made the suggestion that we should go to bed – we had much fun and a fight over that. It was a very cold evening and I felt very tired, but we went down Weston Lane and looked at the stars. I said that the happiness one got out of love was worth any unhappiness it might (and generally does) bring. I can't remember what Rupert said but he wasn't so sure about it not having had the experience I suppose.

22 September. I helped Rupert to pack – he went in a hat and looked about 17! I would have loved to go to the Lakes with him and Miles. It was seriously rather awful parting from him, we'd had such a heavenly week together. I'd never imagined it would be so good. I actually wept a bit!

Michaelmas Term

9 October. Met Rupert in New College Lane at 12, and went back with him to his digs. Then we met Miles in Stewart's and had lunch. A happy reunion – it was marvellous.

13 October. Went to the Bod. On the way back met Rupert in dark suit and white tie – he persuaded me to have lunch at the Randolph with his mother and brother Edmund. I was, of course, terrified, but my fur coat gave me some confidence! Mrs G. is very nice and talkative, not like Rupert in any way. Edmund is vaguely like him – uglier – but he has 'personal magnetism'. We trailed into the Sheldonian where I explained various things such as the Proctor's Walk. Miles was also having his degree – he and Rupert were the handsomest men there, as far as I could see. Then, when the ceremony was over, and we had admired their white fur, we adjourned to Fullers for tea. Edmund was funny and kept putting things into my hand (sugar, pennies) when I stretched it out in my characteristic way.

15 October. Today I must always remember I suppose. I went to tea with Rupert (and ate a pretty colossal one) – and he with all his charm, eloquence and masculine wiles, persuaded . . . . [Here several pages have been torn out.]

23 October. I went to see Rupert in the morning and stayed to lunch. We had a delightfully domesticated time over the fire and nearly went to sleep – then we had to go just before tea, as he was having it with Professor Myres. I went and had tea with my female friends, and went to St Mary's in the evening.

3 November. Rupert called for me and we went for a long and energetic walk it being such a fine afternoon. I was hatless and Atalantesque in blue.

5 November. Guy Fawkes day. In the evening we ventured out – first we went along to Norham Gardens to call for some Bradfordians. (I was with Mary Sharp and Dorothy Pedley.) We took a bus and it nosed its way thro' the Corn – which was very crowded. We took many buses and then plucked up courage to walk down the Broad where it met the Corn. We saw a lot of drunks though – one being carried in the Broad – shouting 'Blast you, you bloody fools – you're busting my braces!' – also (when we had ventured into the Corn by Woolworth's) one who called me Charlotte – two propping themselves up in the middle of the road. Nothing thrilling happened – people rushed about in crowds – everyone followed but it always seemed to be a false alarm. Very few fireworks were thrown. We were back by 11.10.

1933

17 January. Nichol Smith's lecture on Swift and Pope at Schools. Lorenzo was there. Found a letter from Rupert awaiting me – he called in the afternoon, and I found myself remarkably glad to see him. After tea we went out and Rupert bought a B.A. gown. Sharp, Pedley and self went out with the intention of seeing *Grand Hotel*, but we found the queue so long that we abandoned our efforts. We had a coffee at Stewart's, and then went to a show at the New Theatre – Variety – but Jack Payne too! The variety was bearable – all the jokes extremely vulgar – they were applauded uproariously by the largely undergraduate audience! Jack Payne and band were heavenly – they played mostly things one knew, and did a lot of comedy stuff. I liked the 'rendering' of 'We Just Couldn't Say Goodbye' – also 'Round the Bend of the Road' and of course 'Love is the Sweetest Thing'!

18 January. A full day of lectures. Percy Simpson at 12 was singularly amusing – he read some priceless letters of the 17th Century describing a masque where everyone was tight. Lorenzo was there. I'm convinced that he hates me. Our gazes meet, and he half smiles – but it is a cynical sort of smile. His affectation intrigues me.

25 January. This diary seems to be going to turn into the Saga of Lorenzo. In P. Simpson he sat next but one to me – so that I was able to observe him. He has beautiful hands – rather too beautiful but eminently the right thing for him. He has twinkling (but not pleasantly twinkling) hazel-brown eyes, like a duck's I think. And what a mouth! He is able to curl it in the most fascinatingly repulsive sneering smile. He walks swiftly in his effortless yet affected manner. His writing is very small and mingy – the lines sloping upwards to the left (he uses plain paper).

26 January. I didn't see Lorenzo at all until the evening in the Bod. at about 4.50. I sat nearly opposite him – not on the same row. He doesn't like being observed but often looks at you in his malicious way. (I hope I may be wrong – but I'm not optimistic about it). He had with him his nice herring-boney grey tweed overcoat – also the pathetic green scarf and little brown leather gloves – lined with lambs-wool. He had lots of books out spread over the desk next to him as well as his own. He had a book I wanted, I believe, but my courage failed when it came to asking him – in fact I couldn't really consider it at all. He was writing a lot, sprawling over his desk and tilting his chair in his peculiar manner, evidently he had a tutorial – he seemed in a hurry because he actually ran. He seemed to have a cold (his nose was a little red) – and coughed several times – also a vaguely hectic flush – or was it my over-solicitous imagination? At about 7 coming past Magdalen I saw him in the lodge – looking lovely and rather flushed. Oh dear!

29 January. During this week Lorenzo – whose real name is Henry Stanley Harvey – has been much in my thoughts – in spite of being very conscious of each other, nothing seems to happen!

12 February. Bod. in the afternoon, but I did no work. Lorenzo was there – all hectic finishing an essay. We went back to the Bod. at 6. Lorenzo was still there – even more dishevelled than he had been 2 hours previously. He rushed out to his tutorial, wearing a hat (brown) and looking very sweet. We progress not at all.

11 February. Lorenzo was at the Christ Church play. So was I. He was with Robert Liddell – what a long neck Lorenzo has. Black flannel bags and a curious striped coat.

12 February. A very nice intimate tea party with Mr H. H. Harker, St John's. He gives me so much enjoyment.

13 February. I love Lorenzo – I mean *love* in my peculiar way. And I had thought I was getting over it. I don't think he cares a damn about me – but sometimes vague and marvellous doubts arise – I went to the Dictionary and looked up a word – (an entirely fatuous word) becoz he was there – i.e. *'Pentatremite* – an echinoderm of the genus Pentatremites belonging to the extinct class Blastoidea, allied to the Crinoids'– Is that a definition of me – Lorenzo – or both of us?

1 March. Yesterday a delightful lunch party at Trinity. Barbara Flower and Cordelia Wintour, Rupert, Frederic Wells and Hal Summers. Wells is sweet, but too intellectual – the girls were too intellectual and didn't have the compensation of being of the opposite sex.

Vacation. March–April. Oswestry.
The weather has been perfect – and this is my favourite season of year. It has been very right for all this Lorenzo business. Chestnut trees just coming out – pale, almost-too-good-to-be-true green – blue skies, daffodils and best of all cherry trees in half and full flowers. My attitude to Nature is 18th century I know. But oh marvellous days!

Trinity Term

21 April. Good to be back again! Bought a lovely fat book at Blackwell's to write my novel in (plain paper). In the evening – after dinner Rosemary and I went along to Laurence Whistler's rooms – but he wasn't in. I amused myself by looking at his books – and read some poems by James Bramwell – bad!

27 April. I saw my darling Lorenzo today. Just a fleeting glimpse of his profile – but so divine. His hair is more auburn, and his skin lovely, pale brown with a faint flush.

29 April. Oh ever to be remembered day. Lorenzo spoke to me! I saw him in the Bod. and felt desperately thrilled about him so that I trembled and shivered and went sick. As I went out Lorenzo caught me up – and said – 'Well, and has Sandra finished her epic poem?' – or words to that effect. He talks curiously but very waffily – is very affected. Something wrong with his mouth I think – he can't help snurging. I was almost completely tongue-tied. I said 'Er – No'. He asked me if I was still keeping up the dual personality idea – he had caught me out. 'But you don't know who I am' I said. 'Of course I do' replied Lorenzo. 'Everybody does'. Oh Misery or the reverse! Then I said, 'By the way I hope you don't mind my calling you Lorenzo – it suits you you know'. 'Oh does it – how *awfully* flattering!' He snurged and went on up the Iffley Rd while I walked trembling and weak at the knees into Cowley Place.

30 April. I was very happy thinking about Lorenzo and the funny way he talked and everything. I had that kind of gnawing at the vitals sick feeling if that describes it at all – that is so marvellous. In the afternoon I went out to tea with Rosemary and Laurence at 105 The High. Laurence is charming. We ate a lot and listened to Stravinsky's *Sacre du Printemps.* I couldn't think of anything intelligent to say about it. I was dressed all in grey with a blue and white check blouse. Anthony Baines had lots of peculiar cigarettes – French Woodbines and Spanish ones that you have to roll yourself. He has a grandfather living in Oxford who is a bit potty – and spits on the floor. We left at about 6. I couldn't eat any supper – but drank a glass of water – amazing what love will do!

10 May. After tea I went to the Bod. and it was sultry sort of weather – one expected it to thunder at almost any moment. I wasn't looking awfully beautiful. I was wearing a brown check skirt, yellow short sleeved jersey – yellow suede coat – brown hat and Viyella scarf – flesh coloured fishnet stockings, brown and white ghillie shoes (blue celanese trollies – pink suspender belt – pink kestos – white vest) – brown gloves – umbrella. I sat down opposite where Lorenzo usually sits. In a minute or two he came along and sat in his usual place. We took no notice of each other – but of course I couldn't resist staring. At 10 to 7 they rang the bell and we stayed a bit. I walked out before Lorenzo. We got to the bottom of the stairs – just by the door I felt someone catch me up – I looked up – Lorenzo stood by my side – saying would I like a lift anywhere? I accepted and walked with him to his car YR 4628. I commented on the fact that I'd seen him in another car – he said 'I sometimes hire a car'. Said he shared YR with 'The man with the presumably false moustache', i.e. John Barnicot. He said he liked me and my sense of humour and thought me quite mad. We went to the Trout and got a room to ourselves, where there was a pingpong table. We played till it was time to eat – he generally beat me. We ate mixed grill and drank beer – he's fussy so I had to pick out all the least greasy of the fried potatoes for him. Over supper we talked of general things – but everything he said seemed so marvellously significant. I think I must have told him quite a lot about how I felt for him. Oh cruel Lorenzo.
We finished eating – I can see the romantic surroundings – now dusk – falling water – the wistaria on the Trout. I picked some. Lorenzo said 'It will wither'. It did too – although I put it in water – my char threw it away. I put on Barnicot's mac. Driving back we talked strictly practical things – 18th century literature – the Wartons – Young's conjectures on original compositions – 'Think

you this too bold?' . . . We got back to Oxford. I was still almost in a daze. Outside St Hilda's I kissed his bitten cheek.

And so I began to hope – and what a lot of misery was this evening responsible for. But it was wonderful while it lasted.

14 May. Rupert came to see me in the morning but I couldn't possibly kiss him – because the last mouth to touch mine had been Lorenzo's.

17 May. Lorenzo came into the Bod. in the morning – wearing a dark green shirt and tie – he walked in very artificially, preoccupied and reading a book. He actually came and spoke to me and showed me two books he'd bought, one the saga of Hrolf Kraki and the other a humorous book in Latin with some funny pictures that he said were like me.

24 May. Got ready for the Keble concert to which we (Sharp and I) were going. I wore my black frock – too charmingly decolleté back and front plus the Pym pearls and my fur coat. Keble quad was covered with striped awnings etc., and there was a red carpet all the way up the steps into the hall. Harlovin and Frank seemed rather bored by the actual concert! Frank said that rooms in Keble are like a very small grave – the kind you get when you're buried at the public expense! After the concert we had refreshments sitting at a table on the grass in the quad – *not* in the marquee, where most of the unselect went. Then we passed on to Davies' rooms which are in Museum Rd. The party consisted of Davies – very chirpy and getting gradually more and more intoxicated – a girl called Angela Camus who sat at the table – silent and sullen (apparently she'd had 5 glasses of sherry). Unfortunately we only had time to swallow a hasty glass of sherry – and as it was we were in St Hilda's a few minutes after 12, but luckily it was the nice porter.

27 May. This day I went to Cheltenham with Harlovin and Harding. It was very wet – so we all squashed in the front. Harding continues to be very funny and Harlovin was as sweet and charming as ever. They teased me a lot about my appalling reputation! Poor Sandra!

June. About this time we had a terrific heatwave. We sunbathed in the meadows in our gingham sunbathing frocks. Lorenzo lay low – one imagined him walking about naked in the garden of 252 (if it has one).

6 June. Went on the river in the afternoon. Got to know Leslie

Fearnehough (Queen's) and Michael Rabone (Univ.) because we wanted to borrow a match. I hope they didn't think we were deliberately trying to make a pick up – really I do some unfortunate things but how can you smoke a cigarette without a match? Almost before we'd been in conversation 10 minutes Leslie asked us if we'd go and have tea with them at the Air Squadron. We were amazed – there was something so naif about it! Leslie came for us in his Austin 7 – and we drove to the Air Squadron at breakneck speed. We had tea in rickety canvas chairs under a huge umbrella that needed a lot of adjusting. Leslie seemed to take a fancy to me and suggested that we should go for a ride in his car – ostensibly to fetch a waistcoast that he'd left at a pub in Berkshire. So we went. Finally we arrived at East Leach, a very pretty little place. We wandered about, having found that the people he knew there were out – and looked at some racing stables – lovely horses. We then drank some beer – and I had some port which I didn't much like. The people at the inn could only give us a very frugal supper – and kept on suggesting that we should go to Lechlade, where we could apparently get *anything*!

7 June. Wrote a good-luck letter to Lorenzo. Quite prosaic and hearty – but oh – what wouldn't I have liked to say – still I knew it would be a mistake. Nor did I want Jockie and Barnicot to know any more about the state of my heart!

8 June. Lorenzo's schools began – and I suppose other people's too. I felt sick with apprehension for him. I carefully avoided passing the Schools at 9.30 or at 12.30 and spent the morning in the Bod.

9 June. Today I couldn't resist the lure of the Schools and came out of the Bod. at about 12.15. I met Rupert in the High – so I had an excuse for lingering by Schools. We stood by the Drawda Hall Bookshop and talked. Out poured the masses of people, and at last Lorenzo in his striped suit plus white shirt and tie. I said 'Have you enjoyed yourself?' He grinned rather fatuously and waved his square at me and went up the High and turned up Catte St. Rupert thought he was quite beautiful and merely weak looking – not vicious! Then I saw Leslie and lunched with him at the Air Squadron. Coming back to St Hilda's at a little before 2 – I saw YR by Magdalen College School – coming from the direction of the Iffley Rd. Lorenzo was driving it, and Jockie sitting by him looking prim and proper but v. sweet. I waved and Lorenzo grinned, we *all* turned round, including Jockie. Then back to St Hilda's where I was deliriously happy. We put on the gramophone and I danced all over my room – but when we put on 'Lazy Pete', I was struck with the fact that Lorenzo was going down, and that I probably wouldn't see him any more. That tune will always have sad memories – in spite of its general flower-show atmosphere.

17 July. London [staying with Selways at Hatch End]. Visited several shops – Selfridges where we had lunch at an exciting new snack bar with high red leather and chromium plated stools. We ate huge toast sandwiches and drank iced coffee. We had tea at D. H. Evans. I bought some scarlet rouge and lipstick and some scent – also a brown spotted silk scarf.

22 July. Today we went to Stratford-on-Avon to see *Romeo and Juliet.* Of course I'd seen the theatre before – last September – but I still think it's marvellous. Romeo (John Wyse) was awfully like Lorenzo sometimes. It was all terribly tragic – both Romeo and Juliet were intensely passionate, especially Romeo. 'Thinkest thou we shall ever meet again?' I couldn't help applying these lines to another case. But my answer was not so sure as Romeo's!

23 July. On the river in the morning – Sandra punting. I enjoyed it very much – and had a bottle of ginger beer and an ice cream cornet to refresh me in my labours. The river is very pretty in parts and sometimes very much like the 'upper reaches of the Cherwell'. After lunch Uncle J. dragged us off sightseeing. It was very hot, but I'd put on a cool frock so didn't mind that unduly. But high heels weren't comfortable for walking and I got one or two blisters before we'd finished. However we kept our tempers wonderfully. We caught the 6.25 train home and had dinner on it. I was *very* happy and hilarious, cracking many jokes.

25 July. London. Another very hot day. Went to the flicks: Constance Bennett in *Our Betters* was very good. At about 3.30 we came out and went to the SF snack bar, where we had iced coffee and sandwiches, very good, cucumber and cheese – banana and jam.

27 July. Oswestry. I was very 'glad to be back'. I unpacked and made my room tidy. Hilary swapped her yellow bathing costume for my navy blue one – a very satisfactory transaction – it looks lovely with my sunburn.

28 July. Went in the town and bought a *Times.* My very dearest Lorenzo got a Second – not too bad – I hope he was satisfied with it. In the evening I finished *Point Counter Point.* It's quite cheering to remember that at 16 I thought it disjointed, muddled and boring. this time I loved it – although most of the talk was above my head. He still remains far and away the most interesting modern novelist in my opinion. But I don't really enjoy any of his novels as much as *Those Barren Leaves*.

29 July. I worked at Old English for about 1½ hours after breakfast – Wulfstan's address to the English. Really it gave me the pip. After lunch I started to make a summer frock (deep orangey-pink and white check gingham – 5¾d. a yard!) I think it should be rather nice.

31 July. After lunch I took some Yeastvite tablets and continued to take them after tea and supper. A slightly unromantic way of curing lovesickness I admit, but certainly I feel a lot better now. (Hilary is playing 'Stormy Weather' incessantly – my theme song I think!) After lunch I read Richard Aldington's new book, *All Men are Enemies* – it was rather interesting but intensely depressing. After tea I turned to Burton's *Anatomy of Melancholy* and began to read about Love Melancholy – but I haven't yet got to the part where he deals with the cure. Perhaps I'm suffering from the spleen too – in that case I may be completely cured by taking a course of our English poets – which all points to drowning my sorrows in work. I think I shall try to develop a 'Whatever is, is right' attitude of mind – and quite honestly I suppose all this *is* rather good for me – and an affair with Lorenzo probably wouldn't be!

1 August. In the afternoon Hilary went to tennis at the Blakes – I wasn't asked thank heaven! I dislike tennis parties – here anyway. Too much small talk with people who are generally bores – sometimes one even dislikes them!
At 8, Mrs Wakelam and Maud came to play bridge. I sat in an armchair like a docile donkey and knitted my dark green jumper. I also ate a lot of sandwiches.

27 August. I was reading the diaries I kept when I was 15 and 18, and profoundly depressed by them – I'm glad time goes on. But I mustn't forget 'Soir de Paris' perfume reminds me of John Mott – that 'Pêche Marie Rose' was the nicest sweet we ever had – and I shall never be able to smell the fascinatingly sweet smell of Cyclax Special Lotion without being carried back to last term and the Lorenzo atmosphere. As I write this I have a Boncilla beauty mask on my face – tightening my skin – nice if uncomfortable feeling.

4 September. Reading Gertrude Trevelyan's novel *Hothouse*. I desperately want to write an Oxford novel – but I must see first that my emotions are simmered down fairly well.

9 September. Reading *Acorned Hog.* Shamus Frazer is immensely entertaining – he and I might have a little in common I feel. No need for modesty in a diary. Now I want to write something more fantastic about a girl called Gabriella.

Tokalon Biocel Skinfood is just lumps of lard, scented and coloured pink.

10 September. After Oxford I think I must try and get a job abroad, even if the prospect is rather frightening. After all the excitement of life needn't end when I go down – it's ridiculous to think of all the thrill being finished when I'm only just twenty-one.

15 September. More work. At lunchtime while I was eating my ham, chicken roll and HP sauce, a band on the wireless was playing the waltz 'But for You' from the Lilian Harvey film. The passion came over me in a wave 'accompanied with an inward sense of melting and langour'. Read *More Women than Men* by I. Compton-Burnett and saw no point in it – unreal people and not much of a story. Spent the evening variously. I had to decide between giving my face a steam beauty bath and doing 'Beowulf'. I chose the former, and I think the result justified my choice. After a baked-beans supper I embroidered my red satin blouse and did some knitting.

19 September. Tried to think out an essay on the Puritanism of Spenser and Milton in the morning. Had my hair cut very short and puck-like in the afternoon, and washed it – it looks suspiciously golden.

21 September. Hilary went back to school. We went to Hamilton Square in the car and by train to Central. An exquisite lunch at Bon Marché, after which we went to Huyton with her. Then we did some shopping. I bought a black macintosh – some brown suede shoes and a chaste green linen bedspread. I withstood the temptation to waste money on odds and ends. The place is quiet without Hilary.

26 September. What funny things one does – I finish an essay on 'The Puritanism of Spenser and Milton' and then dash off to the Regal with Dor to see *42nd Street* which was good – all legs and music.

1 October. Oxford. The 1st day in Oxford and pretty dull – nothing but meals, wandering and lying about wishing for something exciting to happen. A cup of tea at the Town and Gown – Horlicks and sandwiches at Stewart's – then a quiet evening – except that I spilt a lot of ink on the carpet. I *must* fall for someone – so as I can forget Lorenzo – and at present I'm pretty bad.

3 October. this morning lunched off steak and kidney pie at Kemp Hall cafeteria. Jockie Liddell came in, wearing a grey suit and navy blue overcoat. He gave me a poisonous look, but I didn't mind. Then at about 2 o'clock I was walking to St Hilda's and on Magdalen Bridge I saw Barnicot with an amazing woman – twice as big as him, with a red eton crop – hearty and not ravishing.

After a solitary tea in the Super, where the band played 'Young and Healthy', I went to see *The Kid from Spain* with funny Eddie Cantor and its marvellous tunes. I wish there'd been more of those.

4 October. In the afternoon I walked a little and changed some gloves at Webber's – a 3/11½ pair for an 8/11! In the afternoon Harry Harker came and I had tea with him in Elliston's. We then went to the Bijou wine lounge and I had sherry while he had a Green Goddess – and lots of salted nuts. Feeling thus elated we wandered to St Hilda's – just between the public lavatory and the Cape of Good Hope we saw Barnicot. I smiled brilliantly but he took no notice – is he afraid, ashamed, or merely short sighted?

5 October. Worked in the morning and had coffee with Harry at Elliston's. I ordered a copy of Ernest Dowson's poems in Bodleiana and spent some time in finding appropriate lines and poems. I'm beginning to enjoy my pose of romantically unrequited love. Jockie was in Kemp Hall. I had no tea, and supper in Kemp Hall with Rosemary. Afterwards we went along with Laurence to his digs – 7 Long Wall – and had a lovely time, drinking beer and eating nuts. L. is charming and wore a delightful black hat when he took us home.

6 October. I'm terribly enamoured of my new room, and have it most artistic and aesthetic. Chaste green cover for my bed – check cushions – beautiful pictures – books and bookends – bronze golden chrysanthemums on the table in the window alcove. I hear Magdalen and Merton clocks all the time.

7 October. Went to get some visiting cards printed at Emberlin's. In burst Rosemary with the news that they'd seen Lorenzo – I was terribly excited and couldn't eat any tea, although it was nice hearty buns which I usually enjoy. After tea I prepared to go over to Blackwell's to buy some Shakespeare books – and to find him. I was wearing my grey flannel costume, black polo jersey and no hat. I had an orange marigold stuck in the collar of my jersey. I was coming away from Blackwell's for the 2nd time when I met Lorenzo and Jockie. There was no escape – we walked towards each other and met about by Trinity. He took off his hat and gave me a marvellous smile – a slightly mocking bow I thought – but it's difficult to tell with him. I was horribly nervous and grinned I imagine. He was wearing grey bags and the familiar tweed coat. Then I wandered some more until I came upon them by Elliston's but they didn't see me. I tracked them down St Michael's Street but I couldn't follow because it was so deserted.

8 October. Worked for about 2 hours in the morning, and did a few odd jobs such as writing home and trimming my eyebrows. After lunch we put on the gramophone and I gave my nails a careful manicure and varnished them a becoming shade of rose pink. At 4 o'clock I went to have tea with Harry at Stewart's – it was hot and full of people. I kept having visions of Lorenzo and they played 'Isn't it Heavenly'.

10 October. An amusing lecture in the morning – Professor Tolkien on Beowulf. I bought at Boots some Amami Henna application – but doubt whether I shall have the nerve to use it strongly!

11 October. Having renounced Lorenzo I'm trying to find someone else, but so far no one has specially taken my fancy. In the afternoon I put some henna on my hair – only a little, but it made it quite a nice colour. Next time I must be bolder! JCR meeting – I wore my scarlet satin Russian blouse over a black frock – and had my hair straight, with the short piece hanging down almost into my eyes.

12 October. At the Bodleian – all morning. Barnicot came in – his hair a nice golden corn colour. We stared at each other for a long time. Jockie also came looking rather dissipated – I am intrigued by the way in which he lifts one corner of his mouth in a disdainful sneer. I spent quite a lot of time looking thro' the stained-glass windows by the Dictionary to see if I could see Lorenzo – but it was not to be. The trouble is that although I've renounced him I still love him – or I suppose it's love. Miss Rooke's class at 5.30. I showed neither intelligence nor knowledge.

14 October. What happened in Elliston's this afternoon ought to amuse anybody. I was there with Harry, and it was very full. At about 4.45 Lorenzo came in plus another man and sat down quite close to us. He and I were almost opposite each other. He began the conversation by asking me why I imitated his black macintosh. I replied, 'Why, because I think it's so charming'. All the time I answered him in his own vein, although I was feeling somewhat trembly. I don't know what Harry must've thought. Lorenzo was singularly amusing if a little rude – it appears he is staying up to read a B. Litt. He looked very attractive. His skin deliciously smooth and creamy brown – his hair and eyes so nice too.

16 October. Lorenzo was in the English Reading Room in the afternoon – wearing a pale blue shirt, and looking very sweet. He says he's doing Palaeography – I didn't know what it was!

17 October. At the Bodleian in the morning I saw Jockie and liked him immensely – funny how I alternate in my feelings for him. He was wearing a dark brown suit which fitted him beautifully – he has a very nicely proportioned little figure – but what I liked was that when he was sharpening his pencil and I was reading in the Encyclopaedia – I happened to look up and see that he was nearly laughing and he looked so sweet. I wish he and I could be friends. I didn't see Lorenzo – except in the High at about 12, and he gave no sign of recognition.

18 October. Lectures, then to the Bodleian where I talked to Lorenzo for a few minutes which seems to be the highest point of happiness in my life at present. He tells me that he and Jockie are having a flat in the Banbury Road which is at present half-furnished. He asked me to go and see him sometime and said I must go and eat with him one day. I think I should love to go – but probably it mightn't be wise. Jockie has got a job in the Bodleian.

20 October. Saw Lorenzo waiting for a bus with the red-haired girl – his hair does need cutting – but it looks very decorative all the same. On arriving back at college we made coffee in Sharp's room – I raved and soliloquised as usual.

23 October. Work, work....Jock is in pale blue socks and suede shoes – Barnicot smiled at me (all jolly together). Lorenzo ignores me – and I ignore him. Oh Sandra, cheer up – you'll forget one day.

28 October. Harry took me to the Walton St cinema in the evening to see *The Virtuous Isidore* – a superbly funny French film. Life is difficult, I don't feel I'm treating Harry fairly – and yet what can I do. I'm sure he knows the position but he never says anything. If only he were more explicit.... Life would be considerably easier.

1 November. What a bad sign it is to get the *Oxford Book of Victorian Verse* out of the library.

6 November. Sharp and I went to tea with Frank Harding and a man named Naylor, to the Moorish. I like the Moorish exceedingly

– the decorations and the divans and cushions in the corners. Harding is terribly amusing – he told us a good Groups limerick:

> There was a young man of Pretoria
> Who said 'Things get gorier and gorier'
> But he found that with prayer
> And some savoir faire
> He could stay at the Waldorf Astoria.

7 November. My Lorenzo is *so* beautiful – even if he has had his hair cut rather shorter than usual – the shape of his face and the line of his cheek fill me with rapture. He grows more affected – his smile of self-conscious fatuity is sweet – but one day it may seem silly. This afternoon he was in the Bodleian from 2.30 to 3.10. He snurged at me, but said nothing.

11 November. Armistice Day. I went to St Mary's and everything outside was almost more silent than I've ever known it before. In the evening Harry took me to the flicks – Bebe Daniels in *The Song You Gave Me* – which was bad but amusing. Then to Harry's rooms where I let him kiss me properly, and so gave up the 'Lorenzo was the last person who kissed me' pose – sad, but what's the use. H. seems to be in love with me if he meant what he said – anyway we got on better than usual. I also had some beer and borrowed a book on Modern Art and some Proust.

14 November. In the afternoon I went to the Bodleian and he was there. My wretched heart was beating so fast I thought I should die or something – in the course of conversation he asked me to go and see him at the flat tomorrow afternoon and I implied that I would. When I got home I wrote him a long letter telling him the position and saying I could not go – it was a great relief to me to be able to pour out some of my griefs etc.

15 November. Found the following note awaiting me: 'Do come this afternoon. I should very much like to talk to you. Thank you for this morning's letter but don't be mean. Try to get there before 3. I am not going anywhere at 5.30'.
I didn't go – but oh how I wanted to! Can it be that my darling Lorenzo is sorry? Anyway I think still that it will be best if I can forget him.

23 November. Rather a depressing day. I went to the appointments committee and I broke the pencil sharpener in the Bodleian. My foot was bad so that I couldn't walk properly. I also burnt my fingers on a kettle in the evening.

24 November. I discovered Samuel Butler's *Notebooks* in the library which gave me great pleasure. At 5.30 Sharp and I went to the Yacht Club's bottle party in Michael Rabone's rooms at Univ. When we arrived Michael hadn't come, nor was there anyone there that we knew. So we just sat drinking sherry, smoking, and eating salted almonds and potato crisps: feeling rather bored, especially as nobody knew our names to introduce us to anyone! There weren't many women there and the men had collected into a group and were talking about yachting. When Michael arrived things brightened up a lot. The party had begun in the room adjoining Michael's but we eventually migrated into Michael's, where a noisy gambling game was in progress. A pity one always has to come away when things are getting amusing.

25 November. Went out to dinner at the George with Harry, and had the loveliest cocktail I've ever had – a sidecar, very iced. Also hock and good food. I wore blue lace – with three real red roses pinned on to the front. Also my long crystal earrings and makeup to match the roses. Very nice!

5 December. This was definitely a good day. In the morning I had 2 telegrams from Hilary saying that she was coming for interviews. That made me so excited that I couldn't stay in College and work – so I went to the Bodleian. As I was going up the stairs cheerily half-whistling 'In the Park in Paree in the Spring' – I met Barnicot coming downstairs – we grinned broadly at each other and both said 'Hullo'. He is a cheering up sort of person to see. I met Hilary at the cold and dreary LMS station. After taking her to LMH we came along to St Hilda's and had tea in my room, then took her back again for her interviews. Then we went along with Pedley to the Museum – to see if her results were up. Of course she had got through, as I knew she would. She bought Sharp and me 50 cigarettes to celebrate. Lovely flat tins of Goldflake.

6 December. After tea I paid my Blackwell's bill and bought a book of Restoration verse – then more Bodleian. After supper I went on a Banbury Road crawl – in spite of great weariness. There was a light in Lorenzo's bedroom – is he ill, or packing, or was he just there. Anyway it gives me a little hope – and Jockie hasn't been at the Bodleian for days.

7 December. In the afternoon we went to see Lord Irwin installed as Chancellor. It was a good ceremony – we, the rabble of the University, were consigned to the upper gallery but had a good view. After it, Roland Rahtz – Harry's friend from Keble – approached me and asked me to tea – I couldn't very well refuse. We went to Elliston's – I can't see any prospect of being interested in him – what shall I do. I don't want to be unkind. Still there's all the vac. for him to simmer.

9 December. I wrote a little note saying Goodbye to Lorenzo. A nasty tea all by myself in Hall (a new experience). Then a taxi to the station and into the 4.30. Quite a dull journey – going Paddington way one was able to catch a glimpse of the dreaming spires in the twilight of a December evening – romantic time to leave.

11 December. London, Hatch End. Betse, Aunt Nellie and I went into town at about 11. I wore my fur coat – navy blue skirt and fez, and looked rather Turkish–Parisienne. We went to the Carlton and saw Mae West in *I'm No Angel.* She is said to be the rage of everywhere. Fat and not attractive – at least I didn't think so – a purely physical appeal and crude technique. Her clothes were too fluffy and feathery on the whole. The shops are full of the most tempting things. I saw the divinest black velvet dresses in one shop which makes me determined to have one.

13 December. Heard the glad news that Hilary had got into LMH.

14 December. We had a good look round the shops without buying anything. Selfridge's first – where what I liked almost best was the zoological department. There was the most adorable kangaroo there with eyes like Lorenzo and a long pointed nose. It loved having its neck stroked and closed its eyes in ecstasy. I would have loved to have had it – but it was sold – and anyway what would I have done with it?

22 December. Oswestry. I would love to be able to write a book like *Moll Flanders* which I'm reading slowly and thoroughly. And then there's Christmas – Harry has sent me *Peter Abelard* by Helen Waddell which I'm sure I shall like. He is good to me. Lorenzo can't even send me a card.

23 December. In the evening I had a card from Lorenzo. It was addressed in Jockie's writing and inside was the inscription 'Sandra from Lorenzo'. It was a reproduction of a picture of St Barbara – sweet and quaint – the sort of thing that accords well with Jockie or Lorenzo.

25 December. Christmas Day. A very happy day in all ways – it made more happy by the card from Lorenzo and/or Jockie, a little thing but it helped to make the day perfect.

Hilary and I went to church at 8, where there was the usual large congregation, but we managed things well and managed to get into the first row of communicants. Then home to breakfast and the exciting ceremony of opening the parcels. I had some lovely presents. Besides food I had: From Auntie Nellie a glorious jumper in rich royal blue with white buttons – short sleeved and knitted in thick wool and an intriguing stitch. The welt is very deep and it fits beautifully. Little Annie sent a parcel for the family with pyjama cases for Hilary and me. From Pedley I had some lovely silk stockings and from Sharp a black crêpe de chine evening bag with a quilted front with SANDRA embroidered on it in pale blue silk – lovely. We listened in to a service broadcast from Christ Church, Oxford. Beautiful singing – the way they do the psalms is such a delight. Then Hilary and I went down the road to meet Ack and Winifred and they gave us a lift back. Winifred gave me a nice hankie and an elegant lemon coloured swansdown puff in a georgette hankie. From Ack I had a box of Dubarry bath salts, a painted matchbox and some sweets. We had a lovely Christmas dinner. Sherry to begin with and an 18 lb. turkey done to a turn. The afternoon was spent in laziness and eating, also listening in. I am knitting a most exciting scarf-of-many-colours from all the bits of 4-ply wool I've had left over from jumpers etc. After tea we went to the pictures to see *Smilin' Through*. Leslie Howard is so lovely. In the evening the second act of *The Mikado* was broadcast which was great fun, and to end up the evening Henry Hall and the BBC Dance Orchestra gave the best programme I've ever heard from them. It included some lovely tunes full of memories sweet and poignant – 'Stormy Weather', 'Won't You Stay to Tea'.

1934

4 January. I have a new frock, crimson jersey – with a collar of red and white crochet which makes me say 'Lo the poor Indian' for some obscure reason.

7 January. I am reading *The Belief of Catholics* by Ronald Knox – but have not yet got far enough into it to know whether I shall become a Catholic or not.

8 January. At Marks and Spencer's I bought a peach coloured vest and trollies to match with insertions of lace. Disgraceful I know but I can't help choosing my underwear with a view to it being seen!

13 January. Oxford. In the morning I went to see Miss Everett, who seemed almost paralysed with horror by my red nails!

18 January. In the afternoon I went to the flicks with Harry – *The Blue Angel* at the Walton. It's a horrid, depressing flick, and Marlene Dietrich revolting – but it was interesting. Coming down the High at about 5.50–5.55 saw Lorenzo on the other side of the road. I only really saw his back view – all romantic in the twilight. Leaving Harry hastily I sprinted up to Carfax, just in time to see my darling getting on to the top of a 2 bus, and so gliding out of my arms so to speak!

19 January. At Blackwell's I bought a lovely set of Young's *Poems* in 2 volumes – for 12/6 – green and gold with lovely mottled edges.

22 January. Having discovered that Lorenzo goes to some lectures on Mondays and Thursdays at 5, I arranged things so that I should be passing the Schools on my way to the Bodleian, just before 5. I timed it beautifully and met Lorenzo as I had hoped. I made no attempt to stop, nor did he, but he smiled and put out his tongue a little and said 'Hello!' He was looking very beautiful in a hat and overcoat, and was carrying his B.A. gown. At about 6.30 he came into the English Reading Room and looked at a book for a few minutes. We took no notice of each other. His hair needs cutting terribly and looks awful at the back; he was wearing a brown pullover, which goes with his eyes.

23 January. As I was going round Carfax I nearly walked into Lorenzo who was coming from the opposite direction. He smiled at me, I was so thrilled, and touched him. The rest of the day was dull. I bought a vivid scarlet cardigan to keep me warm in the Bodleian.

24 January. An exciting thick fog in the evening – Sharp and I took the opportunity to sleuth round the Bodleian. I had all the luck. I followed Lorenzo to Balliol – then Jockie down the snicket and we all of us met at Kemp Hall. Poisonous looks from Jockie, and amused ones from Lorenzo.

25 January. Tutorial and all that. I looked elegant in my fur coat, but of course saw neither of them!

26 January. I went out to the Bodleian in my little grey suit with a red hankie knotted round my neck. I sat reading – Chaucer and the Roman poets – when Lorenzo came and sat down beside me. I did not speak to him but we smiled at each other. I found it difficult to work. I looked out of the window at the nice little lower bits of All Souls against the pale blue sky. I remembered having done the same on the evening of May 10th 1933. *'Sed sic sic fine feriati'*.... I thought. I was in fear lest he should go, and eventually he looked at the clock (it was just before 12) and showed signs of going. But first he leaned over and said 'Come and have tea with me today'. I refused but said I would next week. He suggested Tuesday. He asked me how I liked my Christmas card – and apparently he had sent it. After he'd gone I picked up a piece of paper he'd left on the deck. It was written in a kind of palaeographic script (I imagine). Of course I have kept it among my Harvey–Liddell relics (of which I now have 3).

27 January. In the afternoon I went shopping by myself. I saw Julia Pakenham looking superb in a turquoise blue frock and new halo hat. She was wearing a fur coat, so one couldn't see how fat she was.

5 February. A helpful Spenser revision class with Rooke. Very funny too, as she had a great cauldron of marmalade boiling on the gas ring!

7 February. In the English Reading Room the only vacant seat I could see happened to be by Lorenzo. He was looking particularly nice. Blue shirt, blue spotted tie, brown pullover and the usual brownish coat – and most delightful of all – his black trousers. I glanced at him occasionally and thought how much I loved him. Sometimes he looked my way and made a remark, such as 'We do work hard, don't we?'

13 February. In the afternoon I looked up Jockie's brother in the Cambridge University Calendar. He is called Donald Stewart Liddell and is a Senior Wrangler. Lent begins tomorrow – I light my last cigarette!

21 February. Up early helping to feed the Hunger Marchers at the Corn Exchange. We piled up blankets – took round tea and porridge – cut bread – buttered it – made and packed meat and jam sandwiches. There was a lot to do, and I did enjoy it. Hilary Sumner-Boyd was there in green velvet trousers – he is pleasant to talk to and looks so exactly like a girl – somehow one doesn't associate him with Communism. At about 9.45 we left together with the Hunger Marchers – the idea of me marching behind the October Club banner (which I did) was ludicrous – also shouting, under the direction of a kind of cheer-leader '1–2–3–4– Who are *We* For? *We* are *For* the *Working Classes* – *Down* with the *Ruling* Classes. Students join the Workers' struggle' etc. Still I wish them luck even if I do disapprove of much that Communism stands for.

26 February. In the afternoon I went to have some passport photos taken at Elliston's. They will be pretty terrible I expect, as I was grinning a large teethful grin. At Bodley in the afternoon Lorenzo came in. He has a new coat – greyish, rather nice. He looked extremely beautiful and stood quite a long time by the Bibliography books where I could see him. I must be still pretty badly in love with him, as I trembled all over when he came in, and could hardly write.

Coming back from Blackwell's at about 3.30 I met Lorenzo in the snicket and he invited me to tea tomorrow, but, having a tutorial at 5.30, I couldn't go. He asked me to go on Friday and we left it uncertain – he saying he'd expect me. I want to go, but I will not be treated in this rude and casual fashion.

1 March. He has not answered my letter – perhaps I should not have expected it. I do seem to mess things up so hopelessly and there is no one to help me. At 4.45 I met him in the street and almost cut him dead – fool that I am – He came into the Bodleian twice but he did not speak to me – and when I heard his footsteps disappearing out of the picture gallery I nearly burst into tears there and then.

8 March. Lorenzo was in the English Reading Room, he smiled sweetly at me. I was jealous because he spoke for a little while to a girl – and so I said 'Goodbye you hound' as I left. Tea with Harry and then a hilarious dinner at the Town and Gown which I enjoyed a lot.

9 March. In the Bodleian I observed the girl Lorenzo spoke to the day before. She is my rival and lives at 105 Banbury Road – and is called Alison West-Watson. To look at she is remarkably like Lorenzo, same sort of colouring, mouth and eyes, and I think she is rather attractive, although not made up or particularly well dressed. I am really rather jealous of her as Lorenzo is always praising her up, and comparing her with me, to my disadvantage. Some of it may be only fun, but it hurts. I was setting out to go tea with him, and just as I'd got to the Botanical Gardens YR drew up beside me and I got into the back where Lorenzo was. Barnicot and Edward Gardiner were in front. We did some shopping and then all went to the flat where we had tea. Barnicot and Edward were nice, but Lorenzo was horrid to me, teasing me about West-Watson and saying rude things. Edward and Barnicot went before 5 so that Lorenzo and I were left alone. We sat in silence and I felt miserable, then into his room. He was not kind to me and his attitude towards me was made so cruelly obvious – and he would not stop talking about W-W. All the time I was getting more and more unhappy, until suddenly I burst into tears and cried more than I've done for years. It was as if I'd felt it coming for days – my love for him, his indifference to me, the mess I'd made of my affair with him, and the fact that I was leaving him probably for another woman to have, was simply too much for me. When he saw my tears he was quite nice to me – and promised that next term we should be good friends and go on the river together. By the time I was more or less clothed and in my right mind Jockie came in. I was terribly glad to see him. He and I went and cooked the supper and talked a lot, while Lorenzo more or less sulked in his room and put on the gramophone – *Tannhäuser* too! Jock is so kind, and amusing, and I like his laugh, and the way he wrinkles up his eyes when he's amused. He told me a few things about Lorenzo which made me realise even more than I had hitherto done, what a terribly difficult person he is. And Lorenzo himself was frightful at supper – he just sat and sulked with his glasses on and stared down at his plate. He did not speak to me at all except to be rude. If it hadn't been that Jockie was so nice I don't know what I would have done. I stayed until nearly 10.30 and I had to do all my packing when I got back to St Hilda's, and was too tired to think much about the way Lorenzo had behaved to me and my miserable future prospects. the worst of it is that the more I know him the more I seem to love him, in spite of all his faults.

13 March. Oswestry. My photos of Lorenzo lying in the punt came and I am so pleased with them – they are awfully good and like him too. I felt quite happy in the evening – I wish I could be certain that it would last. What a perilous thing happiness is!

23 March. A lovely long letter from Jockie, which although it contained rather depressing news, made me feel happy and excited. It seems that Lorenzo is really in love with Alison West-Watson, because she has not fallen into his arms straight away as he expected she would. Lorenzo wrote a peevish postscript to the letter which makes me even more determined not to write to him. He had cut his finger and drops of his blood were decorating the letter – there was also a page with HENRY written on it in large bloody letters. Jockie was sympathetic and the letter was a witty and a charming one. I am beginning to feel the weest bit hostile towards Henry, and to think that the glamour of being his doormat is wearing off. I don't look at his photograph, and I must not let him spoil my Schools.

17 April. Oxford [in lodgings in Ship Street during the vacation]. A busy and pleasant day. Work at Hamlet and the Ghost in the morning. Pedley and I went to the Super and had an excellent programme for our 1/3d. *Love, Honour and Oh Baby!* was gloriously funny. 'What

37

about the man who wears the red pyjamas?' 'Yes but he doesn't wear them in the afternoon!' *By Candlelight* was the big flick and very entertaining too. Paul Lukas and Elissa Landi. It made me determined to marry a rich man.

A long letter from Friedbert, all in German – which I've not yet deciphered, and a lovely snap of him. Also a book containing a speech of Hitler's (in English). I resolutely worked till nearly 1.30! I am writing this at that hour and have almost earned a rest – but I'm longing to decipher my letter.

18 April. At about 1 o'clock I had my first glimpse of Lorenzo/Henry for nearly six weeks. He walked along Ship Street in his black macintosh. I didn't quite know how I felt – rather excited I suppose. At about 6.30 he passed by and invited himself in. He asked me to supper that evening. I went at about eight o'clock. Jockie came to the door in a ravishing pastel-coloured Paisley dressing gown – looking very sweet. We had supper – very nice it was too – and I felt happy and excited. Henry, by the way, had insisted on reading some of Friedbert's letter and had translated a little of it – very satisfactorily! We had much amusing conversation. Barnicot came and he and J. tried to play Jockie's flute. Henry was being quite nice, then he pulled me over to the divan and made me lie down with him. The others went out. He said he had a headache and was very sweet and gentle with me. I had to stop myself from asking whether I didn't still love him as much as ever. There is no doubt that I do love him in some sort of way, but I can't quite make out how, because I certainly don't feel the same as I did. Then Jock and Barnicot came back and I was furious because Henry wouldn't let me go. We had a struggle on the floor – I was simply furious and burst into a passionate fit of crying. They were all rather embarrassed – even Jockie – and left me for a while. Then Henry came back and was very solicitous. I had begun to feel tired by this time and was very subdued when my crying had finished. We had some tea and they were all very nice to me. Finally Barnicot drove me home in YR, very tired and feeling that life was too much of a good thing.

19 April. Just before lunch Henry called and tried to persuade me to go to tea. But I resolutely refused. After lunch he came in again and stayed all afternoon and moreover was quite nice most of the time. Is he trying to win me back or something? Just before going he said 'Oh you're common property'. He tried to be nice to me when he saw he'd hurt me. In the evening I did some more deciphering of Friedbert's letter and found (or thought I found) in it much that pleased me.

27 April. After dinner I changed out of my chiffon into my scarlet satin blouse and black skirt. I had a delightful evening at 86B Banbury Road. Jockie was very amusing and looked so pretty – but he has heaps of socks to darn! Henry was rather rude to me on the whole. Barnicot came after a while and he and Henry played chess while I darned socks and talked to Jockie. I only managed to do about 4 pairs – but I am going to do some more tomorrow evening. Henry was very anxious for me to go to tea and said he would teach me about Chaucer and Langbaine – but I am not going. He actually walked with me to the bus stop and tried to persuade me. When I got back to College I looked at my photo of Friedbert and said aloud 'Oh my darling – it's you I love'. I wonder.

28 April. When I went to 86 this evening I had 10 minutes alone with Henry to begin with. He and Jock quarrelled rather a lot – and I left in a furious temper with Henry. Of course Henry and I fought.

2 May. At Bodley again. Henry was wearing a pure white shirt and one of those plaited Austrian ties – orange and brown – which matched his eyes. He looked as if he wasn't going to smile at me, but gave me a sweet one when he saw I did. Very depressed about work in the evening – a disquieting feeling that I may be in love with Henry still. I wish Friedbert would write, that would cheer me. Then there's my wretched future career too.

3 May. Alison was in Bodley this morning – also Henry. If Friedbert doesn't write soon I shall find myself as deeply in love with Henry as ever I was before. In the meantime Jockie smiles at me adorably and looks kind.

4 May. In the morning I had a most touching meeting with Henry on the steps of the Radcliffe Camera. I always think that Providence must arrange little incidents like that. He looked charming and was wearing a black pullover. He tried hard to persuade me to come to tea – but I would not, although I felt very tempted. He swore that he would not even touch me – but how can I believe him after all the other times he's sworn and promised? When I met him I was moved instinctively to put my hand out towards him. Deep down in my heart I know I love him, although I hardly dare admit it to myself. As it is – because I didn't go to tea – I am thinking of the happy time we might have had – and am loving him far more than I probably should do if I had actually gone. It's rather horrid not being able to trust someone you love – or anyway think you love.

9 May. In the morning I worked hard in Bodley. Honor Tracy came in and I showed her where to find some books. She asked me to have tea with her at the Cadena tomorrow. Then Henry wrote in German on some of my Milton notes *'Kommst Du – Ja?'* and a few other things. I went and he was extremely nice – but Jockie came in and caught us reading 'Samson Agonistes' in bed with nothing on. Really rather funny. I stayed to supper. Jockie forgave me as I was penitent and was very sweet.

10 May. Honor Tracy was awfully nice. She is on my side and thinks Henry has treated me badly. She advised me *not* to get involved in an affair with him.

15 May. Honor was in Bodley after tea, also Alison. I want to see Henry again or I may think him nicer than he is. I felt myself inclined to do that this afternoon. I want so terribly to go to Germany again and I'm 12/10d overdrawn at the bank.

20 May. Church at 8 and at 11.30. All my worst thoughts seem to be brought up to the surface on such occasions – like a poultice drawing the poison out of a boil perhaps – !

21 May. Henry and I walked round by Brasenose and the Camera. And he squashed me for liking All Souls better than the Radcliffe.

24 May. Met Henry on the steps of Bodley. He said I looked quite mad – perhaps I did. He added because of the navy spotted hankie round my neck but actually I was concave inside and was rather peeved that he didn't ask me out to coffee.

If only God would arrange that Friedbert would write to me things mightn't be so bad. But as it is I can only conclude that F. meant not a word he said or wrote (possible) or that I've offended him (vaguely possible). Or perhaps I didn't translate his letter rightly or – lots of other things! Anyway, I have very little faith in mankind now – although Hope does spring eternal in the human breast, especially in Sandra's!

26 May. No work all day – a *passionate* desire to go to Germany. I got quite brown (my face at least) in the afternoon on the river. Heard a delightful remark made by a man finding the end of the pole muddy and getting his hands dirty: 'I'm covered with the most *utter* dung'.

28 May. Had a very affectionate letter from Hanns Woischnick in the morning – written in good English with many darlings in it. Apparently Friedbert has told him that I am going there in June – if so I wish F. would write! I did not realise that Hanns was at all fond of me. He says he will never forget me, but seems to think I am irretrievably Friedbert's. I suppose the truth is that I belong to a cruel sweet Englishman called Henry Stanley Harvey, but at the age of not quite 21, it is not possible to be certain. Henry does not write, nor do I see him. The Germans at least appreciate me if the English don't.

1 June. The last day of being sweet-and-twenty. And very sad it made me to think so. In fact at about lunch time I could have been in tears about it. In the afternoon I went with Harry to the Bath and West Show – it was lovely, though very hot. The fine bulls and pigs took my mind off Schools for a while. Among those present (also looking at the pigs) were Mr Barnicot and Count Roberto Weiss.

Supper with Jock and Lorenzo was lovely – they said I looked blonde and Aryan, like something on the cover of *Die Woche*! We drank sherry and Liebfraumilch and I felt a little dazed and amorous.

2 June. My 21st birthday – and in many ways not a happy day. Was excited in the morning waiting for Links and Hilary to come. We had a good meal at the Cadena and tea in my rooms – it was very hot. They went quite soon afterwards and down the Banbury Road too. They took me with them some of the way. And I called on Henry on spec. as I was rather depressed by then. He was in, as it happened, and just going to have his tea. Then he had a bath while I read Spence's *Anecdotes* to him. The bath put him in rather a bad temper though. I retired to the other room and was sitting on the floor reading Goethe when Jockie came in and he was very pleased to see me. He was frightfully funny imitating Bodley's Librarian with whom he'd been to tea. I had supper with them and slipped away before 10.30. Jockie read Jane Austen to me and Barnicot played chess with Henry. When I got back I felt miserable and conscience stricken – so that I cried much in bed. Silly Sandra, but I suppose it was a relief.

4 June. I did 7 hours revision today – Wordsworth and Beowulf. It was rather cheerless. After dinner, at about 9.15, I got into a panic about Gawain and longed for congenial company. So I rushed to 86 Banbury Rd. Henry came to the door but seemed bad tempered and not pleased to see me. But Jockie was sweet – also Barnicot in his silent way – and together they managed to calm me. Henry drove me home, and was surprisingly sweet. He told me to try and get to bed early and said I was to come and see them whenever I liked. I loved him for being a little kind – it made such a difference.

6 June. A nasty day – it was the last before Schools and the weather was uncertain. I hurried to Bodley to do something on Beast Fables. Jockie, in his brown suit, came in and reminded me that this was probably my last day in Bodley. Alison was also in. Henry came through – his hair all fluffy and washed – he spoke to Alison but not to me. I was a fool, but it hurt me terribly. I cried on the stairs coming out. In the evening I dined with Harry at the Town and Gown and was very hilarious and excited about Schools.

Schools. I shall have to write this up all together, as much as I can remember. I enjoyed the experience of Schools and the papers were quite nice, if rather dull at times. I always did the morning ones best. Henry, divinely beautiful in B.A. gown, white fur etc., was taking B. Litt. papers – but I saw very little of him.

8 June. That evening I went to the flat and found Jockie there. We talked till 10.30 and he was very sweet as always. Henry had gone to *The Invisible Man.*

Every afternoon I had tea with Harry and sometimes we would wander about until 6, and then have some sherry in the Bijou.

At nights I used to stay up late, working and talking, and I always worked after breakfast and in the lunch hour.

It was a good time, especially as I got my second.

17 June. A wonderful day.

Henry suggested that we should all go and have dinner at Burford. We set off in YR. Henry drove and Anton [Fendrich] and I sat in the back. The noise it made was so terrific that we couldn't have much conversation. The Lamb was a charming place and we had a very good dinner, at which Anton said some very funny things and Henry gave me a character, saying that I was kind-hearted and didn't demand much. We wanted to go to some place where we could walk about, so we decided to go to Bibury. The village was lovely and we spent much time wandering there. It is completely unspoilt with some lovely cottages and cats. Anton behaved in a delightfully lighthearted Friedbertian manner – turning cartwheels on the road, and walking along the wall by the river. It got dusk – later and later, and we were nearly 30 miles out of Oxford. But I didn't care and was blissfully happy. Henry was so kind and they were all such good company. Coming back I sat behind mit Anton. We lost our way rather at first. Anton was very sweet to me. He wrapped me up in a rug and I half went to sleep in his arms. It was all comfortable and lovely, and because Anton was a German I didn't feel as if I were being unfaithful to my real love. Somehow I could never take a German very seriously, but they are glorious to flirt with.

We were at Carfax at 11.55 and at St Hilda's just before 12 and it was impossible to get in legitimately without making more fuss than I wanted to. So my last evening at Oxford, I had to climb in – but not straight away. We went to Magdalen Bridge and got a punt. The river looked so tempting and YR was broken. We did not go straight to St Hilda's but turned round and went right past Addison's Walk and round the corner where we moored. It was all lovely – the river dark and still with a few stars. Then we went back and to the St Hilda's landing stage. Anton and H. climbed ashore with me – and helped me over the wall and barbed wire. They waited while I went to see whether there was any possible way of getting into the building. There didn't seem to be, so I went back and Henry came into the garden with me to help me – it was romantic to be walking in St Hilda's garden with him at almost 2 in the morning. We went round to try and wake Sharp – and as luck would have it – I noticed Celia Evans' window was open and the gates undrawn. Henry lifted me on to the sill – held my hand and said goodnight. I managed not to wake Celia, although I made a frightful noise. I wasn't in bed till dawn was breaking and the birds were starting to sing.

18 June. I went along to the flat with a big bunch of red and yellow roses for Henry. I had to knock a long time before anyone would come – they were both asleep. The char. arrived – I felt it was rather strange to be there at 10. Henry was in a lovely temper and very pleased with the roses. After breakfast I lay on the blue divan and Henry put on a Brandenburg Concerto and some Sibelius. Despite the fact that Anton would sing 'Stormy Weather' I didn't feel really unhappy. Henry came up behind me and kissed my mouth very gently, which was my real farewell to him and the sweetest thing that could be imagined.

16 July. Went to Oxford from Oswestry on the 9 train. Coming up Beaumont Street I saw Henry. He seemed genuinely glad to see me. The flat is now beautifully furnished and they have a heavenly sofa in tweedy stuff, very long and comfy. In spite of the fact that Henry was talking much of a sweet Finnish girl he'd met called Pääviki we proceeded as usual. He said we'd probably go on meeting each other like this many times in the future and I think so too. We had a frugal supper after which Mr Barnicot came. Then it was so thrilling, Henry got a letter saying he'd got the job he'd tried for in the University of Helsingfors – Finland. He was so excited he thought he'd be sick – so he sat in a chair and I calmed him down and stroked his lovely head. Then we rushed out and bought a bottle of whisky – and we celebrated. I drank to my sweet Harvey in the first whisky I'd ever tasted. We danced and sang, played the piano and made a glorious noise – Sibelius on the gramophone too, and we spoke German nearly the whole evening. I made up Henry's mouth with lipstick and he made up Barnicot and me like clowns. Finally they took me home at about 12, and I walked arm-in-arm with them both. Henry gave me a pair of slippers – red leather and brightly coloured wool.

17 July. Very hot. I was going to Bodley at about 12 but was waylaid by Barnicot and went and drank lemonade with him. We talked much – the poor dear always seems to want to talk about Honor.

18 July. My Viva was short and sweet, purely formal and my class obviously decided – but what? I had tea with Henry and he took me to the station. He said I was part of his background, like Jock and Barnicot, which pleased me. It is what I've always wanted – I love him too, but don't want him for my very own yet awhile.

I got a 2nd. With comparative ease too.

1 September. Sometime in July I began writing a story about Hilary and me as spinsters of fiftyish. Henry, Jock and all of us appeared in it. I sent it to them and they liked it very much. So I am going on with it and one day it may become a book. It is interesting in more ways than one. It is of course 'for Henry', and in it I seem able to say what I cannot in the ordinary course of events. Barbara keeps looking back to her youth, and so I have an excuse for revealing some of my present feelings about Henry. No change has been wrought in them, as far as I can see. He still remains the only person. This time not even a visit to Germany made any difference, but perhaps that was merely chance. Anyway I am content about that.

Germany was delightful and more than usually interesting, as we arrived in Hamburg on the same day as the Führer and were able to see him. I thought he looked smooth and clean, and was very impressed. The elections were held on the Sunday, 19 August (we had arrived on the Friday). There was plenty of publicity etc. urging voters to say '*Ja*' for Hitler. The ones I can remember best were: '*Führer wir folgen dir*'. '*Alle sagen Ja!*' '*Ein Reich, Ein Führer, Ein Ja*'. At the station – '*Reisende! denk an eure Stimmpflicht*'.

4 October. The position at present is this. I am staying at home this autumn and not taking a job. I think I am going to enjoy it very much, being naturally contented. But I am not entirely idle, as I am writing my novel of real people which is getting on quite well, though not really as fast as it ought to. I try to type 2 sides every day, and today I haven't done quite that, although on occasions I can do more.

Henry went to Finland on the 19th of September, and according to Jockie's account is happy there. Naturally he hasn't written to me, although he did in August about my story, a very nice letter. Still I hope that he will keep the promise made at viva-time in July. I still love him very deeply as far as one is able to judge, with no men to compare him with and absence making the heart grow fonder – but I am calmer about it. It is not as easy to be jealous of various vague Finns as of some definite people in Oxford.

7 October. I wrote 4 pages of my story today, and enjoyed doing it. After lunch I thought all inspiration had gone, but later it came back quite surprisingly. I gave way to a hysterical outburst because Links was cross with us about laying the tea. And I haven't really cried for ages. I do try my best to be honest with myself and ask myself whether I'm really in love with Henry, and whether I really feel a kind of *Sehnsucht* for him. I do believe that Absence makes the heart grow fonder and lends a sort of glamour to the beloved person.

9 October. Wrote in the morning and went in the town. Cold weather is coming upon us and I feel the need for my waffy coat. I started my white polo jersey and have done quite a lot. It is in a nice rather thick 4-ply wool. All afternoon I thought about clothes and decided to get myself a new evening frock. I've not had one for three years! I also decided how to make my blue velvet and how to renovate my green frock. Not a bad afternoon!

23 November. I went to Oxford. It was lovely seeing people again. Jockie and Barnicot, Sharp, Hilary, Harry, etc. I also had a letter from dear Henry and took my degree of Bachelor of Arts, which was rather boring.

10 December. I was to have returned to Shropshire this morning, but after much thought decided not to, but to wait until Henry came. It required a lot of thought, this decision, but Jockie and Mr B. persuaded me to stay. I knew that if I went home I should only 'fret' at not seeing him, but I knew also that if I stayed I might have to endure much misery. And yet the thought of unhappiness couldn't make me run away. I had to face up to it, and I wanted to know if I still loved him. I called for Jockie and we had tea at the Moorish – he was deliciously amusing as ever. We decided it might be rather fun if Henry were drowned at sea then we might write a *Lachrymae Musarum* – rather in the style of the elegies for Edward King – in Latin English. I should do rather a Clevelandic poem –

> My pen's the spout
> Where the rain water of mine eyes runs out –

or whatever it is.

11 December. At about 8 o'clock this evening I saw my Henry, for the first time since July 18th. He greeted me with derisive laughter, but said he was glad to see me. It was not a happy evening and during the end of it I was in tears. They were all there. Henry was excited and he and Jockie squabbling rather a lot. Henry has a navy blue hat, which I think I don't like. Somehow I lamented the passing of the brown hat and the big grey coat – and yet he was not really much changed in his attitude towards me – there wasn't really a chance to show it.

12 December. A lovely morning and I was with Henry. The intense misery of the night before had given way to a state of 'calm of mind, all passion spent'. I was content just to be with him and tried hard to live in the present as I drove down the Banbury Road with him in YR in the sun and said goodbye at about half past twelve – hours of his company and so little of it alone – he really hardly seemed aware of me! He will not be in England again until May, and so much could happen in these next months, with the Spring coming – that same Spring which in 1933 afflicted poor Sandra with that divine madness for which she can only be thankful. For, in spite of unhappiness, it has brought me Jockie and other friends – and a little of Henry which I shall never forget.

> How small part of time they share
> That are so wondrous sweet and fair!

as I am always quoting in my novel. If I'm in Oxford in the Spring who knows what may happen – or shall I just content myself with remembering last year and the year before? And still be desolate and sick of an old passion.

29 December. Oswestry. Dear Jockie sent me a select Rochester – *Poems on Several Occasions* and *Valentinian* (1696). I was delighted with it, in spite of its expurgations! But as I've read the real thing from Phi while I was at Oxford it didn't much matter.

1935

3 January. Actually I miss Jockie more – his company and conversation, but I am still enslaved by Henry's baser charms. I've not written to him – mainly because I'm not sure of his address. He goes back to Finland next Wednesday.

Now for more trivial matters. I am knitting a sock, dark blue – but ah for whom? I suppose much will depend on the size and general elegance, but it seems thick enough to withstand the rigours of a Finnish winter. My novel progresses not at all – Auntie Nellie is here and we are without a maid, so that at present I seem too busy to do much at it. Nor am I reading anything 'worthwhile' just now, although our greater English poets in their completeness lie in my bookshelves. Tonight we went to see Claudette Colbert in *Cleopatra*, which was quite entertaining and unintentionally amusing.

9 March. Oxford. I went to see Jockie at the flat and yearned for Henry, as that atmosphere always makes me. Henry had left behind his grey overcoat and I sat in it sentimentally the whole evening.

19 April. Germany. We started from Victoria at 10. This year going to Germany wasn't quite so much to soothe an aching heart, though I had been rather bored. I hadn't written to Henry since February 25th nor he to me. There is something satisfying about such silence.

20 April. We arrived in Cologne about 6. I was very tired but sufficiently awake to notice who of last year's German students were there to meet us. To my pleasure I noticed Hanns. It was so nice to see his familiar face again that I felt comforted although there was no sign of Friedbert. I spoke to Hanns and we had a little conversation in German. The drive to the *Kameradschafthaus* was rather long.

Friedbert was angelic to me. Such kindness as his one can never forget.

May. Oswestry. Why can't I write this diary properly? But now that I've seen Henry again I must make myself write. Otherwise his biographers (or mine) will be disappointed at the break in the otherwise continuous account of my acquaintance with him.

After Germany I was in love with Friedbert *in a way.* I put it so because I realised even at the time that most of it was probably glamour. His being a foreigner – the little Americanisms in his speech like 'terribly' and the way he said 'Barbara' – it being in a foreign country with the Hohenzollern Brücke by moonlight and *zwei* Manhattan at the Excelsior and his Nivea Creme that I rubbed on my arm to remember the smell of him – for all these things I loved him and yet I hardly knew him as a person and didn't at all agree with his National Socialism, although I tried to read Feuchtwanger's book *The Oppermans* and a lot of German poetry just after my stay in Cologne and my interest in the language was reawakened with the result that really I learnt a good deal more. Now that I've seen Henry again I suppose it will be Swedish, which he seems to speak and read fluently and gets quite annoyed when I can't do the same.

I heard from Barnicot that Henry was in Oxford when I arrived 22 May. On Friday 24 May I saw him again for the first time since 12 Dec. The meeting was quite as I could have wished. I came upon him face to face in the Broad. He was pleased to me me, genuinely I think. He made fun of my pink toenails, saying that I must hide them under a table as quickly as possible. This we did, by having coffee in Fuller's, although it was almost lunchtime. Funnily enough we saw Alison there and it was pleasant not to feel jealous of her. Henry was extremely nice and I went back to lunch full of hope. I went to see him at 30 Banbury Road at 6 o'clock that evening and he was still nice and seemed more interested in me – which was perhaps natural. 'There is no future, there is no more past'.... When I quoted that to Henry in a letter I was writing while with him one morning I'm sure he didn't in the least know what it was, and naturally he wouldn't ask. That is so unsatisfactory, not being properly understood, and not being given the chance to explain. I suppose I imagine that I must be more interesting and intelligent than the other unwanted lovers of this world. However, I had dinner at the George with him and Jock. Henry said – 'It's no use looking at those strawberries, because you won't get any'. I had actually been contemplating a fine lobster. I was happy that evening. Then, although Henry and Jock argued somewhat (about Jock's desire to leave Oxford and cut himself off from it entirely) we had pleasant conversation and things seemed better than they had been. Afterwards we went back to 30 Banbury Road and were turned out for being noisy, and perhaps the woman heard my remark about it being so sordid to be seen in one's suspenders. I was on Henry's knee at the time and Jock was playing 'Holy, Holy, Holy' on the recorder. A strange combination of circumstances.

After that I didn't see Henry for four days which made me rather depressed. At least I only caught glimpses of him. And on Sunday night I heard from Jock that he'd gone to live at 5 Pusey Street. I spent Sunday night wandering about Oxford trying to console myself and perhaps catch a sight of him. Monday too was spent in looking for him, without success, for I didn't like to call at his house and would have preferred a chance meeting. I went to his room and left him a note. On top of his tin of Nivea, which the mean creature refused to give me. The note I left was in my best style I think. He thought it charming and wrote me a nice letter next day, which I was surprised and delighted to get. As a result I went to see him on Wednesday morning at ten o'clock and saw him eating his breakfast. He was not particularly good tempered, but then he seldom is in the mornings. He will never talk about him and me and always gives evasive answers that are unsatisfying to me, as I want so much to know how things *really* are between us. Is it any use hoping even for his friendship – and is that enough? Is it not rather worse than nothing? At present I can't decide. Barnicot thinks I have no hope at all and that his friendship would be of no use to me. But I think somehow that I'd like it. I don't mind being part of the furniture of his background, or even hanging over him like a gloomy cloud, as he said at tea one day. He himself has admitted that I have a special place in the little world he has built for himself and of which presumably J. is the centre. And I suppose too that he feels this is so in the novel where I have brought us all together in our later years. But at the present moment it seems as if this world is falling to pieces – so what becomes of me then?

After supper we all went on the river. We landed at the Victoria Arms where Jock left us and strutted away across the ferry. When Jock had gone Henry proceeded to get rather drunk. I had a little beer but not much, though I was quite hilarious. We got mixed up with a party of tight undergraduates, one of whom was rather funny, and asked Henry to sleep with him. Henry, rather getting the worse of it in the wit combat, diverted attention to me. From then I was for it. We had been speaking foreign languages, as one naturally tends to under the influence of drink, and he pretended I was a German. None of the undergraduate party could really speak it, so we were able to deceive them. Henry (by this time rather drunk) insisted that we should punt along with them and kept trying to put me in the other punt, which he eventually succeeded in doing with the help of another man. Barnicot (who was punting) was silent. Up to now I had been quite enjoying things but when I found myself in a punt with five drunken undergraduates I didn't feel so happy. Also I was being taken further and further away from my own people, who seemed unable to catch up. I think I am to be congratulated on the way in which I kept up the deception to the end. Anyway I'd have felt even more of a fool if I'd admitted to them that I was English and a graduate of the University, so I more or less had to and my German was adequate. There was rather a terrifying moment when turning and we were standing up and the punt began to fill with water. I suppose I should have felt very much ashamed of myself but I wasn't really, especially as it was all H's fault. At the time I wasn't in the least angry with him although I should have been, for he behaved like a complete cad. We went on to Jockie's flat where we had tea and Jock heard all the story. I think he was amused about it, though of course he pretended to be shocked. Of course when Henry told it, he made me out to be much worse than I really was. But I was feeling very loving towards him and sprawled all over him on the sofa.

30 May. I went round to Henry's at 10. This was a very nice day for me. We spent the morning quite lazily, I was sleepy and so was he. I read aloud to him then he wanted the book to himself, so that all he could lend me was Colley Cibber's *Apology* for his life which I wasn't really feeling in the mood for. So I slept a little and thought much and rubbed Nivea and Eau de Cologne on myself and wrote a love letter to Henry and then he said I could stay to lunch. We decided to go to Basingstoke to fetch the Bentley – just me and Henry. We caught the 3 o'clock train and had a carriage to ourselves and it was upholstered in lurid shades of red and rusty brown in a large bold pattern. I'm sure I shall always remember that upholstery.

We smoked Finnish cigarettes and talked about travel in Finland and the English countryside. We also read the *Telegraph* and I meditated on how strange and wonderful it was to be in a train with Henry, and who would have thought it two years ago and the sort of thing I always think whenever I do anything with him. I suppose this is inevitable, as the most ordinary things done with someone one loves are full of new significance that they never have otherwise.

In Basingstoke we wandered through the streets till we found the garage, where we were told that the car would be ready in about half an hour. So we wandered in the streets once more and looked at the shut shops. We saw some cottages for the poor, aged and impotent but somehow it was difficult to imagine that either of us would ever be those things. Basingstoke is a very ordinary town with rather a hideous Jubilee (1887) tower, which doesn't match the rest of the architecture. But I suppose I shall always remember it luridly. I think Henry and I must have looked like two characters out of a musical comedy – the comic characters. As I caught sight of our reflections in shop windows I couldn't help smiling. I was wearing my German hat, turned up all round, so that it looked like a kind of parson's hat, or dish, and there is always something faintly ludicrous about Henry's blue hat with him inside it. It was rather hot, thundery weather and I expressed a desire for a drink of Eno's which Henry thought rather shocking. We looked about at men's clothes in the shops and then went and had tea at a place called the Golden Gate Café – all orange. We sat in the window and Henry said that if he was very rich he would buy me a cottage in the country, only I couldn't have a wireless. Also an establishment in Oxford which I insisted on.

The ride back in the Bentley was marvellous. It was the first time I'd ever ridden in one. We ran into heavy rain and thunder when we'd gone a few miles and had to put the hood up, during which I cut my finger. Henry made a somewhat unnecessary fuss about it, but it was nice to be poor Pym-ed at intervals. When we reached Pangbourne the weather was nice again, and stayed so all the way back to Oxford. I was wearing the Barnicot waffy coat which I liked very much. It is so enormously spacious and opulent. I'm sure we must have looked very caddish. I found myself wanting to gaze all the time at Henry's divine profile, particularly those lovely hollows in his cheeks which delight me so. But if I gazed too much I had to make conversation so I contented myself with remaining huddled in the huge coat, wishing the journey needn't ever come to an end.

After supper went for a ride in the Bentley – Henry and Jockie in front, Barnicot and I in the back. It was very pleasant intrinsically but Henry's good temper had worn off and though we were together in the back of the car on the latter part of the ride he said he was bored with me, and seemed in the sort of mood when he would be nasty whatever I said.

The next time I saw him properly was Saturday the 1st. I had lunch with John Barnicot and we talked a good deal about Henry as we always do. He thinks I have absolutely no hope at all, and it's a waste of time me hanging around. Naturally this wasn't really news to me, but I couldn't help being a little cast down when he told me that Henry found me boring because I always agreed with him. J.B. thinks it would be better if I were a little rougher with Henry. Consequently when we met him I tried to be rude to him and he was also rude to me, which made me annoyed. However it was difficult to be really effective in public and the afternoon was rather futile and pointless. We walked down St Aldate's and through Christ Church meadows and then went in the Botanical Gardens, where I took them into the very hot hot-houses. But there was nothing exciting there – only a few orchids. We were all rather fractious and I chased Henry with a stick and argued with him about the date when the place was founded, although I hadn't really the faintest idea. Henry and B. and I had tea in the Union Garden – the first time I've had a meal in the Union. That was nice and there was a charming cat in the garden, but Henry was rude about my teeth, which always makes me unhappy. Henry and I then walked back to my digs in St Margaret's Road somewhat drearily and I tried to talk to him and find out how I stood. I said it hadn't been delightful seeing him but quite nice, to which he agreed saying that nothing could be delightful any more.

25 August. Oswestry. Henry, Jockie and Mr Barnicot all came to Oswestry. It was lovely. Henry was absolutely at his best. He wore his grey flannel suit, a bright blue silk shirt with a darker blue tie and blue socks. He wanted me to return to Oxford with them, but I feel it is better that I remain here, thinking lovingly of him, with more real fondness than before. He goes to Finland on the 11th of September. I don't know when he comes back or when I shall see him again.

3 November. I take up my pen after a long interval, not as seems usual in this diary because I've seen Henry again or because anything particularly exciting has happened to me. There's no point in trying to write up all past events so I shall just have to begin now.

10 November. No letter from Henry. No news of my novel. Last Monday I sent two stories to the *London Mercury – Unpast Alps* and *They Never Write,* but have so far heard nothing. On Tuesday I had a driving lesson with Price and got on well.

11 November. Armistice Day. My novel came back from being typed while I was having breakfast. They seem to have done it well and in spite of a few mistakes it looks very nice. I may call it *Some Tame Gazelle. Some Sad Turtle* is also another possibility but somehow it reminds me rather too much of turtle soup and the rest of the quotation isn't quite so suitable. I spent some time going through the novel in the evening and did about 13 chapters. I am alternately cheerful and depressed about it.

For the two minutes silence we went to the Park gates where they had a nice service.

15 November. I am reading *Gaudy Night* by Dorothy L. Sayers and enjoying it so much. Pleasure and pain in an agreeable mixture. That's what I feel when I think of Oxford and my days at St Hilda's.

16 November. No letters today or indeed any other day it seems. Henry, Jockie, Barnicot, Friedbert, Sharp, *London Mercury* – all silent.

I packed off my novel (*Some Tame Gazelle* it's to be) to be bound into 2 volumes (in limp covers!). We had lunch in Shrewsbury and did a little vague shopping. I bought a 6d. lipstick. Now I'm trying to think of a plot for a new novel. Possibly another me, in the character of an undergraduate this time!

19 November. This morning I had another driving lesson and got on very well except for a few lapses, notably when I went on the pavement at the Sun Corner. However I'm getting better at it. I had a nice Austin 2-seater to drive. Yesterday I started another novel and wrote about a thousand words or more. It promises to be quite fun. This evening Ack and I went to the pictures to see Charles Boyer and Loretta Young in *Shanghai*.

21 November. My novel came back from being bound – very nicely with green backs and soft yellow covers. I had a nice letter from Jockie. He says Henry has given away his kitten and wonders how he had the heart to do it. Personally I'm not so sure about Henry having so much kindness in that heart of his. He is coming back to England sometime between December 9th and 12th. I don't feel any special emotion about it, but I certainly shan't stay in Oxford as last year.

23 November. My novel was sent to Chatto and Windus yesterday. I didn't feel half so emotional about it as when I sent it to be typed. Today I have spent most of my time knitting a brown peaked cap. It is now finished and quite snappy.

26 November. Had a nice note from Harold Raymond acknowledging my novel. At 11.30 my last driving lesson. We went through the town then Whittington, Queen's Head, Wolf's Head then through Oswestry again and the Race Course. We talked of dogs and monkeys and the Big Wheel at Blackpool. I got on quite well and gave him 10/-. He seemed quite pleased.

27 November. Refused yet another invite to Mrs Moon's dance. Nowadays one cannot undertake such engagements lightly. Most of this day was spent in getting ready for Oxford – packing. I am pleasantly excited about going away, and hope I'll meet somebody nice and not be brooding too much over Henry.

28 November. Oxford. Once more in Oxford and so far it seems to be very much like any other time since I left. Only I notice even more that everywhere is full of strange young faces – Elliston's, the Bodleian, the Corn – I've seen Barnicot – yesterday evening in the Radcliffe Camera and had a long talk with him. They've altered the place and made a great round enclosure in the middle of the floor – wherein sit Barnicot and minions. We talked for a long time and he was rather depressing about my novel. About that one can only wait. I sent a postcard to Henry, a highly coloured one of Christ Church – the Light that never was on sea or land, I called it. It's good to be here again though I can see nobody to fall in love with.

2 December. Yesterday I went out to dinner with Jock and had a long talk afterwards – he gave me a peculiar photograph of Henry. On seeing photographs of Henry in his album I was so moved that my eyes filled with tears, whether from love, memories of the past, regret of the present or anticipation of the future, I don't know.

After tea with Hilary today at Elliston's we went on to Martin Watkin's sherry party at 99 Botley Road. It was very much as sherry parties usually are when one really knows none of the people there – a small low-ceilinged room full of people and cigarette smoke. Noise of talking and a radiogramophone makes all conversation impossible – one can't be intelligent shouting remarks at a person. There was nobody I passionately wanted to know. After it we had some food at Kemp Hall Cafeteria and then I called at 30 Banbury Road to see Mr Barnicot. Fortunately I found him in and I spent a very pleasant evening talking with him and Meurig Davies who came in later. They seemed impressed by the fact that I was looking so elegant, which I was more than usual – in my turquoise frock, black fur cape and high heels. We talked of course and then they wanted me to read, so I read a chapter from *The Brothers Karamazov* for which they each (B. and Meurig!) gave me one penny. Mr B. also read some Italian (Ariosto I think) while Meurig recited a few speeches and bits of things. Later we turned the light out and had music from Budapest, which always makes me a little melancholy. There we were, the three of us – Mr B. in love with Honor, Meurig with Ann Sitwell and Pymska with Henry. It was a most pleasant evening.

3 December. I went in the town this morning – very poor. I tried to get back 6½d. from Elliston's for a pair of knitting needles, but they would only change them and wouldn't let me have the money. Then I wrote home for some books to try and sell them.

6 December. I forgot to say that yesterday my novel was rejected by Chatto, but they wrote me a very nice letter. They think it's too long and my character drawing too detached, but I have a style which is a pleasure to read, etc. I wasn't as depressed as I thought I'd be and even looked forward to cutting and improving it. Jockie and Barnicot were very sweet and sympathetic. 'There is a world elsewhere' anyway.

On Friday David Tree – Viola Tree's son – was at a party I went to. He is a charming young man (about nineteen I think) and very good looking. He is however interested in Hot and Swing music to such an extent that he can talk of nothing else. He will sit with a profound rapt look on his face and then all he will say is – 'wonderful, that entry after the vocal'. He made no real effort to divert.

7 December. I went into the Bodleian to say goodbye to Jockie. He said he had had a postcard from Henry, and that Henry had sent his love to me. J. was very sweet and quite at his best. I hope he doesn't go to Cairo, because I shall miss him very much. I bought two postcards in the picture gallery – one of the outside of the library and another of the familiar *'Plurimi pertransibunt et multiplex erit scientia'*. I wonder when I shall pass through again. I seemed to be telling myself that I shouldn't visit Oxford for a long time, but it seems hard to imagine not going there for a termly visit, although each time it gets a little sad. A slow wrenching away indeed.

9 December. Oswestry. This morning I sent my novel to Gollancz.

12 December. Went to Brian's dance. We kept getting lost and missing signposts but eventually arrived at Petersfield about 6. We changed hastily and had a magnificent dinner at the Red Lion. We had a good start for the dance with cocktails, champagne and port, so that I felt quite dizzy! The dance itself was great fun although having to dance and make conversation with so many different people was rather a strain.

20 December. Today I had two stories rejected by the *London Mercury,* so that I only need my novel back from Gollancz to complete everything. But in the bustle of Christmas shopping I seem not to care overmuch.

29 December. I must start reading our greater English poets again. *The Heir of Redclyffe* is rather a comfort though. At present I am depressed. I want Liebe but I would be satisfied if my novel could be published.

1936

2 January. My novel came back from Gollancz with a polite note. I also had a long letter from Henry, but as it was written in Latin, German, French, Swedish, Finnish and the English of James Joyce I could not well understand it. We went to Shrewsbury and saw Katherine Hepburn and Charles Boyer in *Break of Hearts*. Very good.

11 January. I sent Hilary a scarf, also an eyebrush and comb for her birthday. We went to Shrewsbury and saw Conrad Veidt in *The Passing of the Third Floor Back*.

17 January. In the evening I tried to write a story about Budapest, while Links and Ack were at the pictures.

19 January. The king was much the same all day. While washing up I began to wonder how I could get hold of a typewriter, for without one I am lost.

20 January. The king died tonight at 11.55 p.m. It was a very peaceful ending.

22 January. King Edward VIII was proclaimed. We heard it on the wireless from London.

To Henry Harvey in Oxford   *Staying with her cousin*

Newburn,
Hatch End,
Middlesex.

15 May 1936

Dear Henry:

I don't know whether you intended me to answer your letter or whether it was just written in a hurry and you didn't mean a word you said. However it was quite sensible and much that you said I agreed with (look out!) but not all. If you want the truth straight away here it is. I am fed up with the whole business. Of writing gay flippant letters to you and expecting you to see that I didn't really feel that way. Of meeting you at regular intervals and finding that if anything we get on a little worse than the last time. Of having my peace disturbed for no purpose. And of your promises to write which never came to anything – although fair play to you – you always have plenty of excuses – and of finding that as time goes on you don't improve or grow any older – I mean grow up in the sense that people ought to. In fact I daresay I've become thoroughly selfish and I feel like staying that way. Of course *all* this probably isn't your fault, although some of it certainly is. As you said, we have never been real to each other. This may be because of the way Jock has treated us by refusing to take anything seriously – but it is really because you haven't been sufficiently interested in me to make much effort about it. And of course when things are like that between two people there just isn't anything that can be done about it. I don't know whether you agree with me over this – or whether you've even thought about it, but I think I am right. But however much Jock may be responsible for the state of affairs between *us*, I can never forget that he saved me a great deal of unhappiness by his way of looking at things, which I adopted too, at least in our correspondence and conversation. It is an amusing game, and I don't see why it should affect one's real self unless one wants it to. I know that as far as I'm concerned, although I've learned to treat things in his way, the other side of me is still there to be brought out when necessary. I have no wish that it should be annihilated altogether because I know I couldn't find any happiness unless I were a real person as well as a 'flat' one. (I use your word because it seems a good one and I can't think of another. I'm finding it rather difficult to explain myself clearly, but I hope you'll see what I mean).

Did I tell you I had started a new novel? I am just beginning to get into form, although at first I found it something of an effort. It is about time my first novel came back from Macmillan – it has been there over two weeks now.

My best love to Mr B. and Jock, and to you,

from Barbara

Oswestry. I've got to start writing again. I've fallen in love, and with Henry. I feel just as bad as I did three years ago – almost worse because he has been extremely nice to me and we have got on much better together than ever before. We have been together day and night for the past three weeks and yesterday he and Mr B. brought me home and now I'm wretched and missing him terribly. I have been acting as his secretary since June 17th. I've typed and taken dictation and copied pages out of the *Dictionary of National Biography* for him – worked all night for him – and received 30/- a week.

7 June. Oxford. On this day H., J., Mr B., and I went out in the car for the day. Into the Cotswolds. But somehow I didn't get on very well with them. It was largely my own fault as I was inclined to be rather aggressive in my 'lowness', talking about dance music etc. I think I did this because I felt intellectually inferior to them all, especially Henry, who always makes you feel it more than the others do. I felt that they were all against me and I made things worse by my obstinacy. But I felt resentful of being dominated by them and not being allowed to be myself at all. Also I was so conscious of being much better on paper than in speech. Anyway it was a nice day and we had a very pleasant dinner at the Old Swan at Minster Lovell, where we made up verses to celebrate the approaching nuptials of Count Weiss.

8 June. After tea Henry came round in the car to fetch me to hear a record of James Joyce at the flat. He was morose and bad tempered, hardly speaking to me and arguing with Jock. I felt miserable and left rather abruptly before seven o'clock. Just as I was going Henry came to the door and said goodbye in that lovely gentle way of his which is so surprising. I often think that Henry is never so nice as when he's standing at the door of the flat saying goodbye.

9 June. I had a long talk with Mr B. I can remember telling him that I thought I didn't care for Henry, in fact almost hated him at times, and wouldn't now marry him at any price, as I once thought I would.

15 July. Oswestry. Gerard Langbaine the younger was born on this day in 1656. I was very unhappy in the morning and cried (a) because I missed Henry (b) because I loved him and could see no hope for the future (c) because I couldn't get any of my works accepted (d) because Oswestry was so frightful after Oxford (e) because it was a dull day. Quite enough reasons for feeling wretched I think. But at lunch things improved. To begin with I had postcards from Scotland from Henry and John Barnicot. Then we had strawberries and cream. And last of all the sun came out, so that I was able to sit in the revolving summerhouse. Here I read Mr Huxley's new book *Eyeless in Gaza* and went to sleep. In the evening I realised that I had served nearly half my seven years for Lorenzo – or Henry as he has now become. The service began on 13th February 1933 (as nearly as such things can be dated) – it will therefore be finished on 13 February 1940.

16 July. I remember how hard we were working this time last week. Henry, Mr B. and I in the flat. I was, I suppose, at this moment typing Chapter III (Dramatic Bibliography), all that complicated stuff about the 1680 Catalogue, which I didn't very well understand. Certainly I know that it was dawn before Henry took me home and several birds had started to sing. The last day of all I worked all through the night – with two hours sleep in Henry's bed. He had slept between nine and eleven. And at about six o'clock in the morning, I tucked him up in an armchair with a rug, while I went through one of the copies marking in notes. Without me he couldn't have done the thing at all. I can say this, knowing that it is true. Between seven and nine, or thereabouts, he dictated the last pages of the chapter on the Account. I have been given a taste of how lovely things *could* be with Henry – and before I had often guessed and imagined it, but never *known*.

17 July. Henry will be back in Oxford today and I shan't be at the flat to make tea for him. I can't help hoping that he will realise this, but naturally he will only look upon it as a fact, it will have no sentimental significance. I am now on the 6th chapter of my second novel [*Civil to Strangers,* unpublished] and am intending to get on with it as fast as possible.

18 July. In the morning I wrote a little of my novel, and then I have been reading a book on Bibliography and trying to fold pages in 12mo and 4° etc. I got a book about it from Blackwell's. I must *work* at my novel, that is the only thing there is and the only way to find any happiness at present.

19 July. I haven't done very much today. I went to church, knitted and talked and listened to a play about Keats.

Tonight I have been looking through my early works – poetry and prose!

20 July. I compromised by sending Henry a postcard in cheerful style – but ending with a quotation from 'Tears, idle Tears'.... 'Oh Death in Life, the Days that are no more!' But he will not perhaps know how seriously I meant it. Today I wrote about 8 pages in a large foolscap size notebook. I'd like if possible to get the whole thing done by November. It will be something to work for.

21 July. My *Life and Times of Anthony à Wood* came – it is a lovely book, although I wish I had the complete one.

I had my hair cut and got two new pairs of trollies – a peach and pale yellow. In the evening I did some typing and finished my socks.

22 July. After supper I wrote about four foolscap pages of my new novel. I don't quite know what to think of it – I can't feel it's really as good as *Some Tame Gazelle,* but it may stand a better chance of getting accepted.

24 July. Naturally I've ceased to miss Henry so agonisingly, but I still hope – though faintly – to hear from him. When I think of him apologising for being irritable with me, and standing in the room in the early hours of the morning, looking like an unshaven Russian prince with a turquoise coloured scarf round his waist – of course I love him!

I have now written 8 chapters, or a hundred pages of my new novel, and feel that I am getting into it. I have worked hard at it today and yesterday.

14 August. Last Monday I had a letter from Jonathan Cape – saying that he was interested in my novel *Some Tame Gazelle* and thought he might be able to offer to publish it if I would make some alterations. They are quite minor ones – so I hope I shall soon be able to send it off again. And then – I dare not hope too much, but it would be marvellous if he took it.

To Henry Harvey

I imagine you are at
30 Banbury Road?

Morda Lodge,
Oswestry,
Shropshire.

20 August 1936

My poor Henry:

Thank you for both your pathetic letters. They were a good deal better than nothing. I doubt if either of us will ever be the same again after Gerard and as you've had the examining as well you may be worse off. But I don't think you will be, because your heart will be quite whole and you will have £37.10s.

I am quite worn out although we have only just come back from the sea. I daresay Jock has told you about Jonathan Cape and my novel. He is going to consider it again – after I have made a few alterations. They are quite minor ones, but so wearying to do. I'm sure I know it almost by heart – certainly the first few pages. I am greatly cheered about this, but only vaguely hopeful. Why should Jonathan Cape want to publish my novel, when Macmillan and Methuen didn't? (I don't count Chatto and Gollancz as nobody but a fool would have published it in its early form.) And anyway I'm only twenty-three. But all the same I shall probably cry if Cape don't take it. Adam and Cassandra [*Civil to Strangers*] are getting on quite nicely, though I haven't done much to them lately. Adam is sweet but very stupid. You are sweet too, but not as consistently stupid as Adam. But I wish you were here to show me where to put commas and to help me with my novel. I can type frightfully fast after doing Gerard, but find that instead of being able to type words like Archdeacon and Belinda I want to type Langbaine and Architypographus.

I am all alone in the house, except for the wireless, which you despise so much. I am writing rather slowly and laboriously and every time I think of something nice to say I stop and consider it well before I put it. I don't believe letters should be written like this, especially from people like me to people like you. It would be better if I could write you a poem and I have written one or two fragments since I last saw you. But I don't think I shall own them. Your little poem was very touching and far more acceptable to me than your letters in the style of Joyce. I wish I knew something about the modern poets. Nobody will listen to me (except Jock) when I say that I am very fond of Young's *Night Thoughts.* I wish you would teach me about them and tell me which ones to read and how to understand them. Even the Finns know more than I do. You ought to try and educate me in things I don't know about.

I hope you have recovered from your spleen. I haven't been really unhappy since the week after you went.

Just such a letter might poor Elsie Godenhjelm write to you, only perhaps she has more respect for you than I have – though I have still a certain amount. I hope you will think this is a nice answerable letter although it is rather dull. (*Very* dull, I think, on reading it through – but there is not much news and I have forgotten how to write a real love letter. I have now for so long mistrusted the spontaneous overflow of powerful feelings.) And at present I don't really pine for you – I mean my eyes don't prick with tears every time I think of you as in July.

Take care of yourself and be happy.

All my love,

Barbara

30 August. I wish my diary were as interesting and instructive as Anthony à Wood's. It must be dull reading with nothing but the falseness of Henry in it. There should be more talk of prodigies in it and more intelligent accounts of what I have been doing.

7 September. A very pleasant day with Henry, Jockie and Mr B. They came for me at about 9.30 – having spent the night at the

Wynnstay.We went to Port Meirion. This is a very charming, very Henryish place with pink and blue and yellow Italian villas and statues all about in odd corners. Henry was very nice and it was all very pleasant. He goes back to Finland on Tuesday. I envy Elsie Godenhjelm – after all I love him too!

1 October. In the morning I finished (typing) Chapter XIV of *Adam and Cassandra.* I have now reached p.170 and think I can finish it. It seems to get better as it goes on, I think.

1937

On 12 December – a Sunday – Henry Stanley Harvey married Elsie Beatrice Godenhjelm in Helsingfors at the English Church.
So endete eine grosse Liebe.

3 December. Oxford. I was having lunch with Denis Pullein-Thompson in Stewart's. We had been to a sherry party and were still feeling the effects of it. I was talking like a Finn. When we had almost finished lunch a young man came and stood by our table. He was about my height, slight and dark with a quizzical, rather monkey face. He wore a camel hair coat and a spotted tie and looked sleek and neat. Denis introduced him as Jay and me as Päävikki Olafsson. He sat down with us. I went on talking like a Finn. After a while Denis had to go to an OUDS rehearsal so Jay and I were left alone. I gave up being a Finn. We talked about my writing. He said that he sometimes wrote poems and that he thought it might be a good thing to spend five years writing a novel. I said I couldn't do that. He asked me to go back to his rooms in Balliol, which I did. He asked me what I would like to drink but I wanted nothing. His rooms were rather untidy, with papers and letters all over the table and desk and a rather ill-drawn map for some subject of Pass Moderations. The books were just work books. We sat on a sofa – he took my hand and told my future and then kissed me. I was surprised – it was the first time anyone so much younger than he had done such a thing, for he was only eighteen and I twenty-four.

He had so much charm and a kind of childish simplicity, combined with Continental polish that was most appealing.

He stole my handkerchief – a Woolworth's 1½d paisley – and wouldn't give it back. Before I went he put some German and Hungarian records on the gramophone and made me say that it would be *Auf Wiedersehen* and not *Adjö*. He came out into the rain and walked with me to the bus stop, arm in arm, with fingers linked. I was happy.

4 December. I went back to Oswestry and later had a letter from him

I went to a ball at the Austrian Legation last night. Everyone wore peasant dress or pre-war Austrian uniforms. Occasionally swarthy Hungarians smashed their glasses against the wall. It was your party. I wish you could have been there. They played nothing but Viennese waltzes and *Bauermusik*.

Next Friday I leave for Kitzbühel. I'm afraid the atmosphere will be anything but central European, but I'll send you a postcard of some mountains and some peasants.

I send you a handkerchief that you may dry your tears when you read *Werther*. I'm afraid it's not as nice as yours but it will make up for it. When am I going to see you again my *'vaend at Elske' Vikki* – when do you come to London? and when you come will you be a Shropshire spinster? a Finnish student? or just a novelist up to see her publisher?

Servus

Jay

1938

January. Hilary went back to Oxford and met Jay – a funny little thing but rather fascinating, she said. After they met he wrote to me, saying that her voice had reminded him of mine. And

I am angry with you. You have been in my mind all day and stopped me concentrating on Louis XVI – I simply can't believe that I've only seen you once for an hour and a half. What will you be like when I see you again? Budapest is on the wireless, the songs have all been very melancholic so far – I feel very Hungarian. Write to me and tell me what you're doing and thinking, and don't forget to tell me when you're coming.

This was especially welcome at this time because I was still feeling rather unhappy and lost about Henry's marriage – I was thankful for any interest to be taken in me.

25 February. I went to Oxford. After tea I went shopping and when I came back there was a light in my room. I went in and saw someone standing in a camel hair coat with his back to me. He turned and faced me and held out his hands to me. I scarcely knew him as we had only met once before. Soon I was talking rather nervously and rapidly and found out that he was writing for a newspaper called *Oxford Comment*, that he hadn't been well and was going to Spain in March. He thought perhaps that I was disappointed in meeting him again but soon we had our arms around each other and I knew it wasn't so.

26 February. When I got to Balliol three blond Etonians like teddy bears were there. I was nervous and forgot my Finnish accent. They went soon after I came. Jay embraced me with such force that he hurt my nose and made it crooked.

For some reason I was vaguely unhappy all evening – either because it was raining or because I had forgotten my lipstick, or for some other, less obvious reason.

After dinner we went to see *Ghosts* at the Playhouse. It was quite the most terrifying play I have ever seen and I felt unhappy all the time. We talked in the intervals about ourselves and our ambitions. He said that he couldn't bear to die without having done something by which he could be remembered.

At the end of the play – which was horrible – we were both frightened and disturbed and walked back to my rooms apart and almost without speaking. There was a tremendous wind in Pusey Street, so that we could hardly stand. It was cold and refreshing.

28 February. Jock depressed me about my Finland novel and I was in tears all the time I was at his flat, especially as I was also unhappy about Henry and my own life seemed pointless and just a waste of time if I wasn't even going to be able to write. I went home and cried – there seemed to be nothing to live for.

The next day I tried to pull myself together and succeeded in thinking about a new novel although I was still unhappy and thought I would have to get a job somewhere at once.

3 March. I was better. A man came along the street singing and I threw some money to him. He wished me luck – I thought how I needed it. I did some writing and then read a book about the Oxford Group – *For Sinners Only* – which brought a curious kind of consolation as well as making me laugh. I thought how nice and easy it would be to be 'changed'.

I went to the Pacifist Meeting in the Town Hall. I saw Don Liddell – he and Jock were there selling literature and carrying posters. Just before it was about to begin I saw Jay standing up in the front. I felt rather excited although I had resolved to put him and all such diversions from me – but I managed to attend well enough to the meeting. The speakers were George Lansbury, Mary Gamble and J. Middleton Murry. After the meeting I talked to the Liddells and John Barnicot. We walked along the Corn. Just by Marks and Spencer's Jay walked past us. I caught him up and asked him if he was going to sign the Peace Pledge. He took my hand and held it very fast. Walking along with him all my unhappiness vanished. We went into the the Randolph and, as it was only five to ten we were able to buy a bottle of Niersteiner to take back with us. In my rooms we drank wine and talked and loved and I made a half-hearted effort to convert him to Pacifism, though I wasn't entirely converted myself. But he said that he thought there were worse things than war, and that if he thought all Beauty was going out of his life he would simply shoot himself.

4 March. I met Jay by the Ashmolean and we leaned up against it and stood looking up at the Randolph and the blue sky behind it. We were like two people having a coltish flirtation. He bought me a bunch of violets and I gave him half a dozen – one for every occasion we had met. Then we parted, he to write an essay and I to write him a Betjeman poem:

> ...Oh the sky is blue behind it
> And the little towers of stone
> Of the Randolph Hotel will still be there
> When this present day has flown.
>
> When Jay has quite forgotten
> That one early closing day
> He leaned against the wall with me
> And I would not go away.
>
> And I went back to my lodgings
> And there I made a shrine
> Of *Oxford Comment* and violets
> And the bottle that once held wine.
>
> And I took a glass I had used before
> And filled it to the brim
> And I thought as I drank of the night before
> When I had been with him...

5 March. I went to lunch with Jay in Balliol.We had eggs with cream on top, chicken and chocolate mousse. And Niersteiner, of course. Just before three we decided to go out. Jean-Pierre Giraudoux came in for a moment to ask Jay to go on the river but he didn't stay when he saw I was there. We walked out into the Broad and down Holywell and talked about going to Italy or somewhere in the Cotswolds. Up to town on the 10.10, breakfast on the train... *Ach, jenes Land der Wonne, Das seh' ich oft im Traum....* When we got into the Botanical Gardens we lay down on the grass under a tree. There were branches of mistletoe in the branches so we kissed. After a while we went into the hothouses and looked at the goldfishes and the palms. Jay kissed me by the orchids and stole a spray for me. They were pinky-mauve with purple centres like velvet. I thought they had a sweet smell but Jay said they smelt like the tomb. I remembered Marvell and so did he:

> The grave's a fine and private place
> But none I think do there embrace.

I said that perhaps it would be nicer to have a marble vault together than a house in North Oxford.

11 March. I went to lunch with Jay in Balliol. We had fish, duck and green peas, peaches and cream, sherry, Niersteiner and port. Jay was wearing his elegant East-End style suit, made in Savile Row – slate-blue with nice padded shoulders and trousers with no turn-ups, touching the ground at the back.

Jay was lying on the sofa and I was sitting on the floor beside him when Woodrow Wyatt, the editor of *Oxford Comment*, came in. I remembered my Finnish accent. After he had gone away we were happy and then incredibly it was five o'clock and he had to go and see his tutor. I knew it would have to be goodbye and perhaps not even *Auf Wiedersehen*. I was calm and sat down at the table to write something on a farewell card. Jay stood in front of his mirror and combed his hair and put on his coat. Then he came up behind me and said *'Servus'*. That was the last time I saw him.

I inscribed a card of Boecklin's *Die Insel der Toten* with our initials and the dates of our first meeting and our last and added a line from my favourite poem by Heine... *Neuer Frühling gibt zurück....*

I was pleasantly sad at leaving his rooms. I took a red anemone from my buttonhole and left it on top of his pale blue pyjamas. I walked round the room touching things. Then I walked slowly down the stairs.

I walked out of the St Giles' gateway in a happy daze and then into Elliston's for tea. I was so happy I could hardly speak coherently to Ruth Brook-Smith and Alison Ross whom I met there. Still in the same state I went back to change to go to dinner at St Hilda's. Just as I was ready to go out I saw that there were some flowers in the hall. Two dozen of the loveliest daffodils and with them a card from Jay saying in German that although he had to go away I knew that he had thought of me. I felt it was a perfect ending to what had been one of the happiest episodes of my life. I was so glad that I didn't see him again in Oxford.

Joint letter to Robert Liddell and   Oswestry
Henry and Elsie Harvey in Helsingfors   *early 1938*

Spring, the sweet spring, that season wherein everything reneweth itself, even the unhappy lover, Miss Pym

Now it is spring and the garden is full of beautiful flowers, primroses, violets, daffodils, scyllas, grape hyacinths, anemones, *und so weiter*. And Miss Pym is looking out of the window – and you will be asking now who is this Miss Pym, and I will tell you that she is a spinster lady who was thought to have been disappointed in love, and so now you know who is this Miss Pym. Well now, as I am telling you, this Miss Pym is looking out of the window, and she is looking into the field opposite the house, where there are many lambs frisking, it being spring, the sweet spring, when maids dance in a ring. But this Miss Pym, although she is, so to speak, a maid, is not dancing in a ring, no sir, and she is not frisking, no buddy, no how. She is seeing an old brown horse which is walking with a slow majestic dignity across this field, and she is thinking that it is the horse that she will be imitating and not the lambs. Old brown horse, she says, we have had our moments you and I, and she is singing in a faded voice an old song she is remembering and it is all about great big moments of happiness and such. No, Jock, it is not about *sin and such* – you are not rightly understanding this Miss Pym. I must ask you to remember that we are here today and gone tomorrow, Heigh-ho.

Well, as I was saying before you interrupted me, this Miss Pym is feeling oh-so-happy in this beautiful weather and she is sitting outside in the garden in a green deck chair and she is reading a book. She is reading the Poetical Works of Lord Byron – no, not the whole poetical works of this said Lord, but *Don Juan* – and you are thinking well, that is enough, *nicht wahr?* And she is beginning at the beginning of the poem and she is reading these lines:

But if there's anything in which I shine,
'Tis in arranging all my friends' affairs,
Not having, of my own, domestic cares.

And she is laughing ha-ha – she is laughing, is this Miss Pym and thinking Oh, this is like my dear friend Jock who is in the frozen north, where the sea is frozen, and the snow is frozen, but the people they are not so frozen she thinks, else how could there be any *lilla flickas?* Well, she is thinking of her friend Jock, her dear friend, and she is wanting to thank him for his beautiful letter, which is the most beautiful letter she has ever had from him. I must write another letter, she thinks, that is what I must do. So cheerio chaps and here goes, she says, not being by any means one of your old fashioned spinsters. And it is evening and she is sitting by the fire in the drawing room smoking a cigarette and the wireless is on and dear Aunt Janie is knitting a white jumper, and this white jumper is always going wrong, oh, you have no idea how wrong it is going. Anyway here is Miss Pym in the middle of a happy domestic scene, so you can think of her in this same happy scene, and I know you will like to imagine her in the drawing room with Aunt Janie, rather than imparadis'd in Mr J's arms in Balliol, or getting into a merry state of condition in the St George's restaurant with Mr Pullein-Thompson, or walking in the Parks and telling her so sad life story to Mr B. H. de C. Ireland. Well, now you have what you like, so I hope you are content, because it is not often that we have what we like in this life.

And now you are asking, what is this Miss Pym doing with herself in Oswestry? And I will tell you, she is writing, simply that. And she is writing a new novel, and Chapter One is nearly done, but it is not in rhymes, no sir, not even Miss Pym is as clever as that. And this novel it is oh-so sober and dull, and there are no parties of young people getting *beschwipst,* and there are no Finns or Swedes or Germans or Hungars and the *Magyar bor* is not flowing at all freely, and there is no farm on the *puszta*...no, there is none of this. Well, there can be really nothing, you say. And you will be right *die ganze Welt dreht sich um Liebe* you will be saying in a furry, *sentimentvolle Stimme* as you see darling Henry and more darling Elsie and how happy they are. And you will be coming back to England, and you will be meeting this so dull spinster which is like the old brown horse walking with a slow majestic dignity, and you will be saying Well-fer-goodness-sake, Miss Pym, like they say in the films. But this spinster, this Barbara Mary Crampton Pym, she will be smiling to herself – ha-ha she will be saying inside. *But I have that within which passeth show* – maybe she will be saying that, but she is a queer old horse, this old brown spinster, so I cannot forecast exactly what she will be saying.

And what else is she doing you ask me? Well, she is reading, and she is reading *The Christian Year*, and *Don Juan* and Rainer Maria Rilke, and the *Daily Mirror*, and the so nice poems of Mr Betjeman, which remind her of standing looking up at the Randolph on early closing day, and having a coltish flirtation with a young man. Ho-ho, you say, wagging your finger very avuncular, so this spinster is having a coltish flirtation. *Das ist nicht gut* you add in a guttural voice, shaking your head, but Miss Pym, this so prudent sensible spinster, she is agreeing with you. *Nej*, she is saying, *det ar dalig*. For she thinks that may be Swedish for saying that it is not good to have a coltish flirtation outside the Randolph on early closing day, even if the sun is shining and you are only four and twenty. *Then come kiss me four and twenty* – but no it is not that, not at all – Miss Pym is four years too late. And Mr Liddell is chuckling because she is four years too late.

And Miss Pym is reading the newspapers and listening to *Wien du Stadt meiner Traüme* on the wireless. But it is not that any more. No it is Deutschland. *Ein Reich, Ein Führer – Heil Hitler!* that is what it is. And she is receiving letters from her so dear friend in Dresden, and he is saying that it is *Schade* that she is not in Germany to experience these so great events which have shaken the heart of Germany, or something similar. And Miss Pym is remembering how... but no she is not remembering, she is just writing back a very cautious letter because she does not like to be rude to a dear friend who has been always so kind to her when she was *allein in einer Grosstadt*, like Marlene Dietrich in the song, which her dear friend Jock wouldn't know about. And Miss Pym is getting a letter from her dear little, young boy friend Mr J., whom her dear friend Jock thinks unprepossessing, which is not true. For Jock has not seen him in his pretty blue suit, looking like a handsome little boy out in the East End, and taking a pride in being so because it is so much more *Stimmungsvoll* to look like the Mile End Road than like Mayfair. Well, as I was telling you, Miss Pym is getting this letter from Mr J., and it is written from Dover where he is spending two hours because he has missed the boat which shall take him on the beginning of his journey to Spain. And Miss Pym is very angry, oh she is, you have no idea how angry she is with Mr J. It is coming over her like violent wave. Yes siree. And do you know why she is angry? You may think you can guess why, but even you are not so clever, Mr Jock Liddell. Your first in Greats availeth you nothing here. Well, I will tell you, I am not one for keeping you in suspense. She is angry because Mr J. writes oh-so-calm in his letter that he forgot to go to the Schools to do the French Unseen in Pass Moderations, and so he will not be able to get through his two subjects, no, not even though Miss Pym wrote him three beautiful letters and offered up so many prayers for him. Now do you see why Miss Pym is angry with him? And do you not think her anger is right? *How shall thy fortress ever stand...* well no, the rest of the quotation is not suitable, but how will Mr J. become oh so celebrated and famous if he is doing silly things like this? asks Miss Pym. And she is going to his tutor in Balliol and they are weeping together and drinking a glass of sherry wine to steady their nerves, and his tutor is saying *Where were ye, nymph*, and Oh, what the influence of a good woman could have done at this time, and they are weeping again, and Miss Pym is wishing she had stayed longer in Oxford, so that she could have led young Mr J. by the hand into Schola Magna Borealis, or whichever it was, and she and his tutor are very broken. but Mr J. is not broken, oh no, nohow is he broken, he is in Paris, kissing people's hands and paying nice compliments and being charming. And Miss Pym is quoting Gray's 'Ode on a Distant Prospect of Eton College' and shaking her head, and being very wise and old, like as if she had a house in North Oxford and asked young men to tea on Sundays.

Well, another day is come, and the sun is shining all the time and it is as hot as summer and this Miss Pym, this spinster I was telling you about, is sitting outside in her green deckchair and she is reading *Don Juan* and smoking a Russian cigarette (she is quite a dog, this old spinster) and knitting a pink jumper. And then she is dropping off to sleep and the sun is shining on her face and making what we would call sun-kisses if we were not *verboten* to be all romantic. So we will say freckles. And Miss Pym is oh-so-pleased, and she is looking in the glass, and thinking how her face is a little brown, and she is singing a song ho-ho, and it is a song about somebody who is tall and tanned and terrific – you know how, like these so glamorous American playboys are that you see when you are in the Ritz in the two shilling seats. And Miss Pym is very pleased and happy and she has just had tea and when she finished writing to her dear friend Mr Liddell she will be writing that oh so dull and full of nothing novel I was telling you about in our last. And she is writing it in a fine book with a marbled cover, like I don't know what unless it is a fine pulpit in the House of God. And Miss Pym is chirping out a poem

> Of marble brown and veinèd
> He did the pulpit make...

[John Betjeman]

She is chirping, oh so merrily with a hey nonny nonny, is Miss Pym. Miss Pym is asking tenderly after the Herr Lektor Harvey and his beautiful wife. And she is envying Jock because he is with these so dear people and he is seeing new things and he is filled with the *Stimmung* of the northern winter. And she is hoping to see dear Henry and darling Elsie if they come to England in the summer, and she is hoping that marriage has improved dear Henry, and that he will not any more be rude to her. For this Miss Pym, this spinster, she is getting to a good age now, and she is got very touchy like and crabby. And she is sorry that she cannot send dear Jock any beautiful cards and pictures like he sent her, but she has only a card of Balliol College Chapel and one of that place, and she thinks he would not be liking that. *Plurimi pertransibunt...* she is saying and her eyes are misty with tears and she is reaching for the *Oxford Book of Victorian Verse*. But then she is remembering poor Henry, and how he thinks Swinburne very fine, and she is giggling and thinking it is oh-so funny that he should now be reading this poet which she read on Sundays after evening chapel when she was a plump *Backfisch* of sixteen summers. And she is saying ho-ho, you *brown bright nightingale amorous – so ist die Liebe, nicht wahr?* And then everyone is angry with her because she says these things, and is not behaving like the old brown horse I was telling you about, but she is not minding that everyone is angry, no not at all. She is thinking of herself eating dinner in St Hilda's College on the last night of last term, wearing a green chiffon dress and pearls and diamonds. And she is feeling oh so happy because why? Oh, you want to know everything, you old people, with your wagging fingers. Well, it is because she is eating a brown soup with no taste, and some slices of pork and some stewed plums – that is why she is feeling oh so happy. Do you think that is why? Well, you will never know now, because this Miss Pym, this old brown horse spinster, is all shut up like oyster, or like clam. And she is an old stuffed-shirt is this *gnädiges Fräulein* Pym vacker – no sir, no how, but she is a devoted friend, oh yes, she is so devoted. And she is sending so much love to Finland, to dear Jock, to the dear Harveys. Oh, she is so loving.

Joint letter to Robert Liddell and   Oswestry
Henry and Elsie Harvey in Helsingfors   5 April 1938

> *Ach! der mich liebt und kennt*
> *Ist in der Weite*

says Miss Pym, thinking of her dear friends so far away

Well, it is the last day of March. *It is the first mild day of March,* and it is
the last. Perhaps the Herr Lektor will explain this so *nische* poem of
Wordsworth to his dear wife if she does not know it already. And
after this little digression Miss Pym, this old spinster I was telling
you about last time I wrote, will continue her letter.

Well, now, what is she doing, this Miss Pym, what has she to tell
her dear friends in Finland? She cannot write such an interesting
letter as her dear friend Jock, but she can tell them about the lovely
spring weather and the beautiful flowers which are growing in
Shropshire. And the cherry tree at the bottom of the garden is out,
and Miss Pym, this old learned spinster, is quoting A.E. Housman
to herself, and she is picking flowers to put in her room, and she is
wearing a black jersey and sandals, but she is not saying *Hail Mosley!*
no sir, she is singing. Now what is she singing? *Will no one tell me what
she sings?* I will tell you.

But now it is the third day of April, so now you will never hear
what it is that Miss Pym was singing, but it was probably the *'Horst
Wessel Lied',* 'God moves in a mysterious way,' *'Still wie die Nacht',*
'Ungeduld', and 'St Louis Blues', and now while she writes she is
listening to the lovely wailing music from Budapest and it is
reminding her of so many things, but they are not the sort of things
you would wish to know about, so we will say no more about it. But
now the music is finished and they are playing the Hungarian
National Anthem which is so sad and beautiful like the Eton
Boating Song and the Randolph and so many other things in Miss
Pym's life. But you would not want to hear about those either.

You will perhaps be more interested to hear that Miss Pym has
written 60 pages of her new novel, in her lovely marbled notebook.
Now this is not so much because during this last week she has
written only about fifteen pages, because she has been doing other
things. Yes, she has been sewing and buying new clothes. And she
and her dear Aunt Janie are going to Liverpool on Thursday
because Aunt Janie's nice blue costume, well, it is oh-so nice this
costume but there is something about the back of the coat that is not
quite as it should be, which is like so many things in this life. So this
coat must be altered and Miss Pym and her Aunt will be driving to
Liverpool in a motor car and they will be spending much money, for
Mrs Pym went yesterday to London and has left behind the
housekeeping money with her daughter, and oh fancy! if Miss Pym
should spend it on herself instead of on food for Mr Pym and her
Aunt Janie and the dear servant Dilys – that would be a very wicked
thing, would it not? And Miss Pym is thinking, it is no end of a
nuisance all this food business, what should I do if I were married

and had to be always bothering about it like the poor Fru Lektor? But if I were married I should be rich and have many servants and I should be sitting down writing a novel and at one o'clock lunch would appear, just as it does in Balliol or Trinity, where Miss Hilary Pym and Mr Peter Potter of the OUDS are eating oysters. But Miss Hilary Pym is now in Athens and she enjoyed so much the voyage from Brindisi when she watched the sunrise with a nice young man from Cambridge, while Mr David Hunt lay sleeping, not caring to do such romantic things. And Miss Pym says she is just oh so little disappointed in Athens because it is rather dusty and there are people squatting on the pavements wanting to weigh you and clean your shoes and sell you things. And the shops are not so beautiful as she had expected, but oh, one can see the Acropolis every day and there is dear Mr Dunbabin at the British School and dear Mr Casson coming too, and not so dear Miss Benton and they are all jolly chums together.

Miss Pym is praying every day for Mr J. in Spain and she is writing him a beautiful poem for his birthday, and it is in heroic couplets, and it is such a clever poem because it spells his name down the side, and it is not sentimental, no sir, it is most unique. But she cannot send it to him because he has no address in Spain and so she will send it to him in Balliol at the beginning of next term. And he will read it through once and then it will be lying on his table with all the letters from his admirers. And Monsieur Jean-Pierre Giraudoux, that so charming French boy will be coming in and reading it, and Mr J's rich Indian friends will be coming in and Mr J will be putting a record on the radio gramophone, and can you guess what the record will be? It will not be the sad German record, or the funny Russian one, or the *romantisch* Hungarian one that Miss Pym likes – it will be Josephine Baker singing *Si j'étais blanche* – oh, fancy, says Miss Pym to Mr J, if your black friends should understand French! And she is remembering how she played bowls in Balliol with the late Mr Harvey and Mr Wall and Mr Sundarum. Oh, so many summers ago. But she is not sad, oh no *Sie ist nicht traurig*, because she is always happy when she is in Balliol.

And she is happy again now because she has had another letter from that so kind, nice Mr Liddell out of Helsingfors. And she is so especially, so *immensely* pleased with the photographs of her dear sister Elsie, who is so charming and who can speak Finnish, which is the most difficult language in the world. She is putting these photographs in her album, and hoping so much that she will be able to meet her dear sister in the summer. Snow we have not in Oswestry, she says in a low, sad tone, and oh for the *Stimmung* of the northern winter, and how I wish I were a man and could be invited to stay out in Finland. Oh how true it is that to him that hath it shall be given!

Well, every time she gets a letter from her dear friend Jock, Miss Pym is conscious that she has not so many interesting things to write about as he has. For the people she thinks so nice, he just thinks dull – and will not be wishing to hear about them, perhaps. But as long as this Miss Pym remains an old brown spinster, reading the poems of John Betjeman with calm of mind all passion spent, it is okay, *nicht wahr? ¿no es verdad?*

So cheerio chaps says this Miss Pym.

To Robert Liddell in Helsingfors   Oswestry
                                                     12 April 1938

Well, this is a lovely letter from Mr Liddell, and fancy, there is a page written by darling Elsie, and she shall have a separate letter all to herself from her loving sister. And there is a page with the Herr Lektor's writing on it, but what he has written does not make sense, and he is not sending any nice messages, so he shall not have a letter to himself. He shall have Mr Liddell's letter. But is there enough for two? It is hardly worthwhile dividing a cherry, as my dear mother is fond of saying – Well, we shall see. Hope springs eternal in the human breast, as I said to Mr Jepsen in August 1937, and I daresay that if it did then it does now.

Life is so beautiful here, so *ganz entzückend*, the weather so fine and the garden so full of beautiful flowers. I was looking in my Shelley the other day, and I found a collection of flowers there which brought back a rush of memories. Oh, it came o'er me like a violent wave. Those flowers were some I picked in the garden of St Hilda's in the spring of five years ago. It was a Sunday morning and I thought oh, if I could give them to Lorenzo – (but I didn't talk like that in those days) but here they are still, brown with age but one still keeps its colour, it is a bright blue scylla and it was pressed in Marlowe, at the beginning of *Edward II*. Well, that was five years ago, and this old spinster this Miss Pym, she has some new pressed flowers now. They are a daffodil, an orchid and a violet, and they are some of the flowers given to her in Oxford this spring by a dear young friend. So, dear Lorenzo, would you like these poor flowers that have waited five years to be given to you? No? It was what I thought. You would not wish me to be deprived of any sentimental token that would give me pleasure.

'No,' said the Herr Lektor in an emphatic voice – 'I should not wish it.'

'I think Miss Pym is not quite herself today,' said Mr Liddell, in a nervous, hurrying tone. 'This talk of pressed flowers and sentimental tokens, it is not good. I understand that she was perfectly content at Oswestry. That there were no regrets, no…' he stood holding a beef in his hand, making vague nervous gestures with it.

'Oh, fancy if all passion should not be spent!' said the Fru Lektor in a high, agitated tone.

'Oh, do not speak of it. It is more than I can bear,' said her husband sinking down on to the couch, and taking a glass of schnapps.

'It is more than I can bear,' said Mr Liddell, casting the beef away, and sinking down beside the Herr Lektor.

'Well, well,' said Miss Pym, coming into the room. 'Two old men bearing an imaginary burden, that is what I see. It must be the more heavy because it is not real.'

'So there is no burden?' said Mr Liddell, rising to his feet.

'I will not say that,' said Miss Pym, in a quiet thoughtful tone, 'but you do not have to bear it.'

'Oh, I know who will bear it,' said Mr Liddell in a loud triumphant voice, 'It is that handsome tall Etonian, that Mr Michael Benthall of the OUDS. Miss Pym admires him, I know that, he has a scar above his right eyebrow, she admires that, he wears a black polo jersey, he takes her out to dinner, he gives her orchids, oh, I see it all now, that is what it is. Those young shoulders can bear this burden better than ours can.'

'Oh, do not say any more. My head is reeling. I cannot keep up with this,' said Mr Harvey in a low groaning voice. 'I think it is simpler if I bear the burden myself. We do not wish to be hearing about these dreadful people that she is associating with.'

'Oh, fancy that the Herr Lektor should end a sentence with a preposition,' cried Mrs Harvey in a delighted tone.

'Well, it is the first time he has ever done it in his life,' observed Mr Liddell in an open tone.

'There must always be a first time,' said Mr Harvey, in a dull flat tone.

Now this just shows what idleness and a wandering mind and sitting out in the garden to write a letter can do. Poor Henry will now think there is a burden and really there is none.

There is an aeroplane flying above my head, but it is so high up that I can't see it. Fancy! And now I am getting all anxious about little J. in Spain. I look every day in the papers to see if he is dead yet.

'I see that the Reverend R.G.T. Gillman, rector of West Felton is to take the Three Hours service on Good Friday,' said Aunt Janie.

'Oh, that will be interesting,' said Mrs Pym, 'I have heard that he is continually crossing himself and saying "I am not worthy" in the middle of the service.'

'We are none of us worthy,' said Barbara in a low tone, spreading some Gorgonzola cheese on a biscuit.

'Why here is Mr Boulder!' said Aunt Janie, as the curate was announced.

'How is your fiancée?' asked Barbara in an open tone.

'She is better, thank you,' said Oswald.

'How old is she? She is older than I am, is she not?' asked Barbara in an eager tone.

'Yes, she is older than you are,' said Oswald in a guarded tone.

That was the gist of a conversation I had with the curate when he dropped in to tea last week. He and Miss Carfax are to be married in the summer, just fancy, a real curate's wedding in Oswestry. They say he is to be married in a cassock. Oh, fancy! Shall I never know how old she is?

Now it is Easter Sunday and Miss Pym intends to finish this letter. But it isn't a very good letter, what with all this talk of pressed flowers and Mr Benthall, or is it J. or Pullein-Thompson? I hardly remember which one it is, it seems not to matter very much. Benthall is handsome, J. is charming and has beautiful manners. Pullein-Thompson is unique, and one wants all those things and more. It should be a consolation to know that they can be found, even if not in the same person.

I have written nearly 90 pages, very restrained, very trivial round and common task, not many laughs but quite nice in parts and in a mild way. Shall I ever make a novelist? What a genius I had when I wrote that book! I feel I can almost be saying that with Swift. How long do you stay in Finland? You must be very useful to the young couple as you appear to be doing all the cooking. How nice if they had a little stranger! I should be expected to look at it with tears in my eyes, should I not?

With love to you all –

Pymska

To Elsie Harvey in Helsingfors   Oswestry
                                                   17 April 1938
                                                   Easter Sunday

My dear sister!

Thank you so much for your nice letter, but oh, why didn't you finish it? I am now burning with curiosity to know why you are glad that I have a...? Did your husband or the censor stop you from writing any more?

I send you a piece of blossom and a cowslip, pressed in *Pilgrim's Progress.* Perhaps you already have flowers in Helsingfors though I read in the Encyclopaedia that spring comes in the middle of April. We are having lovely weather and it is warm enough to be sitting outside in the sun, and your dear sister is browning her face, so that she shall look like a Scandinavian when she goes to Oxford, and then the young men will take her out to dinner and ask her to sherry parties.

I would so much like to learn Finnish. I know 'excuse me' (*anteeksi*) and *oletekko*...How many dear Finnish brothers could I get with those two sentences?)

I hope you and Henry are coming to England this summer, and that I shall see you. Perhaps we shall meet in Oxford, or you must visit me here and see the beautiful Welsh countryside.

You can imagine your sister Barbara very busy making new clothes, because it will soon be summer, and fancy, if Elsie should be smarter. Your husband and Mr Liddell will no doubt have told you what I look like, but it is known that their opinions are often unflattering. They do not think that an unmarried female novelist should have any interests but her work. You have no idea how harsh they are to me.

You see, I am pouring my heart out to you. I have had toothache which is very painful and I lie in bed at night in great agonies, knowing that I shall have to endure it until the Easter holiday is over and I can go to a nice dentist who will have to be cruel to be kind. But in the day it doesn't ache so much, only in the night when one's courage and physical strength are at their lowest ebb.

What a depressing letter I write to my dear sister! She will say, Oh, this Barbara, she is always weeping and ill-treated and suffering, *nicht wahr?* Whereas in reality, she is smoking, eating, drinking, using much lipstick, making new clothes, writing letters to dear friends, thinking out a new novel, reading nice poems by Mr John Betjeman, making plans for visiting a foreign country, and dreaming at night of somebody she loves very much. But it is not anybody you know, so she will not tell you any boring details.

Dear sister Elsie, I long to meet you. I think of you frying beefs and walking in the Esplanadsgatan in your new brown walking suit and send you my love.

Barbara

To Robert Liddell in Helsingfors　　　　　　　　Oswestry
early 1938

Friends and Relations

'You and Janie have been asked to lunch at Bryn Tirion,' said Mrs Pym, one Sunday morning. 'I hope I did right to accept the invitation for you, Barbara?'

'Yes, you did right,' said Barbara, in careful, considered tone. 'It would have been impolite to refuse when I had no previous engagement. I think Uncle Frank and Aunt Helen would have thought it so.'

'Well, dear, I daresay they would have thought nothing,' said Mrs Pym absently. 'We will have a boiled fowl for lunch and then we can have it cold for supper with some ham.'

'We shall not need much supper, Irena,' said Aunt Janie in a prudent tone. 'I expect we shall get a good lunch and tea at Bryn Tirion.'

'Yes,' observed Mrs Pym. 'Helen keeps a very good table.'

'Well, well,' said Barbara in a bright, elderly tone. 'Here we are. Well, Uncle Frank how are you, and Cousin Charlotte I saw you in Oxford but it is a long time since I saw Cousin John. How tall he has grown.'

'Yes, he must be as tall as Emily's second boy,' said Aunt Helen in a full, satisfied tone.

'No, John is much thinner than Billy' said Barbara. 'Billy is very broad.'

'I expect John will fill out,' said Aunt Janie.

'Yes,' said John.

'Are Charlotte's eyes quite well again?' asked Barbara in an interested tone.

'Oh, yes, I am all right now,' said Charlotte, 'but I have missed a term's work. I shall not be able to get anything better than a third now.'

'We got £250 compensation from the Insurance Company,' said Uncle Frank.

'We were very pleased about it.'

It was not enough,' said Barbara firmly. 'Charlotte would probably have got a second if it had not been for this.'

'Oh, no, Charlotte is not clever,' said Aunt Helen in a full, sensible tone, 'she would never be able to get a second. She does not work as hard as you did, and you are not as clever as Barbara, are you Charlotte?'

'No, mother,' said Charlotte.

'And Hilary has gone to Greece,' said Aunt Helen. 'Has she gone alone?'

'No, she has gone with a young man she knows, a fellow of Magdalen, an archaeologist, we have met him, he has been to the house,' said Barbara in a high, hurrying tone.

'Ah,' said Aunt Helen. 'I expect there will be something between them after this. You mark my words.'

'Oh, I think Mr Hunt is just a friend,' said Aunt Janie quickly.

'I do not think there is any likelihood of an engagement,' said Barbara.

'Ah, but you never know,' said Aunt Helen hopefully.

'But I do not think....'

'Well, lunch is ready. We will go in,' said Uncle Frank.

'What do you think about Austria and Germany?' asked Aunt Helen.

'Well, I always like the Germans,' said Barbara.

'Oh, Barbara, surely you do not like the Germans,' said Aunt Helen.

'The ones I have met have been very nice,' said Barbara in a firm, level tone. 'I have a friend in Dresden....'

'Ah, I expect it is a young man,' said Aunt Helen in a triumphant tone, 'that is what it is.'

'Well, yes,' said Barbara, 'it is a young man, but that is not why....'

'Oh, Barbara, you surely would not marry a German?' persisted Aunt Helen.

'No, I have no intention of marrying a German,' said Barbara firmly.

'Well it would be something to talk about if Barbara married a German, would it not?' said Aunt Helen brightly. 'Personally I could not marry a foreigner.'

'Neither could I,' said Barbara in a hopeless tone – 'As I said I have no intention....'

'You would have to live in Germany,' continued Aunt Helen. 'You would not be able to live in Oswestry. I wonder how you would like that.'

*

'How quickly time goes,' said Mrs Minshall, 'it seems only yesterday that you were married.'

'I have been married twenty six years,' said Mrs Pym, in a firm, clear tone.

Mrs Minshall looked surprised – 'But Barbara, she is how old – eighteen?'

'Barbara is twenty four,' said Mrs Pym in a clear, ringing tone.

'Yes, I am twenty four,' said Barbara in a low, mumbling tone.

'Well, well,' said Mrs Minshall.

'Have you heard that Greenfields is to be sold?' asked Mrs Pym.

'Pour Louisa Richards,' said Mrs Minshall, 'I suppose she is dead now.'

'No,' said Barbara, 'I saw her walking into the town yesterday.'

'Well, fancy, I thought she was dead. Your brother Ridley and his wife, are they still living?' asked Mrs Minshall, turning to Mrs Pym.

'Yes,' said Mrs Pym, 'They are very well.'

'And Janie – is she still single?'

'Yes,' said Mrs Pym smiling. 'Janie is still single.'

'Mrs Minshall seems to want us all to be either dead or married,' said Mrs Pym to her daughter as they drove home in the car.

'Well, I do not see what else we can be,' said Barbara in a thoughtful tone. 'I suppose we all come to one state or the other eventually. I do not know which I would rather be in.'

'Oh, there is plenty of time for that,' said Mrs Pym comfortably.

Dresden A.
Strehlerer str. 65,
Bei Rieper.

23 May 1938

Dear Jock –

Oh you really should not do it – making this poor old spinster laugh, so that when she is walking alone in the Strehlerer strasse a broad smile is coming on to her face because she is thinking of Jonathan Cape speaking in a voice drained of all emotion, and the passion fruit cocktails. But oh Jock just imagine – *I* might have been there drinking that passion fruit juice, and I know well how harmless it is because my uncle at Hatch End frequently drinks it. Did you think of me? just for one instant, as you stood among that happy band of pilgrims, those Cape authors? No, said Jock in a harsh, hurrying tone. I cannot say I thought of you. Why should I have thought of you? What could have been my motive? You were talking to Miss something, said Barbara in a low, sad voice, that is why you did not think of me. How can you shake that falser than false Cressid by the hand when you think how he has ruined my life? [Jonathan Cape had rejected *Some Tame Gazelle*] Well, that's a new one on me, you might well say if you were given to talking *Amerikanisch*. It is Cape and not Harvey who has brought this Miss Pym to this state of condition in which her whole life has resolved itself into a question of 'And now what?' or 'Where do we go from here?' Well, we need not be speaking of that now. Good things will always keep and what can be more good than a discussion of the whole purpose of one's life? I can think of plenty of things more good, you may say in a hasty, hurrying voice. Perhaps I can too.

Can you guess where I am writing this? Of course you can. Naturally I am in a beer garden and the sun is shining and the birds are singing and the chestnut trees are in blossom and the band is playing music. And at any moment they may play *Orpheus in the Underworld*, I feel, because I see a trombone in the band and so there is no reason why they shouldn't. But no, just now they are playing a sad Volkslied that I am very fond of . . . you can guess the sort of thing. I needn't tell you. I can see that you are afraid I will. I find this atmosphere has on me the same effect as the meanest flower that blows had on Wordsworth. When I see the palms in their silver painted urns, I think of little Jay, and how I used to force him to appreciate such things. Friedbert is being educated to enjoy the poems of John Betjeman, but naturally it is rather difficult particularly when I have to explain such lines as 'The incumbent enjoying a supine incumbency' but I make him read them aloud which is really a treat. And he has his revenge by translating long passages out of the *Völkischer Beobachter* to me, which I could really quite well read myself. And then he has a disconcerting habit of asking me things which I feel I ought to know and don't.

F.   Let us talk about Cromwell.

B.   (in an interested, condescending tone) Cromwell? What about Cromwell?

F.   (in a firm, direct tone) What was the influence of Cromwell on Milton?

B.   (in a high, nervous, hurrying tone) The influence of Cromwell on Milton? Did you say the influence of Cromwell on Milton?

F.   (giving the the word its full meaning) Yes.

I needn't say any more. you know that Cassandra is familiar only with the more sympathetic parts of 'Paradise Lost', 'Comus' and of course 'Samson Agonistes'. How well she remembers the opening lines of the last poem, and the voice that read them.

Did I tell you that we went to Prague the weekend before last? I sent Mr B. a card from the city where he was shot, when he was just sitting drinking beer, doing nobody any harm. Curiously enough – the day after we came back I was sitting in the Hotel Eden reading the *Times* and in it was a letter from Mr B. about the Sudeten Germans.

Well, we went to Prague via Bodenbach, and it was as hot as August and we sat in the Speisewagen mopping our faces and making rather waspish remarks to each other and then we went back to our carriage and a handsome young Czech began speaking to me in perfect English, and dear F. kept on wanting me to look out of the window at things, but everytime I looked I was too late and saw just nothing, or what one might see any day between Birmingham and Wolverhampton. Well, after $3\frac{1}{2}$ hours in the train we arrived at the Masyrak – Masarak – Masyarak – well anyway you must surely know what I mean – station. And I was so terribly excited in the taxi to think that we were really in Prague, but F. was not at all, although he had never been there. Oh the Golden City, I kept saying, the Golden City. No, I do not think it is Golden, he said. To me it is Golden, it will always be Golden, and the streets are paved with sharp stones – even the pavements which made walking in high heels extremely uncomfortable.

In the evening a sort of Czechish Mr Barnicot attached himself to us – I think he directed us somewhere when we asked the way – I don't remember exactly. Somehow there was never a time when he wasn't with us. He was quite pleasant and helpful and spoke German. He thought F. and I were English as we occasionally spoke to each other in that tongue, and after a time F. said to me 'I do not like to go with this gentleman more' and so after we had politely exchanged addresses and I had coyly waved to him out of the back of a taxi we found ourselves alone – And you will not wish to hear any more, I'm sure.

We spent Sunday morning very conscientiously sightseeing, although I had a vague hankering after the English St Martin's church which was advertised (if one can advertise Divine service) in the hotel. I wondered if I should find the English colony in Prague any more interesting than the Anglo-American one in Dresden. Here is the first of my impressions of the latter.

In the library attached to the church, getting out English books (after Divine Service at 11).

'I am Barbara Pym,' said Miss Pym in the manner of one feeling that she ought to say something. 'I have just come to Dresden.'

'Well, you have not taken long to find us,' said Mrs Bruce in a welcoming tone. 'This lady here –' she indicated a gaunt woman of middle years – 'has been in Dresden five years and this is the first time she has been here.'

'Yes,' said the gaunt woman in a satisfied tone, 'today is the first time.'

'I think we all feel the need for worship in our English tongue when we are abroad,' said Miss Pym in a low grave voice.

'And some of us feel even more the need for English novels to read,' said the gaunt woman . . . .

But now you see my imagination has run away with me, and I think how nice it would have been if I had made that remark about worship. Does one ever make consciously Compton-Burnett remarks in situations where they would be most fruitful I wonder? I must have the courage to try some day.

Supper has been brought in and I am waiting for dear Friedbert to come; it is all so domesticated. I feel I should say 'The Master has to go to Pirna today – he will not be here for lunch.' And then in he comes – the hasty husbandly kiss . . . .

Auf wiedersehen – whenever that may be. Won't it be odd seeing Henry married. I only hope I may not find it too odd or not enough odd. I feel there should be a happy medium. Still, Hope springs eternal . . . .

Best love to you – Barbara

To Elsie Harvey in Oxford   Oswestry.

20 July 1938

Darling sister Elsie!

I shall just be able to start a letter to you before I have to go out into the town to meet my sister Hilary, but I have only about ten minutes and it is known that one cannot say much in ten minutes. Still, it is something to have started this letter, do you not think it is something?

Yesterday we went to Liverpool to do some shopping. My mother has given me a fur coat to go to Poland, and I bought it yesterday. It is a golden brown musquash, quite long – I had only a little short one before. Hilary helped me to choose it. I tried on several, and it was a marvellously hot day, so that I was wondering if the coat would perhaps be too hot! But as my dear sister told me, the Poles are hot but their country is cold. I have had my passport back from Dr Alberg, with a Polish visa etc. It looks lovely, and I don't understand a word of it. He also sent me some books and pamphlets about Poland, so I shall be able to learn something about it.

I had a postcard yesterday from a friend of mine Mary Sharp (Henry will remember her). She was married a few hours after she landed in America and is now on her honeymoon round Lake Michigan. She sent me a picture of a romantic lake and forest. Oh, said Barbara, in a quiet full tone, I do not grudge happiness to other people, although it is something I want for myself. It is known that every woman wants the love of a husband, but it is also known that some women have to be content with other kinds of love. Now, Barbara, I do not quite see your meaning. I do not see what you mean by 'other kinds of love'. I hope you do not mean anything disgraceful. I very much hope it. Disgraceful? said Barbara, in a high nervous voice. Why should I mean anything disgraceful? One is usually silent about disgraceful things. No, indeed, she added, her voice taking on a fuller, rounded tone, I was meaning the love of a dear sister, simply that.

I expect your dear husband is busy with his examination papers, but I hope he has not been reading *Pilgrim's Progress* aloud to you. Give him my love. I am sending a great deal of love to Oxford, so you must divide it up into suitable portions.

Barbara Pymska Fredericovna

To Henry and Elsie Harvey in   Oswestry.
Helsingfors   30 September 1938
Dearest Elsie and Henry!

What will you think of me for not having written to you for so many months? Actually I don't suppose you will have thought of anything, as I imagine you must have been through the same anxiety in Finland as we have here in England. And now here we are with seven gas masks in the house and Mr Chamberlain is safely back in England and thanks to him there isn't going to be any war. Although one hardly dares to believe it after all the worry of the last few days. I've wondered so much where you were and what you were feeling because being here I'm so cut off from all my friends who seem to be all over the world at the present moment. But it was marvellous to be back in England after Poland, where everyone was so terrified. I left Katowice on the 16th – a fortnight ago to be exact – when it was still pretty easy to come through Germany. I suppose I should have had to go eventually if I hadn't left of my own accord.

My departure was in many ways quite dramatic. I left with Dr Alberg and the chauffeur at 8 o'clock in the morning. Mrs Alberg took a bunch of gladioli out of a vase and handed them to me as a last gesture and I was given enough food to feed myself and numerous Germans all through Germany and still have a lot to bring home here. So the fine Polish sausage was much enjoyed by our gardener. Dr Alberg was so nervous all the way to Beuthen – the German frontier station from which I was to catch my train – he told me not to speak at all at the frontier but just to show my passport and money, and not to speak to a soul in Germany. That was rather difficult as I had an eight hour journey from Beuthen to Berlin – and then the night journey Berlin – Hanover – Aachen – about another ten hours. And by the time I'd got out of Poland I wasn't nervous any more, because of course Germany seemed just as usual. Naturally they knew very little about the crisis and I talked to many people and everyone was very kind to me. I had time in Berlin to see Unter den Linden and to walk in the Wilhelmstrasse, and to feel rather disappointed that it didn't show signs of feverish activity. It was so dark and silent. I suppose everyone was having dinner. I had a splitting headache, having to deal with half my luggage being lost and some to be registered to England, all alone. But no, I wasn't quite in tears on the Friedrichstrasse station. I just sat smoking a gold tipped Polish cigarette, feeling as I used to feel when I came back from Oxford and sat waiting on Snowhill station Birmingham, that my whole life seems to be spent sitting on stations all over Europe leaving behind the people I love. Well, Barbara, love is a strong word and now you will be thinking that I fell in love with somebody in Poland and you will be ready at once to be unkind about it (not Elsie!) and say that I had better not be putting any Silesian episodes into my novels. But don't be afraid – if I ever do write another novel – and I intend to when I feel a little calmer in my mind – it will be in the style of my first one.

I can hardly expect you to believe that I ever went to Poland as I didn't even send you a postcard of Katowice, but Jock and Barnicot both had letters from me so you can ask them. It was a curious life and the few weeks I had of it have made me just like I was before only more so. The family were extremely kind to me but I was agonisingly lonely, though latterly I became friendly with the British consul and he was a great comfort to me.

I am going to London some time next week and hope to get Something To Do. But what? My five talents are really so very special, aren't they, and that must always be my consolation. Do I seem very bitter in this letter, by the way? You know I am not really like that. I shall like being in London – Hilary is there too, doing a secretarial course.

This isn't a very exciting letter but it is full of affection and yearnings to see you, which I know can't be satisfied for months. Now do you see why I am so mournfully pathetic about my friends being all so far away? The obvious remedy is to make new ones as everyone else seems to be doing, even at our time of life.

I feel I ought to have told you more about Poland – the smuts on one's face, the bright pink soup, the barefooted peasants, the artistic pattern of the factories on a wet Sunday afternoon, the impossible but beautiful language and all that. But I will write again. And *do please* write to me – both of you.

With best love –

Pymska. Barbara Fredericovna.

To Elsie Harvey in Helsingfors
27 Upper Berkeley Street,
Portman Square,
London W.1.

31 October 1938

Darling Sister Elsie:

As you see by my address I am at present living in London. Hilary and I are in rooms together – she is doing a secretarial course and I am writing a new novel. It is such a pleasant life – I don't think I've been so happy since I was a young girl of eighteen in my first year at Oxford! I work very hard and have done about a quarter of this new novel. It is such a nice change being in London and our rooms are very comfortable and near everywhere – just by Marble Arch and Hyde Park. Jock asks why I loiter sadly in Upper Berkeley Street instead of returning to Poland. I might ask him why he stays in Greece instead of returning to England to be a comfort to his brother and to me. In any case the Polish family don't want me to go back even if I wanted to. It was terribly lonely there and I had no time to write, and I honestly don't believe I can be happy unless I am writing. It seems to be the only thing I really want to do. My parents also want me in England – my mother was terribly anxious about me, even before the Crisis started properly. So you see I have given all manner of excuses and reasons for staying in London. And of course the main one is that I'm happy here, and isn't that enough? Have we a right to be happy, or is it only a rare thing, so that we should be glad if we are happy for a few days in every year? We have no rights, said Barbara, in a dull, flat voice.

I have met Jonathan Cape, Jockie's publisher. He also nearly published my first novel, and spoke quite well of my second. I wondered if it was possible to get a job with a publisher and so I wrote to him and went to see him. Actually it seems impossible to get anything like that, but he was awfully nice to me and said he had liked my novels, and hoped I would go on writing. He asked Hilary and me to a cocktail party at his flat, which we enjoyed very much. He is a charming man and so amusing.

I heard from Jock last week. He doesn't seem to be coming home yet. I have been hoping he would as I haven't seen him since the end of February. Has he told you that his first novel *Kind Relations* is to be published? Actually Jonathan Cape told me, and then Jock said so in his letter. He seems to be meeting a lot of very odd people, but as he is thirty I suppose he can look after himself. It amuses me so much, though, to read the kind of letters he writes now and to remember how annoyed he used to be with me when I wrote like that. I wonder if I shall find him much changed – if I ever see him again. Somehow I cannot call him Robert. I am getting old you know and I am set in my habits and he has been my friend since I was twenty. You would not expect an old woman to change her ways, would you? I think you would be shocked if I were suddenly to marry, for instance. But there seems to be no chance of that.

Fancy that we should have nearly met in Germany – I am so sad now about it and Czechoslovakia and Poland and everywhere in central Europe that I can't think of going there again at present. There seems to be nothing but cruelty and misery in the world sometimes. This 'stand up to them and fight' attitude sounds very fine but I am sure the people who profess it don't stop for a moment to think what a war really means. You'd think that Spain and China would show everyone, but they don't seem to.

This doesn't seem to be a very amusing letter (all the amusing things I think of have to be saved for the novel, so my letters are all very dull!), now that I look back on it, but I hope you don't mind. At least, I am very happy and don't need comforting which is something new! The only thing is to work at something you like and that you feel is worth doing, even if it's only a novel that doesn't get published. I suppose it is all good experience, anyway, and while I'm doing it I'm perfectly happy.

See how serious and philosophical I am! But it is marvellous being with Hilary after being so alone in Poland, and we have the most wonderful jokes about everything. I don't know what Henry will think about me, probably he will think nothing.

Very much love to you from Barbara

1939

London W.1

21 February 1939

My dearest sister Elsie:

I have been working hard at my novel. It is nearly finished now, but I shall then have to go over it and make some improvements before I am really satisfied with it. When you start to write one you always wonder if you will be able to make it long enough, but by the time you get to the end it is always too long – I love cutting out bits and crossing out whole pages.

The best piece of news from London is that spring has come. Has it come to you yet? It started here on February 5th, a Sunday. There was that absolutely unmistakable feeling in the air that sends people mad, particularly old spinsters like your sister Pym who is already rather queer in the head. But now that she is twenty-five she has reached years of discretion and does not do the things she would have done when she was nineteen. And London is so different from Oxford anyway. One behaves much more soberly. But the weather has been lovely – we have had a lot of sunshine, especially today, and for months past the streets have been full of flowers. Now they are selling daffodils, narcissi, tulips, blue irises and of course lots of mimosa. Somehow I always think of my sister Elsie when I see mimosa! I will send you a piece in this letter, although I expect that you do have such flowers in Finland too, just as you have deep armchairs. But I hope you will agree that it is the *thought* that matters, even though the flower will be all dry and squashed and fall on the fine carpet so that Mr Harvey will be angry.

I was so touched at the picture of him decorating a Christmas tree with his own hands – things like that make me want to cry.

We went to two Surrealist Exhibitions last week – one of pictures – paintings and drawings – by Man Ray which I didn't understand or like very much, though he does wonderful photographs. The other – Wolfgang Paalen – was more interesting. The first object that met our eyes as we opened the door into the gallery was an umbrella covered entirely in sponges! Your practical sister's first thought was oh, what a waste to cut up all those sponges, when they are so expensive too. There were also some curious leather objects made of a sort of grey suede. There was something very unpleasant about them, I think because one expected them to be in stone or some hard material and of course they were quite soft. He had done some quite nice paintings, very dreamy and fine like the skeletons of leaves or birds. These exhibitions are very amusing, although I can't say whether they are really good. I think they can hardly be, as so many of the things one could do oneself! But didn't somebody say I was a genius? I think it was a very long time ago, in the old Imperial Russia before the war, or in Oxford in the days of Jowett when one played croquet on the lawn with bearded undergraduates, Henry Stanley Harvey and Patrick Marsden Wall perhaps!

But you see I am raving. Perhaps it is because I am hungry. I have two beautiful cakes and a fine box of homemade sweets from my aunt, but I want *meat*, red meat. You see, it is about seven o'clock in the evening and so it is really a natural appetite I am feeling. Perhaps I will eat an orange when I have finished this letter. It is known that oranges are very good for the health, and I have two fine large ones on my mantelpiece.

I hope Herr Lektor Harvey is well. I had a spare Valentine and very nearly sent it to him, but then I decided it would be more prudent to send it to young Mr Michael Benthall, who has asked us to sherry in his dear little flat. He is twenty years old. Jock thought I was in love with him, but although he can divine all the secrets of the human heart he made a mistake and now of course there are really no secrets in my heart.

Now please write and get Henry to if such a thing can be possible. I long for news of you.

With much love to you –

Barbara Frederickovna

To Henry and Elsie Harvey　　　　　　　　　　London W.I.
in Helsingfors

11 May 1939

Dearest Elsie and Henry!

I hope you are both well and that you will soon be coming to England. I shall be terribly disappointed if you don't! I am imagining that Jock will be coming back too and we can all be dear brothers and sisters together, except that some will be husbands and wives, which is an even more satisfactory relationship.

Now I am back in London, in my minute little room at the top of a lodging house in a quite good district of London – conveniently near all the shops and art galleries and Mayfair – though why I should want to be near there you may well ask. Hilary has just got a job on the secretarial staff of the B.B.C. and she is very pleased about it. It will last till September and if she is good enough she will be able to get on the permanent staff. I think we may get a little flat in the autumn as it would really be more convenient than rooms. We can't cook anything here and there isn't much space to put things. But we are very happy and the people in the house are nice and we are near Marble Arch and Hyde Park and Oxford Street (and the Edgware Road which is not a very *nice* district for two young women to wander about in late at night). (I have rather a fancy to live in Kensington, but don't know if Hilary would agree.)

Today I had lunch with the wife of the British vice-consul in Katowice – the place in Poland where I was teaching English. Things seem to be about as bad as they can be there – she and the children have come back to England and see no prospect of returning to Poland yet, and the Embassy and Consulate in Warsaw have sent all their women and children home. So if I had gone out again I should have had to come back a second time probably! As you know, we now have conscription for men of 20 – 21 which may make things a little better. If there is going to be a war – and we can't be sure that there won't be one – we may as well be prepared for it. I don't know what Jock would say to these views, if he is still a Pacifist, but with the world in the state it is now, it seems to be no more than common sense. But yet the whole thing is such a farce, everyone spending millions to get ready for a War that nobody really wants! I am going to get a First Aid certificate which ought to be quite useful even if there isn't a war – I am going to classes every week. Fancy me learning how to make splints and bandages! I rather look forward to it. I made some boxes for gas masks when I was at home – it is rather a pleasant sensation to fool oneself into thinking that one is doing useful work!

Apart from all this I have been working very hard at a new novel which I finished before Easter. I am now making some alterations in it though, so heaven knows when it will be ready to go round the publishers. It is really quite a nice novel in its way but needs to be made more exciting. 'Be more wicked, if necessary,' says my agent [Ralph Pinter], who is very kind and helpful. Can you imagine an old spinster, frowning anxiously over her MS. trying to be more wicked? Or rather trying to make her people more wicked? It is difficult to imagine, is it not?

. Do write very soon – I hope you are both well. Hilary sends her love.

And so of course does your affectionate sister,

Barbara

May

What is the heart? A damp cave with things growing in it, mysterious secret plants of love or whatever you like. Or a dusty lumber room full of junk. Or a neat orderly place like a desk with a place for everything and everything in its place.

Something might be starting now that would linger on through many years – dying sometimes and then coming back again, like a twinge of rheumatism in the winter, so that you suddenly felt it in your knee when you were nearing the top of a long flight of stairs.

A Great Love that was unrequited might well be like that.

So many places where one has enjoyed oneself are no more – notably Stewart's in Oxford – shops are pulled down, houses in ruins, people in their marble vaults whom one had thought to be still living. One looks through the window in a house in Belgravia and sees right through its uncurtained space into a conservatory with a dusty palm, a room without furniture and discoloured spaces on the walls where pictures of ancestors once hung. One passes a house in Bayswater with steep steps and sees a coffin being carried out.

Walking in Mayfair just before eleven on a Sunday morning (21st May), the air soft and warm and lovely, trees in leaf and red hawthorns in flower. There is a delicious nostalgic smell of churches and new paint and later a Sunday dinner coming up from the basements. His [Jay's] house is newly painted in cream and royal blue and a window-box next door has petunias in it. How all things are in tune to a poor person in love. A fine, sunny afternoon in May, Beethoven and German lieder. I go to my irises, thinking to throw them away, but find that each dead flower has a fat new bud at the side of its stem. And so I take off the dead flowers and the new flowers begin to unfold. The photograph of him at the Union stands on the mantelpiece and in front of it a spray of red roses – but they are artificial ones from Woolworth's.

Whitsuntide weekend – an old lady with a curious bakelite *apparat* – perhaps an ear trumpet – talking about spiritualism in a restaurant. A clergyman composing hymns, where perhaps emotion and fervour get the better of reason.

6 June. On the hottest day of the year I saw two nuns buying a typewriter in Selfridges. Oh, what were they going to do with it?

17 – 18 June. Prescription for a lonely weekend in London. After getting into a good emotional state over Charles Boyer and Irene Dunne in *Love Affair* go into Lyons and have tea. Then walk in the park and back through the deserted streets of Mayfair. Such of the aristocracy as still lives here is away for the weekend. Turn off Park Lane and stand at the bottom of Park Street – you can look right up over Oxford Street and along Gloucester Place to some distant view of trees and spires which is comforting. One day you will really go and see what it is. But not yet. You must go back and read your new *Vogue* and wash stockings – for that is an essential part of a lonely weekend in London. A great deal of washing and tidying must be done, and if it is the Oxford end of term, well, so much the better.

July
On the 4th of July I met one I loved and had not seen for more than a year [Jay]. Such meetings should be avoided if possible. On this same day I went inside that curious house in Mayfair with its oil paintings and smell of incense and met his mother, a splendid character for a novel.

> In a drear-nighted December,
> Too happy, happy tree,
> Thy branches ne'er remember
> Their green felicity.

I used to quote that two years ago but it was only recently that I read the whole poem. Here is the last verse –

> Ah! would 'twere so with many
> A gentle girl and boy!
> But were there ever any
> Writhed not at passed joy?
> To know the change and feel it,
> When there is none to heal it,
> Nor numbed sense to steal it,
> Was never said in rhyme.

> [Keats]

And so it is, I suppose, with this gentle girl and boy. But now when the world is in this sad state, when one hardly dares to look ahead into the years, all this is a warm comfort . . . the remembrance of meetings, letters, a photograph (absence – cheek pressed against the cold glass), all the little relics, all the jokes, everything that did happen and didn't quite happen and might still happen. Twenty hours – but perhaps twenty years of memories.

Part II

THE WAR

1940-1945

In a small provincial town in wartime life resumed some semblance of normality.

Went to the pictures for the first time since the war started. Took gas masks but felt rather silly.

Budget out. Cigarettes up – Players $1/1\frac{1}{2}$d – and income tax. All drawing in our horns.

Put in some hyacinth bulbs. Reading a biography of Caroline of Brunswick. *Band Waggon.* This is a war diary but this seems to be our life.

There were some excitements:

Postcard from Don Liddell to say that Jock, Henry and Elsie are leaving Finland. Flight from the Bolsheviks in an open boat. Somehow, though it's serious, I can't help laughing.

But everyday life supervened:

Made 16/- by selling old clothes to Mrs Ramage.

All this time she was writing steadily and conscientiously:

I did a little writing – it is getting involved and I don't quite know what I am driving at. That's the worst of a plot.

After supper I did some writing which quells my restlessness – *that* is how I must succeed.

She had already, in 1938, completed Civil to Strangers *and a novel with a Finnish setting, half jokingly based on Henry's life there (both unpublished). During 1940 she wrote the first draft of a novel with a wartime setting, which she called 'my spy novel', which was more remarkable for its observation and humour than for its plot.*

95

When one is tired one gets strange fancies. On one occasion when we had the evacuees I fancied I smelled rabbit cooking in church and the altar looked like some celestial Aga.

I like to see that all lights are put out and never trust anyone but myself to do it. Also it has become doubly important since the war as our Air Raid Warden is the grocer with whom I am not registered.

During 1940 and part of 1941 she worked in the YMCA canteen at the local military camp:

Did my nails with Pink Clover but later, doing the money at the camp, it all peeled off.

A Scotsman called me 'a wee smasher' but what he meant is rather obscure.

Busy poaching eggs in little machines.

A ravishingly handsome Second Lieutenant poured into an exquisitely tailored overcoat came in, but he studied his book of Gas Drill rather than me.

But there were quite a number of soldiers only too happy to flirt with her a little. One of them, a Scot, inspired her to start learning Gaelic, as she had learned German for Friedbert and Finnish for Henry.
She also helped at the baby clinic in the town:

I'm learning quite a lot about babies and their feeding. I am gradually learning to pick up a baby with a nonchalant air.

And at the First Aid Post:

Long First Aid lecture. Shall I *ever* grasp the circulation of the blood?

In the evening an anti-gas lecture. Went into the tear-gas van – a snouted figure – got my badge.

Like all women in civilian life she was busy with housework, making over her old clothes now that there was clothes rationing, and constantly preoccupied with food:

Links managed to get a 7lb jar of marmalade – such are the joys of going without. Not even love is so passionately longed for.

She did not have to brave the perils of air raids though enemy planes passed over:

A big bang in the night, reputed to be a bomb at Bagley.

And the sirens went most nights:

Had a bath after tea in case the sirens should go.

We have a rota at the First Aid post now and if I hear the siren I don't have to go tonight. It went at 12. All clear 4 a.m.

In October 1941 she had to register for war service and after various suggestions ('Had a phone call asking me if I'd be interested in a political intelligence job in the country') she was offered a job in the censorship at Bristol, censoring civilian letters, mostly to Southern Ireland.

Hilary was already working as a secretary in the BBC Schools Department at Bristol, living in a large house called The Coppice in Clifton, a suburb of Bristol, overlooking the Suspension Bridge. Barbara joined her there in December 1941.

Barbara compared life at The Coppice to a play by Tchekov and certainly the inhabitants, all working for the BBC and living in close proximity, were an interesting collection of personalities, and there was a very Tchekovian mixture of comedy and tears. They were: Dick Palmer with his wife Mary, their three children, Liz, Gill and Sally, and Tamara, a Polish friend; Flora Meaden; Hilary, and Honor Wyatt with her two children Julian and Prue. Honor had separated from her husband, the writer and broadcaster C. Gordon Glover, when she got her BBC job, and moved to Bristol taking the children with her. Gordon was based in London on the staff of the Radio Times *but was living at Arkesden in Essex. He used to visit Bristol to see the children, since the separation had been amicable with no bitterness.*

Barbara fell in love with Gordon and they had a love affair, very serious on her part, perhaps less so on his. There is no written record of this period in her life, apart from a few letters to the Harveys, since Barbara burned her diaries for this year (see her notebook entry for 17 February 1976), but she started writing a kind of narrative which she called After Christmas *in 1943 after she and Gordon had parted.*

It was a strange, ironic situation, to be living in the same house as Gordon's wife Honor, to whom she was deeply attached, following with sympathy and anxiety Honor's love affair with George Ellidge (whom Honor later married), then on active sevice in North Africa, and the progress of her divorce from Gordon. The interrelationships and emotional undertones were complicated and painful and in July 1943, to make a break in an impossible situation, she wrenched herself away from the warmth and familiarity of The Coppice and joined the WRNS.

She served as a rating at HMS Westcliff and was then promoted to Third Officer and worked in naval censorship. A testimonial from Director of WRNS on her demobilisation described her as 'an intelligent and adaptable

*censor officer with a keen interest in her work'. But Barbara could never quite
believe that she was part of service life.*

Gradually people will begin to discover what a fake I am — how
phoney is my Wrennish façade.

*She did, however, find herself immersed in social life, especially when she was
stationed at Southampton:*

There is plenty of social life whether you like it or not, because most
of the invasion forces, both English and American, are concentrated
in the South-West and there are always far more men than women at
dances. The Wrens get so many invitations they hardly know which
to accept.

*In 1944 she was posted to Naples where social activity was even more
hectic:*

In the evening went to a party at Admiral Morse's villa, quite
enjoyable but I am never at my ease there, feeling Jane Eyre-ish and
socially unsuccessful. Danced with Flags and Astley-Jones, both
doing their stuff – charm etc. How artificial it all is. I wonder if they
feel it.

*She returned to England in June 1945 and went to Oswestry to be with her
mother who was very ill and who died in September.*
*A fellow Third Officer, Frances Kendrick, introduced Barbara to her
aunt, Beatrice Wyatt, then Secretary of the International African Institute in
London and it was arranged that Barbara should work there as an Editorial
Assistant.*

H.H.

Adapting to the War

Addressed to Robert Liddell but   Oswestry.
also intended for the Harveys with whom   12 January 1940
he was staying in Stockholm

Dear Jock –

How can you possibly know that I was delighted with your letters when I do not write to tell you so? I feel I should write nearly a whole novel to make up for my neglect. 'Oh, surely that will not be necessary,' I can hear you saying, in a high nervous tone. 'I really do not think you need put yourself to such trouble. Is it not true that the Government is exhorting us to save paper?' 'We are digging for victory,' said Barbara, in a deep resonant tone. 'I suppose that is what you mean.' But as you will have seen from my letter to Elsie I somehow imagined you would all be coming back to England soon, though I now see that it is not so easy for you as I had at first supposed.

And now, as I had your last letter yesterday morning, I feel we need not have any more of this reproaching. I am answering it now. I am sitting in a comfortable chair by a blazing fire, and realize that I am lucky to be in such a position. In about half an hour I shall be going with my mother to see *The Lion Has Wings*, and so I can look forward to a nice emotional evening, though I believe it is a very fine film. So I shall start this letter and then go on with it and perhaps on and on until it breaks into *ottava rima*.

A very happy New Year to you and may it be not quite as bad as we expect, and even bring the end of the war in sight. We are told now to prepare for much grimmer things, and certainly we have not yet been called upon to endure anything except the evacuees. As I expect I've already told you – they have gone to another billet and we are having a rest.

Rationing has started but there is Plenty of Everything Here. It is always better in the country anyway. Mrs Pym says she will take her sugar ration with her when she goes out to tea or evening bridge, but Mr Pym ridicules the idea. 'One should be able to get a special container for it,' she says.

You are so nice wishing good things for my poor novels. I do not see much prospect of getting them published just now, though I believe they are the kind of novels some people might like to read at a time like this. (That sounds very cautious). Anyway I shall try. I am now getting into shape the novel I have been writing during this last year, and which I have had to lay aside because I have been so busy [provisionally entitled *Crampton Hodnet*]. It is about North Oxford and has some bits as good as anything I ever did. Mr Latimer's proposal to Miss Morrow, old Mrs Killigrew, Dr Fremantle, Master of Randolph College, Mr Cleveland's elopement and its unfortunate end . . . I'm sure all these might be a comfort to somebody. I have also done nearly half of a novel about the war. There is a nice vicar's wife called Jane, her daughter Flora (a comic character) and evacuees etc. And there is always my poor *Tame Gazelle*.

Your new work sounds very fine and I hope I may see it soon. It might even console me (in a nice way) to find that you have human frailties in your writings. The influence of Miss Compton-Burnett is very powerful once it takes a hold, isn't it? For a time there seems to be no point in writing any other way, indeed, there seems not to *be* any other way, but I have found that it passes (like so much in this life) and I have now got back to my own way, such as it is. But purified and strengthened, as after a *rich* spiritual experience, or a shattering love affair. I'm afraid I never had the former, unless one can say that they are the same thing. Somehow I do not believe one can. Who knows what the war may bring though? Already to think is to be full of sorrow, but I am never without hope. The winter has never seemed so long or so cold as this year and I am sure I never had chilblains before. And now that I have come down to the ridiculous I can tell you that most of my hopes are rather small ones and my pleasures too. Getting letters, finishing my blue tweed jacket, watching my bulbs sprout and flower (that's not so small), imagining that one day I shall see my friends again. I suppose everyone lives from day to day now and it is really the best way, if you cannot see anything pleasant in the future. The present is at least dull and peaceful and there is much writing and reading to be done. Or do you think I should join the ATS. Would you not be proud of your friend Sergeant Pym?

Poor Michael Benthall has sent me a photograph of himself in the uniform of a private. He looks very fine, almost like a Field Marshal and with a noble expression on his handsome face. He spent Christmas with Osbert and Edith Sitwell in their ancestral home somewhere in the north of England. We had thought of writing a play together which was going to be very successful – the sort of chintz and teacups comedy that the matinée-goers like so much and Lionel Hale is so scornful about. I have no recent news of Friedbert for you as I have not written to him since September – 'nor he to me,' added Miss Pym, her tone losing in fulness. 'Henry has not written to you either,' said Jock in an open interested tone. 'One does not expect letters from enemy aliens or from married men,' said Miss Pym.

Well, I seem to have written about as much as I can. I hope the CENSOR will not open this letter and think that my crossings-out are of any significance. Your first was opened but not the second.

'Oh these are dull people,' said the Censor, in a low dragging tone. 'They do not seem to realise that we are at war. They write only of trivialities and the young woman does not know her own mind. All these quotations too, it is not natural.'

We have got a new Shakespeare calendar in the lavatory. So far all the quotations seem to be from *Troilus and Cressida* – the more noble parts. Last year we had Golfing Hints. Well, you dear people, know that you have all my love. My mother and I have sent money to the Finns. Take care of yourselves –

BMCP.

March
But *I remember, I remember*.... I was never more happy in my life than with him [Jay] in the spring of 1938. I am sure that I truly loved him and do still. I put this in writing so that in the years to come I may look back on it and reflect about it (as poor Friedbert would say) and smile and say, 'No, no, it was only a passing infatuation,' or 'Yes, yes, you *did* love him....'

Oh how absurd and delicious it is to be in love with somebody younger than yourself! Everybody should try it – no life can be complete without it. 'When we have before us such *objects* as excite love and complacency....' Love and complacency – and children should be flattered! So I will leave this notebook to Jay in my will.

27 March [on holiday in Wales]. Pwllheli looked lovely – the sea calm and sparkling, the cardboard hills clear in the distance.

Today was my darling Jay's twenty-first birthday and I was able to drink his health in Burgundy (not Empire). I wish I knew where he was. As it was there was a beautifully religious effect in my room at night – a single candle before his photograph, lighting up his lovely, sparkling Russian eyes. Like an ikon – he would have appreciated it. One day I must remember to tell him. But I will not tell him that the reason why I had the candle there was because I had no reading lamp and wanted to read in bed. Children must still be flattered – even when they are twenty-one.

Wednesday 3 April. Oswestry.
This morning I polished up an old box I found upstairs – it is of walnut with black and yellow inlay and a brass crest on the lid. It makes a beautiful box for relics – so in went all the letters, pressed flowers, Niersteiner corks, handkerchiefs, *Tilia platyphyllos* etc. It will still hold a few more letters, though it is quite nicely filled. I wonder what will happen to it. If I were to die tomorrow I should either have it sent back to him or buried with me (probably the latter) – but as it seems not very likely that I shall, I daresay it may be in my possession for years and years, until one day it becomes junk again and the box returns to the place where I found it – perhaps with the relics still in it. Dust to dust, ashes to ashes.... What a great pleasure and delight there is in being really sentimental. I thought about this as I picked flowers in the garden this morning – violets – a great patch of them smelling lovely, sweeter than the lids of Juno's eyes, primroses plain and coloured, scyllas and wild celandines, so very much spring flowers. People who are not sentimental, who never keep relics, brood on anniversaries, kiss photographs goodnight and good morning, must miss a good deal. Of course it is all rather self-conscious and cultivated, but it comes so easily that at least a little of it must spring from the heart. I could write a lovely metaphysical poem about the relics of love in a box. Perhaps I will – for his seventieth birthday (in March 1989).

Sunday 7 April. Today I have been reading *Of No Importance* – Rom Landau's diary of February–October 1939. Many things in it I understand so well – the reluctance to sit down and begin writing so that one finds oneself doing all sorts of unnecessary tasks to postpone that moment of starting. And also the feeling that no day is really satisfactory if one hasn't done some sort of work – preferably a few pages of writing, but anyway something useful. Why is it that one is still surprised to discover that other people feel these things too? I am beginning to be less surprised now. I used to think that I was the only person who the night before setting out to go abroad –

even for a holiday – had the feeling that I'd give anything not to be going. But Jock says he feels it too and Mr Barnicot – both hardened travellers.

My days pass so pleasantly and uneventfully but really with nothing *accomplished*. I have done so little writing this year. But writing it not now quite the pleasure it used to be. I am no longer so certain of a glorious future as I used to be – though I still feel that I may ultimately succeed. Perhaps I need some shattering experience to awaken and inspire me, or at least to give me some emotion to recollect in tranquillity. But how to get it? Sit here and wait for it or go out and seek it? Join the ATS and get it peeling potatoes and scrubbing floors? I don't know. I expect it will be sit and wait. Even the idea of falling violently in love again (which is my idea of an experience!) doesn't seem to be much help in the way of writing. I seem to have decided already the sort of novels I want to write. Perhaps the war will give me something. Perhaps the Home Front novel I am dabbling with now will get published. Perhaps....

But women are different from men in that they have so many small domestic things with which to occupy themselves. Dressmaking, washing and ironing, and everlasting tidying and sorting of reliques. I think I could spend my whole day doing such things, with just a little time for reading, and be quite happy. But it isn't *really* enough, soon I shall be discontented with myself, out will come the novel and after I've written a few pages I shall feel on top of the world again.

Friday–Sunday 19–21 April. In Oxford once more and it is melancholy because I know absolutely nobody except the Liddells – and they are charming in their ways, but it is not a way which fits all my moods. Respect and Esteem, the dry bones picked clean of flesh. To one who has known Oxford in the spring with Jay they are not enough.

How differently one behaves now though on a melancholy evening! Instead of the abandonment of tears and the luxury of a good cry one thinks philosophically about what is the best thing to do – to smoke, get ready for bed, read a nice light novel and then sleep a long sleep. It is always better in the morning. It would be interesting for a novel to trace one's development (if it is development) in matters of emotional restraint.

I went to Evensong at Christ Church and there was a pretty girl there (rather like Jill Furse) looking sad, almost weeping. But the service was soothing and the singing exquisite, so I hope it comforted her.

Friday 10 May. Oswestry. Today Germany invaded Holland and Belgium. It may be a good thing to put down how one felt before one forgets it. Of course the first feeling was the usual horror and disgust, and the impossibility of finding words to describe this latest *Schweinerei* by the Germans. Then came the realisation that the war was coming a lot nearer to us – airbases in Holland and Belgium would make raids on England a certainty. People one met were either gloomy (Mr Beauclerk, the electrician and Mr Cobb, the wireless shop), slightly hysterical (Miss Bloomer) or just plainly calm like Steele. I think I was rather frightened, but hope I didn't show it, and anyway one still has the 'it couldn't happen to us' feeling. Then there is the very real, but impotent, feeling of sympathy for these poor wretches who are the latest victims. In the news the Dutch and Belgian Ministers spoke and the Dutch Minister sent a greeting to his wife and children and grandchildren. Then it was the most difficult thing to control oneself, and I know that if I had been alone I couldn't have done. Later came the news of Mr Chamberlain's resignation and his speech, in that voice which brings back so many memories mostly of crisis. But even if he has failed, and we can't be sure yet that he has, there is no more courageous man in the government or indeed anywhere, I'm sure of that. But Winston Churchill will be better for this war – as Hilary said, he is such an old beast! The Germans loathe and fear him and I believe he can do it.

It was odd to remember that this day used to be a great anniversary for me. Seven years ago, on May 10th 1933, I first went out with Henry. Imagine a lovely summer evening at the Trout with the wistaria out and the soft murmuring of the water. And my heart so full of everything. And now, emotion recollected in tranquillity.... dust and ashes, dry bones. Or are they not so dry as all that? I don't suppose I shall ever know.

Thursday 20 February 1941. This evening I was looking for a notebook in which to keep a record of *dreams* and I found this diary, this sentimental journal or whatever you (Gentle Reader in the Bodleian) like to call it. Perhaps it is hardly a diary, for I keep a bald record of everyday happenings in a neat little book which has a set space for every day. And I write in this book only when the occasion seems to demand it. In the spring, when I think of past loves like Jay or when something momentous happens, like the invasion of Holland and Belgium (but not when France gave in – perhaps I'd got used to shocks by then. Now all I remember is sitting in deck chairs on the lawn with Hilary, the garden full of sweet williams).

It hasn't been such a bad winter as last, although there has been all the frightful bombing. We've had sirens too and a few bumps in the distance (in August) but nothing worse than long nights at the First Aid Post, smoking, knitting, talking, eating and trying to sleep in the stuffy air, covered with scratchy Army blankets.

I've worked hard in the YMCA canteens at the Tented Camp and Parkhall. I've even been temporarily – though it was quite violent while it lasted – in love. Anyway it has all passed now and my heart is free again with Jay's memory warming it, especially with February and March coming on – his months. I hear no news of him – I don't write.

I have been doing quite a lot of writing lately [her 'spy novel'] which is satisfying and pleases me if nobody else. I have also been improving my mind – I've read Jane Austen – *Emma* most lately, Scott – *Redgauntlet*, Johnson's *Tour in the Hebrides* with Boswell – I've had a Scottish craze lately. At the Tented Camp I grew fond of a young soldier who had been a waiter in many of the best Scottish hotels – LMS on the china, stags' heads and palms. Anyway, because of that, or for some more subtle reason, I took to listening to the news in Gaelic and poring over maps of the West Highlands.

I've also read *Vanity Fair*, after hearing it as a serial on the wireless. That marvellous Waterloo chapter was especially appropriate this summer although I had nobody in France or at Dunkirk. But perhaps one could almost enjoy it for that reason – only enjoy isn't at all the word.

This very evening on which I've written all this I was looking among my books and took out John Piper's *Shell Guide to Oxfordshire*. I went all through it, a nostalgic pilgrimage in churches and churchyards – most of which I have never seen at all but shall see one day – and lingered over the view of Blenheim's park and lake by which are quoted some favourite lines of Matthew Arnold from *Thyrsis*.

Friday 4 July. Here it is – summer and at least the dream of flowers has come true. In my room delphiniums, sweet williams, roses and sweet peas. Tonight (rashly) I wrote to Jay. Afterwards picking flowers I thought of 'Go Lovely Rose' and

> How small a part of time they share
> That are so wondrous sweet and fair

Also of the chicken without any bone, the cherry without any stone and the baby without any crying. The first poem is obvious, the second ['I gave my love a cherry'] less so but still fairly obvious.

I have been reading Katherine Mansfield's scrapbook – and I feel that I might do more with this. I have my commonplace book for extracts and poems, but this could be bits of stories and ideas as well as a kind of superior (and very sentimental) diary.

When Mrs Morris comes she brings her grandchild Dorothy with her. Dorothy follows you about or if you are sitting in the garden stands and peers at you through the trelliswork by the back door. One morning when I was washing up the breakfast things she came and stood with her hands at the draining board, staring at me. 'Wordsworth could have made more of this,' I felt, but I could think of nothing to say except to tell her to be a good girl and go and sit down at the table. We are embarrassed when children stare at us – there is something unnerving about it.

I have written a story called 'Goodbye, Balkan Capital' which I have sent to *Penguin New Writing,* but three weeks have passed and I have heard nothing. Shall I ever succeed – I begin to doubt it sometimes and now is a hopeless time to try. All the same I might write something for Woodrow Wyatt's *English Story.* Something nostalgic, faintly Russian and true – period (for me) July 1939.

A table too near the band in Lyons and thoughts, a flashback to the dark house in Mayfair and his eyes looking out over Lake Maggiore. Very sad but gradually the music puts me in a better frame of mind and I go back cheerfully to wash stockings in Bayswater. Or could I meet somebody thinking to be consoled and finding that they need consoling too? It must be logical and yet it seems that the best stories nowadays are more atmospheric than anything else – incomplete rather than rounded off – anyway it mustn't be too long as my things generally are.

Or I might do something about a child like Dorothy or evacuees.

15 July. Pwllheli. To see an airman or soldier with Poland or Czechoslovakia on his arm makes me think that there could be a story about him. He is at a dance in a ramshackle place like the pavilion with the band playing an old Continental tango like '*Regentropfen*' and he thinks of his estate in Poland and the great dogs or his forests or the peasants sitting on the ground drinking vodka. Or he is in a provincial hotel with stags' heads and dim stained mirrors. The Czech could remember that glass restaurant in Prague on a Saturday afternoon with dancing and very full of gay young people – it looks over the water. And lilies-of-the-valley being sold in the streets.

20 July. It is extraordinary how the slightest emotional disturbance (like hoping to have a little German conversation with a Czech officer) can put all other ideas out of one's head, making one stupid and unable to concentrate on anything intelligent like writing or any book but the lightest novel. It is humiliating to discover that one has not grown out of this sort of thing, but enlightening too, a useful experience and happily it passes so that it is all the more satisfying and peaceful to be normal once more. I suppose it can go on happening indefinitely, at any age, or I shall know when I get there – if anything like this ever happens to me again. It was so *very* slight too, and had really nothing to do with the Czech personally – just the desire for a little *Stimmung*, which conversation with an attractive foreigner can bring.

14 August. Oswestry. I have been reading Virginia Woolf's *To the Lighthouse.* Although I have read her before this is the first time I have really taken note of her special technique. It is one that commends itself to me – I find it attractive and believe I could do it – indeed, I already have, in a mild way. Sitting by the kitchen fire drying my hair, a cat, a basket chair and a willow tree and Mr Churchill and President Roosevelt meeting in the middle of the ocean to discuss War and Peace Aims.

Tuesday 7 April. 1942 Bristol. Today Hilary came back from a weekend with the news that Jay is a Major in the Persian Army. How beautiful, how right, how more than mildly amusing!

And it is spring again and I have noticed that almond trees and forsythia blossom in Clifton as in North Oxford, and the clear evening light comes into the house and one can pick daffodils in the garden. But I think I have noticed a little less joyousness and hope in myself – a more sober, damped down, possibly more suitable frame of mind.

> The foot less prompt to meet the morning dew,
> The heart less bounding at emotion new,
> And hope, once crush'd, less quick to spring again.
> [Matthew Arnold]

I recited these lines to myself last Friday evening when, at blackout time, I was drawing the dusty red baize curtains across the windows of the ramshackle building where I work and firewatch once a week.

But the heart can still bound a little at the idea of Jay in a fez (dark red, I hope) and the idea that people might one day whisper about me and say – 'Wasn't there once something about a *Persian Major*?'

To Henry and Elsie Harvey in Stockholm
[As this letter was going to Sweden, a
neutral country, it had to be written in
guarded terms as it would be censored]

The Coppice,
Leigh Woods,
Bristol.

2 July 1942

My dearest Henry and Elsie!

Today I had a letter from Betty saying she had had a cable from you last week with the news that you were in Stockholm – and that you have a daughter! You cannot imagine how pleased I am at this news and how happy to know that you are safe. I have thought of you constantly during these last two years and it has been awful having no news, though Betty always passed on to me anything she heard, which wasn't usually very much. By the way she didn't mention Elsie in her letter today so I presume it is my darling Swedish sister who has the daughter and not somebody else! If you have to take a second wife, Henry, you know who it is to be. 'We need not be speaking of that just now,' said Henry in a low, hurrying voice. 'It is not a very suitable way to begin a letter.'

I haven't got on with this letter very well – I think I was a little depressed by being told that I couldn't possibly send a letter to Sweden. But as I haven't asked anybody who really knows I may as well go on writing, and if I can't send it I will keep it until that happy day when we are all drinking tea together in 86B Banbury Road. (As I write I can still smell the peculiar smell of paint and carpet and new furniture that used to linger in the hall and see the china horse and the Degas and the long satin curtains in the sitting room. And old Barnicot coughing over a Craven A.)

I had a lovely long letter from Jock today. It was dated April 15th and he had just had the letter I wrote in January. A long time, but it is a comfort to know that letters *do* arrive eventually. Of course all his news is very stale now and with the position in Egypt being so bad one doesn't know whether he is still in Alexandria, where he was when he wrote. I daresay he has gone back to Cairo – the Germans were supposed to be about 60 miles from Alexandria at the weekend and we have been hanging on pretty well but of course one never knows what may happen. Jock wrote very cheerfully and seemed to be busy teaching Greeks, lecturing in the University of Alexandria, teaching Latin in the British Evening Institute and also running a Literary Society, with lectures on Gerard Manley Hopkins, Compton-Burnett and even Mr Huxley (against his will, he said). He has sent the translation of the Greek novel *Eroica* to Jonathan Cape and Jonathan doesn't like it at all and advises him to offer it to John Lehmann at the Hogarth Press. I wonder if it will appear. It doesn't seem right somehow to think of Jockie with all the *New Writing* people. I once sent a story to John Lehmann but of course he rejected it. He always looks so fierce that I hardly thought he *would* like it.

I haven't written anything for ages – I have really no time now as I am in a full time job and also assist in running a house. I am working in 'a Government department' [the Censorship] but am not allowed to say what when I write abroad, so you will have to guess what would be most suitable for me as you remember me. I find the work very interesting, though the secrecy is rather annoying as I can't talk about it or share jokes with any except my colleagues. I manage to live comfortably on what I earn as Hilary and I (she is here in the same Institution [the BBC] as in London, if you remember) have taken a share in a big house in this most select residential district of Clifton – a really beautiful position, high up over the Suspension Bridge with the woods in front of us. We share with two families, who work with Hilary, and there are altogether six children so we know all about communal living, though the house is big enough for us to have our own sitting room and to keep ourselves to ourselves if we want to. We cook all our own meals as domestic help is nearly impossible to get now, and so by the time we are in from work (about 6.30) and have cooked, eaten and washed up an evening meal there isn't really much time for intellectual pursuits – though I try to read a little and have lately finished *War and Peace*. But there won't be a new Compton-Burnett for another year I suppose. It is depressing to go round the bookshops and find how little there is that one really wants to buy. I hate reading books about the war – I get quite enough of the war in my job – and so in bed at night I read Jane Austen and Byron and Anthony à Wood – (I might read *The English Rogue* if I had it or even *The Gallant Hermaphrodite*). You see, Henry, she still remembers the names.

Hilary is going to be married in August – her future husband is in the Air Force and is called Alexander (Sandy) Walton. He was at Cambridge and did architecture and has been out in Greece doing an architectural survey of the island of Chios – this was before the war, of course. It's funny that he didn't meet Jock out there as they must have been there about the same time and probably knew some of the same people. Strangely enough he reminds me in some ways of Jock – he is fair and tallish and very musical – he has set some of Betjeman's *Continual Dew* poems to music! I am hoping he will be able to get a nice best man for me as I am to be bridesmaid. It is going to be quite simple, we shall wear day clothes, Hilary a pale blue crêpe dress and coat and I a dull pink crêpe dress with a lovely romantic black hat with a heart-shaped halo brim, which I bought yesterday in Bath. (All this description is for my dear sister Elsie, of course.) We now have to give coupons for clothes, as you know, so it is no good buying something that won't be useful afterwards – but it needs great ingenuity to plan everything. We shall get shabbier and shabbier but who cares. In many ways you would hardly realise we had been three years (almost) at war. We still have plenty to eat and although we can't get oranges and grapefruit and bananas (Do you remember bananas?) we have excellent lettuces and cabbages and carrots etc. fresh from our garden and raspberries and blackcurrants too.

Of course the raids have done some damage. Oxford is quite untouched I am glad to say. I should hate anything to happen to it. I am very sad about Cologne, I did love it so, and although it is satisfying to know that we can do these 1000 bomber raids I can't feel any elation about them. Still, I suppose it must be done. Wars aren't what they used to be in Victorian times, when they were fought abroad decently by professional soldiers!

I wonder what you both look like now? And who is the baby like? Perhaps it's a good thing she isn't a boy – how heartbreaking for some poor girl in the English Reading Room twenty years hence! If you ever get this please write to me. God bless you all. My love to you.

Pym.

To Henry Harvey in Stockholm Bristol.

22 October 1942

Dearest Henry:

It was lovely getting your letter, a week ago it came. And a charming baby, so intelligent looking. It was nice too to get a glimpse of Elsie's face. Why not send me a photo of yourself? I don't think I could send any – anyway I haven't any recent ones. I look just the same except that my hair is longer, as is the fashion now. Still pretty well preserved, still sometimes admired. But why tell *you* this who didn't admire anyway!

You know, that was the nicest letter you ever wrote me. Why do you say you can't write letters? It's an idea you seem to have got hold of which makes a very good excuse for being a bad correspondent. This was so exactly like you – I knew you hadn't changed at all. It is over four years since we met. Solemn thought. Oddly enough I have a great friend [Gordon Glover], made since I came to Bristol, who reminds me very much of you in many ways. He is a journalist, very amusing, a great philanderer but very sweet and kind, and as I haven't fallen in love with him I see only his best side. So strange being reminded of you – I didn't think anyone ever could do that. (He wouldn't say 'Otway is remarkably fine' though.)

You will see that I have become a very *bad* letter writer! As for other writing, I haven't done any for ages. I just don't have time in the evening, after work, what with meals to get etc. If I do write it is letters to my friends now literally all over the world. All that you say about my work is quite true and one day perhaps I'll be able to put it into practice.

Later – Tuesday 10 November

Oh how ashamed I am, not to have finished this before now! I've been busy writing other letters, I've forgotten all about my old Harvey. I seem to be embarked on a kind of love affair, not exactly of my choosing, it just seemed to happen very unexpectedly and well, it is all very nice so far – I'll be seeing him next weekend. I don't suppose we shall ever be able to get married, so perhaps Belinda and Harriet will come true after all – though Harriet would have to be a widow or divorced or something! Hilary has a cold at present and I have been taking her some blackcurrant tea in bed. Sandy (her husband) is coming next week.

I haven't heard from Jock yet. I might write tonight after finishing this. I seem to get so little time now except evenings and weekends are taken up with our little amusements mostly drinking in Bristol's nice pubs, and occasionally, as last weekend, films – *Gone with the Wind*. Four hours wallowing in it, so much so that at the end my eyes were quite dry even through so many deathbeds. It's odd to think that I now have a completely different circle of friends and that you don't know darling Honor Wyatt or Gordon or Sandy or George (now probably on the coast of N. Africa somewhere). Isn't the news wonderfully exciting – perhaps it really will end some time though not as soon as most (some) people seem to think. Of course we have hardly felt anything of it, but I often wonder if anything is worth all the suffering and misery there has been already. But I suppose it would have been worse if we hadn't fought.

You seem to be surrounded by nice persons of culture and

intelligence. How I would love to see you again. It would be so nice now – we should get on better together than when we were both young and silly. Do you remember Langbaine?!!

With love to you and Elsie and 'the baby'.

Pym

17 December

Henry, this is *awful* – to have left this letter so long unposted – what with censorship and everything – (happy Christmas to the Censors – I always think they must have a very arduous job especially at this time – bless them!) heaven knows when you'll get this.

Since I finished it there is nothing special to report. I am very, very happy, but the future is rather dark, as far as my personal affairs are concerned. We just do not know what is going to happen to us – but at present we are happy and that is a lot these days.

With love,

Pym

After Christmas I

January 1943. Bristol. Having time to kill I walked down Park Street and turned off by a notice which said *To St George's Church*. I went in by the back way. Surprisingly it was not locked. It was almost dark inside so that I could hardly see what it was like but I said a prayer there and then walked round the churchyard. This consists of a few overgrown slabs, sadly neglected, which merge suddenly into an allotment with cabbages etc. Solemn and rather horrifying thought, what may be nourishing this soil. 'When my grave is broke up again . . . .' And at the end of it all a kind of cement mixer (I think). An unusual churchyard. My walk brought me round to the front with an eighteenth century façade with heavy columns. I couldn't see much inside, except the glint of stained glass in the dusk. I am suddenly thinking of that other little church in Marylebone, St Luke's, was it, into which I walked at Harvest Festival and the vicar's wife made me go round and admire the decorations. The vicar had just returned from Italy and gave a curious pagan sermon – about the decorations hiding the vileness of the church, as far as I remember.

I went into the Public Library. It is open till seven and was now full of ruins of humanity, come into the reading room for learning. And on my blotting paper I write 'A Testing Time' in Red Pencil – to remind me.

Gordon said he would die about the time when the evenings began to lengthen and birds sang. I had the first taste of it today. I had imagined it, little knowing that it would be *this*, not death but parting. That eternal dustbin in the dawn, with lines of Donne (?) floating above it.

> The Day breaks not, it is my heart,
> Because that thou and I must part.

Thursday 21 January. I'm firewatching – for the first time since Gordon and I parted. I'm sleeping downstairs in my favourite room, with the plaque of Ernest Wyman Savory on the wall, where I so often wrote letters to my darling. I have been dreading this occasion and now here it is – and it is as if I had taken some soothing drug which gives me a sort of remoteness and detachment from my pain, so that I know it is there but do not feel it. Only calmness and love and certainty, almost. As if the happy atmosphere of this room still lingered and was lapping me round.

It is a wicked thing to want time to pass and not to try to enjoy one's days. Now I try to make things to look forward to, however small. At lunch yesterday I read this in *Trivia* –

So I never lose a sense of the whimsical and perilous charm of daily life, with its meetings and words and accidents. Why, today, perhaps, or next week, I may hear a voice and, packing up my Gladstone bag, follow it to the ends of the world.

Well, of course, following voices to the ends of the world isn't possible now, but there's still the whimsical and perilous charm perhaps. I don't want to lose that.

I hope I shall sleep tonight.

Friday 22 January. It wasn't so bad at all, but I didn't sleep very well, mainly because as usual, it was very hot and there were various strange noises, loud voices outside and howling cats. (But no yaffling woodpeckers in the cypresses.) I dreamed of Gordon a little, but mostly of Jay. (Darling Jay, *mein Kleines*, this is half your book. Imagine after my death two old men wrangling over it. One a dried-up politician, the other a burnt-out old ruin, the most waspish member of the Savage Club. Both so unpleasant that it is difficult to imagine how either of them could possibly have been loved by such a delightful person as the present writer obviously is!) I woke up at a quarter to six, dreadful sentimental time. (In continental trains, seeing the faces of strange Germans, the young airman who sat opposite me during that night journey back from Germany – Dresden – in May 1938). I suddenly decided to cycle home for breakfast which I did in 'the darkness which precedes the dawn' (who said this?). Julian, coming out of the gate, greeted me with the news that Daddy had sent him some liquorice allsorts. Rush of ridiculous emotion, of course! Plenty of intolerable birds. A green Christmas means a full churchyard . . . . We haven't really had any winter yet.

When I came in at tea-time today the Coppice seemed gay and amusing – Viennese waltzes in the kitchen and the chickens madly eating the beans and the cabbage.

How satisfying is a phrase in music when it goes where you want it to go – you anticipate its ending confidently and fulfilment satisfies.

I have got to realise that it is no longer anything to do with me what Gordon does. Although it is a month since I saw him, there are an endless number of months to be got through – a long dreary stretch until it doesn't matter any more. And heaven knows how many that will be.

Oh what a clever book this is! Really I haven't got a beautiful character at all. I suppose I should have been *delighted* if Gordon had said he was miserable. I ought to be glad that he is getting on all right.

Wednesday 27 January. Every time I go past the big windows leading on to the balcony I stand for a moment and look out over the stone lions, towards the Victoria Rooms and the 18 bus stop. Lately I have begun to realise that I do this and I ask myself sardonically – 'Well, and what do you expect to see?' What I do see is sometimes sunshine and crowds of people, other times the rain glancing off the lions and few people. Always a rather dreary prospect. Well, that is what things are likely to be at the moment, a rather dreary prospect. It is impossible that I shall be really happy for some time to come.

Monday–Tuesday, 1–2 February. I am reading Robert Graves's novel *Wife to Mr Milton*. He has in it a phrase, 'I had my enemy the spring to contend with.' Enemy because of the cold winds etc. Oh yes, I have the rheumatics in my back and neck and arms, but it is the intolerable birds that are the enemies, and the primroses bravely pushing up in the tangled Coppice garden. And yet not enemies really – they never were before. Winter would surely be much more of an enemy.

Today on my way home I discovered a beautiful pre-Raphaelite tomb. I had got to the top of the hill into Victoria Square when I was suddenly filled with a desire to go along the paved stone alley leading to St Andrew's Church. So I walked into it with my bicycle and discovered on either side of me tombstones in a rather well-kept grassy churchyard, with trees, palms (which seemed odd) and a forsythia coming into flower. And towards the end of this alley on the right hand side is the pre-Raphaelite tomb. A square, box-like affair supported by angels at the corners, and the angels are beautifully Rossetti with flowing hair parted in the middle. I can't remember who is buried there. I must notice next time I visit it, for I feel sure there will be a next time. At the end of the alley one comes upon the church, a dramatically empty shell, blitz, of course.

Thursday 11 February. This evening there was a pre-Raphaelite sky. Bright blue with orange clouds like Thermogene wool. And a monkey puzzle dark against it, and none of us getting any younger.

I am reading Newman's *Apologia Pro Vita Sua,* but not really getting very much from it as I do not understand many of the theological terms and arguments. And how reasoned and logical is his account of his conversion – I am still waiting for the miraculous act of faith, that finally sent him over. The sort of dramatic thing Gordon or I would expect. But somehow I don't think it's going to be like that. He says – 'From the age of fifteen, dogma has been the fundamental principle of my religion: I know no other religion: religion as a mere sentiment is to me a dream and a mockery.' No Abbotsleigh or pre-Raphaelite tombs there.

I like the account of how 'Lead, kindly Light' came to be written. It was in 1833, when he was 32, I had imagined it much later. After a tour of Italy and Sicily, during which he was ill with a fever, he waited for a ship home at Palermo for three weeks. 'At last I got off in an orange boat bound for Marseilles. We were becalmed a whole week in the Straits of Bonifacio. Then it was that I wrote the lines "Lead, kindly Light . . .".'

Today I took Saroyan with me and read it at lunch. I like the picture of myself dipping alternately into Newman and Saroyan.

Friday 19 February. Avonmouth again and a pleasant ride back in the top front seat of a 99 bus, feeling very sentimental and quite pleasantly melancholy as today Julian was going up to London to spend his half term with Gordon.

Wednesday 10 March. Last Friday I joined the Wrens. It is done – inevitable now, I suppose, though I *can* still withdraw if I want to. I am calm and happy about it and sometimes excited – all settled. Like Going over to Rome. And Cardinal Newman has gone, and I'm still reading *The Daisy Chain.*

In Shirehampton Vicarage garden there is a chestnut tree with green uncurled leaves – and almond trees galore, daffodils a few, and an afternoon alone at Avonmouth. Working hard, answering the telephone, making tea, and finally, looking out the window with silly tears in my eyes, because I suddenly remembered Gordon with his hair smoothed down sitting opposite me at breakfast in the Coppice kitchen on a Monday morning.

Oh, a bad day. Beware of complacency, and you must fight all the time and have the same struggles. Tears on top of the bus going to Avonmouth, up into Sea Mills, down into Shirehampton and Johnny Doughboy in the park. And at lunchtime when I was alone,

I *howled*. . . . At teatime I went to the office in Bristol, feeling very Rip Van Winkle, to find people away and on the point of leaving and the blackout *stuck* halfway across the skylight of our room, casting a gloom, *quite* a gloom as they say, over the place.

Later, ironing and humming the Warsaw Concerto, and later still listening to a Brandenburg Concerto and Dvorak's New World Symphony, and reading *The Daisy Chain,* which is so well written, very Compton-Burnett and very sad, and then eating eggs and bacon for supper. Then Hilary came in wearing a pretty little hat and I cheered up. And now – after midnight – I'm glad to say I feel better. But that bat hovers around (rather like a squander bug) so I won't say any more. Dusty old creature, to think I've still got you, after ten weeks.

Thursday 11 March. My own darling raving dilettante, what is 'a leaf-nosed bat'? (see *Introducing* this week). It sounds a gentler creature than the thing you left with me. (Gordon's broadcasting tomorrow and I'm firewatching – so . . . .)

Sunday 14 March. Well, on Friday, she came back from Avonmouth, loitered a little at the Academy and then, with a sudden wave of inspiration, went and had some tea in the Berkeley. Ludicrous place with palms and mirrors, but no orchestra now. It was the end of the day and she felt rather a ludicrous object sitting there drinking tea, eating bread and butter and smoking a cigarette. There *ought* to have been an orchestra and she ought to have been at a table rather too near it, with two curious women – but of course things never happen quite like this. At 5.35 I left and thought of Gordon just beginning and wondered if he was feeling nervous. Then home, very tired, drained of all emotion.

Firewatching was quite peaceful. There is a curious timelessness about it, as if one were *really* in one's marble vault . . . but *Now* therefore while the youthful hue Sits on thy skin like morning dew . . . and . . . Spring will not wait. Anyway it might have been one of those times before Christmas instead of After Christmas. *After Christmas* . . . that's the title of this part of this book.

Saturday 20 March. Watching Honor writing a great long letter to George this evening, I thought, the greatest luxury now would be to be allowed to write a great, long silly letter to Gordon. As it is I suppose I must go on drearily in this book. My clever book. I seem to write in it only when I am depressed, like praying only when one is really in despair – on the whole I've been fairly happy this week though. Tonight rather low. But after all that is to be expected. Low and dull.

Tuesday 23 March. Firewatching. West wind and small rain and I thought all the usual things coasting down through the dark on my bicycle – riding or walking in the dark, especially to firewatching, is surely the most detached and lonely time. One cannot feel really sad because one seems to be outside oneself. It's the state I once described to Gordon – it gets on very well, like 'Social Success', until suddenly it's 'Oh God, it's awful, I wish I were dead.' And now I'm sitting in this uncosy high-roofed room with no sound but the ticking of my common little clock and the click of my companions' knitting needles.

The other day I thought 'And now it's Spring' and decided that this would be quite a good title for a novel. Well, why don't you write it? Ah, but *is* it Spring? I know that the air is warm and sunny, birds sing at dawn and twilight and the daffodils are out in the Coppice garden, and violets blue and white, sweeter than the lids of Juno's eyes – I know, but what about the dusty heart? Not much spring there – yet. Turning out of Manilla Road this evening I heard the sound of dance music in the dark. And the tune was 'My Devotion' – is oh such a *dreary* emotion . . . . Very suitable.

I often pass the pre-Raphaelite tomb, or rather the path leading to it, but I have never been there again. But I will go one day. You (reader) may say, Why do you make such a thing of it all? To which I will snap (like *Trivia*) Well, what about your own life? Is it so full of large, big wonderful things that you don't need tombs and daffodils and your own special intolerable bird, with an old armchair or two and occasional readings from Matthew Arnold and Coventry Patmore?

On Sunday we [Barbara, Hilary, Honor and the children] went to Weston – it was a gloriously sunny day and we were lucky getting taxis. It is a large bright Betjeman place – surely he must have written something about it – with many hotels and boarding houses. We walked into the middle of a very serious invasion exercise and were twice turned back for unexploded bombs. After that we walked along the beach to the pier, eating sweets and gathering little pink, yellow and white shells. At the pier the sun was very hot. We looked at the naughty peepshows and Hilary and I went on the figure of eight and the Racing Speedway clinging together and shrieking! What a place to come to when one is lonely and miserable, as Honor did in the autumn when George first went and she wasn't hearing from him.

Saturday 27 March. In the afternoon Honor and I made sandwiches and cut bread and butter for Julian's birthday party. We had the Yehudi Menuhin concert on. He played the old Mendelssohn and of course I wept a little over the slow movement, alone in the back kitchen, my hands immersed in the washing-up water, need I say. It was a very successful party. After tea I gathered fresh flowers for my room. Once there was a Saturday when all I could find was two November roses, rather browned off at the edges.

As dusk fell I grew melancholy. I am ashamed to say that I am sometimes just plain jealous when I think of other people who can be with Gordon. It is sometimes intolerable to be a woman and have no second bests or spares or anything. I struggled with this feeling – I hope I have got the better of it, for now, at any rate. It only makes me more miserable when I feel angry and resentful. Testing Time . . . . Well certainly I am being tested. I cannot answer for him. Does the road wind uphill all the way? I asked myself, waiting for kettles to boil tonight. Yes, to the very end. And remember, one step enough for me. Sunday tomorrow and plenty to do. One step . . . .

Sunday 28 March. Afternoon we sat in the sun and listened to the *Messiah.* I wrote home, went to the post, pumped up my bicycle, put cotton over the peas. And then lay on a mattress with my face close to the ground, thinking about that poem by Robert Graves, the man seeking lost love, who has become so sensitive he can hear wormtalk and moths chumbling cloth etc. Hilary and Sandy went at 5.30.

After supper Honor and I Baldwinned our legs – she was delighted, never having used a Baldwin before. We listened to a Stephen Potter poetry programme, where, curiously enough, that Robert Graves poem was read – then Scott Goddard's Theme and Variations programme. Very nice. Brahms–Handel (I like the 1st) and Strauss *Don Quixote.*

Monday 29 March. Better today. When I got back to the Academy the first thing I saw was a new examiner sitting at a table, wearing earrings, gaiters and a hat. By teatime she had removed the hat, as if (somebody said) she had really decided to stay.

There was much talk and agitation about a circular which had appeared that morning, dealing with the release of Examiners [in the Censors Office, making them liable for call-up] under 41. Thirty-five yesterday but forty-two today. Anyway I felt a little smug having already volunteered, but it unsettled a good many people.

Honor had had two letters from George – written not much more than a fortnight ago. It brings things nearer if we can recall what we were doing when he wrote, so I have decided to put down the events of each day anyway. And of course the usual dreary reflections when

I am miserable. Oh mumbling, chumbling moths, talking worms and my own intolerable bird give me one tiny ray of hope for the future and I will keep on wanting to be alive. Yes, you will be alive, it will not be the same, nothing will be quite as good, there will be no intense joy but small compensations, spinsterish delights and as the years go on and they are no longer painful, memories. Too many like the curate's too heavy eiderdown which he flung off him in the night.

Or it may not be like this at all. You don't know. Nobody does.

Tuesday 30 March. This morning I had a notice from the WRNS asking me to go for my medical on Thursday – unless I'm having a period, which I will be. So I was almost inclined to write as in Crews Mail letters – 'Well, I might be seeing something, you know what I mean'.

At tea Honor read from a letter from Pen. She wrote about Gordon – that of course he wasn't happy, but that it might be a good thing for him to have to work things out for himself. I'm so glad he is with nice, sympathetic people like David and Pen. Pen says they don't allow him to dramatise himself, which is of course a very good thing! But oh I hate to think of him being unhappy and me not being able to do anything for him. Well, we are neither of us happy and nobody can help us but ourselves. One day, perhaps . . . .

Wednesday 31 March. Quite a good uninterrupted working day. Blustery weather. I bought 2 pairs of fine utility stockings. After tea fitting a dress on Prue and doing a little sewing.

Thursday 1 April. Well, the beginning of the fourth month and a donkey, then *two* donkeys eating the cabbages in the garden. (April Fool.) Felt very weary and aching all over. At 6 o'clock Honor and I went to the concert at the Colston Hall. We had supper in the [BBC] canteen, caught the last 89 home and walked the rest of the way. Windy coming over the bridge. That walk at night is still painful to me – I can't help remembering. The place where we first kissed and such sentimentalities!

Monday 5 April. Had my day off and lay in bed till 9.30. It was a glorious, unnaturally hot day with sun shining all the time. I went without stockings. Hilary and I had lunch at the Buttery and afterwards did some shopping. Quite like pre-war – it was the kind of day for spending and wending and squanderbugs, but we didn't buy much. I had my hair cut and styled – quite nicely and read a novel all about Censors – then did more shopping and arrived back at about five. In the evening Yehudi Menuhin broadcast – he played the Brahms Concerto. We also listened to a prodigiously long play by

Val Gielgud. After tea Prue walked down to the Bridge by herself and we were all feverishly looking for her.

There are certain notes on the violin (or is it a certain way of playing) that gives me the same lovely, out in the cold feeling as walking or riding down to firewatching in the dark. Why, this is strange, I don't know the reason, probably just some chance association.

Tuesday 6 April. Today I had another summons for my WRNS medical – I am to go on Thursday. I do hope everything goes all right – then I can start Part II of *After Christmas.* I've never before felt so conscious of 'making a life for myself' – I suppose the continuous effort is good for me, some people probably have to do it all the time.

I got home in time to have some of Elizabeth's birthday tea – Mary had made some lovely things. Julian had a good report – Honor said 'Gordon will be pleased'. Yes, I know. How could I bear not to have as much of him as she has had and still has in the children. No, I couldn't. Julian is going to see him next weekend. And I am going to stay with Rupert and Helen Gleadow in Chelsea.

Honor and I have *groats* last thing at night – Lovely!

Wednesday 7 April. I got back to the Coppice in time to share in yet another birthday party. Honor seemed rather depressed – she hasn't heard from George for over a week. She told me Julian is going to Gordon next weekend and not this – they will be at Arkesden. She also said that Gordon has now 'supplied the evidence'. This news flung me into a *turmoil* of emotion so that I spent a most miserable evening. Now *why* was I so miserable? Well, for one reason – I couldn't help thinking how joyous I *might* have been at this stage being reached. Whereas now I have no reason to hope – I don't even know if Gordon ever thinks of me and nobody can reassure me on that point. So I went round in miserable circles – to know what one wants and see no prospects of getting it – what pain, sometimes I feel I must talk about it, and let go for a minute (yes, there were some tears privately) – then I can start again being drearily splendid. I also had the idea Honor might know definite things – future plans of his that didn't include me – oh – I can't write about this futile wretchedness. There it was – and I didn't go to sleep till comparatively late. Darling Honor made me groats.

Friday 8 April. A cold day. I washed very carefully, having also had a bath the night before. For today was my WRNS medical. I felt very weak at the knees and found it difficult to work – I left at twelve, had lunch at the Buttery where I fortified myself with roast pork. By this time it was sunny, so I walked down to the army Recruiting Centre where the medical is held. It was one o'clock by this time. There were several other girls there. We were put into a waiting room decorated with ATS posters and a 'No Smoking' notice. I read my novel, *Table Two* by Marjorie Wilenski (obviously about the Censorship) and talked a bit to the others – various types and ages. First of all we filled in a medical form – then went upstairs and undressed, except for shoes, knickers and coat – then produced a 'specimen' into a kind of enamel potty with a long handle like a saucepan – of which I was quite glad. Next came examination of eyes, ears etc., weighing and measuring by an elderly doctor, then heart, lungs etc., by a woman. All quite quick. After that I dressed again and had an interview with an extremely charming WRNS 1st officer – she had my London forms and correspondence but couldn't really tell me much, except that my application was marked 'urgent' and that they probably had something in mind for me. And I mustn't be *too* impatient. Oh, but I do hope I get in now. My heart is set on it. The whole thing took over two hours and I felt terribly tired, really exhausted after it. A thorough emotional upheaval, what with everything.

When I got home I lay on Honor's bed. She was upset at having told me about Gordon and the 'evidence' last night. I told her what it really was that upset me and we talked about it. Really there is no reason to feel more depressed than usual – nothing has changed and Honor has no inside information about Gordon's plans. But she thinks Gordon may not be the right person for me – and that I am probably brooding over an idea. Oh, I don't *know*. It may be – but oh it was good wasn't it – Surely I *didn't* see what wasn't there? Patience and Courage still – And struggle on. Lead, kindly light and one step enough for me.

Friday 9 April. And what exactly, may Posterity ask, *was* all this 'struggle' about? Why this need for Patience and Courage? And the bewildered English spinster, now rather gaunt and toothy, but with a mild, sweet expression, may hardly know herself. Really, if I ever have any children I think I must call them Patience and Courage. Twins – rather dreary stolid little girls.

For the first time I had lunch in the British Restaurant. Very good hot food, rather too many potatoes, but a lovely steamed pudding. Masses of dockers etc. And this spinster with Tchekov's *My Life* on the table, but not reading it.

I got home to find the kitchen *very* tidy and silent. It reminded me of the last day I saw Gordon (December 28th). But then it was dusk and I walked through the house crying.

Saturday 10 April. Today I went to London to stay with Rupert and Helen Gleadow. I travelled on the 1.45 train, in a carriage full of silent people who insisted on having the windows too wide open. I went straight to Chelsea and found 22 Cheyne Walk just on the corner, opposite the bridge and looking over the river – I rang a likely bell and in a minute the door was opened – 'Are you Helen?' – 'You must be Barbara.' I've done this before, in the summer of 1938 when I met Elsie for the first time in 86 Banbury Road. Helen has fair curly hair and very blue eyes, is vivacious and sweet – we were able to have a good gossip before Rupert arrived. I saw him out of the window on his bicycle. He was wearing blue corduroy trousers and looks so nice without a beard – quite his old self. We had cowslip wine and beer and a nice dinner and much pleasant amusing talk. I was conscious of feeling happier than I have done for a long time. We went to bed fairly early. I noticed in the bookshelf in my room Francis Stuart's *Try the Sky* which Gordon had once spoken of – I glanced at it but deliberately didn't read it!

Sunday 11 April. Rupert and Helen went to Morley College to 'pursue the arts' leaving me with a lovely tray of breakfast and *Tristram Shandy* of which I read a little. It seems a nice inconsequential sort of book – the sort of book one would like to have written – or might even one day write. I got up about eleven and had a delicious bright green bath with pine essence and bright pink Spanish geranium soap. Rupert and Helen came back about half-past one and we had lunch – they opened a tin of apricots for me and we had a flan. Also some olives. Afterwards we went for a walk in Battersea Park – all the flowering trees were out – lilacs nearly, double cherry and magnolia. There is a nice pond (or lake) – also deer and wallabies (?).

I was back in Bristol about nine – I was like a drowned rat when I got home. But Honor was there with a lovely supper, so I undressed and ate.

I really feel it did me good going away and being with Rupert and Helen, who are so blissfully happy together they hardly seem to be real. Oh, but it *can* be done! They said my eyes had far too much sparkle for one who had been crossed in love. Honor had to send £25 to the solicitors yesterday.

Monday 12 April. I changed from one unglamorous pair of stockings to another. I worked quite hard all day. Honor had been speaking to Gordon on the phone. And he had sent a message for me – asking when I was going to the WRNS and that he would be thinking of me. This made me feel absolutely terrific – how it helps, just a word like this.

And cigarettes have gone up to 2/4 or 2/6 for 20 – so life's consolations grow less and less – and soon it *will* be just Matthew Arnold and memories. Or the future and the whimsical and perilous charm?

Tuesday 13 April. I went into Bright's and looked vaguely at materials – red spotted chiffon for a spinsterish nightdress. Hilary and I are going to have our rooms spring-cleaned tomorrow so we moved all the books and things – now my room is bare and dusty and echoing. We began playing and singing hymns – and I remembered some things I'd forgotten, favourite bits and lines – 'the angels' armour and the saints' reward' – 'the drift of pinions, would we hearken, beats at our own clay-shuttered doors' – and of course my dear old favourite 'God moves in a mysterious way'. But of *course*

> 'His purposes will ripen fast,
> Unfolding every hour,
> The bud may have a bitter taste
> But sweet will be the flower…'

Wednesday 14 April. I made a potato and leek soup for supper – then went firewatching. It was a beautiful evening. On the bridge I saw a girl warden (rather plain) being kissed by a Doughboy (a hidey-ho, a sweet and lo, a come and go boy). Lucky pigs I thought. The atmosphere reminded me of those summer evenings when Gordon and Honor and George and Hilary and I used to walk down to The Rocks and The Commercial and the Club. But in those days G. and I, though arm in arm, would talk only of British Israelites and other general subjects.

Thursday 15 April. Had breakfast at the Copper Kettle after a hot, restless night. My bed had a rock in the mattress and I couldn't avoid it. We were served by the usual inefficient waitress, who is like 'Can I do you now, Sir' in *ITMA.*

I went to Woolworth's in the lunch hour and bought various beauty aids – also looked longingly at ginghams and cherry-red linen in Jolly's window. Oh, but the sun was shining, and in the afternoon a bird sang so that it could be heard even among the censors.

When I got home I found everyone in the garden, so I washed my hair and dried it in the sun lying on a red blanket on the rockery, of all places. Masses of birds singing – I wish I knew what they were.

Gordon would know, Honor said, and I remembered one summer afternoon last year when we were sitting under the beechtree and he told me to look at a spotted flycatcher on the telephone wires. All these things one discovers about people, how nice they are.

Hilary made a salad for supper and we had it with pilchards and then some rhubarb. We listened to *ITMA* and then had a long technical conversation about Tampax!

Earlier in the evening one star came out in the twilight.

Julian is going to spend the weekend with Gordon – so I must be good and sensible. My stolid little girls Courage and Patience are on either side of me – I will cut out my blue satin nightdress (which was nearly black chiffon) and I am going to embroider it with little sprays of flowers and sentimental bows.

Weekend 16– 17– 18 April. Gloriously and unnaturally hot weather. On Friday I went to Avonmouth and sat in the Park during my lunch hour enjoying the sun and reading Tchekov. What attitudes we strike!

I had ironed my dirndl on Friday night, very hopefully, and by Saturday lunchtime it was hot enough to change into it. Hilary and I gardened fiercely – digging buttercups out of the front rockery – so much so that Hilary threatened to make a salad of the leaves, and we dreamed of digging them.

On Sunday it was again hot – I spent most of the morning scrubbing potatoes and making salad, but I enjoyed it. Surely my spiritual home is in the Coppice back kitchen? After lunch lay in the sun. Honor seemed rather miserable and when I came up with the tea I found her crying. We talked and decided that the burden and continual strain of being 'splendid' was sometimes unbearable – sometimes something snaps. Honor said she thought I'd been very good never to have written a word to Gordon. Funnily enough it had never occurred to me that I could – and now of course I'm glad I haven't. Of course I've wanted to – not so much long miserable letters as small darling jokes and funny things. Then Honor told me that a week or two ago Gordon said he had nearly taken a train to Bristol and gone to Mrs Weedy's in the hope that we might be there. And he had seemed surprised when Honor said we never went there. Oh, darling, how peculiarly insensitive your sex is! Anyway, as far as I was concerned it wasn't such a bad weekend as I had feared – you wait, says the bat. All right, I know I'm ready. As ready as I can be. What a lot one learns about the technique of misery! We ate an enormous supper, soup, omelette and potatoes, and then to bed. Prue was an adorable film child all the weekend.

Wednesday 21 April. Felt not exactly low but well damped down all day. Julian came back – I thought Honor looked depressed at tea – perhaps G. has been tearing her to pieces or it may be just not getting a letter from George – one doesn't like to ask all the time. Anyway after lighting a fire and having soup we felt better. The weather seems colder but all the lilac is out and the chestnuts.

Thursday 22 April. Up in the Morning Early [a radio keep-fit programme] certainly helps to dispel that feeling of lowness with which one usually starts the day. One gets instead an agonising stiffness in the backs of the legs, so that one feels trembling and doddery.

Quite a tolerable morning at Avonmouth. I was back in Bristol at lunchtime and bought a utility brassière which makes me look a *very fine shape,* not at all like 'this English lady'. The afternoon seemed long. When I got back we had a large late tea – Honor has received a letter from the solicitor to say that G. refuses to divulge the name of the woman or rather the address – Joan Leslie Glover – I shall always think of rows of spring onion seedlings in Honor's patch when I hear that name, as it was there she told me the name – sometime last week.

In the evening we listened to Walton's *Belshazzar's Feast* – a fine dramatic work. (Remarkably fine, as dear *Henry* would have said or might still say!)

If G. isn't the best and the real thing, well, I will get it with somebody else. But it's got to be pretty good, to be better than 'Sweeney Todd' and that November afternoon in Christmas Steps and our conversations in the Rocks [Hotel]. No words will describe this wonderful nebulous lover that may one day materialise.

Friday 23 April. Up in the Morning Early, but still stiff. Honor said how Gordon would laugh at us, and oh dear I could just see him laughing! I was working in Bristol all day and it seemed long and tiring.

Hilary has gone to the cottage this weekend – so Honor and I are by ourselves. We talked about things – the folly of day-dreaming amongst others. She thinks I ought to have a really good affaire. I quite agree, but OH DEAR.

Saturday 24 April. Today is an anniversary – I mean six months since my poor darling declared his ill-fated love and started me on this great chunk of misery.

After breakfast Honor and I went shopping in Clifton and came back with our string bags bulging – treacle and Shredded Wheat and cakes and buns. We discussed the technique of misery on the way back, then had tea in the kitchen. In the afternoon I washed my hair and parted it in the middle again.

Tuesday 27 April. Went to Avonmouth. The day started brightly but afterwards rained. I had my half day, but Bristol was only half alive with some shops still closed so I came home and did some sewing and gave myself a little concert of Dohnanyi, Brahms and the Classical Symphony. The latter is quite spoilt so I may well count it a dead loss. The nicest lover I never had, and the rest of it and A ring is round but not round enough and The sea's deep but not deep enough and I will fight for what I want and if I can't have it, then I will have nothing, but NOTHING!

The beech trees are out in tender green leaves – the spinster feels like going rushing into the garden and embracing them, crying Thank you, *thank* you! you at least do what is expected of you and never fail.

> How happy is he born and taught
> That seeketh not another's will,
> Whose armour is his honest thought
> And simple truth his utmost skill.

Why that *now,* I don't know. I must have many bats (all with broken wings) flying around in my head.

Wednesday 28 April. Had a most miserable cold day at the office and also had toothache. At 5.30 I went to the dentist and had 2 teeth out – he did it very nicely, but now my jaw is aching. I have a great bloody gap and feel rather pathetic. I got home about 7 to find poor darling Honor very low, though she didn't say anything, and worried about George. Oh God, if there were something . . . . At the moment the only thing that seems to matter is that he should be all right. She has so much to bear and can't even have Gordon to comfort her. Tomorrow she goes up to London to sign the petition and 'discretion' statement – oh it's all so beastly, if only it were over.

Thursday 29 April. Slept until ten and woke with blood on my pillow which very much intrigued Prue. Mary came in bringing a cup of tea and the news that there *was* a letter for Honor, but of course she had left before the post came. We discussed how we could let her know and eventually Mary sent a telegram to Hilary, as they were meeting for lunch. After tea I did some washing for Honor – this dreary spinster pounced on it joyously – here at last was something! Honor got back about 10 – Hilary hadn't had the message, so the joy of getting the letter was all new. It was written only a week ago – probably while we were listening to *Belshazzar's Feast* – the quickest yet. The visit to the solicitor went off very well – he seems very pleased with everything, but thinks the case won't come on till October – so that means perhaps a year before it is all through. Oh, what a long time I would have had to wait. I have got a much more calm and sensible state about the whole thing – I can now, after all this time, understand exactly Gordon's feelings about the affair and why he acted as he did, and how he could hardly have done anything else. This is surely an advance because though I could *see* it in a way I never really *felt* it.

Sunday 2 May. (Much colder). Busy morning making salad, scrubbing potatoes etc. Drank tea with Honor and listened to Hubert Foss talking about and playing records of Berlioz's *Fantastic Symphony*. Honor crouched on the floor, pounding potatoes in a saucepan. We talked about Gordon's play. Honor says she is afraid that it is the one he wrote about his breaking off with Anna. One night, in the early stages of their affair, they were at a concert at the Queen's Hall. Gordon said that the last time he had been there was with Mollie and that if she were to come back again he wouldn't feel a thing about her. And Anna burst into tears – And he couldn't understand why. Thought she ought to have been pleased. What a haunting scene for a novel – it could have also taken place in a churchyard where he has been with someone he once loved. And she, the new one, sees it happening again and again. (Oh, of course you *would* make it all happen in a churchyard – wouldn't you?) Gordon, if you ever take any other woman to Abbotsleigh, may you never rest peacefully in your grave with the marble chips on top.

Monday 3 May. I am afraid one of our elderly censors will think me not such a beautiful natured girl after all. This afternoon I was washing, or waiting to wash my hands when I said, 'I wish people wouldn't clutter up this basin with flowers.' And of course they were hers and, worse, she was taking them to an *invalid*. Oh dear, and perhaps she was a pathetic old governess or a decayed gentlewoman. Now I can never make amends, though I did feebly apologise.

At teatime Honor and I had one of our long, thorough talks about Gordon and their marriage. And she showed me the petition and it has to be resworn as they left out one of Honor's names. It is rather a horrifying document, but perhaps faintly comic. Really we have discussed Gordon so much, that one would hardly think there was anything left to love. I seem to know everything bad about him, there surely can't be much more.

Tuesday 4 May. Lovely vigorous up in the morning early exercises. A bright cold morning. It got very hot at teatime and I went out on the balcony. Today (or yesterday) I went and put my arms round the broken unicorn who knows everything, all my joy and misery and is always the same.

Thursday 6 May. Will the tune 'Dearly Beloved' always remind me of dreary rides to Avonmouth, and the bus stop at Shirehampton? The cuckoo has started now and it is real Matthew Arnold weather.

Friday 7 May. Had a rather dreary day at work. Saw a dilapidated pigeon on the balcony with ruffled feathers. In the evening felt very elated, dangerously so. For no special reason. Good News – we are in the suburbs of Tunis. Very loud cuckoo outside and the beech tree so green.

Saturday 8 May. Heard on 8 o'clock that we have got Tunis and Bizerta. After six months. A wild and stormy day. Icy wind and driving rain – we all got soaked coming back to lunch. I made curry for supper. Late in the evening, cutting dreary sandwiches for work tomorrow, I let myself go for perhaps half an hour. But one always has to pick oneself up again and go on being *drearily splendid.*

Sunday 9 May. Worked – a cold miserable day. Shivering and watching the pigeon die, while I ate my sandwiches. Work was intolerably boring. How delightful to come back to tea and a boiled egg and warmth. Listened into various things – high spot was a Stephen Potter poetry programme ending with Latin gender rhymes to a background of Dohnanyi, *Variations on a Nursery Tune.* Honor said she was going to write to Gordon – I envied her and she said I could write to him if I wanted to. But oh *no,* I can't yet. Not till six months at the earliest – unless the giddy heavens fall.

Monday 10 May. A filthy day, very wet and stormy. But I wore my fur-lined boots and took an extra jersey. Now I can see how people get eccentric. Came home, had tea, ironed etc. Listened to a lovely Louis MacNeice programme *The Death of Byron.* Today is the tenth anniversary of my first evening with Henry. Wistaria and the Trout. Every detail is imprinted on my mind. How small a part of time....

To Henry Harvey in Stockholm   Bristol
                                                                   11 May 1943

My Dear Henry,

Of course I should really have written to you *yesterday* as May 10th is the anniversary of the first time I ever spent an evening with you! What's more it is the *tenth* anniversary, a solemn thought! Yes, it was in 1933 and we went to the Trout and played pingpong and ate mixed grill and the wistaria was out.

Well I will start to tell you my news. The biggest thing is that I have volunteered for the WRNS. I decided that I had been long enough in my present job and that a change would do me good – also practically all young (sic) women, especially single ones are liable to be conscripted now – so I thought I'd rather choose what I went into. The uniform is very becoming but of course this dreary spinster wouldn't be influenced by considerations like that. But those little hats – You can have no conception what England is like now with so many women in uniform. And elderly women are flocking into Government offices and becoming 'Temporary Civil Servants'. Our new recruits get older and older. And more and more peculiar. The other day one of them came into the tea room wearing a turban and carrying an umbrella. Well Miss Pym and what about yourself? Were you not seen only yesterday, wearing fur-lined boots in May wrapped in a rug and your head tied up in a scarf? It is the cold and the Government ban on Central Heating that does it. We had a glorious heatwave in April but that has now gone. Still all the lilacs have been out and I can imagine the dear old Banbury Road with the lilacs – no the laburnums and red hawthorn all out. It is a long time since I was in Oxford. It would be almost unbearably nostalgic now. Hilary goes there more often as her husband is stationed quite near there. She says you can still eat at the George and it has the best drink. Which is all one cares about, but *all.* And now, after that, what an unpleasant person I shall make myself out to be. The Censor [this letter would have been read by a Censor] (probably a woman, too) will not realise that the writer is a woman who will be thirty next month, who reads Coventry Patmore and often lunches off Welsh rarebit in a teashop, run by *ladies*, called Nell Gwynn – who patches her underwear in the evenings, wears lisle stockings (except for special occasions) and weeps when she hears the old B Minor Tchaikovsky Piano Concerto. And lots of other things. But she (the Censor) will no doubt wonder at the relationship between writer and addressee. 'Old friends, simply that,' said Miss Pym, giving the words their full meaning. By the way how nice it would be if this letter could arrive in time for your birthday, which is on May 31st. And you will be thirty two, won't you?

I can't exactly remember what I *did* tell you in my last letter. Did I tell you that I was in love and that it was all hopeless? I expect so – well if I did you may be interested (and relieved?) to hear that we parted at Christmas and haven't seen or written to each other since then – a really dramatic Victorian renunciation – the sort of thing I adore in novels, but find extremely painful in real life. Of course we may come together again in the future – time alone will tell (sorry!) but in the meantime he thought it better I should try and find somebody else who can marry me, which he won't be able to for at least a year – we neither of us wanted any other kind of relationship so a complete break was the only thing. Luckily we both are rather comic people so it isn't as bad as it sounds. It has been hell being away from him, as he understood so well and we had all the same ridiculous jokes and things together. I haven't told Jock but I believe you do know something of these things, even if you have never been in a similar situation. My parents didn't know either – though everyone here did of course. I am quite resigned to it now and can even visualise the possibility of marrying a dashing naval officer – what – at nearly thirty, with lisle stockings and patched underwear?

Dear Henry, I don't know why I'm telling you all this – but I have a feeling that as we have known each other so long and you were once so much to me that it doesn't matter. Like some comfortable chair and everything turned to mild, kindly looks and spectacles. I once wrote something of the kind in a novel which I never finished. I'm afraid I haven't written anything for ages, though I fully intend to when I have time. And I expect it will be better than any of my early work.

I was tidying a drawer this evening and came across a photo of poor Anton Fendrich! I wonder where he is now – also my dear Friedbert. I don't suppose you ever hear any news of Anton, do you? I imagine that you would be able to write to him, being in a neutral country, though perhaps you hardly could being English. They might think you were a spy. I cannot send any messages through you either, as it is not allowed. and, I, even with the lisle stockings and welsh rarebit lunch, might also be a spy.

Oh dear why did I write all this – most unnecessary and melodramatic. Probably they are dead in Russia – one cannot know and does not like to think. Or taken prisoner by my cousin in Tunisia.

I have made no comment on the war news, but things do seem to be going well for us at last. It hardly seems three years since Dunkirk.

I'm afraid it will be a long time yet though. But you wait till I am in the WRNS.

Of course this letter is meant for my dear sister Elsie as well as you. I am sure there is nothing in it I would not wish her to see. I hope we shall be meeting again sometime before we are too old to be helping each other into our graves. I've chosen a churchyard here or rather my love has – I am going to have marble chips put on top of his grave which he much dislikes.

Much love to you and Elsie and the child –

Barbara

Tuesday 18 May. Got my release form signed so that I can really join the WRNS – also the Admiralty have written to the Censors asking for my character!

Wednesday 19 May. Rose early and did the exercises – we are now stiff in the waist muscles! Gloriously hot weather. I am firewatching in a cotton dress and in the light. Well, summer's here now. Spring has not waited....

Thursday 20 May. Bought my *Radio Times* which contains a photo of my Gordon at the darts board and the announcement of his play *Farewell Helen* to be broadcast on Wednesday next. Spent a pleasant, almost happy evening feeling generally at peace with everything. Drank beer. Listened to a very funny *ITMA* and *The Armchair Detective*.

Friday 21 May. Everyone much shaken over the call-up – only I in calm of mind all passion spent!

Saturday 22 May. I went down to the hall to look for the afternoon post and would have given anything to be able to produce a letter from George for Honor. But I couldn't.

> Oh Love hath he done this to thee
> What shall (alas) become of me –

At tea we talked all about Gordon's relations and discussed various things – we also read to each other little extracts from White's *Natural History of Selborne*. A nice book but one is continually reminded of the Agony of Not Knowing Latin. As Gordon said at Arkesden when we were reading Ezra Pound or Eliot.

Sunday 23 May. Honor, Julian, Prue and I went to Weston. We had a taxi to the station and there were crowds travelling. To think, as we said to each other, that most of these people *could* have stayed at home if they'd wanted to!

It was chaos on the station at Weston. Prue started to grizzle a little and Honor said, 'All right – we'll go straight back to Bristol!' Idle, grown-up threat. We managed to slip away for a pint at a rather gimcrack pub with a great many red leather and chromium chairs. Lunch at Rozel [BBC Hostel]. Afterwards the beach, where we lay on my mackintosh. And then the pier with its grinding noise and everything going round and round. We put Prue on the children's roundabout and stood watching her. In the centre there is a pillar which revolves, made of mirrors (rather distorting) some of them painted with birds and butterflies in bright colours. As I looked at this I thought out a scene for a novel or short story – the governess with the children – in the same unhappy state of mind as Honor was before Christmas and I after. Behind was the Hoop-La and the only object at all nice was a white china swan, hollow in the middle. She plays for it and a Commando seeing that she wants it wins it and gives it to her. There were a lot of Commandos there, incidentally. It was an exhausting day and we had to come home by bus which meant a lot of walking and waiting. Still there was beer and cold beef and chips at the end of it, then a bath and bed.

Monday 24 May. A very wet day. On such a day what is more depressing than the cloakroom at the Censorship – cold and vault-like anyway, but hung with dripping mackintoshes, stockings trying to get dry on the cold radiators etc. Honor had cooked a lovely supper, shepherd's pie and rhubarb with sponge on the top. Mr Slope proposing to Eleanor Bold in *Barchester Towers* [BBC radio] was very nice.

Tuesday 25 May. Worked drearily hard. Honor seemed low at teatime – it is time she heard from George – that he is all right after the fighting. It is the one thing I want at the moment – that she should have a letter. It's so awful not being able to comfort a person you love – all I could do was vain words, half a bottle of Drene and a large sheet of blotting paper I had got from the office. Hilary came back and later we were all quite merry and had a large supper of omelette (very good, made by me) and chips. I washed my hair. We listened to V. S. Pritchett's programme about Dostoevsky and Turgenev (Stephen Potter produced) – an excellent programme. Good to listen to something really exciting that one couldn't possibly have written oneself. There was a phrase about nobody having a business to turn away from things in life – one must feel

things to the marrow of one's bones. (I wish I could put it better).
Anyway it was *good*. Gordon's play tomorrow. We rather dread it.

Wednesday 26 May. Honor had a letter from George, so he is all
right. With that worry off my mind I sunk low in myself and spent
rather a gloomy day – being rather depressed and yet sharp with
myself writing snappy comments on my blotting paper like 'Snap
out of it' and 'Testing Time' – all the time. At tea time I wept rather
decorously in my room. Then entered the kitchen full of people –
consciously bracing myself, eyes all bathed in cold water. Sally had a
child to tea. I had some remains, scones and brandy snaps and
cherries with an impossible number of stones.

I prepared a cold supper – asparagus, hardboiled egg, potato
salad etc. Honor and I were rather tense and nervous about
Gordon's play. I knitted feverishly – the sleeves of my black jumper.
The time came. It was exciting and funny and clever and rather
embarrassing. None of it really applicable to me. The bit of La
Rochefoucauld he once quoted to me in a letter came in – how little
the beginning of love is in our power, therefore you shouldn't blame
your lover or mistress when it ends and all that. I was very excited
and yet depressed after it and couldn't get to sleep for quite a long
time. I began thinking of a play *I* would write.

Thursday 27 May. Received from the WRNS a summons to a
selection board on Monday next – so that may mean that I'm being
considered for a commission in Censorship. Very excited and
agitated and still brooding over the play.

After supper I went to have coffee with Mrs Green and Inky
Woodward – in Inky's flat at the Paragon. I wore the blue-green
dress with a full skirt that I made specially for Christmas and haven't
worn since – and rode down Sion Hill by the Rocks and the
Portcullis – where he said 'My bright and shining Ba' and the bridge
was lovely in the twilight and horrid people sat in the window of the
Rocks and I was filled with indescribable nostalgia and love for him.
Our Sunday morning drinks and talks about food and Roman
Catholicism and Oxford and Cambridge and the September
evening when we discussed the Barbellion passage [*Journal of a
Disappointed Man*] we both like – about the dead haunting the places
where they have been happy....

It was fun at Inky's. She told me all about the WRNS. I tried on
her uniform and look Divine in it!

Saturday 29 May. Lovely hot day. In the afternoon Honor and I
scrubbed her carpet and floor (good practice for me). It looked

wonderful, when we had finished we could talk of nothing else. We were very tired at the end of it and scrubbed in our dreams.

Monday 31 May. Went to London for my Selection Board. Had lunch with dreary people – myself no less dreary than any of them.

The journey was uneventful and went quite quickly. Two impressions – sheets of ox-eye daisies growing by the railway and a patch of ground full of bird-baths and dainty garden statues. Yes, that dwarf with the broken head, that solid unfluffy stone rabbit might well have been among them.

London was bright and pleasant – streets crowded and shops full of nice things. It makes me intolerably sad to go there – although I have now been three times since Gordon and I parted. We took a taxi to WRNS Headquarters and had a long gossip with Betty Rankin. I was then shown into a room where about seven or eight girls – all Wrens – were waiting for the Selection Board. It was most nerve-racking as I was last of all and although my interview was for 5.10 I didn't get in till about 5.50. It was a real War of Nerves atmosphere – we sat round in a bare dingy room with nothing to read and the windows half blacked out. Each candidate knew whether she had passed or not as she came out. When they were ready for the next victim they rang a piercing bell which made everyone jump. I felt nervous and quite *erschöpft* and was conscious that my face had got beyond powdering and needed re-doing from the beginning. I thought for a moment – all this is quite *fantastic*, I've no need to be afraid. But then it occurred to me that everyone else was taking it seriously therefore I must too, as I was aiming to be part of it.

My turn came. There were three Wren officers sitting at a table – one grey-haired and soignée, another motherly and wearing a hairnet, and the third dark and massive and ominously silent. I saw her writing something on a piece of paper at the end. They asked me various general questions – why I wanted to join the WRNS – whether I liked Censorship etc. and were very nice. But at the end of it I wasn't very much the wiser. They said they would let me know in a day or two which rather flattened me, as I had hoped I might know straight away. So now more waiting – I almost felt I would rather be in the ranks as the lowest of the low, though to fail in anything is rather humiliating and I've had enough failures lately. After it was all over I felt exhausted and depressed and would have given the rest of my life for the comfort of Gordon and a drink with him. As it was I staggered unthinking into the first train I saw at St James's Park and then realised that I wasn't really sure how to get to Gunnersbury. So at Victoria I got out and sat on a seat and meditated and smoked and finally asked an official.

And finally I arrived [at Kew] – Sybil was there, then Rosemary and they were kind and sweet. It was bliss to relax and drink beer and eat and flop into the green sheets – wearing my new blue satin nightdress – my body spread-eagled like a corpse. It was a very hot night – at about 2 a.m. the sirens went and there was gunfire in the distance. I lay awake thinking of Gordon, wondering where he was and if he was awake and longing hopelessly for him and panic came over me at what I had done and the life that was before me. But I thought – well this is the worst time to think of things. Everything seems gloomy and dark when you're lying awake in the middle of the night. One day, perhaps quite soon – it will be better.

After Christmas II

8 June. London. In large shops full of women I always feel safe from Gordon. But in the street, especially round Oxford Circus, I must be careful!

I had a happy wandering in the shops. It was a hot sunny day. I went into Zwemmers and bought a volume of Rilke – the young man there is growing older. His hair is receding. I remember the first time I saw him – it was at the Exhibition of Picasso's *Guernica* in the winter of 1938 – nearly five years then. And since Guernica, Rotterdam, Belgrade, Coventry, Athens – just like a poem by one of our young modern poets. But even they aren't so young now.

I took a taxi to 271 High Holborn for my interview at 3. It is a large grey non-committal looking building called Princeton House. I went in a lift to the 8th floor, and was deposited in front of a pair of swing doors. Inside behold, a dear, familiar scene – tables of censors – so much like our office except that some of them were Wrens and there were one or two naval officers padding about. I was put to wait by an open window looking out on to city roofs. I was given a cup of tea which was most welcome as I was very thirsty. Then I had my interview with First Officer Salmond – a charming person with curly hair and a faint Scots accent. Apparently I must serve three months in the ranks and after that I am pretty sure of my commission, provided I behave myself. I was very pleased and happy with this interview – *very* different from last week – and am now longing to be called. I had a discreet tea in Marshall's, wandered on to Selfridge's and bought a few things then took a taxi to Paddington to get the 6.30.

Wednesday 9 June. Bristol. In the evening we went to the Theatre Royal to see Bridie's play *Susannah and the Elders*. Very amusing. It's curious how unreal a play seems at first but how you soon get into it. It really does *take you out of yourself* as they say. We had some beer in the interval and ate a whole bar of Fry's sandwich each! I wore the turquoise dress I made for Gordon at Christmas with a grey jacket. The theatre is charming inside – green and gold with nice slender pillars and designs – masks etc. It was a lovely evening.

Whitsuntide. 12–14 June. Hilary and I got a train to Compton and from there cycled to the cottage [belonging to Hilary and Sandy], which is literally in the middle of the downs and has a pretty overgrown garden full of delphiniums. Tom Marriner was there and had started to get lunch. We had sausages and potatoes and salad. Later George [Murr] came bringing a ham and a chicken – we had the chicken on Sunday. Baptista disembowelled it and I watched her. It was most delicious. I slept a good deal and felt quite happy but rather remote and lonely. One feels so without a chap especially when *one* has had one. A nice lump of misery which goes everywhere like a dog. Isolation. Still, I wasn't unhappy. But I couldn't help thinking how nice such a place would be with Gordon.

Tuesday 15 June. In the evening Honor told me about a communication in which Gordon has apparently demanded the big Armchair in the sitting room, so of course that at once suggested Eliza Cook and

> I love it, I love it, and who shall dare
> To chide me for loving that old armchair.

But oh darling – can my love stand this. May it not be the beginning of the end. Could it be because of an armchair that I first began to fall out of love with you! But of course one doesn't fall – it's a slow wrenching away painful at once, afterwards just sad and dreary. Or so I imagine. It hasn't happened yet.

Wednesday 16 June. Once – a few days ago – I dreamed that when a certain period was up – six months I believe – Gordon wrote to me and suggested that we should go on again, but what as I never knew – I woke up before that was made clear. Well I'm afraid it won't be six months – because that's less than a fortnight from now. He seems to be rather sticky about the allowance for the children – that's the thing that maddens me most about him.

Thursday 17 June. At supper had to fight a little pang of jealousy when Honor talked about ringing him up. Must go now and see if the boiler is in because it is *our bath night.* So there is romance and wild longing and death in life the days that are no more all in the chaos of the Palmers' kitchen. My clerihew – made this evening.

1 "A new term in a new year. Oxford really is intoxicating."

2 a *(left)* Links with Mrs Vernum

b *(below)* Links, Dor, Buddye, Poopa, 1938

c *(below left)* Barbara with "the brethren dwelling in unity", Oswestry, 1935

d *(below right)* "Orangey-pink and white check gingham, 5¾d a yard"

3 a (above) "Henry said I was part of his background like Jock and Barnicot." *Left to right:* Barnicot, Jock, Henry, B.P.

b (right) "Henry was absolutely at his best. He wore his grey flannel suit, a bright blue silk shirt with a darker blue tie and blue socks." 1935

4 a *(left)* Dresden, 1938.
"... zwei Manhattan at the
Excelsior"

b *(below)* "It's marvellous being
with Hilary and we have the most
wonderful jokes about everything."

**5 a *(right)* Gordon Glover *(standing)*
with Lionel Hale**

b *(below right)* The Coppice: "Like
something out of Tchekhov." *Left to
right, back row:* Gill, Tamara,
Honor, Hilary, Dick; *centre:* Mary
with Lindy, Julian (with bird),
Lulu with Dan; *front:* Prue, Sally

6 a *(left)* "My officer's uniform is really smarter than my Wrens' . . . made to measure and fits better."

b *(below)* Rome, March 1945. "Lunch at the Officers' Club in Pincio Gardens"

7 a *(right)* Among the Excellent Women: "The fancy-work stall . . . was considered to be the most important."

b *(below right)* "Shall we have moussaka or do you like those little meat balls or kebabs or something?" Greece 1964

8 a *(above)* Office party: Barbara and Hazel. "People standing around clutching glasses of sherry or hoping to be offered one."

b *(below)* International African Institute, Fetter Lane: "Smothered in a mass of intractable seminar papers."

9 a *(right)* Skipper

b *(below)* "Bob and I have lunch and then walk in the park . . . but he feels that Nature is not enough so we go into the Church of the Annunciation at Marble Arch."

10 *(above)* Barbara with Philip Larkin. "He's shy but very responsive and jokey. Hilary took our photo together." 1977

11 *(right)* Tea with Lord David Cecil for the television cameras. "We agreed that the whole thing might easily have lapsed into farce like the Mad Hatter's tea party."

12 Booker Prize dinner: "B.P. . . . black blouse (C & A, £4.90)"

BARTOK
is my stumbling block.
I am in some doubt
As to what he is talking about.

Julian found some rubber objects in the Gorge and told Honor what they were used for.

I have sunk very low. I emptied tea leaves out of the window.

Sunday 20 June. Surely it is the height of decadence to listen to Richard Strauss before lunch on a Sunday morning. As I am doing now – Scott Goddard doing a programme about Strauss's *Don Quixote.* Such lovely music, rich, exciting – cold shivers of delight – breezes of spring (in the Banbury Road)! – like the *Rosenkavalier* waltz. Earlier in the day I chopped off some of my hair and gave myself a new style, curled up all round. The idea is for it to look shorter and neater.

Oh Coppice back kitchen full of kisses and jokes and tears – and the blackcurrants are ripening.

Tuesday 22 June. Ann lent me *Cocktails at Six* [one of Gordon's novels] which I tried to read at Arkesden. But I can't get up any interest in it – so brittle and unreal.

Thursday 24 June. Well, it came this morning. And when it does come, it's like Love – make no mistake about it, you *know.* A long envelope with a railway warrant Bristol to Rochester (Single, this time there is No Return). Also a list of clothes to be taken. No food or drink (not the smallest of double gins) to be taken there. I am to go on July 7th. My feelings are a little mixed but mostly I am excited and glad. Everyone at the office very nice. It was a hot day, hard to work. In the afternoon we had a lecture, very interesting, then our birthday tea party on the balcony. The table was decorated with flowers, wild strawberries and cakes to eat. It was gloriously sunny.

Tea in the garden when I got home – did some rather spectacular weeding among the roses – enormous things two or three feet high and even a potato plant. Pleasant evening with Honor – very few of these left now – how I shall miss her. I wonder what Gordon will say.

Saturday 26 June. Oh dear, oh *dear.* I'm afraid I had a bad outburst this morning – in the kitchen. Honor advised me to forget Gordon (I had been lamenting that we had no news of him) and then it suddenly all came over me and I had a good weep all over Honor and didn't start for work till after nine!

I picked a lot of raspberries and went over the whole Gordon situation. I feel at the moment that I still love him as much as ever and nothing will alter that except meeting somebody else. It is no use worrying about *his* feelings because even if they were still the same I shouldn't want him to do anything about it (though I long for just some word of comfort before I go into the Wrens).

Sunday 27 June. My last Sunday at the Coppice and there was a sweetness and sadness about everything and everybody. Breakfast in the kitchen, tea on the grass after lunch and in the evening a supper for me and my health drunk in cider. Looking through a book of Honor's press cuttings I came across the wedding picture of her and Gordon – the two people I love best in the world. One can't help feeling sad and sentimental. Gordon looks so young and so absurdly like Julian.

This evening heard the *Epilogue* [BBC radio] – the parable of the Prodigal Son, which I love, and we are now listening to a programme about Gluck.

Monday 28 June. My last afternoon and so hot and airless, there was an extremely good looking Air Force officer in attendance most of the day. Got home and tea under the beech trees with Honor and the children – read our novels for a bit. Listened to some of the Brahms Piano Concerto (early one) on the gramophone. Hearing that lovely rounded melody in the first movement, I thought, yes it *could* be all right. There *might* be somebody else – it's just possible. He must like music and, if possible, Matthew Arnold, and have a ridiculous sense of humour.

Tuesday 29 June. Work as usual in the morning and I was even able to concentrate on all the usual things as I had all time before me. At about 12 I started to say goodbyes which was very sad and everyone was so nice. Well at least I have got on with people and made friends – that's something. I was given a lovely extravagant box of talcum powder, a nice expensive gift I would never buy for myself and therefore all the nicer to have.

Trying not to feel sad, though I'm excited too – worrying now about what clothes to take!

Wednesday 30 June. Had a very pleasant day at the Coppice. Listened to Dick's broadcast and Honor doing bits in Hilary's Unicorn programme [for schools]. Very nice though of course it didn't sound a bit like my Honor. I did a lot of clearing up and packed a suitcase of clothes to take home. Gave Prue my wreath of flowers I got in Salzburg and Honor the scarf with Edelweiss from Dresden.

Friday 2 July. Oswestry. Did more tidying and packed a large suitcase to come home.

I had a hot journey but managed to catch all the connections – I slept a little and read *The Lover* by Naomi Royde Smith which G. says (in this week's *Introducing*) he thinks would make a good Radio Play. It's rather sad, the cold places in the heart, the ashes and Devouring Time or Time the Great Healer – anyway Nor in thy marble vault shall sound my echoing song . . . .

Sunday 4 July. Independence Day, and we were not allowed to forget it! Quite right of course, but I wonder why I can't listen to modern American music. Strawberries for lunch – afternoon in the garden reading an excellent novel *Two Days in Aragon* by M. J. Farrell. Very penetrating – about sorrow going to the stomach too!

'I leaned my back unto an oak – I thought it was a trusty tree' – the other day Honor and I were discussing the versions of 'Waly, Waly', especially the verse about gathering flowers and pricking my finger right to the bone. She quoted the oak verse and I wondered if the same thought was in both our minds – Gordon. But we neither of us said anything.

Monday 5 July. Bristol. Crowded journey. I stood as far as Hereford – trying to read Browning but the train was going too fast. So I meditated and planned a grand future for myself including a new love to smooth out everything! At Hereford I got a corner, ate my sandwiches and slept. Managed to get back to the Coppice in a taxi by way of Blackboy Hill. Climbed in through the kitchen window. The house was locked. Lovely to see Honor again, and Prue. We had tea then I cycled to the BBC and had a drink with Hilary – then to *Uncle Vanya* – a wonderful play and well acted. So very like the Coppice – except that we don't sit down under our sorrows – no we are drearily splendid and even join the Wrens. And we have a more positive hope than 'we shall rest'. But comic too. And we know we are comic – don't we, my relique?

Tuesday 6 July. A very busy typically Coppice last day. How can I bear to write about it. It's raining, trees – the beach tree swaying in the wind – Julian shouting and Scarlatti on the wireless. Well, I will write – and I just can't take it in. It just doesn't seem real . . . . I went out in the pouring rain and shopped – then came back to a hasty lunch with Honor and preparations for Prue's birthday party – she looking intolerably sweet in a white smock with my wreath of Austrian flowers in her hair. I wore my Christmas frock – we had a lovely tea. I did a lot of packing and tidying and we had supper – then

I began writing this. After supper we listened to a John Betjeman programme in the *How* series – *How to Look at a Town* – simply delightful of course – ending up with a Non-conformist chapel! Then talking to Honor and telling her all the last minute things – news of HIM etc. In the morning I gave the first volume of this diary and his letters to her to keep.

Wednesday 7 July. The worst time is definitely when you wake up on the morning you're going. I woke at six, having set the alarm for seven. I took Honor the last cup of tea for some time. The taxi came very early, soon after eight. Then goodbyes and I felt very wretched and couldn't keep back my tears. They stood in the doorway, the dear Coppice porch with the antlers. Honor held my hand tight in the taxi and she was crying too. She and Prue and Julian came with me some of the way. As she said she and I were the worst possible people to be left together at the end. I was early at the station and got the best sort of corner – i.e. in control of the window – carriage empty except for two W.O.4's – we talked all the way, so I hadn't much time to brood. At Paddington I queued for a taxi and eventually got one – calling down the queue to find if anyone wanted Charing Cross I was joined by a stout jolly businessman from Birmingham and might have been seen driving through the park with him. He insisted on paying for the taxi. I left my luggage, looked out my train then went to Oxford Circus and into D.H. Evans, where I soon found myself in a queue explaining the intricacies of the Quick Lunch Bar to two Miss Moberlies [BP's generic name for elderly gentlewomen]. I looked at a few shop windows but had little heart for it and less coupons so I took a taxi to Charing Cross where I had a cup of tea in the Buffet – now feeling calm and drained of all feeling. I got the 2.27 to Rochester – a bright green train that stopped at every station – including Greenwich. (How lovely if I were there one day.) Got to Rochester just before four and staggered along with my suitcase (helped by two kind Wrens) to the Training Depot.

Pro-Wren at Rochester

Well, the Nore Training Depot is a big North Oxford Victorian Gothic house, that looks like a Theological College – actually it was a school. I was in time for Tea Boat – afterwards changed my ration books etc. and got sheets. There was a lot of queueing and I felt a little low and strange – but not very. I have a cabin – Beehive XI – which I share with a girl of 19, my own class and quite nice. She has a long rather melancholy face and I can see her when she is older as an English gentlewoman – one of her names is Mildred. There are about fifty new pro-Wrens – most of them in teens and early twenties. I don't think there are really any of our kind of people, though there are one or two pleasant ones.

Making up a bunk is difficult, especially when you have the lower one and it is fixed against the wall. You must do hospital corners and the anchor on the blue and white quilt must be the right way up.

For supper we had toad-in-the-hole and bread and jam. After that a talk from First Officer Dixon who was very kind and Third Officer Bolland – Quarters Officer, who was also very nice. A rather restless night, as there was thunder and the mattress and especially pillow are *very* hard.

Thursday 8 July. Woke very early, still not feeling too bad. Rose at about 6.10 but couldn't get into 7 o'clock breakfast as I have a No. 3 meal ticket – so had some rather melancholy hanging about – I was glad not to be a steward when I saw them sweeping and scrubbing the coloured tiled passage by the mess. (Yes, we have varnished pitch pine too.) Made my bed and had breakfast 7.30 – scrambled egg and bacon, tea, bread, also cornflakes. Good! At 7.50 we had to muster on the parade ground and were taken in two lorries to R.N. Barracks, Chatham. Chatham is a cold windy place, as far as I could see, absolutely full of the Navy, of course. We stood in queues in various places for what seemed a long time. We are, on the whole, a silly giggly lot and look rather dreary in our motley civilian clothes – most of us wearing turbans. We are not allowed to go out without a hat or turban, but must not wear one in the mess. One soon gets used to it.

First of all we had X-Ray of our chests – a rather impatient Surgeon-Commander who seemed rather irascible and one could hardly blame him. Then a visit to the dentist who said my teeth were all right. After that into the lorries again and back to Rochester in time for Tea Boat. After that we waited in the fo'c'sle for our separate interviews with First Officer. She said a few words to each of us – I heard her saying something about me – I must be made a note of or something – I suppose my white paper entry or something. I can see now that one *must* be in the ranks first!

After lunch we went into the Captain's office and had our qualifications taken down – that is all the writers, who have a 'school'. We were given a list of ships in the Nore command and various naval abbreviations to learn.

After Tea Boat we had a lecture on pay and allowances, during which I found it terribly difficult to keep awake – my head kept jerking and sometimes I was even dreaming! After that supper and letterwriting and cigarettes in the fo'c'sle. Then I went out and met two others and went to the majestic Cinema – we had tea there. It is architecturally what one would expect – very pretentious and modern with steel chairs and palms – but all right for a cinema really.

Friday 9 July. Woke quite early and got up just before seven to wash up for 7.30 breakfast. One washing up a day is all the fatigues we have to do. At 8.45 we attended our first Divisions – which is really prayers. We muster on the parade ground with the five Petty Officers and three officers. After various salutings First Officer reads prayers – we first have a roll call.

After that we had our first squad drill with C.P.O. Penny. We learnt how to stand at attention and ease etc and also saluting which is more difficult than it looks. Then Tea Boat – then again in the writers' school – there isn't very much to do apart from learning the commands, ranks and abbreviations. So sometimes, as now, I can write this diary. The shorthand typists practise but there's nothing for the rest of us to do but chew over the abbreviations etc. Oh M.A./ S.B., D.E.M.S. and R.H.M. – Praise Ye the Lord etc.

We had a lecture on Naval Customs and Traditions from a very amusing Lieutenant-Commander, quite good looking and not more than about forty five!

After that I went to the YWCA with a girl called Vera Potts and we had supper there – baked beans, gooseberries and custard and tea. I never thought in the days when I used to serve in the old YM that I should be one of the Troops myself one day. Anyway one certainly appreciates it. There is a reading room with a wireless where one *might* be able to hear a little decent music. The wireless is always on in the fo'c'sle but always at the Forces Programme.

Now as I write (Saturday 7.10 p.m.) there is 'Ah Sweet Mystery of Life' but very often it is 'As Time goes By' – 'A kiss is *still* a kiss' – well I wouldn't know about that. After supper I went for a walk by myself. I walked up the Vines (a park opposite our house) and towards the Cathedral. There are some very decent Georgian houses around it – from one in a row I heard the sound of a Bach Prelude and Fugue on the piano – so I stopped to listen for a moment. I discovered a nice little old teashop (perhaps run by a widow of one of the Canons – or sister of the late Dean) with a lovely old rounded glass window – Also a nice set of tombstones and a well kept churchyard belonging to the Cathedral. And to crown all – as I looked through an archway into the main street I caught a glimpse of a rather pretentious GORDON HOTEL restaurant and grill room.

And for about half an hour I was my old gothick self – the self that I've had to put off while I've been here – and it's been quite easy – in fact I seem to have adapted myself quite happily to this life – and haven't felt at all miserable yet. And it's *very* hard to brood about Gordon or even the darling Coppice. Is this like an anaesthetic and will the effects wear off sometime? I can only wait and see.

Saturday 10 July. A very long morning in the class room, not doing very much, but learning Plymouth and Portsmouth commands and writing this diary. It's rather a bore sometimes not having very much to do. After lunch (a good one) we went to the pictures. I think the pictures are slightly nostalgic, also radio – they take you out of yourself, your new self, into your old one – but not too badly. I went with Peggy Wall, a quiet dark girl who seems to be about the best of our lot – she used to be secretary to a literary agent. She said as soon as she saw me she thought – I bet she's going to write a novel about it. Well – who knows.

Sunday 11 July. At 9 o'clock we had a short service in the Mess taken by a naval chaplain – it reminded me irresistibly of school – the chairs and the pitchpine-panelled hall and us singing 'For all the Saints' rather badly. After that we had an inspection and then were free for the rest of the day. I went to the Cathedral to hear the Archbishop of Canterbury preach. I noticed some nice wall-urns etc. – one to Henry King – young officer – Victorian. I had an excellent view of the Archbishop and also of an Admiral and a Vice-Admiral. My attention wandered rather during the sermon but I enjoyed the service and the singing.

After Tea Boat I went out to post some letters and called at the Museum – it is quite well arranged, but has a great variety of things – mammoth's tusks, Victorian shell and wool flowers under glass, arrowheads and of course Dickens. Various nice engravings – Sir Philip Sidney and Laurence Hyde, Earl of Rochester, but not John Wilmot, 'the dear Earl'.

When I came back I washed my hair and went into supper with it rather wild and flowing but it is now setting in curls, very decorous – I am sitting in the comparatively deserted fo'c'sle – but the wireless still goes on – *Happidrome,* Sandy Macpherson and now *Memories of Musical Comedy.* This evening I should like to be at the Coppice with Honor, talking, having a cup of tea and then listening to *Edward II* – Marlowe's – which is at 9.30. But I'm quite happy really – I keep expecting to be miserable but it hasn't come yet. Just occasionally a phrase somewhere will strike me.

Monday 12 July. We had Divisions and squad drill out on the grass in a fine drizzle of rain. AFS men and other Wrens drilled near us. It is quite fun except for the hanging about. I had a slight feeling of desolation, coming to myself a little and thinking but what am *I* doing here and why on earth am I standing out on the grass drilling with this curious crowd of women. Then Tea Boat and work – I laboriously copied out the Rosyth command and the functions of the Admiralty. A lovely letter from Honor, which cheered me up a lot, though I shed a few tears in the lavatory. All the dear Coppice scene was so beautifully painted – Honor in her curlers, Flora finding a nest of insects in her desk and Dick joyously examining them under the microscope – and my letter being passed round the Palmer teatable. After Tea Boat we had a lecture on Hygiene by a Surgeon-Captain – everything, but everything.

At about 2.45 a.m. the siren went and we all had to troop down to the shelter – sad amid lines of washing. This is a bad time to be woken – we were there only about twenty minutes, then back to bed where I tossed and turned a little, with sad thoughts of Gordon.

Tuesday 13 July. Went on a route march which was rather pleasant – we went by the river and had a nice view. After Tea Boat I had to go to Chatham again with eight others to have X-Rays done again. We went by bus with a rather plump wanton-looking Wren with gold rings in her ears and dark hair – and pink nails. It was all rather alarming and I felt as if I were going to cry! Of course I began imagining all sorts of things – I was in a Naval Hospital – I was invalided out. The Surgeon-Commander didn't come near us, and we were X-Rayed by a young man, who was very reassuring. Still, he wouldn't be able to tell us, even if he knew. My companions were so dreary, and there is something very alarming about medical apparatus – but I've never had anything wrong with me, so surely it's all right. But we still didn't know for certain. After supper we did some washing and romped like jolly schoolgirls in our cabins. But I'm not one really and it doesn't come very naturally. The others are all so much younger. But if I'm at all desolate (and I'm not really) it isn't in the same way as it was before. And I suppose there's always the whimsical and perilous charm *somewhere*.... Another siren but we didn't have to go down.

Wednesday 14 July. I suppose I have become too introspective during the last six months – the luxury of having somebody to *talk* to, which of course I haven't here.

After that we had a practice Air-Raid Warning and went down to the shelter. When First Officer was taking the roll call she asked 'Which is Pym?' so out I came from behind the washing. But why did she ask – because of my white paper – or *what?*

Thursday *15 July.* A hot day. We went on a route march of nearly 4 miles. We passed a remarkably fine cemetery on a hill, white angels, and fine grass, which was being cut by a motor mower. I think it must be a public cemetery. Every day at the start of our march we pass a very nice eighteenth century church with a beautiful churchyard full of waving grass – and a lovely urn tomb. Nearby is always the sound of children's voices singing – there must be a school here.

It was a day of endless queueing and altogether TOO MANY WRENS, so that I could almost have packed my bag and gone. After a half hour's queueing and waiting, we got PAY – £1 and 2 soap coupons – but I can't work it out at *all*! After tea a lecture on Ranks and Badges – the Mess was very hot and crowded and I looked forward to a weekend in solitude.

Friday 16 July. In the morning we had our writers' test – it wasn't so bad. I got the rates of pay right purely by luck as I hadn't learned them properly. At 2.30 we had a lecture about firefighting given by a P.O. from Chatham. It was intolerably hot and crowded in the Mess and a great relief to go outside for the practical demonstration of the hose. After that a few volunteered to be lowered from an upper window in a rope sling – I couldn't have done it – it made me quite sick to look at it. After Tea Boat we were FREE – it was a glorious afternoon and a lovely sensation to be able to walk out to the shops – I went into Smiths, got a book to read at the weekend and bought a copy of *Tristram Shandy,* which I feel will be nice to have about. I also bought apples and cherries and a *Radio Times.* I spent a happy hour lying in my bunk eating and reading a Graham Greene novel.

Saturday 17 July. Lovely hot day. We wrote our essay after Tea Boat. I wrote, as did most other people, on my impressions of Life in the Nore Command. As I write this I am in a nearly deserted fo'c'sle. I have heard the whole of Liszt's Piano Concerto in E flat and am halfway through *Hary Janos,* though a group of stewards have suggested we should have Jack Leon.

I feel apologetic for Kodaly when he makes a specially peculiar noise! And one eyes anyone who comes near the wireless with suspicion.

Sunday 18 July. This was a Day of religions, or religious observance of different kinds. I began the day feeling very sad and aching for Honor and my friends and the Coppice. Tears pricking behind my eyes, terrible lump in the throat. Also I'd had no letters for a week, which is a long time in a strange place. The weight (or burden) of unshed tears – there was a phrase to that effect in the novel I'm reading now (*Long Division* by Hester Chapman). But as the day went on I gradually got better. It's nearly always in the morning that one feels most homesick – by evening one is generally very happy and exuberant.

We started off with a service in the Mess. We had a very good-looking Padre but with such an affected voice that it was difficult to concentrate on what he was saying. I got nothing from it. Then Margaret Earp and I went to the Cathedral – it was dark and cool and the service was very sparsely attended – the usual sprinkling of old ladies – a soldier or two, a few Wrens. We sang and prayed and there was a dry theological sermon about original sin from an old withered man. I felt yes, this is the end. What can one get from this but peace and the pleasure of music and the loftiness of the Cathedral? You couldn't expect anyone to come in and be inspired or even very much comforted – at the best soothed a little. Or even rather damped down and saddened as I was. Age and dry bones.

Later on we had quite the opposite. Margaret and I had gone to the YWCA after supper and were sitting in the room opposite the canteen when two young clergymen came in with hymn books and said that they usually had a short service – so we stayed. Somebody at once chose 'Rock of Ages' – so we sang then had a very nice little address, then some prayers and finally more hymns which people began to choose. I could only think of 'Lead, kindly Light' and the one about keep our loved ones now far distant 'neath thy care. Anyway it was all very nice.

Monday 19 July. Too Many Women. Has this ever been used as a title? It would do for my life in the Censorship or this Wren life – squashed among them in the queue for breakfast.

In the afternoon we were enrolled – 3/O Rendel did it – she is rather nice, with a kind of babyish air which is a contrast to her parade ground manner. I had been feeling depressed but at teatime I got 3 letters, including a lovely one from Honor – Gordon knows now – he said he was glad I had got into the WRNS and hopes it will turn out to be a nice thing to have done – My only reaction is – well, (*dear*), it had better be! I was a little disappointed, having expected some message a little less dreary.

Tuesday 20 July. Today we were kitted. We were taken in lorries to Chatham at 8 a.m. – a great herd of us – I was standing in a mass of suitcases, lurching all over the place as we drove very fast. My hat is lovely, every bit as fetching as I'd hoped, but my suit rather large though it's easier to alter that way. I have also a macintosh and greatcoat – 3 pairs of 'hose' (black), gloves, tie, 4 shirts and 9 stiff collars, and two pairs of shoes which are surprisingly comfortable. After that we had to get respirators. One girl and I got left behind at the clothing store so had to hurry through the barracks – on our way we came across a little company of Greek sailors being drilled – in Greek. Service respirators are a good deal more comfortable than civilian – we went in the gas chamber. Then had lunch in the WRNS mess.

It all sounds quite simple written down like this, but it's a long dreary business and we all looked very tired and fed up as we sat (or lay) in dejected groups in the WRNS fo'c'sle – I wished I was out of it all – but suddenly, drinking the dregs of a cup of indifferent coffee my spirits began to lift and when we got back I was quite excited – I packed two large parcels of civilian clothes and sent them off. At 4.30 we had a lecture by a Padre, but all the time I wanted to shorten my skirt and there seemed to be so much to do. I got down to it eventually and little Peggy Wall very kindly marked all my things for me. After supper we mustered in the mess and 3/O Rendel read out the draft list – most of us are to go to Westcliff which is a holding depot where we wait indefinitely for a draft. Days or weeks. I envied Palmer, a dark evil-looking little steward, who had got a draft to Drake at Plymouth! The evening was spent frantically packing and worrying about how we were going to get our heavy suitcases to the station in the morning. I couldn't sleep for thinking of what I had to do.

Wednesday 21 July. After a rush to the station with heavy suitcases we heard that we'd missed the 9.29 which was almost a relief. It felt funny being in uniform – more like fancy dress than anything, but I don't look too bad. Hair is a difficulty. I think I must have mine cut.

This journey was noteworthy as being one of the longest and most tedious I have ever made – as the crow flies it isn't far from Rochester to Westcliff but it took us about four and half hours to get there – rain and carrying luggage and laughing and hating Vera Potts (who always managed to get her suitcase carried) and over the ferry from Gravesend to Tilbury where we had hours to wait and had tea and cake in the refreshment room (3rd class) and Beatrice Pizzey and I stood and watched the rain pouring down. Tilbury obviously has been a large exciting station, but now it's bare and deserted, though not decayed, just empty and waiting. We arrived at Westcliff and it was still raining. We were given a meal in the mess then went to our quarters – Pizzey and I are sharing a cabin in 7 Clifton Drive – a typical seaside villa in a row on the front – there is a good view of Southend Pier and plenty of ships to be seen – but no beach to speak of. Was asleep literally as soon as my head touched the pillow. I was on fire watch duty – but no siren luckily.

Thursday 22 July. There are no clocks here at all except one by the Regulating office, but there are various bugles, bells, bosun's pipes etc. which sound in the camp and are some guide. First bugle is 6.30. Pipe down 10 o'clock. We had to rush into breakfast – I was unwashed and wore my hat – a contrast to our decorous behaviour and dress at the Nore – also smoked, though this has now been stopped. We had an examination by the M.O. after breakfast – at least when I say 'examination' it was hardly that – 'Are you feeling quite well?' – 'Yes thank you sir' – no more than that. After that Beatrice and I scrubbed a larder – saw masses of butter etc., large tins of golden syrup like petrol tins. The food is good here, though everything is rather slapdash – there's plenty of it, but we often have to wait for knives etc. After dinner we had P.T., *very* strenuous with a very fine upstanding young man who puts on an Oxford accent. After Tea Boat a lecture from 1st Officer Bowen-Jones in a sad room littered with benches and piled-up chairs at the back – and round the walls large square mirrors, rather misted over and spotted – not with gold baroque frames, but the place had an atmosphere – the room where the children played on wet days or there was a dance in the evenings or pingpong – before it was table tennis I think.

After supper we walked a short way along the front – sadness and decay – closed cafés, Tomassi's ices, and Rossi's – the idea for a radio programme came into my head – about a seaside town before and during the war. Now rolls of barbed wire everywhere, but gardens decently kept.

Friday 23 July. The most strenuous day I've ever had in the WRNS so far. Gardened till lunch, then squad drill, then scrubbed a room in Palmerston Court. Quite worn out. One's spirits go up and down. After supper we walked into Southend and had a look at it – it is definitely a *common* place with no charm as far as I can see – one great street of shops – Woolworth's, Marks and Spencer and cheap stores – pin-tables and amusement halls – cinemas – the whole place smelling of fish and chips – raffish – and an enormous hotel, the Palace. Much of it decayed, but in a very depressing way, no beauty or dignity or even nostalgia about it. We finished up at the Women's Services Club, which is a house with various rooms, library etc. and refreshments – very convenient.

Sunday 25 July. Why am I always depressed at Sunday Divisions and church parade? We marched (rather badly) in shirt sleeves and were inspected by the Captain, who hurried along our ranks with his head bent. The service was awful – I was choking with tears and longing for the Coppice and Honor and everyone, so that I could hardly sing. The place was very hot and the sailors restless and irreverent. I was surprised at their bad behaviour. After dinner I had a good howl in my cabin! Then washed my face, powdered and lipsticked and went and sat in the public gardens and read G.D.H. & M. Cole, which I'd got out of the Services Club Library. It was terribly hot and I began to fall asleep and dreamed of a field of waving corn but when I opened my eyes it was just the sea and the ships and Southend pier if I could see it. I had tea at a little café and then decided to explore the amenities of Westcliff – to see if there was anything to see – any churches or fine buildings. Well, there's nothing – I walked down a road of dreary suburban houses called Valkyrie Road which led me into what seemed an interminable street of shops, many of them shut up, ruined and otherwise decayed. One felt that the whole lot might just as well be wiped out and started again. I don't think Westcliff or Southend has much for me now. I noticed an undertaker's shop – 'H. W. Whur – Cremations arranged'. I wonder if it's any relation to the author of 'The Female Friend' in *The Stuffed Owl*. Walking along carrying my coat and feeling like a braised owl it all began to seem quite funny as it usually does and I gradually came out of my depression. For supper I changed into a cotton frock and sat on a seat on the front – really very pleasant like being on holiday. But I'm not.

Wanting Gordon still comes into it. Now that the novelty of being a Wren is wearing off. WRNS – you aren't giving me enough. I'm doing my best, trying to see the funny side, looking out for churches and buildings, writing it up, talking to various people and trying to take it all as a great chunk of experience – an extraordinary bit of life – but I want music and intellectual companionship and affection – to be able to lavish it as I could at the Coppice. Well – perhaps I'll get all that, one day. Don't forget the whimsical and perilous charm – there'll come a day when you really will have to pack that Gladstone bag and go to wherever the Admiralty thinks fit. And in the meantime there are little things to look forward to, letters and the unexpected.

Monday 26 July. It was *terribly* hot – and now I know how hot one can feel in uniform even without a coat. I scrubbed out a room in Palmerston Court. We visited four ships – ordinary looking middle-aged men in navy blue suits and trilby hats climbed perilous rope ladders. Somehow one didn't connect them with the sea.

I stood looking over the side – humming 'Dearly Beloved' and that took me back to the early spring and trips on the top of a 28 bus to Avonmouth, and I knew that the thought of Gordon is *still* an ache, a longing, a regret, a sadness....

Two sirens in the night – I had to get up – oh wretched, looking at the stars and hearing muffled guns towards Sheerness and Canvey Island.

Tuesday 27 July. Another grilling day. Was working at Mount Liell which appears to be rather junior officers' quarters. Cleaned windows and a bathroom and swept. It amuses me to pay exaggerated respect to very young sublieutenants and even midshipmen, flattening myself and my broom against the wall as they pass, less than the dust indeed. The F.O.I.C. was coming down to inspect us so we were urged to make ourselves very scarce indeed – consequently we did nothing from 12 to 2.30 except have dinner and sit under the apple tree in the backyard of our house, reading – *The Constant Nymph.* At 2.30 P.T. inside the gym – he was more merciful than last week. At 6.45 I had my hair cut and set – pageboy again which is more my style really, then tea at the Services Club and finally a walk in search of churches or other interesting buildings – so far I've only seen chapels, but tonight I found St Alban's, modern and rather ugly outside but somebody was playing the organ rather well so I went in – it was a girl, her bicycle was in the porch. The church was dark and smelled comfortingly of incense – there were little lights burning and a statue of the Virgin Mary. It has no tablets or monuments worth mentioning – I should think it is quite new. I think I must try and go there on Sunday to take away the depressed feeling that the service here gives me.

Wednesday 28 July. I was sent to sweep and clean in the V.A.D.'s quarters, but I had just started on a room when I was summoned to First Officer – so into uniform again, and after waiting for a time I went in – apparently she has just discovered I am a white paper (Rochester hadn't told her) and I am to be given a job to do in Whitehall Regulating office. I saw 3/O Patch and spent the rest of the morning and afternoon trying to learn a little about my job which is to take over Green Watch – rather formidable but P/O Williams is very kind and helpful and I hope I'll be able to pick it up.

Thursday 29 July. My first day in Regulating Office – quite enjoyed it, especially being able to smoke and drink tea – there's so much to think about one has no time to brood! We were paid – about 32/- – the Paymaster is a thin harassed looking man, as he might well be. I officiated at 3/O Patch's lecture and held up charts for her - - had to march a squad of Pro-Wrens back – managed quite successfully. What will I turn into at this rate.

Saturday 31 July. Had a rather hectic time looking for people to do the washing up and trying to hunt out those who weren't there. Not like me at all, but it will be good for me to learn.

Sunday 1 August. We had Divisions and I couldn't swing my arms properly so Third Officer Honey had to move me. Gradually people will begin to discover what a fake I am – how phoney is my Wrennish façade. My Wren façade – no that makes it quite different. We had the service outside this week – it was much nicer, though singing was a little difficult as the harmonium accompaniment dragged rather. After that I went to the Regulating Office and made out my list for Monday. I am going to try hard to be really efficient – it doesn't come naturally to me, no use pretending it does, but it will be good for me to learn to be.

I went to a concert in Southend with Beatrice and Eileen Starinovich. Pouishnoff was giving a Chopin recital, the first concert I've been to since goodness knows how long. I became drowsy and thought all sorts of strange dreamy surrealist things – none of which I can now remember – of Gordon, of course, and it's still a raw wound. And will I ever meet anybody here to divert my thoughts from him? Ought I to go dancing feverishly at the Queen's? *Is* there anything for me in the future.

Monday 2 August. In the afternoon we went on a tug trip – had some jolly conversation with some Irish Merchant Navy. One had a little sacking bag full of cockles which he offered to us, also cigarettes. The sea was rough and sometimes the spray drenched us. We visited several ships, two quite large ones. One felt very nautical, especially climbing back out of the boat on to the pier up a rather scarifying ladder. I was the first to set foot on it.

Wednesday 4 August. A very busy day – went into Southend on a bicycle and enjoyed the ride – carrying a Petty Officer's coat for which I was trying to buy buttons and an Admin. Crown.

Friday 6 August. I was standby so did some ironing and talked to a strange girl with flowing blonde hair who asked me if I drank a *lot*.

Gone are the days of round about Christmas when through a glorious haze of Guinness I was happy in my own little piece of world enough and time.

Sunday 8 August. Did not go to Divisions, but watched from an upper window – no I mean from above and thought sentimentally how nice the sailors looked in their blue collars. After dinner I went to the Services Club and managed to get some chocolate – then lay reading and sleeping, listening to *Johnny Canuck's Revue*, writing to Honor and talking to some ATS.

Monday 9 August. I am officially drafted to HMS Westcliff as from the 11th. I'm pleased – Busy today as 56 are going out and 44 coming in on Wednesday.

Thursday 12 August. Writing in my new single cabin, having just had a *hot* bath, great luxury. Spent the evening at the Services Club drinking tea and writing letters. Was called Leading Wren by one of the new ones!

Friday 13 August. The Superintendent came. P.O. came in with a rumour that Holding Depot might be increased to 500 – Palmeira and the block of flats by us might be taken – awful speculations.

(Oh dear, what value will this journal be to posterity with its nautical jargon and incomprehensible daily routine – the puzzled reader of *After Christmas* plodding hopefully on to *A Happy Ending* will stick in the bogs of *Wren Pym* asking plaintively but what *is* Holding Depot and what do you *mean* when you say you were standby?)

Saturday 15 August. Went to Divisions and service. The dear boys behaved a little better than usual. But the Padre has no idea of what to say to them. In the evening went into the Queen's with Margaret Earp to have a drink and listen to the band – orchestra I should say. It was nice in a way but I couldn't help feeling sad. It would have been better if we'd had some male company of course. There was a full moon when we got out. I went doggedly to bed and read a novel by Stephen McKenna. On how many evenings, when one is older, does one just go 'Doggedly to Bed'. (Obviously the title of something.)

Tuesday 17 August. Busy coping with tomorrow's drafts – everyone grizzling so that one feels harsh and inhuman and would like to knock their heads together and send them to some filthy place.

Wednesday 18 August. Had a letter from Honor – it was over a week since I'd heard and this was a short letter – one page – I unfolded it, wondering.... And I read that she had had mumps and George had arrived suddenly in England on Saturday. Naturally I was quite overcome – the thing one had never dared imagine – and oh what does it feel like to have one's love come back like that.... I wonder if it will ever happen to me. But I'm so happy for her.

We had quite a busy day – 23 out and 14 in. I staggered with luggage from the station. Like a seaside landlady showing them round anxiously pointing out the delights of a front cabin.

Thursday 19 August. In the evening, I went to the Palace in Southend with Joyce Gresham. It is a large jolly smoky place, rather pleasant, crowded with people, mostly soldiers and cadets, a few odd Navy, Poles and Americans. We got some drinks, harmless little half pints, a Cadet asked Joyce to dance and bought us some drinks – I had a dance with one of his friends – not quite my height; but I found I still remembered how to dance. Afterwards Joyce's cadet saw us most of the way home – we got talking about classical music. It was quite an enjoyable, queer kind of evening – and I know I should love it if I had someone nice (and tall) to dance with. Funny moment when, sitting in that vast smoky place I realised that I didn't care twopence for a single person there!

Thursday 26 August. Busy and weary in the evenings. Not busy with doing things entirely, but with wondering if I've forgotten things and coping with people. And yet it doesn't really worry me – and I'm not frightened of anyone. It has given me confidence – and I feel I can do something I thought I couldn't before.

3–6 September. Had my first weekend – went to the Coppice. Off on the 10.16 train – then from Fenchurch St to Paddington, and it wasn't till I was in the train there that I began to realise it – the real places – Reading, Swindon, Chippenham, Bath, Bristol. Hilary had expected me at 7.30, so there was nobody to meet me – but by a miraculous chance I was seen going up the steps by Honor and Julian – We had a taxi to the Coppice. No need to say what the reunion was like. And they think I look nice in uniform. A boiled egg for my tea. And what strikes me is the luxuriant *greenness* of everything – the lovely trees and the weeds in the garden!

On Saturday morning Hilary brought me breakfast in bed – toast seems a luxury – and the softness of the bed. I got up in uniform and went into Clifton with Honor. We talked about Gordon as we walked down North Road. I said I was trying to forget him and she thought it much the best thing to do. He will, obviously, never be any good to me. All this I acknowledge and it hurts me – but – wasn't he like that always? And didn't I *know*? I can't say more – we had coffee at Lloyd's Café and then I went into the Censorship where I stayed nearly an hour. I felt homesick when I saw the letters, but knew I couldn't go back there.

A real Coppice Saturday lunch with Sally grizzling and Gill looking beautiful in a red dress with a black peasant jacket. Heard a lot of music during the weekend, all the things I've longed for – Berlioz Fantastic Symphony, Brahms Piano Concerto No. 1 (in D minor), Mozart Sinfonia Concertante, Brahms–Haydn Variations, Dohnanyi, and the rest. Lovely and all too short – so that I began feeling sad on Sunday morning at the idea of going back. Honor and I went to church and heard a sermon about up with your listless hands and strengthen your feeble knees – for me, surely. Julian looked angelic. He is going to learn the piano – lovely picture of his aged father at his first concert, weeping in a box while he plays the old Tchaikowsky. Honor dreamed I had told her the whole Wrens thing was a failure – of course it hadn't been – even though it hasn't done anything positive and concrete for me yet – it has at last given me a change, less opportunity to think of G. – no associations – and the feeling that I am trying to do something about it.

Monday 6 September. I got up at 6 and managed to say goodbye bravely – it was a lovely morning and I rode down to the BBC on Hilary's bike – then got the 7.50. I tried to read Pater's *Marius the Epicurean* which I've always found soothing, but somehow it didn't work and I found myself thinking instead. Wandering round Oxford Circus trying to get silk stockings I had an insane desire to see Gordon, who may be still in Scotland, and in the taxi to Fenchurch St and at the station I was very near to tears. That funny raised-up station in the middle of the city and Poor Jenny sits a-weeping, trying to eat a very stodgy sausage roll. In the train I noticed a nice churchyard, very green and overgrown with little leaning tombstones, in the middle of buildings and ruins and a curious Russian-looking edifice.

Italy gave in and we are all so busy dissecting shrimps that we hardly noticed. I've been working in the Mail Office and though at first I didn't like it I'm getting to now as we are really busy and were working till 6 today – Saturday.

Gordon has written another Radio play to be broadcast on 14th September – but I shan't hear it – I haven't even bought the new *Radio Times*.

How exciting it is when the men come in from abroad in their white hats and shorts, looking sunburned and ragged.

Sunday 12 September. After supper went to St Alban's church. I like to see some other side of the life of Westcliff. In my enthusiasm I brought away an English hymnal and prayer book. I shall read some of *Marius the Epicurean* before Tea Boat.

Wednesday 15 September. Tuesday was Gordon's play and this is the first week I haven't bought a *Radio Times*. I went to the Services Club and saw from the paper that it was at 10.30 – too late for me to listen anyway. I felt dramatic standing there in the dusk alone in that funny little room, too lazy to do the blackout. It's better to be dramatic than just a lonely spinster, though it comes to the same thing in the end.

Friday 17 September. I am thinking of finishing that radio play I started, also an amusing spy novel. And of learning German at the Southend Municipal College. I'll think ahead. After the war.

Last night had a very nice dinner at Gavon's with P.O. and Priestley. How long is it since I had dinner out with a nice chap! We had loud blaring music all the afternoon, which was pleasant at first, but later one wanted to escape from it, as there was a loud speaker in every house.

In the evening I enrolled as a student at the Southend Municipal College, to take the Intermediate Course. A crowd of spinsters, spectacled young men, nondescripts, Forces men and women – crowded into the great hall and up to the little tables where the various departments were stationed. At the languages table was a little elderly woman in a grey cardigan with some feather or bird in her hat. When I said I already knew some she nodded eagerly and said 'Splendid, splendid'. Then we all queued to pay our fees. It was all like an early H. G. Wells novel – *Kipps* or *Love and Mr Lewisham*. Surely there ought to have been a beautiful young woman teaching wood-carving?

Saturday 18 September. London. Went up to London on the 12.37 train, together with a crowd of liberty men – but got a seat. Had tea with Muriel Maby and Betty Rankin in the flat belonging to Muriel's friend – I loved it all. We walked round Chelsea afterwards. and I began to feel really human and myself again – as if something were thawing inside me – Mulberry House and Mulberry Walk – and I don't approve of a garage being called after Carlyle. And do you remember Jane writing: 'I died yesterday and was buried at Kensal Green – at least you have no knowledge to the contrary....' Some *nice* houses, with dignity, which is what Southend and Westcliff hasn't got. We rode to Piccadilly in a bus and then had dinner at the Berkeley Buttery – cocktails and baby chickens – and oh I *enjoyed* it all so – seeing different people, and we also walked in Berkeley Square then back to Fenchurch St with no miserable feelings – only anxiety lest I should fail to catch the train and be *adrift*!

Sunday 19 September. Another good day – worked in the morning – – mechanically at checking and victualling sheets and talked to 3/O Hawksworth about all sorts of things, German poetry, churches, censorship, and will my face fit at 271 High Holborn?

In the bath Marvell and Matthew Arnold and Heine. And what literature can compare with English poetry for variety and richness – and people who like the same thing find it the hardest thing in the world not to like one another – so if there *could* be a marine who liked Matthew Arnold and Brahms.... Anyway a good weekend. On the way back from blackberrying, chapels and meeting houses – Christadelphians, a small square house in an overgrown leafy garden. And a chapel with a curious obelisk-like monument – which might have been a chapel or a rather ornate garage and petrol pump. It adds to the pleasure of life to notice things.

Monday 20 September. Had a letter from Rosemary – she is worried about Emile who may even be prisoner of the Germans now. Oh, it's terrible what people are having to suffer.

Went to Intermediate German class at the Southend Municipal College – enjoyed it very much. Found it quite easy, though it will do me good to revise the grammar.

Monday 27 September. Things seem to have begun to move for me – – I mean about a commission – Do you play any games? Not if I can help it. Or the greatest indoor sport and you know what *that* is, dear Reader. And what is my degree. And Pym must take squad drill – and we are all laughing about Pym in the Wardroom. And will you sign a paper saying that you are willing to go overseas. And no I'm damned if I will – but I do it and think, well I'll deal with that when I come to it. If I ever do get it it will be the biggest laugh ever – I shall be quite the phoniest thing in the navy. A grown up person playing a fantastic game. You see, Reader, I am now completely myself again – the most unlikely person to be in the Wrens – but there's no reason why I shouldn't do it as well as other people.

On Sunday I went out to Kew to see Rosemary and Sybil. We went into the Star and Garter and had a pint, and while I was there, hat adrift, face flushed, glass in my hand and voice talking loud Naval jargon, a woman came up to me and asked how she could join the WRNS! Then Rosemary and I walked to Kew Gardens. We talked about our lives as we walked. Of course we're both pretty splendid. We both want the same kind of things. And fancy people not getting married and having children when they are able to. She encouraged me by so obviously thinking I had done the best thing in joining the WRNS. I gave her a pretty comprehensive picture of what it's like and how people of our sort feel about it.

We went back to the flat and had high tea about six – beautifully arranged salad – if all else fails we can always start a teashop.

October
Just to think, I've been saying to myself that it will soon be a year since G. declared himself and we had that brief, stormy but heavenly two months. It's *Sunday October 3rd*, a gloriously sunny morning with an undercurrent of cold air, rather like a spring day. I'm sitting looking at the sea and listening to rather too many seagulls. I am reading *A Room of One's Own*. Most delightful and profound – if I had the time I would write an essay about life in the WRNS.

Officers – pay them the respect due to their uniform but otherwise assess them as people.

On Being Yourself, and how you cannot be *too* much yourself or the life wouldn't be endurable. On Friday evening I was having supper when Marion Booth, a very attractive looking MT driver came and sat by me and we talked about German and Rilke and the necessity of hanging on to the things that matter – painting for her, writing and literature for me and music, of course. This is important, otherwise you will lose yourself completely, as you do in the first week or two. '...it is much more important to be oneself than anything else.' So Virginia Woolf. I wonder what she would have made of service life.

Sunday afternoon. At 3.15 I went to a CEMA concert at the Queen's. The singer sang a group of Schubert songs and apologised for having the words with him but he was using a new translation and might otherwise burst into German. How stupid that one should have to use a bad English translation – this kind of thing makes me bristle and wonder if we are worth saving! The pianist was good. He played Brahms, Chopin and Ravel.

Wednesday 6 October. The Wondrous Dance. I feel I should write something about this, but I don't quite know *what*. I had been inoculated in the morning, Dr Levy. 'Now nurse, be sure that the needle is sharp. It is better to have a sharp needle. I do not believe in economy in these matters – it is foolish to economise in needles when the war is costing us 11 millions a day' etc. Anyway after inoculation I wasn't feeling quite at my best. But I managed to get partners at the beginning, though I didn't dance very well. I felt very tired, probably because of the inoculation. Left at 10.40, alone in pitch dark and drizzling rain. When I got back into my cabin leaned my head against the wall, not unhappy, but thinking the obvious thing – where in the whole world, etc. But mixed with this feeling was a kind of satisfaction – well, I've been to the Wardroom dance. I'm trying.

Saturday 9 October. Leave started....

Had breakfast and caught the 7.45 train to Fenchurch St. Very cold and misty. Went to Paddington by Inner Circle. How I love Paddington Station. Already a mass of people was beginning to queue for the 10.25 Cornish Riviera Express. I went to the Restaurant on Platform 1 and had some toast and coffee – the room has pretty pale green walls and on the table a notice reminding customers that the GWR have NOT adopted the principle of adding a service charge. Got home about four – changed into a red dress with unwrenlike red bows in my hair. Then wallowed in the luxury of bed.

Sunday 10 October. Oswestry. Breakfast in bed – enjoying my room – sunshine, books, light clean walls and pictures – the bright Raoul Dufy over the mantelpiece. After lunch lying outside in the sun.

Tuesday 12 October. Being on leave one is humanised again, listens to the news more, gets more into touch with the war. Coming home in the train I was reading the *Spectator* and an article by Harold Nicolson, in which he mentions looking up his diary for 1940 – the Battle of Britain period. It occurred to me that were I to look in this volume in three years time what dreariness I should find. One would hardly know that there was a war on at all, and certainly not have any idea that I was an intelligent and presumably thinking person. Or perhaps I do think a little, but not about anything that really matters to anyone except myself.

Thursday 14 October. Yesterday Italy declared war on Germany. What a strange mad war. A pity they didn't choose our side three years ago.

I am a wretched melancholy creature when I would like to be noble and strong and very intelligent. I lie in a hot bath brooding about G. (yes I still do in spite of putting him right out of my life) when I ought to be thinking about the Metaphysicals in a scholarly way or planning a great comic novel.

Friday 15 October. Bristol. Hilary met me at the station yesterday and we came straight up to the Coppice in a taxi. A lovely welcome of course – but poor little Sally lying on the sofa looking rather plain and peaky, just like a child in a novel by Charlotte M. Yonge. And Dick in his dressing gown – Lulu and Dan and darling Mary. Prue is ill too, and now as I write is sleeping through the Fantastic Symphony of Berlioz.

I asked Honor if there was any more news about the divorce – and she says it is going to be heard NEXT FRIDAY! They had not intended to tell me until it was over.

Well, there it is.

My first feeling was one of elation – I went upstairs to change and stood for a long time looking out of the window, over the trees and gardens of Brackenhill. But now of course I'm sobered down. There is really no cause for rejoicing as far as I'm concerned.

Saturday 16 October. A very melancholy day, but in some ways a satisfying one. Because I've really faced up to the fact that Gordon doesn't really love me as I love him and will never ask me to marry him when he is free. He told Honor a week or two back that he didn't intend to make any more 'experiments'. And she also told me, when I asked her, that according to Pen Lloyd James he regarded it as a pleasant sentimental episode which was now closed. He must have said that as long ago as the winter. So now what becomes of my illusion that this was a great renunciation and that he had ever for a moment wanted the same things as I do? Well, the illusion is dead or dying. But I'm not bitter about it. I still love him of course and in the months (or years!) that follow I shall no doubt ache for him sometimes – sweet, hopeless person, the most delightful companion. I was of course wretchedly miserable in the evening and tore up all his letters. But I have been realising that it would come to this soon and am really glad that I have had the courage to ask Honor and face up to it.

Sunday 17 October. Had breakfast rather late. And a surprisingly happy and calm day. Had lunch with Honor and the children – Julian amazed us all by saying that the king was in church, but we haven't really got to the bottom of it yet – I mean how *could* he be?

Monday 18 October. London. When I got out of the train at Paddington in the twilight full of dim hurrying figures I felt about the most lonely person there. Oh, to be cherished and comforted at a journey's end. It was nearly seven o'clock and I hurried on to Platform 1, hoping that the restaurant might be open. I sat at a table with a young Canadian officer who offered me a cigarette. We got talking and he finished by paying for my meal. I couldn't say to him – you've brought comfort and friendliness to a rather lonely and miserable person, but that's what he did.

Wednesday 20 October. Westcliff. Hawksworth thinks I ought not to be a Censor Officer, but suggests Intelligence or Staff Officer. But how could this be managed? I mean, nobody ever tells one anything about anything – but it would be lovely.

Friday 22 October. Was very busy today on the Marine index and thinking all the time about Honor and how she was getting on with the divorce.

About 5 o'clock they rang through from Regulating to say there was a telegram for me and should they read it. It said 'Successful and Painless. Love. Honor.'

Sunday 24 October. London. Caught the 7.40 to London and now am sitting in the Tottenham Court Road Lyons Corner House having had a second breakfast. It's nice to be in London on one's own. Had some coffee and an almost continental fruit flan in Old Vienna. It's nice, red plush and a chandelier and the waiters surely were once eminent Viennese businessmen and lawyers. I felt I had to have a glass of water with my coffee even if I hadn't felt thirsty. I had decided to go to a concert but wasn't sure which one as there were three to choose from – the L.P.O. were playing, and it wasn't till afterwards that I discovered their programme contained both the old Tchaikowsky Piano Concerto *and* Prokofiev's Classical Symphony – so I could have been nicely torn to pieces. But I chose the Albert Hall and heard a lovely programme with Boyd Neel conducting.

After the concert went into the big Lyons where I soon got a seat at a table with two young men – (one very dark and good looking, who reminded me of poor Friedbert) and a sergeant. We soon all got talking about music and so I had quite a jolly tea. Talking about Lyons the dark young man said that one needn't ever feel lonely there, which was a new aspect of it to me, as I've always thought of it as the sort of place where one was essentially lonely, especially with all the crowds and music and glittering decor. It was the first time I ever haven't been and I enjoyed it.

Sunday 31 October. Winter will soon begin. I often used to think it would be romantic to be by the sea in winter. Now that I am by it I scarcely look at it. Though perhaps I meant wild dramatic sea, not Westcliff's tame suburban waters.

November

I had a lovely weekend in Bristol – unmarred by any real Gordon misery – but plenty of tender rather sad memories – it's come round again to that time of year. Our feet rustling through the leaves and the dark mornings. But how completely he is Honor's, really.

Friday 12 November. I was sad yesterday evening and alone in the redirection room began writing a poem. As soon as I'd had supper I hurried out to the Municipal College to a gramophone recital – whirled away from my misery along the London Road in a blue-ly lighted trolley bus. The lecture was at the School of Art – a modern building, rooms full of Greek plaster casts – (Oh God, oh Montreal – surely Westcliff might be such a place?). Our room was full of books and had a blackboard and a screen, and rows of chairs. Mr May, the lecturer, is a tall, distinguished looking grey haired man, wearing a striped flannel suit. A white haired woman in a turban (his wife!) put on the records. The audience was rather scanty – an old man, one or two civilians and three soldiers.

Thursday 18 November. On Tuesday I had my second inoculation. Felt very ill in the evening and I was duty wren. Sat desolately by the fire shivering uncontrollably with an aching head and longing to be cherished. A year ago to the day Gordon said to me, sitting by the fire in Honor's room, 'whatever happens *you* mustn't be made unhappy over this affair'.

This is what it has come to –

> The owl in the attic which is only stuffed,
> The marble vault where one does not embrace.
> Regret that does not even call forth tears
> So dry it is, so old, so out of place.

> The darling jokes, withered as pressed flowers,
> The gay and hopeful person that was me,
> And sentimental love, the white rabbit,
> Outcast and ridiculous at Westcliff-on-Sea.

> Introducing – You in the Radio Times
> Successful, Byronic, rather second rate,
> Me in the Wrens pretending to be a sailor
> Drearily splendid, bravely accepting my fate.

>   (or romantically celibate?)

Saturday 20 November. In the afternoon went into Southend with Prue Leith Ross. A cold bright day – we walked in. Bought two vests and then went into the Odeon to see *Flemish Farm* – very good of its kind. We also had a selection on the organ – bathed in a luxurious glow of rose, green, blue and purple light, one could imagine anything – listening to 'Believe me if all those endearing young charms' – dear ruin and dear Tom Moore – and 'Because' . . . . I like cinema organs, in cinemas – one must have the plush seat and coloured lights, all the right trappings.

Sunday 21 November. Went to St Alban's church, taking with me the prayer book and English Hymnal I brought away from there more than 2 months ago. When I got to the church heard the sound of a piano and inside a thin bald man was playing Chopin – a Nocturne – with great fervour. It seemed rather unsuitable. We had quite nice hymns and the Vicar was very jolly afterwards. When I got out of the church it was absolutely black and I had no idea where I was going, but somehow walking boldly in the middle of the road I found my way to the Hobby Horse! One step enough for me. So I sit listening to Albert Sandler, Indian Love Lyrics, and before that Vera Lynn, surrounded by Marines.

To Henry Harvey in Stockholm
3/O B.M.C. Pym, WRNS
Box 500,
Southampton.

26 May 1944

Dear Henry –

I was so pleased to get your letter when I was in London doing my Censorship course. As you will see I have now got my Commission, and am a Third Officer in the depths of the country – although our address is Southampton we are in fact about 18 miles away and work in a large country house, with beautiful grounds full of camellias, azaleas and rhododendrons. It belongs to the Rothschilds and before that the Mitfords – Unity's family, you know, lived there. It has quite an imposing façade, mock Palladian, with a good sweep of grass and a view over to the Isle of Wight.

I have been here since 13 March and there is plenty of social life whether you like it or not, because, as you can imagine most of the invasion forces, both English and American are concentrated in the South and South-West and there are always far more men than women at dances. The Wrens get so many invitations they hardly know which to accept. Last night we went to a big Anglo-American dance given at the Village Hall – we were allowed to wear civilian clothes which was a pleasant change as a stiff collar and tie isn't very comfortable for dancing. I met there a young Surgeon-Lieutenant, who was up at Magdalen 1936–1939. It was nice to talk to somebody about Oxford again – my dear, I couldn't remember anyone I knew who'd been up at Magdalen except Oscar Wilde and your tutor Lewis. Though before I knew you I used to think *you* were there as I often saw you coming out on my way back from the Bodleian, some starry evening in the very early spring 1933!

Anyway the dance wasn't too bad – naturally I hadn't wanted to go, I never do, would much rather have a quiet evening at home reading. And as for writing I never get a moment now, and have a fine idea for a novel about this place and all the queer people in it. Don't think that because I mention all this social life that I have changed in the least. I don't really like meeting and making conversation with all these people but it has to be done and naturally I manage to see the funny side of it. Last Sunday night I went for drinks with our Captain (an RN type) and some Canadian Commandos, very tough and free with Himself's booze, to which they helped me liberally! The Captain is a great personality with a silver headed stick and a Great Dane – can be very charming when he likes. The other Navy people here are rather varied – we have some Army Captains too who are very nice on the whole – two Oxford ones among them but rather young. Still it is a bond and always makes something to talk about.

I've got your letter in front of me, so will answer it whatever there is to be answered in it. I can't remember at all what my last two letters were like – not very good, I imagine as I know in the first one I was probably feeling very depressed about Gordon – well, that is all over now and I have quite recovered from the misery I felt at the time. It took me nine months or so to recover (just like having a baby). It was really much better when I went into the Wrens last July. Change of scene and new people and now I have met Gordon again and feel quite indifferent towards him – well hardly indifferent but you know what I mean! We had a rather dramatic meeting last December, drinks at the Bolivar, behind the BBC and lunch at Pagani's which lasted till 4. Have seen him only once since then but we write occasionally. I am sure you would like him – he has great charm, though he is hopelessly unstable to lean on, and one does want a little of that, dull though it may sound. Since then I have had one other 'entanglement' with a Petty Officer at Westcliff-on-Sea, where

I was stationed during the winter, but I finished that off and am now more or less heart free. So it looks as if you and Jock may get your way and have me as Miss Pym all my life. I cannot believe that I am still an essential bearing in your lives – it is so long since we have met and we must all have made many other friends in these last four or five years. Still, I do think that we could quite easily slip back into our old ways if we were ever all together again, say in Oxford, preferably. We still all like the same things as we did then.

My officer's uniform is really smarter than my Wrens, I think. Of course it is made to measure and fits much better, has gold buttons and a tricorne hat with a rather beautiful naval badge, blue and gold and crimson. The Wrens wear little sailor hats, as I expect you know. I quite like mine and still have it at home. I imagine you would still recognise me, even in uniform. I suppose I've got to look older but that's about all. How do you look these days – have you still got all your hair? Elsie seemed to look very much the same, judging by the photograph that you sent of her with the baby. Do tell her to write to me – she used to write such lovely amusing letters.

I am vaguely depressed, waiting for things to happen as we all are now, I wish it could be over and done with – we shall know so many people in it and I suppose a good many of them won't come back. Still, I wouldn't be anywhere else now at this time.

I've just been reading a letter from home, my parents are both very well and Hilary too – she is still in Bristol. Her husband is a Sergeant now – Air Force. He's very intelligent. They have started writing to each other in Modern Greek, as they hope to go out there after the war. He is also very musical, as she is, so they are quite a well suited couple.

I must stop now and go over to tea. We still get quite good food, though it isn't always as well cooked as it might be. Anyway there's plenty of it. Cigarettes are plentiful too – at 2/4 for 20! Drink is very short but we do manage to get it.

Love to Elsie and the baby – Barbara

Naples

17 September 1944. Once before, after Christmas 1942, I started a diary because I was unhappy and it helped to write things down. Now I start because I have had a faint feeling of dissatisfaction with life here, the dull day's work and empty social round and the fear that I shall never, never write that novel or do anything at all worth doing. Also a faint nostalgia for the carefree unnatural life on board the *Christian Huygens* and Michael (Lt. RN) and our talks and snatched kisses in the unsympathetic atmosphere of a troopship.

This afternoon we went to Capri. It takes about 2 hours from Naples by boat. It is much bigger than I expected with great sheer cliffs in parts. The four of us hurried ashore, into the funicular which took us past vineyards with hanging bunches of grapes, also lemon trees, but the lemons seemed either green or mouldy. The usual kinds of flowers here, royal blue convolvulus with pink inside, a rich puce climbing thing and another pale blue – I don't know the names but one must be bougainvillaea. At the top we got a car and drove to Anacapri and then walked the last bit to Axel Munthe's villa. The usual beggar followed us – an 'orphan' aged about sixty. The villa is lovely inside – full of old furniture and Roman sculptures which Munthe dug up in the garden – also Roman inscriptions – I wished I could read them – 'oh the *agony* of not knowing Latin!' Very striking is a great stone head of Medusa which he has on the wall over his writing desk. Apparently he *saw* this head in the clear water by the old foundations of Tiberius's bath. How wonderful to have seen it before anyone else did. What I liked best was a cool little courtyard full of these Roman pieces, white walled and peaceful with trees against the sky. I felt tears coming into my eyes and had to turn away. The peace, the beauty, the antiquity, perhaps something of the feeling I have for churchyards came over me. There is also a lovely corner overlooking the sea with a marble seat and an avenue of cypresses. A stone harpy on a corner wall so that it is silhouetted against the sky and sea. Also a large granite sphinx on which you can have a wish. I wished a simple wish that *could* come true.

There is a pleasant little square in Anacapri, full of souvenirs – corals, straw hats, cameos and the little silver bells which are supposed to be lucky. Of course I bought one, being sentimental and a little superstitious. *La campanella porta fortuna* .... I do hope it will. This place made me quite disinclined to go back to Naples.

Naples. From the ship layers of orange and pink and biscuit coloured buildings and in the evening a mass of twinkling lights. No smells for the first week as I had a cold, but afterwards many smells and dirty bits of paper in the streets – and occasionally a good smell, incense or perfume passing a barber's shop. The people, rather ragged and dirty but some girls nicely dressed and pretty, nearly all wearing shoes with very high wedge heels – many priests.

18 September. I seem to be liking Naples better and often feel now the exhilaration of being in a foreign land. We worked very hard. In the evening we went on board the *Sirius*. Was shown all the radar apparatus which is truly fearful and wonderful. We danced on the quarter-deck to a Royal Marines Band. Highly romantic. Then a lovely trip back by the motorboat, wind and spray and stars – dark shapes of ships and the lights of Naples.

21 September. Last night Margaret and I went out with Peter (boredom is an exquisite experience, to be savoured and analysed like old brandy and sex). We were joined by Lt. Cdr. Crabb, who used to be in Major's Gallery in Cork Street before the war – I couldn't think where I had seen him before. We thought we might give a surrealist exhibition here – some of these Naval types would need no alteration beyond the addition of some small incongruity like a fried egg on the shoulder or a bird nesting in the beard. We went to the Orange Grove where I pleased the waiter by knowing the Italian for carnation. Afterwards we took it in turn to shuffle round the floor with Peter. There were a lot of Americans jitterbugging and looking so terrible I began to wonder if I were seeing right. Afterwards we went to the Fleet Club and had bacon and eggs. I am always eating here. Altogether the evening passed more pleasantly than I had imagined it would. Conversation with Peter is an impossibility. At the Landing Craft Mess on Tuesday, by the way, we had a rather nice *Some Tame Gazelle* conversation about baths of hot volcanic mud, how you lie on a kind of slab and an attendant plasters you with mud.

It has been pouring with rain yesterday and today and whites and macintoshes look rather silly.

I wish Michael would write. My morale needs a little bolstering up in that direction, unless I met somebody nice here, which would do equally well, but people seem to be so dreary. They are so rare, one's own kind.

26 September. On Saturday afternooon I went to the Opera and saw *Rigoletto.* The Opera House is very luscious, red and gold and baroque with rows of boxes all round and a painted ceiling. After that to the Admiral's cocktail party at his villa, romantically situated with a terrace overlooking the bay. A crescent moon, dark shining water below and clever artificial lighting – weak cocktails of Ischia wine and something and rather formal conversation with a beautiful Flags (seen in a dim light) and one or two others. Doriel and I went on to a party at the S.O.I.'s flat, which once belonged to some rich Italians and has all the original furnishings and even some of their hats! A lovely big table of mirror glass – portraits round the walls, with one of which I fell in love – a young man, looking like Jay in 17th century dress. Best of all is the bathroom which has paintings of Roman architecture all round the walls, bidet, w.c. and bath at one end and at the other a desk and armchairs. Dinner in their Mess, which has delightful Rex Whistler painted walls. There is also a gorgeous salon or bathroom with much white and gold and rococo or baroque ornamentation and pretty brocaded chairs. A pleasure just to sit and look at it. No need of 'a remoter charm by *thought* supplied'. . . .

The rest of the party was dancing, drinking and talking with a good looking (if rather common) young paybob. The first person in Naples with whom I've had any conversation. About sex! on the balcony overlooking the bay. He has a cynical attitude to life and the technique of outrageous rudeness. He told me I would make a good mistress because I would be able to hold a man's attention by my intelligence.

2 October. Worked all day and in the evening wore myself out writing a long letter to Michael – but felt better for it – purged, I suppose! The trouble is I never quite know what I *do* feel and whether I am being sincere or not. Also I keep myself in check as I think it would be disastrous to care too much and even if it were mutual nothing could come of it. I can't be bothered with these fleeting affairs.

3 October. A letter from Michael in answer to the silly card I sent him from Capri – a boring, slightly facetious letter, very disappointing, but I had imagined that correspondence with him would be disillusionment. I was a little alarmed when I remembered my intimate, affectionate 8 pages, nearly in my best style, of yesterday and hastily wrote off another little note making light of it and gently hinting that I had not remained altogether faithful. Which leads to Starky (the paybob) whom I've seen twice since I last mentioned him. He is rude and impossible and casual, in themselves quite attractively provoking qualities and yet I have a sort of liking for him, probably I am flattered by his attention (such as it is). He is the only person in Naples I can talk to about everything and nothing, though not cultured as far as I know. His cynicism is, I think, a mask of defence, which is always intriguing. He makes me feel fiercely protective because the others don't like him! Also he is goodlooking and tall and has nice short-sighted brown eyes – but his voice gets on my nerves. We went to a party on Friday night and *now* I've just heard that he is returning to England any minute and funnily enough I mind. Morag says I enjoy wallowing in emotion – perhaps I do, but I still mind. I'm in agony wondering if I will hear anything from him before he goes – tonight we should have gone out together and it's now 8 o'clock and no sign and does one *ever* learn not to mind!

12 October. One does learn better how to cope. Sitting on the bed at 6.15 after having pushed a note in at Navy House in the morning and seen him only a few minutes ago standing on his balcony gazing out across the Bay. Oh let him be gone and no more hankering for this, second-rate as it is. But the best Naples can offer.

13 October. And of course in the morning he phoned and orided me for letting sentimentality ort the better of cynicism, in my note. And invites me to go out to dinner with him tomorrow evening after our housewarming party. Oh how foolish one is!

14 October. Began to feel sick inside at the prospect of the party, but it went off well. The Anteroom redecorated, clean and cream-washed – new pictures (in the hideous gilt frames still) – new curtains, flowers, plates of food and surprisingly strong drinks. Starky came early and I spent most of the evening with him, not managing to have a word with Rob Long (Admiral Morse's handsome, conceited Flags). S. is no good socially, he is gauche and rather ineffectual but so sweet. We went to dinner at the Fleet Club and it was quite a successful party – we seemed rather divided into couples and this increased as the evening went on. S. and I danced and then went to his Mess when the others went home. And there was the same good thing between us as we had the evening of Mac's party, and which I felt we had lost in our meetings since then. He goes back to the UK either on Wednesday or next week, so I suppose I shall go all through it again, though I don't think I can run into Navy House with any more notes.

15 October. Went to the 22 Club with Captain Heaven (Jimmy) where we bathed and sat in the sun. Then a pleasant drive round Naples – layers of white and pink houses and the bougainvillaea still out. Then tea at the RASC Mess and walked round the garden which is lovely, green and neglected with green oranges on the trees, wild cyclamen, roses, pink lilies, palms. A pleasant, nostalgic place. It got very cold at twilight. At 7 we went to the Opera House to a concert. The old Grieg Piano Concerto. Gordon and this time 2 years ago and now *this*.

17 October. Starky and I went up to the Orange Grove, drank and talked a lot, danced a little and a little love and more talk and he thinks I am in love with him. Because I call him darling – 'but you say it so many times' – I suppose I must in a funny kind of way. Our relationship is physical and intellectual, but not, repeat *not* cultural. He has awful manners.

18 October. We drove to the foot of Vesuvius. The road is very bad in parts, but improves suddenly winding up. Very pretty woods with a view down over the Bay. We got a guide and long sticks and plodded up through the ash and lava. Starky raced ahead but came through the 'mountain' test very well, carrying my hat and bag for me at the end. We looked down into the crater and then came down hand in hand and hysterical with laughter as I kept falling down – my legs got covered with scars. The ashes are still quite hot but it is very cold on top. We drove back in the dark rather silent – I thinking the day was ending and it was our last meeting, but they came in for a drink and afterwards Starky and Mac called for me and we had more drinks. He's funny when he's slightly drunk. Bold and rude and rather sentimental – makes me feel very maternal! We had dinner in the Mess and then went on to a party at the flat of some Italian girls where some of the Cypher boys were. One has cold hands like a corpse. Ian Macintyre and I talked about Chaucer and Tchekov. Then we moved up to Mac's flat and continued the party. I spoke French and even a little Italian to the girls. I enjoyed myself though I saw little of Starky who seemed rather drunk and kept ruffling my hair. It was a cold stormy evening and the balcony was not very inviting – nevertheless I had a few conversations there, one with a Russian, one with Mac, who accused me of 'talking big' when

A VERY PRIVATE EYE

I said that Starky and I would soon forget each other, and one with Starky himself. We had a ridiculous goodnight outside the Wrennery at 3 a.m. – me saying 'Thanks for a lovely volcano' and him 'Excuse me for kissing you goodnight with my glasses on'.

23 October. Starky phoned quarters just as I got in from the office and suggested coming round for a drink and to say goodbye. I washed my hair, did my face and changed into blues. He came with Jack Fisher soon after 9 and we went into the blue and gold room. I didn't like him at all – he was rather rude and silly and I got to feel more and more low, finally saying can't we go to the Fleet Club and be *madly* gay or something, but it was too late. Still we did go out in the end – drove up to the Monastery in the car. It was too dark to see much, but we talked and he was much nicer and we really said goodbye. But without much hope or wish for the future. It isn't, as we said, that one's cynical, it's that one *knows* from experience how these things peter out. I feel that it's a good thing that he is going.

24 October. Two years ago tonight – if Gordon hadn't said 'In a queer kind of way I'm in love with you' I shouldn't be in Naples now. Told at dinner that Starky isn't going for four more days. Oh dear, I don't want to see him again – and yet I do.

26 October. I am trying not to feel low, knowing that he may still be here but not liking to find out. If only he would really be gone! Last night I went out with Jimmy and Morag and Bruce. We started at Jeni's, continental atmosphere, a man playing a mandoline and singing Italian songs – the sort of place to go to with somebody special to talk and gaze into their eyes! Dinner at the British Officers' Club, then to the Churchill, loud band, good dancing and many gins. Then to the Fleet Club. All through the evening I could feel the pain of missing Starky and even though I know it won't last very long it still hurts. Tonight I don't know whether to go to an American party with Doriel or stay in and go to bed early. Parties and drink are a bad thing when one has a little misery lurking somewhere. Better to bear it with dignity. If I'm not careful I'll begin hating myself again. Not that it really matters but I must keep myself in hand.

27 October. He went. In the early morning by plane.

> Absence is the negation of love.
> Joy fades, but even so fades in felicity

and all the rest.

31 October. This evening I've actually done some Italian – written exercises out of Hugo. If only I could go on with it – it is so satisfying. On Sunday I wrote a letter to Starky, quite a good one, which will no doubt be beyond him – he will pounce on the delicate sentimentallity and miss the rest – or will he?

2 November. At 2.30 started out with Morag for our weekend in Ischia. Sat in the saloon of the ferry for about half an hour but then had to rush to the side. Spent the next hour leaning over the side being sick and trying to keep my balance as the boat rose and fell in the waves. One wave came right over me and drenched me. Also a dead body floated by but luckily I didn't see it. Also being sick was a beautiful young man in an elaborate Italian uniform. How many of them have large melancholy eyes that gaze soulfully at you! I arrived in Ischia, my hair wet and tangled, my face green, which had been so glowing and peach-like when I started off. Early to bed but I dreamed, which I don't in Naples, muddled dreams about Starky. And I looked at myself in a wardrobe mirror and saw I was wearing red plus fours or turkish trousers.

3 November. We walked a little round the island – everything is so beautifully green now. Oranges and orange blossom with shining green leaves, lemons, vines, bougainvillea, mild sunny air – I wore no stockings. We walked to the ruined castle and came to a ruined chapel, the altar with plaster cherubs etc. still distinguishable, also little side chapels and arches all ruined. 'Sentimental delight in decay'... how happy I felt, so different from the artificail life in Naples. After tea we went down to the shops and I bought a basket in the shape of a heart, which I shall use as a workbasket.

5 November. Smooth crossing back. Four letters awaiting me in the office. One from Starky. Iain now!

15 November. Tea at British Officers' Club with Jimmy. Elizabeth Ann was there with a pongo. Whole atmosphere *very* British.

16 November. Party in Maclaine Clarke's flat. Didn't feel like going – sticky beginning but not bad afterwards with Cypher boys. Harry would keep asking me if I missed Starky and enlarging on the merits of his character. Well, it made conversation. Of course it was too cold to go out on the balcony and nobody did. Isn't there an Italian saying about there being no greater misery than to remember past happiness when you are unhappy? Not that one could apply it exactly, but there were *other* parties and *other* people. Once upon a time. And other conversations. Harry tried to persuade me to go to the CHQ New Year's Eve Party – said he was sure Starky would have wanted it – just as if I were Starky's widow! Came home with a splitting headache and sat on my bed for about 10 minutes just doing nothing, with my coat on.

17 November. Dinner at Jimmy's Mess and 22 Club dance – in splendid form, even dancing quite well. I no longer have an ache of misery. Oh how *soon* one forgets....

19 November. Drove with Jimmy all along the sea front through Posilippo down to Bagnoli – lovely view of Ischia in a golden mist. Tea at the British Officers' Club, supper at the Mess, Jimmy, Tony, Auriol and I. The Major was there with a friend called John Baxter, a John Gielgud type, a mouth like Gordon's but blue eyes. *Madly* gay at the Churchill. To the 22 Club and back to the Mess. Driving in the dark in Naples is so pleasant, especially up the roads to Posilippo, the headlights of the car pick out all sorts of exquisite things, a pair of urns set on a gateway, corners of buildings, avenues of trees, grey, deserted streets

20 November. Went out to dinner with Colonel Mote, who belongs to Claims and Hirings – a lovely Mess above the orange grove with a garden full of statues and a glorious view. All in the dark with twinkling lights. Had a rather queer dinner – fish after meat. A charming lot of people – a Brigadier like Charlie Chan and an amusing Scots Major in a kilt.

A description of *me* – somebody said to Jimmy – 'that very blasé Wren officer with a perpetually bored expression' – and he said 'Yes she was born like that. It's rather fun!' I told Cynthia and she gave me another description – 'the girl with the fascinating eyes'.

21 November. Had an airgraph from Gordon, so funny and sweet it brought a sudden rush of tears to my eyes. Oh how much my *own* sort of person he was and is... please can't there be somebody like that again.

22 November. Worked very hard, did [censored] 213 letters, a lot for Naples, but how unlike the weeks before D Day. Had dinner at Jimmy's Mess. The Major came in with lipstick on his face.

23 November. Why doesn't Starky write. But how quickly I forget those bright brown eyes, that sweet smile, that uncertain gauche social manner, those umbrageous remarks. But the blister from Vesuvius still throbs on my heel and I go to sickbay every day to have it treated. And look sadly at my whites packed away in my suitcase, even try on my white hat for a moment.

24 November. Tea with Auriol, Morag and Margaret who are all going to Alex. By train to Taranto and then by sea. I rather envy them the amusement of the journey and feel almost provincial and stay at home here in Naples.

30 November. Went back to work which was very boring as usual. Oh how I am wasting my life in some ways. In the evening we tried to go to Positano in a large American Ford V8. I like driving through the suburbs of Naples to look inside a lighted restaurant where you will see no British or Allied officers, to watch people queuing at some little cinema, to peer inside a flat, to see groups talking on street corners and to drive down the kind of places where you might get a knife in your back. Nothing is more deserted and Chirico-like than a Naples street at night – grey shuttered houses, dark, silent, mysterious, sinister.

Out of Castellamare the car broke down so we went into the sergeants' mess and had drinks (which went straight to my head) and cheese sandwiches. Then back to our mess where we cooked bacon and eggs and coffee.

2 December. Positano in the evening. Drinks at the Miramar, dinner at Bucca di Bacco (soup, squid, steak, omelette). Dancing at Caterinetta. Rich, idle Italians playing cards all night and sleeping all day.

6 December. Positano, Amalfi and Ravello, which is romantic at twilight. Cypresses, olives, an orange grove and a church which is, I believe, Byzantine. Would like to stay there sometime. I believe it has associations with Wagner and Cosima von Bülow. It is a honeymoon spot.

20 December. Vicky's cocktail party. Talked to B.S.O. Astley-Jones, Major Macleod, etc. Went to Robby's party. Lovely food but oh the strain of cheesing.

25 December. Breakfast in bed – opened my stocking from Auriol and books from home. Waited on Wrens at dinner then had our own. In the evening went to a party at Admiral Morse's villa, quite enjoyable but I am never at my ease there, feel Jane Eyre-ish and socially unsuccessful. Danced with Flags and Astley-Jones, both doing their stuff – charm, etc. How artificial it all is. I wonder if they feel it.

29 December. Went to Chiefs' and P.O.'s dance at the Fleet canteen. Very enjoyable, many good dancers. Met a man who had been at Westcliff.

31 December. CHQ dance. Cyclamen chiffon, agonising stiff neck and the magic of 'Long Ago and Far Away' sung by dear Edward Astley-Jones while he danced with me, oh so cheek-to-cheek....

24–25 March 1945. Rome. Went up by Cassino. Country lovely – brilliant green grass, yellow-green trees, blossoms, cypresses as one gets further north. Villages on hills, grey with a church spire or cupola – but ruined with sightless windows. Cassino – literally nothing standing. *Out of Bounds* notices in English and Polish. Little white wooden crosses mark the graves.

Frossinone – much bigger but horrifying damage. Like the Blitz but more desolate.

Rome itself, wide pavements – magic twilight (as I first saw Berlin in 1938). Trees coming into leaf in the streets, flower shops full of fruit blossom and other more exotic things, double anemones, carnations, freesias, violets, irises and funny orange and blue things, tall and spiky, a cross between an iris and an orchid, hardly real. A fountain in the form of a boat in the Plaza di Spagna (in the moonlight you can't see the bits of paper and orange peel in the water).

St Peter's. Vast and unchurchlike. Marble in various colours. Nice Holy Water basins, white cherubs and yellow Siena marble. It was Palm Sunday and outside they were selling palms and little palm crosses and everyone carried sprigs of myrtle. All the pictures behind the altars were veiled in purple. We went up on the roof – the Tiber a yellowish brown – lovely bridges with figures. Palazzo Venezia looks good in the distance, flying statues on the corners – figures everywhere stand out against the sky. Peered into the Vatican City in the hopes of seeing carpet slippers slopping up and down the backstairs. Hens on the roof.

Lunch at the Officers' Club in Pincio Gardens. Tender green cypresses, brown and cream buildings. Lovely greeny fish fountain in Piazza Berberini.

Ideas for Naples Poems or Stories

The Major's Arienzo girl, no longer in her first youth, waiting for him to come back off LIAF in that cluttered salon. Palms in front of the windows – the orange tree that never has any fruit. Then the mimosa. Will he ever come back?

The Officers' Club at Capua. The room with the little baroque birds, bad food lacking salt and half cold, the sweet *spumante* and too many drunken majors.

The Royal Palace at Caserta – like a railway waiting room at one of the bigger stations. Enormous chandeliers with very little light coming from them. Huddled groups of people talking and drinking. (All very like Henry Green's *Party Going*). Marble busts, rather vulgarly ostentatious. Red and gold sofas, very long. Oh, if a romance should begin here and flower!

The Opera House on an April evening during one of the intervals. The dusty plants where we stub out our cigarettes show young green leaves and even buds of flowers. If this can happen, anything can. Upsetting, because one cannot help drawing comparisons with the heart.

Lying awake and seeing dawn come to Naples, hearing the birds singing. One's thoughts so limited to that narrow life that *is* Naples and seems to be the whole world until one thinks of a map and Naples on it.

The suave elegant Flags and the Acting Third Officer in ill-fitting white dress talking on the terrace of an exquisite villa in the moonlight.

The white and gold Lyons Corner House-like atmosphere of the British Officers' Club.

The haunted feeling of places, and objects too, in villas and houses now taken over by the military – the 22 Club for instance.

To Henry Harvey in Upsala   London, S.W.1.

7 November 1945

Dear Henry,

It was very nice of you to write and I appreciated your letter very much – it was a very miserable time for me [her mother had died in September], but I feel much better about things now that I'm away from Oswestry.

I am still in the WRNS waiting to be demobilised really, but in the meantime hanging about at WRNS Headquarters, doing a little, very dull work which calls for very little intelligence. I earn quite good money though, which I suppose is something, and am also in London which I wanted to be. I think I shall be a civilian again by the end of this year or early next. We have given up our house in Oswestry and my father is living in a hotel, Hilary and I have taken a flat – in Pimlico, not a very good district, but perhaps we shall raise the tone. It is on the corner of Warwick Square and really quite nice. Anyway we are so lucky to get anywhere at all, as it is practically impossible to get flats and you really can't choose at all. It will be nice to have a place of one's own and I think I shall be much happier then. If I can get a nice little job to earn me a bit of money I shall then settle to writing again and see if I can get a nice novel or something published. But I don't really want to end my days in London, would prefer Oxford or the country. I suppose it is better than any other town though and as one's nerves are a bit frazzled after six years of war life is difficult anywhere. You know, one is bad tempered and irritable, could nearly cry because a bus doesn't stop when it's too full, would rather go without things than queue for them, and now that the war is over one doesn't seem able to put up with things so easily.

I had a letter from Jock yesterday, he seems much happier and is enjoying the sinshine – oh dear what an unsuitable mistake to make – of course I mean sunshine.

Do write sometime or get Elsie to, and be sure and let me know if you are coming over.

With love,

Barbara

108 Cambridge Street
London S.W.1.

9 February 1946

My dear Henry,

Thank you very much for your letter. It came very quickly. I had an idea that I owed you one, though that would have been rather unusual, I mean, if it had been ten years ago. Yes, I 'did start it', even if I was inspired by you or rather the sight of you in the English Reading Room. I even got Rosemary Topping to go and look in your books when you had left them for a moment to see what your name was. Does anybody ever do that now? I suppose not, though no doubt others are doing it at Oxford. I almost envy them – one seems to feel so little now, and life was certainly exciting then, full of splendours and miseries.

I ought really to have started with facts. I am now a civilian once more and have a flat in *Pimlico* (rather nice, don't you think?) which I share with Hilary, it is really very nice as we have a lot of things from Oswestry. My father has given up the house and is living in a hotel, where he is really very comfortable. I am going up to see him next weekend. He is very well, and though I feel it is very sad for him without my mother he is splendid about it. Luckily he has quite a lot of friends and interests there, which I haven't.

I came out of the WRNS on January 11th and am on my two months resettlement leave (paid!) at the moment. I am going to start looking for a job in a week or two. Heaven knows what I shall get, but I must earn some money. In many ways I would like to go abroad but having just got nicely settled in a flat I want to enjoy it for a while anyway. We do quite a lot of entertaining in a mild way – hardly any drink and mostly foreign dishes like moussaka and ravioli, owing to the scarcity of meat! I have become quite an efficient and resourceful cook and enjoy the domestic side of it very much.

20 February

I am really ashamed not to have finished this letter before now. I have just returned from Oswestry where I found my father very well and the country looking very pleasant, catkins, snowdrops and crocuses, even early primroses and buds on the lilac. I brought my typewriter back with me, so shall be able to get on with some writing. I have done a lot of alterations to *Some Tame Gazelle* and may try it again, after an interval of about eight years it may be more acceptable! There is so much that I want to write now, that I hardly know where to begin. But I feel I must also have a job, not only because of earning money but because I find routine work soothing (as long as it isn't too boring) and the best way of keeping out that *Angst,* from which we all suffer in some degree nowadays. Though creative work is better still.

If you haven't read Cyril Connolly's book *The Unquiet Grave,* you will wonder what I am talking about and say it is just one of my silly German words, but as I expect you have read it you will see that I am keeping up to date with all our clever young men. Not that he is *young* exactly – he is approaching forty, indeed, probably *is* forty now, is fat and given to self-pity and nostalgia. But he is clever and puts his finger on what it is we suffer from now – though maybe you don't in the bracing air of Sweden. He is 'soaked in French Literature' – not my expression, but the kind of thing one would like to be!

I have no very recent news of Jock, but wrote him a long letter some weeks ago. He says he has read all of Shakespeare and all of Proust, since being back in Alexandria. I wish I could say the same. He is certainly more rewarding to write to than you are but perhaps you are more deserving. I have kept some of your early letters, though I destroyed most of the James Joyce-like ones which I never understood anyway. It is pleasant to feel that you and Jock will never go quite out of my life now – who would ever have thought it. I see that Craster has retired and is to write a history of the Library. I hope it may appear in my lifetime. I could give him plenty of material from the human point of view.

With love to you both,

Barbara

108 Cambridge Street

5 June 1946

My Dear Henry,

I have so much news that I had better just fling it at you in Compton-Burnett style. Hilary and her husband have separated and my father has married again and given us a very nice stepmother of suitable age and a dear brother and sister, whom I have not met. He is so happy and it is a great relief to us to think he has somebody to look after him. It was all a great surprise I might add! Life seemed to be whirling too fast for us!

Hilary is happier without her husband – who was nice but much too cold and intellectual and logical to live with. They were not really madly in love when they married but it seemed a good thing, and of course lots of marriages of that kind turn out very well. But personally I would prefer the other thing, even if it wore off, as I am told it does. Maybe I shall be able to keep my illusions as it doesn't look as if I shall ever get married.

I am turning into an anthropologist as I now have a job at the International Institute of African Languages and Cultures, which I like very much. I work for dear Professor Daryll Forde, who is brilliant, has great charm but no manners, and is altogether the kind of person I ought to work for! I never seem to have time to do much writing – I begin to wonder whether I shall ever again send a novel to a publisher – I ought to have been doing that rather than writing to you.

Lots of love to you both –

Barbara

Part III

THE NOVELIST

The Published Novelist

In 1946 Barbara started to work with Daryll Forde, Professor of Anthropology at University College, London, and Director of the International African Institute. He was a brilliant, often impatient and difficult man, but with great energy, efficiency and enthusiasm, who had, immediately after the war, revitalised the Institute, founded in 1926 by Lord Lugard for the study of African languages and culture.

Barbara was his Assistant Editor on the Institute's journal Africa *and on the series of Ethnographic and Linguistic Surveys of Africa. She also helped to edit volumes of Seminar papers and prepared for press the various monographs published by the Institute. She was a capable and conscientious editor but had no real interest in Africa as such, being far more fascinated by the anthropologists and the linguists than by the subjects they were studying.*

She created a comic world around them, embroidering the few facts she knew about the various authors and reviewers into a splendid fantasy so that it was often difficult to remember what was real and what was not. ('I couldn't ask W. if his Mother was better because I couldn't remember if we'd invented her.') She was quick to pick out the ridiculous phrase (anthropological and, especially, linguistic studies are very rich in these) thereby making what would have been a tedious task of proof-reading or editing a constant delight to those who worked with her.

Giddiness continually hurls my goat to the ground.
The hyenas have broken the beer strainers of the women.
Travel with a bicycle in the rainy season is not easy.

No personal diaries other than the briefest entries exist for the years 1946–8. This can most easily be explained by the changed circumstances of her life at this time: the illness and death of her mother in September 1945 which led to more domestic responsibility; the end of the war and demobilisation; the remarriage of her father in 1946; and the completely new experience, for her, of starting a full-time job in London which must have taken a great deal of her concentration. When she did feel able to turn her mind to something else, it was to the revision of her novel Some Tame Gazelle.

In 1949 Jonathan Cape accepted Some Tame Gazelle, *now revised for the third time. It was published in 1950 and had a general critical success. 'Delightfully amusing,' wrote one critic in* The Guardian, *'but no more to be described than a delicious taste or smell.' Between 1950 and 1961 six og her novels were published by Cape:* Some Tame Gazelle, *1950;* Excellent Women, *1952;* Jane and Prudence, *1953;* Less Than Angels, *1955;* A Glass of Blessings, *1958; and* No Fond Return of Love, *1961, They were praised by the critics, enjoyed a modest financial success and delighted an ever-growing circle of admirers and enthusiasts.* Excellent Women, *the most generally popular, was a Book Society Choice and was subsequently serialised in the BBC's* Woman's Hour.

In February 1950 her only broadcast radio play, Something to Remember, *was produced by Hugh Stewart, with Grazelda Hervey playing the archetypal Pym heroine Edith Gossett.*

Barbara always said that she was glad that she could never be a 'full-time novelist' and that she had to earn her living some other way. It was fortunate that she was able to do so in a world as rich in comic material as the I.A.I. Because the Institute was classed as a charity, salaries were very low indeed and Barbara was lucky tha she was able to share a home with Hilary, separated from her husband in 1946 and now a BBC producer. Since 1946 they had lived together in great amity (as they did for the rest of her life), thus making the fictional situation of Some Tame Gazelle, *projected all those years ago, come true. They lived first in a flat in Pimlico (the setting for* Excellent Woman*) and then in Barnes (the suburb in* Less Than Angles *and* No Fond Return of Love*).*

From 1948 Barbara had kept notebooks – partly diaries, partly ideas for novels, or simply observations. At the back of each one detailed shopping lists that may one day provide invaluable source material for social historians. These 82 small, spiral-backed books form the heart of this section. Such was her dedicated professionalism that even in the 17 years when her novels were not published, even when it seemed unlikely that she would ever be published again, she still made notes for novels and recorded observations. In a way these notebooks were her most precious possession, the real raw material of her writing.

In 1961 Hilary bought a small house in Queen's Park (the district described in An Unsuitable Attachment*). There they had a garden and were able to keep cats. Tatiana, the original of Faustina, a beautiful but highly neurotic tortoiseshell, had a short, tragic life, but Tom Boilkin (sleek, black and white, President of the Young Neuters Club) and Minerva (also known as Nana, another, more amiable tortoiseshell whose preferred diet was fried tomato skins and custard) lived long and happy lives.*

H.H.

1948-1963

1948. Mission meeting. Prayers are difficult when choir practice interrupts them – the organist making jokes. We pray for streets. 'Warwick Square', says the vicar, his tone seeming to gain in fullness.

In the vestry I look round with frank interest – two rows of chairs, a grand piano. An assortment of vases and bowls, a small brass crucifix in need of cleaning, rolls of Mission posters.

The conversation – the bishop's letter is feeble, a pity says the vicar. People are so indifferent. Somebody suggests a procession, but people from the pubs might join in.

Worshipping in a Victorian church (St Gabriel's, Warwick Square) – no nice monuments round the walls, but the brass tablets and the atmosphere of Victorian piety is in its way just as comforting.

The new vicar calling – saying a prayer with housewives in their aprons – or the fear that he might.

The electricity man comes – he has to duck among the swinging wet stockings and knickers, but the expression of his serious rather worried blue eyes does not change. He sings in the choir.

Whitsun 1949. Bristol revisited. Coffee at Lloyd's (Carwardines). The comfortable atmosphere of a provincial town. It is this which evokes nostalgia rather than any memories.

Clifton on a June evening. Light on the Regency houses. Wistaria dying, poppies. But it hadn't been like this during the war. Those twinkling lights everywhere and the door of The Rocks standing wide open and welcoming, light glowing in a moonlike globe. Then it had been a blue-shaded light inside the door hastily shut and weeping in the Ladies. And when we looked over the Suspension Bridge it was not into lights but the dark bowl of trees.

The angry, umbraged and hurt postcards coming from the Oxford anthropologists: 'There seems to be no indication that I should get a copy'.

It is the only occasion when one really wants a husband – in a pub with uncongenial company and the feeling of not belonging.

St Michael's Church, Minehead. Morning. Women are doing the flowers – huge dahlias. It smells of floor polish rather than incense.

Old screen and font with stone figures (one partially restored?) The suspicious church-crawler looking out, not for the genuinely old, but the restored.

Sunday 27 November. Tea at the Hope-Wallaces to meet Elizabeth Bowen. Present: EB and her husband Alan Cameron, Jacqueline Hope-Wallace, Philip H-W, Veronica Wedgwood, John Hope (young), old man with white beard, David King-Wood, Hilary and myself. Charming drawing room in little St John's Wood house, first floor. Coral red curtains and turquoise walls – small Victorian chairs and 'objects' – but nothing new or *Vogue*ish – a kind of cosy shabbiness. Elizabeth Bowen is in black with grey and black pearls and pretty ear-rings (little diamond balls). The young author in her nervousness talks rather too much about herself! EB discusses methods of working – better at a typewriter than curled up in an armchair. She is very kind and obviously feels she ought to know more about me than she can possibly know! Her stammer is not really as bad as I had expected. Veronica tells me that both Daniel George and William Plomer were in agreement over Some Tame Gazelle (apparently unusual) and think it very amusing.

Veronica had a relative who 'passed over'. She was heard at a seance, saying in an unmistakable voice that she was 'bitterly disappointed'.

Buying Christmas cards in Mowbrays – one feels one can't push.

The way one betrays one's old loves – getting the new one to read *Trivia* or Matthew Arnold, going to the same churchyard. When we are older there seems no new approach left. The disillusionment of finding out that something (say *Trivia*) has been his thing with someone else.

January 1950. Broomhall Lodge [staying with friends]. The distinction between animals' and humans' dishes is a very narrow one. One feels that when we aren't there, there is *no* distinction.

Fasting before midnight mass. 'Fr X told us to fast for 2 hours.' 'Oh but Fr Y told us 3 hours.' 'I only had a very light meal myself, just a boiled egg and some tea and I did eat a little fruit, but it was over by 7.45 at the latest, so really I was fasting for $4\frac{1}{4}$ hours.'

To Henry Harvey in Göttingen　　　　　　　47 Nassau Road
　　　　　　　　　　　　　　　　　　　　　Barnes S.W.13

　　　　　　　　　　　　　　　　　　　　　1 May 1950

Dear Henry,

Here is a copy of my book [*Some Tame Gazelle*] – published today – with the author's compliments. I don't know if it will amuse you but hope that perhaps it may. Please don't notice all the places where I ought to have put commas – I am only too conscious of my shortcomings. There haven't been any reviews yet. It doesn't seem fair that people should have the power to criticise it!

I haven't put any embarrassing inscription, so you can give it to somebody as a birthday present. I should never know.

Hope you are well,

　　　　　　　　　　　　　　　　　With love – Barbara

Gordon Glover/Fabian. A Gordonish character in the village. His wife, to whom he had been consistently unfaithful, died – his outraged surprise and confusion of sentimental symbols.

'The Chapel Minister has BSc after his name – I feel one gets really everything there.'

1951. It seems rather dangerous, after we have been praying for the unity of the churches, to have a hymn by Newman.

1 February 1952. King George VI's Lying in State. 7.30–8.30 a.m. Very cold. The hall very dim, footsteps muffled on the thick carpet. The still figures guarding the catafalque – the nose and chin of the very young officer of the Household Cavalry so pink and smooth – eyes hidden. The faces of the Yeomen of the Guard – carved out of wood, lined and pale, one with a small moustache. The glitter of the diamonds in the crown and the white flowers on the coffin.

The vicar in the dark vicarage with a broken window, near to the yew-shaded churchyard. Lives with his mother – house said to be very dirty. Vicar has to be roused from his bed (? by an excellent woman) to take Communion Service.

Read some of Jane Austen's last chapters and find out how she manages all the loose ends.

The Riviera Cafe, St Austell is decorated in shades of chocolate brown. Very tasteless, as are the cakes.

To Henry Harvey in Oxford   47 Nassau Road

27 March 1952

Dear Henry,

Many thanks for your letter. There is something irresistible about your finding an old letter of mine in a drawer and answering it! You mustn't mind if I use the incident in a story one day. No, it didn't really need an answer – it was rather a peevish letter as far as I remember. We were both young and stupid in those days [at Oxford] and I can see that I must have been just as trying in my way as you were. Goodness knows what I expected! Anyway, you can be quite sure that I don't bear you any ill will about anything. I even look back on those days with a certain amount of pleasure – or do I mean emotion recollected in tranquillity, 'Samson Agonistes' and Langbaine and Jock being there and our quarrel – some excursions into the country.

Now we can have the satisfaction of being mean to each other – I by not giving you a copy of my new novel [*Excellent Women*] and you by not buying it. I wonder if you'd like it, anyway? I suppose every man I have ever known will see himself as Rocky (the rather shallow character). Doesn't the British Council buy books?

You don't say where you are living in Oxford, so I just imagine you in an office with a lot of filing cabinets and telephones. (Where would they file this letter if they *did* open it?)

I am glad you are going to be able to marry Susi [Henry and Elsie were divorced] now. I should think she has been very good for you and I do wish you both every happiness. Perhaps we shall meet one day – I should think it is inevitable and I shall have much pleasure in buying the young people a drink.

With best wishes,

Yours – Barbara

9 June. London Jazz Club. This is all very proper and formal, there is a kind of controlled enthusiasm. Unselfconscious. Pepsicola and cups of tea and a grey-haired woman collecting the empty cups. It is as respectable as a church youth club. No clergyman there, but a grey-haired man watching the dancers and holding his daughter's handbag and cardigan – for he is the prospective father-in-law (we thought) of one of the young men in the band.

The agony of wondering if he will send a Christmas card! And he, wandering in his provincial town on Christmas Eve, as we used to do in Oswestry.

The Hadzapi will eat practically anything that is edible except the hyena.

The giving and receiving of off-prints brings about a special relationship between people.

1953. The young woman has just read a novel by Rosamond Lehmann about the suffering of women in love – it makes her feel inferior as if she isn't capable of suffering so much. Perhaps when I'm older, she thinks hopefully.

'Gone to Watford to talk about the lineage system,' she said desperately. 'It seems so, well, so *unnecessary.*'

Gems from Crockford:
de Blogue (formerly Blogg), Oswald, Wm. Chas.
The organist of Bristol Cathedral is called A. Surplice Esq.

24 June. Men don't seem to like women in black – does it foreshadow their own death? Or do they think of Masha in *The Seagull* 'in mourning for her life' and fear that a long, dreary tale of an unsuccessful love is about to be unfolded?

Her eyes seemed to beg for a future meeting, but somehow he couldn't suggest one. Instead he asked 'Are you any good at typing?'

Professor Mainwaring had taught his students always to make carbon copies, use inverted commas round certain technical terms and, best of all, that thanks can never be too fulsome.

'It is important that not even the slightest expression of amusement or disapproval should ever be displayed at the description of ridiculous, impossible or disgusting features in custom, cult or legend.' *Notes & Queries in Anthropology.*

Reading a biography of Edmund Campion on a Friday over lunch one feels bound to eat fish.

Title for a Betjeman poem: Despair in the Protestant Truth Society Bookshop, 21st December 1953.

The Christmas card bore the head of a large dog – one of her least favourite animals and an inappropriate message – Kind Remembrances. Perhaps Tom does that to Catherine after they have parted. She almost hates him.

The unsuitable Confirmation presents – books chosen because they were small and in special bindings, e.g. *A Shropshire Lad, The Rubaiyat*, Shakespeare's *Sonnets* – or even Latin poets like Catullus.

After Tom's death, Elaine, who is staying with Tom's sister, wants to meet Deirdre and Catherine for lunch ('He spoke so much of you'). What can they order – Braised heart, thought Catherine wildly. Should they drink? Ought they to feel hungry? Who would pay the bill? T's sister, presumably. Deirdre and Catherine seemed to band together. Who had loved him the most? The nightmare quality of the talk.

For Deirdre it's pass on quickly to the next one (Digby), as it should be. Deirdre had put on rather more make-up than usual, had painted dark, fierce eyebrows – so they would get quite the wrong impression – a tall, thin, rather fierce looking girl, with her hair scraped back in a kind of tail.

Geography learned the hard way by bitter experience on the edge of tears.

But are Christians always and necessarily pleasant people? Who could like the Wise Virgins in the Bible, for example? Is that one of the trials of it all – that one must be prepared to be disliked?

Catherine goes round the back of a Holborn church (St Alban the Martyr). V. strong smell of incense – candles 3d. each. Outside two ladies sitting by a small bowl electric fire on an upturned box talking about the vicar.

Woman like a Henry Moore figure. Tom's mother in the garden?

The viol, the violet and the vine . . . it sounded like – but could he *possibly* have preached on that text?

How irresponsible of Professor Monod to go down in M. Cousteau's bathyscope instead of coming to the I.A.I. meeting.

1954. One woman rings up to enquire about a man friend at his office and is answered by another woman, who gives her full details of his symptoms etc. 'He is taking anti-biotic. . . .'

At the same table in Hill's a man and a woman, middle-aged, perhaps working in the same office, are having a fascinating conversation about immersion heaters.

To Bob Smith   47 Nassau Road

22 April 1954

Dear Bob,

I had a letter from Jock recently. He liked *Jane and Prudence* very much. But the Americans and Continentals most definitely *don't* and now I am feeling a little bruised! In answer to my enquiries Cape tells me that 8 Americans and 10 Continental publishers saw and 'declined' (that seems to be the word) *Excellent Women* and they are still plodding on with *J. & P.* So humble yourself, Miss Pym, and do not give yourself airs.

Best wishes and love,

Barbara

I look out of the window of the Kardomah and see a pale, moony youth, though with a rather sullen expression, selling a newspaper – *Individual Action* – Anarchist Publication – in huge letters on a poster.

September. Portugal. The fluty, well-bred English voices in the Portuguese bus – rising above the chatter of the natives – talk even of Harrods. And 'Everything's so clean – *spotless*. The people are so obliging.' The advantages of holidaying in a feudal country.

7 September. The Englishwoman (about 50) is almost aggressively sunburnt, displays her rather scraggy neck and chest in a low-cut cotton dress. She sits on a canvas chair, wearing sunglasses and a scarf on her head, meditatively picking the skin off her nose which is peeling. NB. This is me, on the last morning at Foz do Arelho.

Driving through the Portuguese villages one notices and comments (British reaction) on some irrelevant things, objects like a run-over cat or dog lying on the dusty road.

Lisbon, Hotel Metropole. Near the Moorish style railway station. Dark little room looking into a well. I can see them washing up at 11 o'clock at night. The lower part of the walls covered with striped canvas like luggage (it's like living in a suitcase), the dim light and the grey iron bedstead like a French film. Setting for a Graham Greene novel.

Estoril is very like Bournemouth except that the beach is much smaller. On the promenade sits an old man with a stall of secondhand objects. Some of the jewellery, rings, etc must surely have belonged to exiled royalty.

I cannot reach up to pluck the prickly balls of a plane tree. Once it might have looked young, charming and gay, now only middle-aged and eccentric.

5 October. This afternoon I painted streaks in my hair with process white; later blew up a paper bag and popped it. It made a splendid noise.

On the 26th of June 1905 (according to the tablet which I can see when I peer down the steps) the men's convenience in the middle of Fleet Street, crossing over to Fetter Lane, was opened.

Since reading *Maiden Voyage* (when I was in Portugal) and the *Journal* I have been besotted with Denton Welch – am collecting and reading everything.

10 October. Today finished my fourth novel, about the anthropologists (no title as yet). Typed from 10.30 a.m. to 3.30 p.m. sustained by, in the following order, a cup of milky Nescafé, a gin and French, cold beef, baked potato, tomato and grated cheese, rice pudding and plums.

In a love affair it comes as something of a shock to a woman to realise that the man does not of necessity feel that everything about her is delightful (the long Victorian ear-rings with the old raincoat).

To receive a love letter and to be eating honey on a June morning (in a bed-sitting room in London). This was in 1939 – me in Upper Berkeley Street. The letter was from Jay and the honey from Jock (Miel d'Hymette) from Athens.

28 October. Lovely warm, windy morning. Rushing exuberantly into a Whitechapel train which seems to have a kind of glamour.

Perhaps to be loved is the most cosy thing in life and yet many people, women I suppose I mean, know only the uncertainties of loving, which is only sometimes cosy when one accepts one's situation (rarely perhaps).

18 November. At lunchtime went into Zwemmers Gallery to see some pottery by Picasso and lithographs by various people. I must have had a distressed look on my face for the man in charge (dark, youngish) told me I could take the price list round and then himself accompanied me round the exhibits. Perhaps he was cold and wanted to stretch his legs. Anyway he was very charming and paid me the compliment of treating me like a person who could afford to buy something. Then a man with a beard came in and he was much bolder than the rest of us and lifted the lid off a great soup tureen with a bold gesture. I shouldn't have dared. There was a wonderful big blue pottery duck, priced £80.

'I thought that Flotum made out that Mbum was a Bantu language,' said A.N.T. 'Oh he didn't try anything of that sort with *me*,' said M.B. indignantly.

31 December. Had lunch with Edward Gardner at the Olde Cocke Taverne – hadn't seen him for 20 years. This makes me feel like Prudence, as when I have lunch with married men contemporaries. With the years men get more bumbling and vague, but women get sharper.

29 March 1955. Today I am cross with D.F. and 'rebellious' but I just have a poached egg at the Kardomah (but a chocolate biscuit with my stewed apple) then go to Bourne and Hollingsworth and Dolcis and don't hurry back, yet I am back again by 2.20. Then I write in this little book.

At St Mary Aldermary (Canon Freddie Hood's church) one hears the shrill whirr of the telephone through the organ music.

From a bus in the Strand I see someone from Oxford days, looking very much the same, red in the face, hair only slightly touched with grey, a little stooping. He goes into Yate's Wine Lodge. Then I seem to remember hearing that he had not done well, been a disappointment, perhaps, even, taken to drink. (Did this occur to me *after* I had seen him enter the Wine Lodge or was the thought already in my mind?)

30 April. At the Women's University Settlement I see Miss Casson wearing a dress that I sent to their jumble sale some time ago – and very nice it looks. Bob and I have lunch and then walk in the park among the young green trees but he feels that Nature is not enough so we go into the Church of the Annunciation at Marble Arch – so near the Cumberland Hotel. Lofty but impressive with the lingering smell of incense. Fine red brocade-covered sedilia and a marble side-table – did the vicar bring them back from Italy? As we are standing there Bob says 'Oh I wish I were still in the Church of England'.

4 May. I give blood in the crypt of St. Martin in the Fields. The donors are all rather ordinary-looking people – the women burdened by shopping baskets. I can imagine (for a novel) a little, frail laden woman saying 'Oh I have given blood' and putting others to shame. My right arm aches so that I can hardly write – is there any connection, I wonder?

5 May. The knowledge might come to me – and I dare say it would be a shock – that one wasn't a particularly nice person (selfish, unsociable, uncharitable, malicious even).

15 May. I went to All Saints Notting Hill with Bob to High Mass. On the way we passed Westbourne Grove Baptist Church and heard records of hymns blaring out. How trying to live opposite! It would surely work on one's conscience to be lying in bed when such music was going on. All Saints is splendidly Catholic – 3 priests. Sean MacAteer (whom I know) was the celebrant. We began with Asperges (later at tea Hilary asked what was the connection between Asperges and asparagus). The three priests in their lime green vestments with bands and birettas look like dolls bobbing up and down. Fr Twisaday, the vicar, is an elderly dried up celibate, irritable and tetchy. He fidgets in the pulpit, times things alarmingly with pauses so that one wonders if he's just forgotten what he was going to say and will fall down in a fit. The sermon, urging us to keep Ascension Day as a day of obligation, was quite good. Then he remembered a notice about a meeting in the Albert Hall and began talking about that, all mixed up – how many tickets to send for, etc. Apparently he lives in a large vicarage with a private oratory – the only telephone is there and he doesn't like the curates being rung up.

WHAT IS MY NEXT NOVEL TO BE? It can begin with the shrilling of the telephone in Freddie Hood's church and end with the flame springing up – the new fire on Easter Saturday in the dark church. Hope and a blaze of golden forsythia round the font. But what about the middle?

When starting to tell a story you have to choose exactly the point to plunge in. Perhaps on a fine Spring afternoon at the induction of a new vicar – 'We had had an early lunch....'

20 May. With Bill H. of Twentieth Century Fox to see a play at the Polish Candlelight Club in Chepstow Villas. The Polish lady apologises because the Ladies cloakroom isn't very nice – but I want to say 'Oh but it's *splendid!*'

Falling in love takes away spontaneity because you're always thinking of things to say or write.

'You never asked about my furniture,' he said.
'No, there seemed so many other things to talk about.'
(They all come before her in her imagination – but in *his* is only a wardrobe or a table.)

'I am no longer convinced of the validity of Anglican orders,' he said rather stiffly – and, indeed, how else could he have said it for it was not a cosy subject – the approach to the door in Farm Street on a cold Winter evening.

2 July. Back at my own church, on a cool greeny-grey English Sunday. We start with a George Herbert hymn – 'King of Glory, King of Peace' – very English, like a damp overgrown churchyard. What different conceptions one could have of God according to the country one was in – those sun-baked cemeteries in Marseilles.

He had solved the problem of how to end the letter by putting 'Yours in haste'. I was astonished – I could not imagine such a thing.

15 July. Went into St Alban's Holborn mainly because I was frustrated at not getting a lettuce in Leather Lane market and it seemed a cool and quiet place. Inside the candles burn to St Alban – big ones. I lit one and put money in the box (like Denton). Over the confessional which has purple curtains, a violet coloured stole is flung. Outside the church is a courtyard, round which are the Stations of the Cross, with a seat where I sit and read the parish magazine. Don't quite like to smoke or read Proust.

20 August. Saw today: a woman with bright purple hair, her expression under it all understandably surprised; two well-dressed upper-class women, chinless; an elderly fragile clergyman and his wife, arm-in-arm, she with the remains of elegance. When the Winter comes we can read Denton again. October to March are his months.

24 August. Saw today a nun coming out of a telephone box. An early Betjeman – Mount Zion in touch with the Infinite.

8 September. In the office 3.55 p.m. Even at this moment some dreadful thing may be happening – a husband deciding to leave his wife, a love affair being broken, somebody dying, languishing with hopeless love or quarrelling about the Church of South India in the Edgware Road as I nearly did with Bob on Sunday. And I sit typing, revising and 'translating' Harold Gunn's ms [changing the American spelling], waiting for tea.

13 October. To the Proust exhibition with Bob – a rather reverent atmosphere – odd-looking, peering women. How Marcel must have driven his printers mad with all his corrections! Many photographs and portraits. Scott-Moncrieff looks not at all as I had imagined – a rather round-faced young man in uniform with tartan trews.

15 October. In the train going to East Croydon. Rereading all of Denton now, beginning with *Maiden Voyage.* 'Nothing could be gayer than a red lacquer coffin,' he says (p.152). Oh darling Denton....
Less Than Angels out on Monday. Rather dreaded. Denton says (p.195) 'I thought how nice it would be to have burnt sacrifices offered to me when I was dead.'

21 October. Reading *In Youth is Pleasure.* D's favourite adjective is 'charming'.

23 October. Went for a walk along the river with Bob – from Hammersmith Bridge along towards Putney, past Harrod's Furniture Depository. It is *vast* when you get up to it, pinky brown brick and 'Grinling Gibbons' decorations, swags of fruit etc. Many blank, blind-looking windows, some a little open. Inside what! One likes to imagine acres of decaying furniture riddled with woodworm and white ants. Great trunks of musty clothes. I suggested furniture brought back from India in 1912 for which the owner had never had a flat big enough. Nearby is a building that looks like a kind of chapel and, of course, the Turkish domes of the main building. Down the front white marks. Bird droppings? We know about the Dominion of the Birds.

I noticed in church last Sunday how young some hymn writers die.

3 November. Evening out with Bill H. pub visiting. Standing with feet hurting a little at bars, one all mirrors and mahogany and happy little queer couples – another semi-Moorish in decor in Leicester Square wedged in between two cinemas.
It was to have been an evening of seduction (?) in the office over the Rialto cinema, the room lit by the pinky glow from the neon signs outside. A balcony with an interesting view – packed humanity round Lyons and the Prince of Wales Theatre. But it didn't turn out quite as he wished. How hungry I was eating ham sandwiches, why don't men think of eating more? Then I wanted to go to the lavatory

but the cloakroom was on another floor and had to be unlocked and we *couldn't* find the right keys! Got the mortice key stuck in the lock. All the time I was striking matches and feeling more and more uncomfortable. But there was such a strong element of farce that one couldn't help laughing! Eventually to a pub in Rupert Street (The Blue Posts) where the landlord preceded me up the stairs apologising for not very good provision for Ladies Toilet. It was a large room with a big mirror over the mantelpiece and tables with chairs piled on them. The kind of room that might be used for a meeting. In a corner and up some steps the door leading to 'the toilet'. Quite adequate! Why are people always apologising to me for such things when one wants only the bare essentials.

December. Feast of St Barbara. I began talking about my novels, whether I should go on writing about the clergy etc. Then it occurred to me what a bore I was being and I had the idea of a young man walking with the elderly female novelist, worrying about the gathering darkness and the park closing and should he take her to tea at Stewart's or the Marble Arch Corner House or would it be sherry time or what?

On TV I thought that women have never been more terrifying than they are now – the curled head ('Italian style'), the paint and the jewellery, the exposed bosom – no wonder men turn to other men sometimes.

Shrove Tuesday and St Valentine 1956. Back at the office 'better'. On these occasions and perhaps on occasions of unhappiness too one might unburden oneself to one's hairdresser and enjoy the cosiness of non-intellectual conversation. Wilmet can do this when Piers has been unkind. Hilary was told by a woman whose daughter was having trouble with her husband, 'You see we have discovered that he is a sodomist.' How dreadful it sounds in a full plummy tone or dark and hushed.

31 May. Corpus Christi. Benediction and procession at All Saints with Bob. It was advertised in *The Church Times* – priests were asked to wear chasubles (?) and 'plain cottas'. Afterwards in the church hall we met Sean MacAteer. He has charm, wrinkles his nose when he smiles. Such a display of charm is surprising, even a little shocking. Later when we are in a pub, Fr James comes in with the thurifer.

Endings: Fr Bode beaming through his spectacles and saying 'Oh but you mustn't leave us – there's the bazaar, the outing to Runnymede, and the party to welcome Fr — .'

21 September. Greenwich. 34 Croom's Hill where Denton lived. It stands back a little between 32 and 36 – square and flat with a nice front door and fanlight. Three floors, white painted windows, dull red brick, net half-curtains. Green plant (azalea?) in upper window. Tiny patch of rather bald grass in front with dustbins. I sat down on the low stone wall opposite by the park with my umbrella up for it was raining and gazed for a few minutes, but I saw nobody.

5 October. Headline in *Daily Mirror*: Secret Love of Vanished Vicar (splendid hymn metre).

All over *The Times* and *Telegraph* ladies (often titled) are forced to sacrifice their minks – sometimes 'going abroad' – the picture it conjures up – one wonders.

January 1957. One talks so gaily about 'old loves', but there comes a time when they really are *old*.

August. At a writers' conference at Swanwick. It really makes one despair when someone gets up and asks if publishers like chapters to be all the same length.
Meet a man who has 'an amorphous mass' of humorous material and a big shapeless novel that can't be controlled.

Dulcie could make some kind of shopping list which might have on it 'Husband for Viola'.

26 October. Staying with Ailsa. In the afternoon we went in the car on a Denton pilgrimage. It was a fine but sunless afternoon, the sky grey-white. Many lovely beech trees in autumn colours – carpets of leaves in the woods. We went through Plaxol to Crouch – notice a pub, the Rose and Crown. Crouch is a straggling village with apple orchards. We drove on then came to a board saying Middle Orchard on the right. There were two houses, one near the road. You go down a short grassy lane, bumpy, to get to Middle Orchard. It is a clapboard house, white (with grey and black) with a balcony on the side nearest the road. Two men were working in the garden or orchard between the two houses. We didn't speak to anyone.

Mr Neale (OUP) entertained Mrs Wyatt, Carol Robson and BP to lunch today. Mrs R. is rather beautiful but nails not quite worthy.

When the woman's daughter (who had divorced and remarried) came to tea with her new husband, the mother shows her disappointment by not making any fresh cakes and giving them 'just a bit of sponge and some biscuits'.

Dreadful scene in library. Viola and Aylwin overheard by Dulcie and Miss Foy. He is talking in a Henry Jamesian way 'There is – as it were – somebody else'. Can it be me? Dulcie wonders, almost in dread, but it is Laurel.

8 April 1958. How would she eat when alone? Half a lobster and a glass of Chablis at Scott's – or baked beans on toast and Coca Cola in the Kenbar at Barkers?

29 April. Last week we went down to the little room (at the I.A.I.), DF, Mrs Nadel and I and opened the trunks of the late Professor S. F. Nadel. In the top of the trunks brightly coloured African rugs or hangings – underneath the notebooks tidily packed. Notes neatly annotated and indexed but some in German shorthand. Even Mrs Nadel cannot read them now.

Sunday morning early. Two strange people in church in front of me. He in a hand-knitted 'Norwegian' pullover, she in a raincoat with tartan-lined hood and black lace mantilla. Both with rather new-looking English missals.

A Glass of Blessings published on 14 April. Only 3 reviews up to 29 April, none wholly good. My humour deserts me when I am dealing with romance, I am tone-deaf to dialogue, am moderately amusing. Reviewers all women. Young?

17 May. A station wagon draws up outside the home of the Siamese diplomats next door and out get two Buddhist priests in orange robes. We wait to see them leave – two of the servants come out and a basket, obviously containing food and drink is put in the car. Later the priests themselves come out and are driven away by the (English) chauffeur. I wonder if the appearance of two English clergymen would arouse such interest in the suburbs of Bangkok.

15 June. Wellington House Lydden. Fête on the Saturday, washing up at the back of the tea marquee among rank nettles and elder bushes. By my bed Honor has put *Memorials of Frances Ridley Havergal* (1836–1879). How almost enviable were the lives of those Victorian lady hymn writers – the leisurely travel abroad, faith and purpose in life. In her study 'her American typewriter', her 'harp-piano' at which she composed hymns. Somebody had given her 'A Journal of Mercies' in which every day she noted down the particular mercy she had received.

Young man from the Clarendon Press. Low Church Anglican, plays cricket, likes chess, bumbling. Married with wife who looks very like him – untidy curling hair.

12 May 1959. The telephone wakes me up ringing – it is 1 a.m. It goes on and on but I don't answer it. It could be the stolid unimaginative persistence of a wrong number or the sly voice of a 'nasty' caller. In a book it might be an inconsiderate woman friend. Young man sitting opposite to me has 3 sausage rolls, a roll, baked beans and chips. Not a very well balanced meal for a hot day. In the little Lyons it's cool and dark with the air conditioning.

In the Buttery reading old *Tatlers*: 'sincere and reverent ceremony' – describing a society wedding – so one would hope!

January 1960. Evensong and Benediction in a N. London church, rather sparsely attended. The young man in the college scarf looking for he knows not what and fleeing when he is offered tea in the Church Hall afterwards, or an older man who has lost his faith coming out of nostalgia and perhaps the memory of a beautiful server or acolyte.

4 February. Going to the vet in Lancaster Gate to fetch Tati. Waiting room has large table with copies of *The Field* and *Country Life.* Round the walls photographs of grateful patients, some with their owners! The whole place slightly shabby as if the animals have made it so. Disconcerting cat's cry from the cattery. Where is it? One is not allowed to see the animals. The vet's assistant is almost excessively reassuring, more so than a human doctor, as if he expects tears, even hysterics, which they must often get.

Laurie Fleming stays at home with his mother – does the flowers beautifully – Is it now the unmarried *son* who does this?

In the church one of the servers appears with startlingly golden hair – curls falling over his eyes give him an air of sickly Victorian piety.

To Bob Smith in Ibadan   40 Brooksville Avenue

21 October 1960

Dearest Bob,

This morning I had the proofs of my new book which is called *No Fond Return of Love,* the title they made me have instead of *A*

Thankless Task. My heart sinks rather as I open the book and begin reading – who can enjoy it? I wonder. Why isn't it much better? Then I look over some of the bits I like to cheer me up. Hazel is going to correct the proofs for me. They say it will come out in the spring.
    Love,

                                                                Barbara

St Valentine's Day. In the flower shop at Ludgate Circus – a queue of people – but they are all women!

[*This is the first letter to Philip Larkin, who had written to suggest that he might write a review article about her next novel when it was published.*]

                                                    40 Brooksville Avenue

                                                        1 March 1961

Dear Mr Larkin,

    Thank you very much for your letter. I was very pleased and flattered to think that you should have had the idea of writing an essay on my books and am grateful to you for telling me about it, even though it was too late to do it. Perhaps, if you still feel like doing it, I could let you know when my next is ready – (so far only four chapters written). It will be my seventh which seems a significant number.
    N.F.R.L. (originally called *A Thankless Task*!) has had a better reception than I thought it would have, and your letter certainly encourages me to go on.
    Yours sincerely,

                                                                Barbara Pym

1 March. Soup, jelly and bread and butter – *that's* not much of a meal for a man I think as I sit in the Kardomah.

8 March. Sophia finds an exquisite piece of claw sheath, like mother of pearl, in the cat's basket.

11 April 1961. Rome. Fr John Francis Gordon knocks back a Tio Pepe at the bar while we wait to be called for our flight. He also buys up all the little bottles of brandy on the plane – but he is nice (and Irish). Many nuns waiting at Leonardo da Vinci airport waving handkerchiefs and with bunches of flowers to welcome back a Mother Superior – we are surrounded by them. Near the hotel an illuminated sign shines continuously in the night BANCO SANTO

SPIRITO (on a par with TAKE COURAGE).

Rome I.A.I. Meeting [meeting of the I.A.I. Executive Council]. Lunch at Roxy Cinema Café (which is very good) then I had a short siesta while Ailsa went to the Officers' Meeting. The first Reunion was at 6. A strange collection of people most of them carrying or wearing raincoats. I felt like Prudence, overdressed in cream Courtelle and a pink and white striped carnation from the spray sent to us by the Tourist Bureau. Then we all moved over to the Ritz for the 'informal reunion' – walls covered with pleated silk, gold plush sofas and chairs, pictures of Roman emperors – a strange decor. Plenty of drinks and canapés. Then a very slow dinner at the Hotel Sporting with DF, Evelyn Forde, Kenneth Robinson and Ailsa. Afterwards for a drink in the bar at the underground station – v. draughty, loud juke box. The Chairman [Gouverneur Mueller] is seen approaching – a bored figure in a Homburg hat, his luggage being carried. He joins us. A strange setting altogether.

13 April. Meeting 9.30 to 12.45 p.m. Then lunch at Ministry of Foreign Affairs, 'too much wine and too much marble' as Contessa Grottanelli said. Each lady had a red rose by her plate and Mel Herskovits told me how he mixed tobacco in a great bowl.

14 April. After the Lugard Lecture we went to a cocktail party at the Grottanelli's flat, high up in a rather squalid building in Largo Arenula. Crossing over the square we went underground and saw the thin cats (mostly grey tabby or tortoiseshell) which are said to be fed by elderly ladies. At the party, as we were leaving, a nice glimpse of Vinigi in his study, handing out offprints of an article to admiring Africans. Then a strange dinner with Ailsa, Lucy Mair, Kenneth Robinson and Nana Nketsia at Checco. Much Chianti. Back in N. Nk's large Ghana Embassy car and the first glimpse of the Spanish Steps massed with red, pink and white azaleas.

20 April. To Amalfi and then went to Ravello on the bus. Acres of lemon groves all covered with matting and branches so that you don't see them until you are close to. It is for the lemon groves that one loves Italy – also for oranges with stalks and leaves still on them and the little bundles of dried lemon leaves which you unwrap to reveal a few delicious lemon-flavoured raisins in the middle. The cathedral at Ravello – pulpit supported by lions of marble, walking, their legs going forward. Also in the garden of the Villa Rifolo a little marble lion licking its cub.

The Church ought to have a lot of summer festivals – Corpus Christi or St Peter and St Paul would do – so that we can have an evening mass with lots of incense, all doors open and hymns with soppy words and Romish tunes.

The new Archbishop of Canterbury has a lovely lap for a cat.

A rather rich lunch hour in St Paul's churchyard. All the people sitting on seats with lunch, knitting etc, raising their faces to the mild September sun. I go round to the back where the pieces of broken marble are – it is all white and beautiful, looks good enough to eat – broken off bits of friezes and urn stands. In the middle of such a pile, as if on the rocks at the sea-side sits a woman (middle-aged of course) drinking tea from a plastic cup, the traffic swirling in front of her. I pass the mulberry tree, but it is too late for there to be squashed mulberries on the pavement. Coming round the other side and down by the shops I go to the secondhand bookshop. There is a band playing on the steps of St Paul's which can be heard in the shop. It is a boy's band and they play the Pilgrims' Chorus from *Tannhäuser* at which point inconsequential conversation starts in the shop between the owner and a woman about dogs/cats. As I go out the band plays 'Land of Hope and Glory!' Surely something for me here. John and Ianthe in the churchyard and Rupert and Penelope hearing the band?

To Philip Larkin   40 Brooksville Avenue
                                                        23 September 1961

Dear Mr Larkin,

When I had your letter it seemed impossible that I should ever get on with another novel, but now I am nearly half-way through and the last part is usually quicker than the first, so perhaps I shall finish something by the spring. Then, if it ever gets to the stage of proof copies, I'll ask my publisher to send you one, so that you can decide if you'd like to do anything about it. But even if you don't I should like you to have it because you seem to like – or at least to understand – poor Wilmet and Keith. I think incubus or familiar describes him well. I'm considering what you said about bringing characters from one's earlier books into later ones and I agree that one does have to be careful. It can be a tiresome affectation. With me it's sometimes laziness – if I need a casual clergyman or anthropologist I just take one from an earlier book. Perhaps really one should take such a very minor character that only the author recognises it, like a kind of superstition or a charm.
    Yours sincerely,

                                                        Barbara Pym

40 Brooksville Avenue
15 October 1961

Dear Mr Larkin,

Your novel I liked was called *A Girl in Winter,* but written quite a long time ago, I think? Did you write any more and why didn't you go on being a novelist? Because you preferred to be a poet or other things pressed too heavily? I apologise for this string of questions. Today my sister was tidying her desk and the old photograph albums reminded me of that lovely poem of yours.

My novel goes on, but slowly, so probably all the Literary Editors (why do I give them capital letters?) will have changed or died by the time it is in proof so you can relax for about a year and not think too much of what may have been a rash suggestion on your part (though I am still pleased at the thought of it!). Unfortunately I *am* the Assistant Editor of *Africa,* though I quite enjoy it, and I also have to see all the books we publish through the press. The only thing is that it takes too much time and energy. A pity one has to earn one's living – why isn't there a fund for *middle-aged* writers to have a year off to write a novel! No – Hull has no anthropology department, so I shouldn't think you'd take *Africa.* Incidentally I have never been to Africa, nor have I a degree in Anthropology, but I know the jargon now – as esoteric as the terminology of jazz!

Yours sincerely,

Barbara Pym

40 Brooksville Avenue
11 December 1961

Dear Mr Larkin,

The novel is getting on – no title yet, of course, and none of the splendid collection I have seems to fit it. Now I have to force myself to type some of the earlier chapters because that's the only way I can tell what it's going to be like – whether it is worth going on, and all those other depressing thoughts that come. But I can see now that it *will* get finished if I am spared. No – nobody has ever written about the 'art' of my books – sometimes they have been well reviewed – other times not at all. *Excellent Women* was best received – *A Glass of Blessings* worst!

I *can't* imagine you writing anything 'knowing and smart' (not even Jazz) so it must be only your own harsh self criticism – of course being so young when you wrote it, it would certainly be different from what you'd write now. Perhaps it is better not to publish anything before one's thirty – I mean novels. I wrote *Some Tame Gazelle* when I was 22. Then rewrote it about ten years later.

I don't think you are a 500-words-a-day-on-the-Riviera sort of writer – perhaps nobody is now. What would one do for the rest of the day, having spent the morning writing? Lead a worthless life, I suppose, and how pleasant it might be for a bit. Then one would get involved with the English church – there would be no escape.

Yours sincerely,

Barbara Pym

40 Brooksville Avenue
25 February 1962

Dear Mr Larkin,

Thank you for your letter which gave me the rather disquieting picture of you sitting, pen-in-hand – before a daunting pile of my novels. You will be relieved to hear that progress on the seventh is very slow, but perhaps sure – I sometimes wonder. In any case, I don't think I've written to you since seeing your very charming tribute in the *Guardian* which gave me so much pleasure that it really absolves you from doing anything else.

If you feel like asking me anything about my 'works' please do – the less great are probably far more explicit than the great, so it wouldn't be like asking Mary McCarthy. On the other hand it is often better not to know things. I liked a poem of yours in the *Listener* some weeks ago – one rather puzzling line, but poets are not to be asked to explain why and how.

The Geography of Communication – sounds like a poem – I will look out for it – not, I think, on *my* station bookstall, which has lurid paperbacks, women's magazines and an occasional surprise like *The Times Ed. Sup.*, but perhaps at Paddington. OUP publishes our books too – we have a sort of joking relationship with them.

Yours,

B.P.

To Bob Smith in Ibadan   40 Brooksville Avenue
                                             9 March 1962

Dearest Bob,

Excuse this Institute paper, but Friday afternoon seems a good time to write to you, as I make it a rule never to do anything that may upset me for the weekend and so like to put *Africa* and our irritating authors out of my mind.

We are now in the throes of Lent at St L's, as you may imagine – Imposition of Ashes on Wednesday *evening* – Stations of the Cross tonight. I hope you are getting some of these things. Lent must seem odd in the tropics, but no doubt you are used to it by now. Hazel thought somebody might have a *bouillabaisse* flown over from Marseilles for Ash Wednesday. But fish and chips in Lyons was perhaps more of a deprivation.

St Barnabas Pimlico: I have only been there once to the wedding of an anthropologist friend (Ioan Lewis who married the daughter of the Master of Balliol whom he met at a bus stop). The church I used to go to when we lived there was St Gabriel's, Warwick Sq., the model of the church in *Excellent Women*, really.

Much love,

Barbara

For my next – the middle-aged, or elderly novelist and the young man who admires her and is taken in by her.

Sister Dew would lower her voice and talk of 'a very big operation', meaning, of course, something female. Men were somehow rendered inferior by this.

22 March 1962. In Gamage's basement I buy (for 1/–) a little Italian bowl with a lemon and leaves painted inside it. It really pleases me, although it is chipped and I begin to wonder if I am getting to the stage when objects could please more than people or (specifically) men.

A woman living in the country who has had a hopeless love for a man (wife still living perhaps or religious scruples), then, when he is free she finds that after all he means nothing to her – is this the reward of virtue, this nothingness? Or an enviable calm – (He then, presumably, goes and marries a young girl).

Mervyn's general dislike of books and reading (commoner than one supposes in a librarian) should be emphasised.

An old woman living in a village with her two husbands (a modern instance of polyandry) one divorced – but, poor thing, unable to cope on his own.

To Bob Smith in Ibadan   I.A.I.

15 June 1962

Dearest Bob,

I am glad you have got the Ife lectureship, though I could really wish you had got a job in England again. The other evening (Thursday late shop-opening) I emerged exhausted from Marks and Spencers wondering where on earth I could go to sit down (without having to order a Wimpy or anything like that) and suddenly thought of All Saints Margaret Street, which turned out to be deliciously cool and restful and only one lady there – no violet-stoled priests lurking to force Anglican ladies to make their Confessions. (That sounds like one of Mr Kensit's pamphlets in the Protestant Truth Society, doesn't it.)

The P.C.s [the vicar of St Lawrence's and his wife] are on holiday and have done an exchange with Fr Francis Ibbott from Norfolk. He has come to the vicarage with his house-keeper whom he acquired in Luton. He is rather nice and sings splendidly. The P.C.s apparently locked up their bedroom and the study. Wouldn't you think that a bit odd, if you were the exchanging clergyman – as if they didn't trust you? Or is that naive of me?

Love,

Barbara

40 Brooksville Avenue

13 October 1962

Dearest Bob,

Hilary has just slipped along to the Jumble Sale at St Ann's Hall. She was curious to see *their* hall and also thought she might pick up a bit of Fabergé or something. We haven't seen Richard Roberts (met with me in summer 1962) again yet as he is still away. We did like him so much and hope to see him again.

The Yoruba is out of print but being reprinted – in the meantime I have sent you by seamail (on Friday) a spare copy of my own. Of course it is a mere summary and rather inadequate now, though it gives one some idea. It contains some of Miss Pym's earliest work though you might not think so from her later writings. How nice of you to want my new novel – a few people do, I think, though not really enough. I asked Wren Howard [at Cape] about paperbacks and Penguins and he said they had tried but without success to get my books done so perhaps it is true what I heard that you must have sold ten thousand in hard covers before the paperback people will consider taking a book. Incidentally Jock is wrong about Daniel George having left Cape – he is still there in his little back room, I'm glad to say. I have tried to read *T. Shandy* and it is the sort of book I should like to like but all that really appeals to me is that marbled page and the blank page – which vary in beauty acording to what edition you have. Perhaps it could be a book for old age.

Love,

Barbara

40 Brooksville Avenue

15 December 1962

Dearest Bob,

I thought, surging through Smith's in Fleet Street today, 'I'm just a tired-looking middle-aged woman to all those (mostly young) people, yet I have had quite a life and written (or rather published) six novels which have been praised in the highest circles.' Did I tell you (I think not?) that I had a charming letter from *Lady* David Cecil (Rachel, daughter of the late Desmond MacCarthy) saying how much she had enjoyed *No Fond Return?* Did you ever read her book, *Theresa's Choice* – a delicious portrait of Lord D. and her other suitors.

My next is getting on, quite flowing now. I am at the depressed stage when I begin to type out some of the early chapters and think that not much of it will do – I can only hope that I will get through this stage, but my first four chapters always seem so dragged out, even when I rewrite the beginning. It is nice of you to have wanted a new BP for Christmas. Angus Wilson has got to look very old, I think, a ruby-coloured face and cloud of snow white hair, not at *all* as he used to look. I heard him give a lecture on 'Evil in the English Novel' at University College – very good, as a matter of fact.

I had Evelyn Waugh's life of R. Knox (out of the splendid public library on the way home) and thought what a pity it was he ever went over to Rome and how beastly it must be for a priest to do it and become a *Roman* priest.

Love,

Barbara

I.A.I.

11 January 1963

Dearest Bob,

I am writing this in the office on a Friday afternoon, surrounded by the raw material for the April *Africa*, the proofs of various books, and a shopping bag containing tins of cat food, frozen fish cakes, packet soups etc.

The first thing you wanted to know was about Richard and Jock. The latter had told me of meeting R and his friend, he thought they were nice but rather overawed by Elizabeth Taylor, who was there at the time. Richard dined with us at the end of November so we got a fuller picture from him of the 'literati' who flock to see Jock. *He* thought Elizabeth seemed very bored, but knowing her I should say it was her usual manner which conceals her shyness. Hilary and I are very fond of Richard – *we* dined with *him* in December – we met Maurice Quick, a nice young man called John something, and a young Siamese action painter just over here and it was all very cosy. Now Richard is in Nassau with his parents and is, I believe, intending to go to Mexico. He sent us a very pagan Christmas card and also a beautiful postcard from Nassau.

I have finished my novel and Hazel has read it in MS, but we are still struggling to find a title. It should really be called *The Canon's Daughter* or *An Unsuitable Attachment* but Cape won't like either of those, so we are casting about wildly and the best we have found so far is *Reserved for Crocodiles*, which is eye-catching indeed – and after all any title can be written into the text! I still have to revise and improve a little – this time there are rather too many references to pink paraffin, as there were to Tio Pepe and gin in *A Glass of Blessings*. I am reading *Morte D'Urban*, an American RC novel, very funny.

Love,

Barbara

40 Brooksville Avenue

8 February 1963

Dearest Bob,

Such an ironical thing happened – I had started a letter to you last weekend on my typewriter, telling you that on Friday last, 1st Feb., we had a burglary and leaving the letter in the typewriter to finish later. But on Monday, 4th Feb., the thief or thieves broke in again, this time taking the typewriter with the letter in it! So I suppose you will never get *that* letter. I can't remember quite how much I told you, except that they hadn't taken the MS of my novel, but only small items of jewellery and Hilary's camera. But on Monday they took the typewriter, an electric fire and some silver. The police of course came very quickly and have the matter in hand though I don't suppose they will ever catch him or them. I think it was having it *twice* that was so horrid – of course it was done during the day when we were both out and the neighbours heard nothing. Everyone is being very careful now, but it gives one an insecure feeling. Yet all our friends have had to undergo this, so why not us – I suppose all experience however unpleasant can be turned to good effect in fiction.

I have finished my novel and the best title seems to be *An Unsuitable Attachment*, though as 'they' are almost certain not to like that I have got several more titles in reserve. Hazel and Hilary have both read it and seemed to like it, but I am still making a few final improvements before sending it to the publisher. I feel the effort of it all is so great that I shall never write another, yet even now vague ideas begin to turn over in my mind.

We had terrible 'voltage reductions', no heat from electric fires and no TV picture till 10.30 p.m. Luckily we have coal and paraffin too, though, and we managed to avoid frozen pipes and bursts which is a great blessing. Even the 'toilet' at the vicarage of St Lawrence the Martyr, Chevening Road, was frozen up on one occasion.

Mrs P.C. [the vicar's wife]. 'How are you off for candles, dear!'

B.P. 'Oh, all right, thank you, and we haven't had any total blackouts yet.'

Mrs P.C. 'Well, don't forget there's plenty of candles in the church dear – I should take some if I were you.'

Love.

Barbara

To Philip Larkin   40 Brooksville Avenue

24 February 1963

Dear Mr Larkin,

Many thanks for your letter – and how quickly the time goes. And yet in other ways this winter has seemed endless. Was there a time when we were not forever on our knees filling paraffin stoves? I hope you are well (perhaps centrally?) heated – poets should not have to worry about how to keep pipes from freezing and all that dreariness – but I suppose it should be part of every novelist's experience. (Though I suppose one could make too much of it!)

I sent my novel to Cape last week but don't know yet what they think of it. I feel it can hardly come up to *Catch 22* or *The Passion Flower Hotel* for selling qualities but I hope they will realise that it is necessary for a good publisher's list to have something milder. It is called (at present) *An Unsuitable Attachment*, which I don't think they'll like, so I have various other alternatives. I don't think they can make one have 'Love' in the title again. Did I tell you that there was a Librarian in it? Of course only in a small way – the Library is rather like ours at the International African Institute – not to be compared with *University* Libraries and *their* problems, need I say....I will certainly let you have a proof copy when it gets to that stage but please don't think that I *expect* you to do anything unless you feel like it, but anything in the way of a review would of course be very welcome, as I don't suppose I shall get all that many! In many ways one gets to disregard reviews or lack of them as one goes on – seeing so many brilliant new works of fiction appearing, almost every week, and new young reviewers. But I am promised *The Naked Lunch* to read some time, so I shall see if I agree with Mary McCarthy or Philip Toynbee.

I was interested to read about you in John Wain's autobiography and also (somewhere else) that you wrote about two poems a year. But I do wish, as I've said before, that you would bring out another collection of your poems – surely the time is ripe?

Yours sincerely,

Barbara Pym

The Unpublished Novelist

The effect of the so-called Swinging Sixties made Barbara's novels seem unacceptable, especially to a publishing house like Cape which was beginning to specialise in what were then called 'contemporary' novels and whose list, as Barbara wryly remarked, consisted mainly of 'men and Americans'. In 1963 they rejected her novel An Unsuitable Attachment. *'Of course,' she wrote to Philip Larkin, 'it may be that this book is much worse than my others, though they didn't say so.' She would have been, as she always had been, willing to make any revisions her publisher thought necessary, but no one made any such suggestions.*

The unexpectedness and finality of this blow (since in that particular literary climate no other publisher would take it) severely damaged her self-confidence. She felt that it was her failure as a writer that was the reason for the rejection rather than that the times were unpropitious for her kind of novel, and for a while she mistrusted her own talents as well as her critical judgement.

She started several novels, one with an academic setting which she though might be more 'publishable' – but she was never satisfied with them and they were never completed or revised. At no time, in spite of suggestions made to her by well-meaning friends, would she ever compromise and write in a style or form that was not her own.

In 1968 she completed The Sweet Dove Died, *inspired, in part, by her fondness for her friend Richard Roberts, a young Bahamian who ran an antique shop. She sent the novel to various publishers (even, at one stage, under the name of Tom Crampton) but, in spite of its 'stronger' theme, it was no more acceptable than* An Unsuitable Attachment. *'Not the kind of novel', one publisher wrote, 'to which people are turning.'*

There were some bright spots. In October 1971 her friend Bob Smith published an article entitled 'How Pleasant to Know Miss Pym' in the journal Ariel, *the first critical appreciation of her work. In 1965 the BBC had serialised* No Fond Return of Love *on Woman's Hour and her novels remained on the shelves of public libraries in the Portway Reprint Series. The demand from her public was still there.*

In May 1971 she had an operation for breast cancer and made a good recovery. In 1974 she suffered a kind of stroke which had a curious effect, as of dyslexia, an inability to assemble the letters of some words correctly, a totally incapacitating disability for an indexer and proof-reader. She recovered from this quite quickly but was advised to retire from the Institute.

Hilary retired from the BBC in 1971 and in 1972 she had bought a cottage at Finstock, about 14 miles west of Oxford. Barbara had been living there at weekends and in a bed-sitting room in Balcombe Street during the week while she worked at the Institute. Now she settled with Hilary at Finstock, immersing herself in country life – jam-making, village activities (Finstock was a friendly, sociable place), the Local History Society. She now completed the novel that had been simmering in her mind for some time about four elderly people in an office and the effect of retirement upon two of them. She wrote it for her own enjoyment and for that of her friends, having, by then, little expectation of its being published.

In April 1975 she finally met Philip Larkin. They had been corresponding since 1961 when he had planned to write a review article of her next novel. Their meeting turned out to be like an incident in a Barbara Pym novel. Two shy and reserved people ('I shall probably be wearing a beige tweed suit or a Welsh tweed cape if colder. I shall be looking rather anxious, I expect'), they met at the Randolph Hotel in Oxford. Hardly had they sat down at a table in the bar when they were joined by a bluff, red-faced man, of the kind who attaches himself to strangers in hotels, who engaged them in jovial conversation for what seemed like hours.

H. H.

1963-1977

24 March 1963. To receive a bitter blow on an early Spring evening (such as that Cape don't want to publish *An Unsuitable Attachment* – but it might be that someone doesn't love you any more) – is it worse than on an Autumn or Winter evening? Smell of bonfire (the burning of rose prunings etc), a last hyacinth in the house, forsythia about to burst, a black and white cat on the sofa, a small fire burning in the grate, books and Sunday papers and the remains of tea.

1963 so far. A year of violence, death and blows.
The bad Winter up to the end of February without a break.
Death of Hugh Gaitskell.
Two burglaries.
My typewriter stolen.
My novel rejected by Cape.
Dr Beeching's plan for sweeping away of railways and stations.
Reading *The Naked Lunch.*
The Bishop of Woolwich's book *Honest to God.*
My novel rejected by Heath.
Tropic of Cancer by Henry Miller (60,000? copies sold on 1st day of publication [4th April]).
Daniel George's stroke.

To Philip Larkin   40 Brooksville Avenue

                                                           12 May 1963

Dear Mr Larkin,

Many thanks for your letter of several weeks ago. I liked to think of you at those Library Conferences – it is comforting to know that such things go on in this violent world. As for the teapots and hot water jugs left standing on the polished table (and it being marked in consequence), I found myself thinking 'What a fussy man' – but then it occurred to me that perhaps the Warden was a *woman*?

Your kind intention to write something about my novels may not after all be fulfilled because Cape have decided that they don't want to publish *An Unsuitable Attachment* after all! I write this calmly enough, but really I was and am upset about it and think they have treated me very badly, considering that I have been with them for thirteen years and published six novels, some of which have been fairly successful, even if the sales of the last two were rather modest. I was not altogether surprised because several other Cape authors have been similarly treated – I don't know whether you have heard any murmur of the distant rumblings in 30 Bedford Square as the new regime gets to work with axe and bulldozer, but the Cape list is now certainly different from what it was and naturally one hopes that Jonathan is turning in his grave.

Of course it may be that this novel is much *worse* than my others, though they didn't say so, giving their reason for rejecting it as their fear that with the present cost of book production etc. etc. they doubted whether they could sell enough copies to make a profit.

But I mustn't bore you with all this and apologise for having written this much in the role of indignant rejected middle-aged female author (a pretty formidable combination, don't you think?). Of course I am hoping that somebody else will have the goodness to take it. Robert Liddell, whom I have known for many years (he was one of the characters in *Some Tame Gazelle*) has suggested people I could approach in Longmans, Gollancz and Hutchinson, and I have also been urged to try Fabers, so we shall see. But it may be that none of them will want it – do you think the title unsaleable? I fear the attachment is not so unsuitable as the public (reading) might wish and perhaps it is altogether too mild a book for present tastes. But then that has always been a sort of fault of mine. It might be printed privately by that man in Ilfracombe who advertises in the *Church Times* – with a subsidy from the Ford Foundation perhaps. Or it could be cyclostyled and distributed privately to a few select persons. You as a Librarian will, I am sure, appreciate the niceties of all this. *How* to enter it in a bibliography and all that.

Having taken up so much with all this I must now say what I ought to have said first – how very glad I am to know that Fabers are going to bring out another collection of your poems. And about time too! This writing of about two poems a year is all very well, but... I presume it will include all my favourite ones (esp. 'Faith Healing') and that you won't leave any out? As for *Jill*, I shall be interested to read that because I have only read *A Girl in Winter* and that a long

216

time ago. In what way are you revising it? – I suppose only in details, because isn't a novel like a poem or a piece blown by a glassblower – once it is formed there is really nothing much you can do about it except tinker with details. Perhaps *I* should revise your novel and *you* mine. That might have interesting results.

Yes, I have a shrinking from publicity too, which is just as well as I seem to be doomed to failure and to sink down into obscurity, at present anyway. Yet I like to think that a few people will read what I have written.

I must again apologise for this boring and egotistical letter but you will, I'm sure, understand and make allowances. It ought to be enough for anybody to be the Assistant Editor of *Africa*, especially when the Editor is away lecturing for six months at Harvard, but I find it isn't quite.

With all good wishes,
Yours sincerely,

Barbara Pym

40 Brooksville Avenue

8 July 1963

Dear Mr Larkin,

Many thanks for your kind letter of astonishment and indignation. It was comforting to think of you leaving for a 'short tour of Midland Universities' and I hope it was comforting to *you* and 'successsful', if that is a suitable word.

Since I last wrote I have sent my book to Longmans, where I had an introduction, but they have decided not to publish it, and say what one had suspected, that 'novels like *An Unsuitable Attachment*, despite their qualities, are getting increasingly difficult to sell', though they did say it was 'most excellently written'. And of course the more one looks at the books now being published, not to mention the stirring events of this year [the Profumo scandal], the less likely it seems that anyone, except a very select few, would want to read a novel by me. I could almost offer my services to Dr Stephen Ward as a ghost writer, for he is a Canon's son and surely I could write about his *early* years if not the later ones.

Anyway I shall try a few more publishers before laying the book aside for ever. I thought I would try Macmillan and then perhaps Faber, though I would feel shy about accepting your kind offer to say a word to Charles Monteith. Because you haven't read the book and it may be hopeless for all you know! It is rather a mild book. I shall try to make my next (which I have almost started) less so!

Excuse this scrappy letter, finished off at the end of a working day, surrounded by material for the October *Africa* – need I explain or apologise further?

All good wishes –

Barbara Pym

5 June. Oh those meals with her – indigestible Italian food in Soho restaurants of which one wouldn't dare to see the kitchen. At least now they would not have to go to bed – no love only friendship or whatever this light irritability and boredom was called.

6 June. The middle-aged woman with an Italian lover (both academics) who comes over occasionally. His hatred of Naples and Neapolitans. Love of Guinness. He eats too quickly whereas she likes to linger over her food. He is preoccupied with death. After a strict Catholic upbringing the pagan layer has seeped through or oozed up to the top.

The (Presbyterian) Minister who complains that he has to work on Sundays and therefore ought to have another day off to make up for it. Yet outside his chapel we see the notice 'This is the day that the Lord has given – let us rejoice in it'.

14 August. A wet day. Hampstead, Keats' House. A pity it looks out on to some ugly modern houses. Inside it is rather austere and simple. The engagement ring he gave to Fanny Braun is a red stone (almandine: 'a garnet of violet tint' Concise Oxford Dictionary) set in gold. The curator has filled the conservatory with begonias, pelargoniums, geraniums, 'We try to keep it a thing of beauty,' he says. There are bunches of grapes hanging from the vine. How full of vines altogether Hampstead seems to be.

15 August. This afternoon to see the Henry Moore–Francis Bacon exhibition. It is a rather hot afternoon and the gallery (New London, Bond St) is underground so that the effect is claustrophobic which seems appropriate. The gallery is small and has all-over black carpet. The Bacon pictures look softer when you see them in the flesh than they do in hard glossy reproductions and the colours are beautiful. Some are of his friend. ('Not very *nice* to show your friend looking like that'). Most of the people looking at the pictures seem to be solitary. And this was better because comments always sound so silly. Later, walking in Bond Street, I see a young man sitting alone in a grand antique shop, presumably waiting for customers. A woman admirer might be a great nuisance always coming to see him.

Deborah has been 'taken up' by Monica an older woman who works as an 'Editor' in one of our great University Presses. She is a devout Anglo-Catholic and wants to have the cottage blessed. The vicar comes and there is a rather awkward ceremony with the cat putting her head in the Holy Water.Monica should go on rather about some man where she works – now getting past the age for loving detachment – gradually hardens into hostility so that she now dislikes and avoids men, is annoyed if one comes and sits by her in a bus.

To Philip Larkin   40 Brooksville Avenue

23 August 1963

Dear Mr Larkin,

Many thanks for your letter from Sark (who can be writing to me from *there*? I wondered suspiciously, not recognising your hand immediately). It was perhaps rash to buy a Panama hat though it will last you for the next thirty years or so – 32/6 seems expensive but not when you think of it as an *investment*.

I hope you did one or two poems – don't you carry your MS book about with you everywhere or write them on the backs of envelopes? I've often wondered what poets did, thinking that perhaps they had no need of the more material aids to writing. On a wet afternoon recently I went to Keats' house in Hampstead (never having been before) and saw that he had written two poems at least – inside his Ben Jonson and another book – Shakespeare, I think.

I like the idea of the Introduction for *The Whitsun Weddings* being anti-twenties – I suppose when you were at Oxford *nobody* came into The George wearing a silver lamé shirt or went around with a lizard on their shoulder or carried a toy kangaroo – and that was the early thirties when I was up. But surely there must have been *girls*, even in the austere one-bottle-of-wine a term forties – (shoulder-length pageboy hair, square shoulders and short skirts?). It must have been strange. *The Meagre Time* – don't you think quite a good title for a novel?

Since I last wrote I've sent my book to Macmillan, but they have returned it regretting it wasn't suitable for their list. So I have decided for the moment to lay it aside and start something else when I can. I don't feel that I can 'improve' *An Unsuitable Attachment* at present; though obviously it could *be* improved. I haven't the energy to do it and it might still be unacceptable whatever I did to it. Three people who have read it tell me it *isn't* below the standard of my others. (I'm incapable of judging now!) I did read it over very critically and it seemed to me that it might appear naive and unsophisticated, though it isn't really, to an unsympathetic publisher's reader, hoping for that novel about negro homosexuals, young men in advertising, etc.

If you would *like* to read it I should be very glad to send you one of my two copies, which are both idle at the moment. But I feel it would probably not be worth approaching Faber with it.

I see I haven't congratulated you on being elected to your College SCR (St John's?) – which I do most heartily – Was it Larkin, the Librarian (some problems of) or Larkin the poet – I suppose the latter.

All best wishes, etc,

Barbara Pym

40 Brooksville Avenue

9 October

Dear Mr Larkin,

Many thanks for your letter. After I had suggested you might like to read *An Unsuitable Attachment*, I began to feel it was rather an imposition, but having said it I felt it would be stupid to change my mind, so I have today posted my carbon copy of the MS to you. (To 'The Librarian' marked Personal). Once anything gets into *our* Library it seems to be swallowed up, so this MS may find itself classified as a thesis or something (not that I mean to cast doubts on the efficiency of your staff!). Anyway I hope it won't prove too awkward to handle.

You will see exactly why a *new* publisher wouldn't take it on, I think; the beginning is too vague, too many characters, and there's not enough plot. And who is the heroine? I think perhaps I *could* rewrite it some time, but not now, as I have started something else.

I hope you will have had a nice 'tour' and return strengthened and refreshed to the north, and 'some problems of'. We have plenty with the next number of *Africa* – trying to avoid having *two* rather dull articles together, and nothing to put in 'Notes and News' but endless Conferences and new African Studies Centres springing up in the most unlikely places.

All good wishes,
Yours sincerely,

Barbara Pym

To Bob Smith in Ibadan   40 Brooksville Avenue

16 October 1963

Dearest Bob,

Who is your wicked friend from Lagos? Do I know him? A taxi from Abeokuta must have been rather expensive. Do you know that Michael Crowder is apparently going to arrange for a performance of *The Palm Wine Drinkard in Yoruba* for the delectation of our Executive Council? At Daryll Forde's suggestion, admittedly! That would be one entertainment Miss Pym would *not* wish to attend. We have so many Nigerians at St Lawrence's now. There is a fashion for them getting baptised, too, started by a pretty girl called Florence (an Itsekiri) to whom I am godmother. Now a young man has fastened on to Hilary and asked her to 'see him through'. Personally, I have the unworthy feeling that it is rather because he is attracted to Hilary than because he wants baptism, but I may be maligning him! Anyway, have the CMS (it would be them?) failed in the Niger Delta, for I should have thought that most of them would have been baptised already. We did meet one, at Florence's baptism party, who was a lapsed Catholic and announced his intention of coming to our church, but he hasn't shown up yet! At the party we drank Coca Cola, British wine and tea and ate biscuits, cake and delicious Nigerian rice and fish with hot peppery sauce.

Richard came one Saturday with the Mrs Beeton and stayed for a drink and an informal lunch. Then he drove us to Cricklewood where he was taking some pictures to be cleaned to an old retired Polish General.

Love,

Barbara

To Philip Larkin   40 Brooksville Avenue

3 November 1963

Dear Mr Larkin,

I was so much encouraged and cheered by your letter about *An Unsuitable Attachment.* In a way I hadn't wanted you to read it, not only because it seemed a terrible burden for you to wade through a second-carbon typescript, but also I feared that you might find it so very much below the standard (if I can say that) of my others that I should feel I could never write another word! Anyway I am so glad it did give you some amusement and I am grateful for your comments and criticisms, which will be a help to me when I come to rewrite it, if

I do, and also in a general way for the future. I can't help feeling that it would be better to start at Faber's with a new book, though, or with this one improved in some ways. I could certainly send them a better typescript, too! You are quite right about Ianthe and John. Ianthe is very stiff and John had been intended to be much worse – almost the kind of man who would bigamously marry a spinster, older than himself, for the sake of £50 in the P.O. Savings Bank! And some of the other people are too much like those in earlier books. I'm glad you liked Faustina.

I have no contractual obligations with Cape now – they had the first refusal of this one. I suppose it *was* money, really, they didn't think they could sell enough copies. However well they do out of Ian Fleming and Len Deighton and all the Americans they publish, I suppose they can't afford any book that will not cover its cost. (I don't think I *really* feel this!)

How well you type – not that I ought to find that surprising. And not a word about your own books – have you written the Introduction yet or are you perhaps even now in the middle of it?

Life in Hull sounds much more carefree than London – is it like *Eating People is Wrong*? A sherry party at *noon* – how civilised that sounds, though there is the question of lunch afterwards. As for a party with twisting, I have really passed that now, though the other day I did go to a sort of Nigerian tea party where we did the Highlife. I was pleased to see that I had guessed the drinks that Granville Jameson [a West Indian in the original version of *An Unsuitable Attachment*] would offer correctly – there was Coke, port, Guinness and tea.

January *Africa* will be rather dull, I fear, but some more promising articles have appeared for April. I have hurt and offended somebody by leaving out an account of their Conference (9 a.m. Lecture in Amhani. 10.15 Tea and biscuits etc) but have written a propitiatory letter and promised to put it in the next number.

Best wishes and thanks,

B.P.

May I say 'Philip', if that is what people call you, or should we go through the academic convention of 'Philip Larkin' and 'Barbara Pym'?

To Bob Smith in Ibadan 40 Brooksville Avenue

8 December 1963

Dearest Bob,

I have received the offprint, for which many thanks – the first time anyone has ever given me an *inscribed* one. How many free ones does *J. Hist. Soc. Nigeria* give its contributors? We give 25, but of course people, especially Americans, order lots more.

Richard has been reading some of my books – I gave him *Excellent Women* and *A Glass of Blessings* – do you think that a good choice? *E. W.* he found terribly sad, but witty – why is it that *men* find my books so sad? Women don't particularly. Perhaps they (men) have a slight guilt feeling that this is what they do to us, and yet really it isn't as bad as all that. I haven't got on very far with the new book I started, though some of it forms in my mind, but the last few weeks I have been terribly busy and tired. Daryll's book on the Yakö is in second proof stage and of course I have to give it much attention, being so fulsomely thanked in the foreword.

Love,

Barbara

To Philip Larkin   40 Brooksville Avenue

12 January 1964

Dear Philip,

I will start by making the usual apology for a typewritten letter, but I am just about to 'do some writing' and so to type something might put me in the mood. I have written seven or eight chapters of a new novel. Of course in the end it will turn out not to be any good, perhaps, but I may as well write something even if only for private circulation among a few friends. I am glad you lent it (my last MS) to a friend to read and hope she enjoyed at least some of it. Catherine used to be quite a favourite heroine of mine but she now seems less real to me than Wilmet and Prudence (my own favourites). Of course I am longing to read *Jill* (which I seem to have missed when it came out first) – I can't believe it can be badly written – I thought, somehow, it was for the poems you had written the Introduction, or perhaps you have written two, which would be better still! I read the new Kingsley Amis on Boxing Day, sitting up in bed, eating cold duck – most enjoyable, of course not one of his best but I would rather have a lesser work by a writer I like than any number of masterpieces by.... I also thought the hero not so bad as the reviews had led one to believe – but it was rather difficult to imagine that somebody like Helène would really have gone to bed with someone made to sound so *very* unattractive? I can believe it was not much exaggerated, though, the American scene.

I hope the horn-players are less noisy. Are they a Thurberish couple or a jazz group or just people learning to play – you didn't make it clear. I suppose 32 Pearson Park is a large Georgian or Victorian house converted into flats – horn players on the ground floor, Larkin on the first, and who up above? Or have you got the two top floors, what they call a maisonette? I do know that your part is newly decorated and that you have a cleaned tufty carpet (perhaps Indian?) in your sitting room.

I hope your driving lessons go well – it must be quite terrifying learning now, though people gain more confidence behind the wheel of a car, I believe. I did learn years ago in Shropshire but I have not kept up my licence as I have never had a car or much opportunity of driving one. I certainly couldn't go to work in one as there is nowhere to park it in Fetter Lane. Which leads me on to speak of our Library (? capital L) and what the staff do. There seem to be more staff in the Library than anywhere else – I suppose their purpose is to discourage Visitors. Still, I expect the staff at the University Library, Hull, do just the same? We don't buy a great many books, but have good holdings of foreign periodicals, some being exchanged with *Africa*. (I have sometimes thought of writing a Pinterish play about our Library.)

I hope you survived Christmas – we had four people staying for part of the time, and it is a rather exhausting ordeal for the churchgoer, particularly as we had two ranting sermons, not quite the few words of greeting and comfort one expects at that time. And Lent begins early this year.... I sometimes think I shall give up going to church for Lent, but have never yet had the courage.

All good wishes,

Barbara

40 Brooksville Avenue

16 February 1964

Dear Philip,

It was a lovely surprise and pleasure to receive (on Ash Wednesday) a copy of *The Whitsun Weddings* – thank you so much. As I immediately began reading it, with the breakfast still to be cleared away, I wondered if I'd ever *told* you how much I liked your poems. If I never did I hope it wasn't really necessary – it was just one of those things that went without saying (which is perhaps why it ought to have been said, as Miss Compton-Burnett might remark). Anyway.... Quite a lot of new ones and a favourite I'd seen in your Anthology ('Faith Healing'), not to mention ones cut out of *The Listener*, now all together in 'handy form' for reading in Lyons or in bed.

Did you see in one of the Sunday papers that my late publisher is to publish a book by one of the Beatles (John Lennon? I think?). That and Miss Bowen should give their list the variety it has seemed to need lately.

All good wishes,
Yours ever,

Barbara

The previous vicar's wife couldn't have presided at Bingo – but this vicar's mother does, rather grimly as if a duty.

When she is grooming her cat she has to put on her spectacles to see the fleas, gleaming red-brown among the combings. 'I must say, she keeps Pussy *spotless.*'

25 March. I take my lunch to the darkest corner of the Kardomah, to the table near the door of the Gents Cloakroom where the silly office lovers used to sit. Where are they now?...

Sunday at Joan's – a bit much to have to listen to Maurice Quick praising Joan and saying what 'a lovely sense of humour' she has when I sit there dumb and uninteresting. How often do women have to listen to praise of other women and (if they are nice) just sit there agreeing. And yet men don't do it maliciously, just in their simplicity.

29 March. Easter Sunday. Coldest since 1903. But the church is warm and full of people. In the evening go to supper with Richard. We eat cosily in almost total darkness (one candle). On the mantelpiece many Easter cards and a telegram. One couldn't really give him anything that he hadn't already got. Not even devotion and/or love. It gives one a hopeless sort of feeling. Roman Emperors (a Coles wallpaper) on the wall facing the bed which is large and covered in orange candlewick.

The Unsuitability of Easter Cards – a gold cross wreathed in Spring flowers (violets).

To Philip Larkin   40 Brooksville Avenue

7 April 1964

Dear Philip,

I was amazed at *Jill.* Such maturity – and detachment and 'Sentiments to which every bosom returns an echo...' it was difficult to believe it had been written by a boy of 21! Of course it is *very* well written and observed too – I don't mean to sound surprised at that, but I hadn't expected it to be *quite* so good. And remembering *A Girl in Winter* one wonders why you didn't go on writing fiction, and regrets it. I suppose you were *too good* and didn't perhaps sell enough, and then you preferred writing poetry? But couldn't you possibly give us a novel now and again – those nine years in a northern university... surely, you are being rather *selfish*? And the Introduction is splendid, though one could have wished for more.

Anyway, that's what I feel about it and no doubt lots of other people will too. I should be tempted, not to write a thesis on the possible origins of the working-class hero in post-war Engl. fiction, but to produce a scholarly note on the occurrence of the name 'Bleaney' (see *Jill* p.73).

I wonder if you have bought a car yet? No doubt you will have decided by now which kind best expresses your personality or gives the impression you would like to create. I think I see you in a medium-sized car, nothing too flashy, but I *may* be wrong.

I never thanked you for returning the typescript of *An Unsuitable Attachment*, which I have put aside for the moment but shall perhaps revise one day. I think it an excellent idea that somebody should 'go over' in Rome. I am struggling with my new unfinished one, which is set in the country mostly and has about ten chapters roughly written. Over the coldest Easter for 80 years I tried to beat the first two chapters into a better shape now that the characters are becoming clearer, but why is the material in a novel so recalcitrant? It ought to be easy when you think that you can do exactly as you like with these people and have absolute power to change them in any way you will. I like writing, but am rather depressed at future prospects for my sort of book. Once you said, I think, that not everybody wants to read about Negro homosexuals. It seems appropriate that I am now reading James Baldwin's *Another Country* lent to me by a young friend. A 'powerful' very well-written book, but so upsetting – one is really glad never to have had the chance of that kind of life!

This letter doesn't really convey the great pleasure I've had from *Jill* and *The W.W.*, but I hope you'll take the will for the deed. (Is that right? One is sometimes wrong about these proverbs and saws?) I was amused to see in Peterborough 'Jazz Reviewer's Poems'. Of course I think of 'Poet's Jazz Reviews' or even 'Librarian's Poems'.

With all good wishes,
    Yours

                                 Barbara

May Day. At Covent Garden with Skipper. He crunches ice as we drink orangeade in the Crush Bar – the great oil paintings, the flowers (real). A happy evening. If 'they' went to Covent Garden Leonora would like to feel the touch of his sleeve against her bare arm (but that would be as far as it would go). Close, intimate red and gold semi-darkness. Here he is *mine* she thinks, the young admirer she has created for herself. Quinton [later 'James'] plays his part with rather self-conscious enjoyment.

12 May. Athens. Jock's party. British Council Representative in Viet Nam, Mary Renault arriving all in gold lamé. Miss Pym (a failure) in her simple black. Elizabeth Taylor – the smile on her face as she looks at me when the band at the taverna (Johnny's Place) is playing 'Colonel Bogey'. The taverna is very much like Cecchio's in Rome, even to the display of food as one enters and the lurking cats. In the beautiful Zappeion gardens, the delicious fragrance of shrubs, the oranges hanging from trees. Here a middle-aged English or American lady might be picked up by a young Greek adventurer.

Drinks with Charles Shoup (a deraciné, rich American painter) in his wonderful flat with views of everything and a lovely terrace. Many bits of marble and odds and ends he has picked up – sculptures, a miniature wooden confessional, a red fox rug on the sofa. Elizabeth is there looking sad as it's her last evening.

20 May. At Delphi, which is wonderful. We pass through Erythrai, where there is a good baker. Thebes (the dump of old cars). Miss the crossroads where Oedipus killed his father (asleep) but saw it on the way back. Helicon and Parnassus. At Levadia the bus stops long enough to visit the 'Toilettes' and have a drink and eat little bits of lamb on wooden skewers.

2 June. My birthday and dinner with Richard at his flat. Champagne and a lovely present. A Victorian china cup and saucer. 'The Playfellow' – a lady and her cat.

To Richard Roberts (Skipper)   40 Brooksville Avenue

                                        30 June 1964 (6.45 a.m!)

Darling Richard,

Here it has been summery and yesterday I saw Bob. We had a large lunch and then I had taken the afternoon off so we went to Bourdon House [a rather superior antique shop]. It was a rich experience, my first visit and should be used in some fictional setting. Of course there were several things I should have liked – a nice pair of mirrors 295 guineas, I think. Even the smallest malachite egg was 7 gns.

Then Bob came back to have tea here. His unexpectedly early arrival and my going away for the weekend meant that the house was dusty and full of dead flowers – perhaps a not inappropriate setting for a not-very-with-it novelist, but he didn't seem to notice. How full of fictional situations life is! I am now making fuller use of all this and have gone back to writing a novel I started some months ago. I am alone so much at the moment that it seems a good opportunity.

Much love

Barbara

40 Brooksville Avenue

18 August 1964 (Night)

My dearest Skipper,

Thank you for sending back the letter. It was perhaps silly and capricious of me to ask for it, but I was punished by the disappointment of finding that an envelope addressed in your hand contained only my own letter back again. So that will teach me ('Behaviour', indeed!).

Anyway this little note will contain all the fondness of the other letter, in a concentrated form like a cube of chicken stock or Oxo. It had been meant to stretch from Wednesday evening last week and to greet you when you got back from where you didn't go! Here it rained incessantly and the office is in chaos anyway with redecoration, tidying and throwing away old files and other melancholy tasks. At lunchtime I went out briefly – it was the kind of day to be horrid to somebody, like that other day, but luckily the opportunity didn't arise. This evening we went to see some friends and they were disposing of some books, so I got a Christina Rossetti (just right for pressing a little cyclamen in) and E.B. Browning's *Sonnets from the Portuguese*, with an inscription dated 1901. Rather the sort of poets Ianthe might have read?

I have thought of a few more good scenes that I might write in, one inspired by the idea of you and Bob having lunch together, though it won't really be a bit like!

I hope you are reasonably well and happy – I really mean *very* well and reasonably happy – no more of those sad looks that cut me to the heart, Skipper dear. I would send you Peruvian heliotrope if I knew where to get it. But love anyway,

Barbara

At Buckland. Trials of a novelist. Miss Conway or Mrs Godwin has read one of my novels, but which? We go through all the titles but none seems to ring a bell – so embarrassing ('*You* read it – I was too busy!').

4 September. (Oh what a month August was too!) Walking in Hampstead with Skipper. Parked the car in Church Row and went up by the Huguenot Cemetery – all beautiful in the dark, warm evening. Into the little R.C. church on Holly Mount, R. lights a candle but I don't somehow like to and don't say anything either. It is a bit too much like something in a B.P. novel. Later we walk to Windmill Hill, Admiral's House, see Galsworthy's house etc, have coffee in the High St. Talk and wander about peering into people's uncurtained windows and even their letter boxes. And on Thursday he is going to Venice.

9 September. The language of flowers...in Gamage's an artificial pond with plastic waterlilies. What do *they* say – the same as Mizpah?

10 September. She (Leonora) thinks perhaps this is the kind of love I've always wanted because absolutely *nothing* can be done about it!

Telephoning me this afternoon Richard asks that I should leave him *all* my notebooks! No. XX [she numbered all her notebooks] he should certainly have. Perhaps this one (XXI) too.

To Philip Larkin   40 Brooksville Avenue

14 September 1964

Dear Philip,

Many thanks for your letter, and card from Northern Ireland. It seemed a very original place for a holiday, but I daresay even that isn't as remote as it seems and I could *hear* the strains of that transistor from that person sitting on the rock. I wish I could have another holiday, but I used it all up going to Greece, which seems such a long time ago now. I sometimes wish I were a University person, even with a 'crushing teaching load' – but I suppose the Library is open all the time, isn't it, even if the Librarian is not there?

You will need to gather your strength for the beginning of your Library extension. It does seem to cost rather a lot, but then estimates for building do seem rather remote and difficult to grasp. I suppose it is a *good* thing that you have joined SCOLMA, which always sounds like a kind of breakfast food or perhaps a tonic for tired academics? *Our* library has been made slightly more interesting – in a macabre way – by a rather peculiar young man joining the staff. He doesn't come in till 10.35 most mornings and is given to cryptic utterances which one can only half hear. I don't have much to do with him myself but hear all this from the other staff. I find it is pleasanter to observe these things rather than actually participate in them.

I have now got *all* your books and wish there were more. It seems *wicked* when there are so few novelists one can bear to read.

I am gratified that you have been re-reading mine and have even spoken of me with John Betjeman, who certainly reviewed me very kindly. I have got some way with another one, but at the moment I have turned back to *An Unsuitable Attachment* and am trying to do something to that in the hope that it might be publishable. A friend who had come fresh (as it were!) to my work read it and made some more suggestions, and as it is now getting on for two years since I finished it I can look on it with more detachment. But every now and then I feel gloomy about it all and wonder if anybody will ever want to publish anything of mine again. When I have finished my revision perhaps I might avail myself of your kind offer to introduce me to Fabers – if it is still open!

Yours etc

Barbara

From the novelist's notebook – Sunday 4 October 1964 – sent to Richard Roberts as a letter

'Are you going to fry them?' he asked anxiously.

'Yes – why not?' Immediately she was on the defensive and saw the kitchen as it must appear to his half-American eyes – the washing-up from lunchtime, the litter of things not thrown away, and the paw-marks on the table.

In silence they watched the sausages lying in the frying-pan. After a while the fat began to splutter.

'They're bursting,' she said unhappily.

'I always prick them with a fork,' he said in a kind tone.

'Well, yes, I *did* prick them.'

'With your fingernail?' He smiled.

'No, with a knife, I *think....*'

...Afterwards when he had gone, it was that part of the evening she remembered – her appalling domestic inefficiency and the meagre meal she had given him when he must have been rather hungry. What was it about him that brought out this curious inadequacy in her? Then another occasion came into her mind. Something to do with a tin of 'luncheon meat' (who, she wondered were the people who ate it for 'luncheon'?). It was only much later, in the watches of the night, one could have said – that the other occasion came back to her, the one for which she *really* needed to be forgiven. Would he, she wondered, put it down to her anthropologist's 'enquiring mind'? That seemed too generous to be expected even of him. Perhaps it had been a desperate attempt to break down the awkwardness and loss of *rapport* she had felt between them, rather than a feminine desire for a scene with carefully thought-out bitter dialogue. (Enjoyable to write, though, she couldn't help feeling with the detached part of the mind that watches us behaving in situations...). And in a way perhaps it had succeeded – *she* certainly felt better in the morning. She hoped he did too.

In church she prayed for them both and resolved to ask him for a proper meal (with cheese) very soon. It gave her a curious kind of pleasure to think of him preparing his luncheon, arranging his table in the elegant way he always did, in the cool clean Sunday morning ambience of Sussex Gardens, in that bright, sparkling air, free from the cats' hairs which caused him such distress in Queen's Park. Any cats' hairs *there*, would be Siamese, as he had pointed out....

So you see, my dear, how with a little polishing life could become literature, or at least fiction! I hope you get its poor little message, or that it at least entertains you for a moment.

My love,

Barbara

11 October. Yesterday afternoon R. called just as I had finished putting my hair in rollers. He had been burgled – now the lovely square gold watch and the platinum and diamond one (in the style of the 20's) left him by his father had gone. He needed company – so we had tea and he took us to a political meeting in Hammersmith to hear Sir Alec [Douglas-Home]. Then we went to Sussex Gardens for a drink. R. was in his scarlet pullover and rather long navy raincoat. Very sweet, but not, perhaps, Skipper ever again.

7 November. Lunch with R. at 231. Sherry, bean and bacon soup, crab and salad and chocolate cake. And Orvieto which (he said) he had remembered as being my favourite. Indeed! (But milk poured from the bottle).

Prof. Beecher is a Reader for one of the University Presses. By his bed is a small manual, almost like a devotional book: *Rules for Compositors and Readers at the University Press* [Oxford] first ed. April 1893.

18 November. Description by R. of the peacocks (on his mother's estate in the Bahamas) being shut up at night 'in a small greenhouse' to protect them from the dogs (or was it one special peacock?). Afterwards he and I went up to the General's and had coffee and collected two pictures. Everyone said how well I looked – 'blooming' – but is that joy at seeing R. again or what over three weeks *away* from him has done –

27 November. Lunched at the Golden Egg. Oh, the horror – the cold stuffiness, claustrophobic placing of tables, garish lights and mass produced food in steel dishes. And the egg-shaped menu! But perhaps one could get something out of it. The setting for a breaking-off, or some terrible news or an unwanted declaration of love.

28 November. Today as I sit in Lyons, a man comes to the table and a middle-aged woman is fetching food for *him* as I have fetched it for my darling R. on more than one occasion.

To Richard Roberts   40 Brooksville Avenue

5 January 1965

My dearest Skipper (yes, that name does seem most suitable for you in the Bahamas)

I'm so glad your going home has been worthwhile for you, and you will be rewarded for going, as one so often is. Your 86 year old aunt sounds marvellous and how nice that you were able to take her on that trip. My father (also just 86) won't even come to London!

I should think that it must be a relief to have somebody less complicated than 'Gary Reindeer' to be with, though of course *we* are drawn to the tortured and tortuous ones, you and I.

Do have some more photographs taken and let me choose the most characteristic even if not the most glamorous.

It says on this Airmail pad that *12* sheets and an envelope weighs less than half an ounce, but I doubt if I can go on at that length. Also, I am writing this in the office in the *morning*, which seems frightfully sinful.

I have practically finished the revision of that novel though I suppose I shall never be really satisfied with it. Now I must read it again with a cold critical eye. I really much more want to get on with the other one I started which will be more amusing. I hate writing 'tender love scenes' and am no good at it – why I wonder? Too inhibited and 'behaviour'-ridden no doubt.

I hope you are well – blessings and prayers and everything

Barbara

31 January. Who but R. would be welcome in the middle of a Sunday afternoon (c. 3 p.m.). Are you still brown she asks idly. He pulled out his shirt and revealed a square of golden brown skin on his belly. She (Leonora) found herself thinking 'All thy quaint Honour turn to dust/And into Ashes all my lust'. Except that he probably hasn't any quaint honour. She reproaches him for not having been to Mass, 'Then you didn't pray for me', since that is the only time he prays.

To Philip Larkin 40 Brooksville Avenue

16 February 1965

Dear Philip,

I have a great curiosity to know *what* you could have been doing at the Inst. of Social Anthropology in Oxford. Some conference, I suppose. It certainly wouldn't matter if you put a hot jug down on a polished? table *there*, from my recollection of it. Yes, Professor Evans-Pritchard is perhaps the greatest of his generation and is of course known as 'E-P'. He has little to do with our Institute these days and spends his time writing articles and books and studying Zande texts. They (the Azande) 'relish putrescent meat' or did in the good old days. E-P is an R.C. convert – rather unusual in an anthropologist – perhaps that explains the reproduction of old masters – if they were of a holy type?

I agree this is a depressing time of year, but November is really my least favourite month – or perhaps December, because that has Christmas too! Only yesterday though I noticed that it is getting brighter in the evenings and this morning there was almost a feeling of spring in the air. (Perhaps only women notice these things?)

Our Library problem, I mean the peculiar young man, seems to have been solved. At least, he was given the sack after Christmas, being told, I believe, that there was to be some 'staff reorganisation'.

Is that always how it's done? Then a woman of uncertain age suddenly seemed to be sixty and she had to retire, and for a time it seemed as if nobody would come. But now there is a young girl... here I stopped writing yesterday, I suppose because I was seeing the procession of young girls over the years and perhaps got thinking that it's only the older, duller and more reliable members of the staff who go on and on. Today, being surrounded by galley proofs, I feel a bit like your poem about the Toad 'work'.

I have revised *An Unsuitable Attachment* – not very well, I believe and it will need some further polishing before it can be sent to any other publisher. I am also going on with another. I like the stage of having work to do on a book, before one actually has to take positive action, like writing to anyone. Revising and polishing could go on for ever.... I really still wonder if my books will *ever* be acceptable again when I read the reviews in the Sundays. I think it might be nice to be famous and sought after when one is rather old and ga-ga – not in one's forties and fifties, or perhaps fame when you're very young is good, if the years after aren't too much of a let-down.

Yours ever,

Barbara

20 February. A sad day. Rang R. in the evening and he felt 'guilty' which I hate. He came to tea on Sunday in his very spoilt little Bahamian mood, full of euphoria, money and sex talk, teasing me and being unkind to Minerva. I get irritated with him.

To Bob Smith in Ibadan   40 Brooksville Avenue

1 March 1965

Dearest Bob,

I am still writing and there is plenty going on inside even though I'm not very optimistic and they may have to be privately printed by that man in Ilfracombe after all. I have revised *An Unsuitable Attachment,* though not very satisfactorily – but I think I can put it right with the help of Hazel's criticisms, then I am in the middle of another book. I haven't thought any more about working part time here, mainly because I doubt my capacity to earn money by writing, at the moment. If only I had a small private income or a husband – how badly I've arranged my life! I really think we do need novels like mine now – did you like Elizabeth Taylor's *The Soul of Kindness*? I lent it to Richard, as he hadn't read any of hers, but I don't think it

234

was really quite his kind of book. As you will no doubt have heard he came back from Nassau almost the day he was expected and looked very well and brown. His life there is full of such rich material for fiction, but I suppose it is really beyond my range. Richard's mother is supposed to be going to Athens and the islands in April – with three American ladies, so that they can play bridge!

Love,

Barbara

24 May. Fortunately all the fury and bitterness I sometimes feel has stayed hidden inside me and R. doesn't – perhaps never will – know!

25 May. All miserable again and determined to 'end it all' between us – but how? And why?

29 May. A letter from R. inviting us to dinner on my birthday. I phoned him and we talked. I must learn not to take 'things' so much to heart and try to understand – don't stop loving (can't), just be there if and when needed.

10 June. Leonora gets the young man to read the menu for her and the programme, rather than put on her glasses.

16 June. Lunch in the Kardomah with R. The salmon sandwiches and coffee and talking 'business' about bidding for a book for him – then a walk in the rain to Smiths to buy books for him to read on holiday. What a change to be happy for a moment – it may as well be recorded after all these weeks.

22 June. Wonderful peace with R. away (Istanbul now, then Greece and *Venice*!). They are altering the Kardomah and 'improving' the ground floor and soon it seems the basement will be gone. Where now will we be able to read and write and brood? First the mosaic peacocks went, now this! What emotions are trapped in that basement.

25 June. Went to Christie's to view 3 books of natural history shell and bird prints that R. wants me to bid for. Very cosy in the basement looking at them – a chaos of books, a man correcting the proofs of a catalogue. A nice girl and an Italian gentleman come in to enquire about books he bought over a year ago and now apparently nowhere to be found.

1 July. Went to Christie's to bid and got Sharpe's 2 vols of *Birds of Paradise* for £1,000! It *was* rather nerve-wracking but rewarding and afterwards lunch at Fortnums.

19 July. R. to dinner – very successful. He brought me a little glass bird from Venice.

Rainer Maria Rilke 1873–1936
Princess Marie von Thurn und Taxis 1855–1934

(18 years difference between them, but *he* was a man of genius)

To Bob Smith   40 Brooksville Avenue

22 July (4th after Trinity)

Dearest Bob,

Just after I had left you after that rather pleasant unexpected tea and Danish pastry in the Kardomah on Thursday afternoon, I ran into Professor Forde, just as I was rounding the corner into Fetter Lane. 'Ah, there you are, Barbara,' he said. 'I went into your room but seeing you weren't there – thought you must be in the Ladies.' (So you see there is no need to tell people when you go out of the office.)
Love,

Barbara

17 August. My novel [*An Unsuitable Attachment*] is with Faber, but surely for not much longer. It may be better to find another interest – antiquarian books perhaps?

19 August. Last night it came back but with a nice letter from Charles Monteith. Now I feel as if I shall never write again, though perhaps I will eventually. Rather a relief to feel that I don't have to flog myself to finish the present one since probably nothing I write could be acceptable now.

To Philip Larkin   40 Brooksville Avenue

21 August 1965

Dear Philip,

Just a line to say that Faber won't take *An Unsuitable Attachment* – rather as I had feared, so I don't feel *too* cast down. I can quite see that it wouldn't be an economic proposition, and not the kind of book to impress a new publisher anyway. Charles Monteith wrote such a nice letter – thank you so much for introducing me to him and for all you have done on my behalf. I don't know yet whether I shall try the book anywhere else – at the moment I don't feel at all hopeful and have even thought now restful it would be never to write another word! But I expect I shall go on. The ideal is perhaps to be 'at work' on a book but never to finish it. After all, I suppose I am lucky to have got six books published.

How are you? Perhaps on holiday at this moment. (Surely *nobody* is in Hull in *August*?) I can't feel you can have got much wear out of your panama hat this year. I am in the country this weekend, staying near Oxford, but haven't had a holiday yet, only odd days – on one of which I went to Christie's and bought on behalf of a friend two vols. of bird prints for £1,000! *That* was an experience, the bidding and the dealers, and might well come into a future unpublished novel.

I've been horribly busy at the office – everything late, proofs not coming, dreadful volumes of seminar papers to get ready for press. But my room is to be redecorated soon and I am to have a new carpet – speckled black and white that won't show cigarette ash. Perhaps I shall then take on a new lease of life, editorially speaking.

It has just occurred to me – perhaps you are 'Visiting Professor' somewhere, though I hope not Los Angeles.

With all good wishes,

Barbara

24 August. Lunching at the FANY Club with R! He seems quite at home among them and his eyes shine when one pays him a compliment. Afterwards choose curtain material in Peter Jones. Then to sit in L'Atelier [his antique shop] for a moment or two while people pass and look at us in the window.

15 September. I find myself going to see Elgar's grave (directed by an arrow) in the R.C. church at Little Malvern. The weather is dull but not unpleasant – rather calming and saddening and I'm glad I have brought Hardy's poems with me. Tea in the Abbey tearooms – very good home-made cakes only 6d. each. In the Priory Gardens the smell of heliotrope reminds me of Skipper's L'Heure Bleue (but one would have to change the sexes for a story wouldn't one?).

To Philip Larkin　　　　　　　　　　　　40 Brooksville Avenue

　　　　　　　　　　　　　　　　　　　　30 September 1965

Dear Philip,

Many thanks for your sympathetic letter! I hope by now you will be back refreshed after Sark, ready to tackle any problems that SCOLMA may present during the coming autumn. I can imagine an Ibsen-ish situation developing now that your building plans are halted – all that latent power and energy – let it go into poetry!

This is only a note to ask if you would be so very kind as to let me know (on a postcard will do) the publishers Charles Monteith thought might be more sympathetic towards my novel. Not that I really think it's much good, but the BBC are doing *No Fond Return* as the *Woman's Hour* serial beginning 6 October and I thought it might be a propitious time to give the book one more try, perhaps. This was quite a surprise to me – and a pleasant one – I shall have to take the transistor to work!

I made some notes in Malvern and Worcester and Hereford on various points, and of course I am now beginning to feel that perhaps I can't stop writing after all. Even if no one will publish me.

All good wishes,
Yours ever,

Barbara

26 September. After the dentist went to the Wimpole Buttery. A delicious creamy cake tasting of walnuts. Now Skipperless one begins to understand 'compensatory eating'. Better surely now to write the kind of novel that tells of one day in the life of such a woman.

To Bob Smith in Ibadan   40 Brooksville Avenue

29 November 1965

Dearest Bob,

Not *much* news though what does one expect? I sent the script (as O.U.P. say) of my novel to Raleigh Trevelyan at Michael Joseph. 'A pleasant book, but hardly strong enough'! almost *exactly* what Cape said of *Some Tame Gazelle* in 1936! Anyway for the moment I am not writing but resting and gathering material since every day gives one something. Miss Pym is still frequenting the sale rooms – a week or so ago R. pushed me into the end of a sale at Sotheby's and made me bid for a book on the Bahamas for him, which I got. Really though I am more at home in Hodgson's in Chancery Lane where Hazel and I spend happy lunch hours and prices are more realistic.

Love,

Barbara

To Bob Smith in Lagos   40 Brooksville Avenue

25 March 1966

Dearest Bob,

Today the window of the Protestant Truth Society is in mourning – a picture of the Archbp. of Canterbury and the Pope against a black drapery and a placard saying 'Archbishop betrays British Protestants' or words to that effect. (I wonder, who arranged the window display and at what time of day or night?)

Did I not mention my own writing when I last wrote to you? The position at the moment is that I have sent the rejected novel (which I rewrote, as I may have told you) to a recommended agent (Hughes Massie) but have heard nothing for two months! (You may well say that is a *very* short time compared with what people sending articles to *Africa* have to wait!) But I hear vaguely from the person who recommended the agent that it is thought to be good but unpublishable at the present time. I haven't heard officially yet, but it seems that is what it will be. Hazel suggests I should get my works printed by private subscription from those who would be willing to support me and I believe there are a few! Curiously enough I find I can still write and have started, or rather got quite well into, another book which looks as if it might be finished some time fairly soon. Whether it will prove any more acceptable though, is another matter.

Love,

Barbara

30 May. Whit Monday. Sitting in the sun reading Beverley Nichols' 'defence' of Syrie Maugham. Made me laugh – people lying ill in the Dorchester and dying in Claridges. It might be a joke, a pastiche of the 20s written by Sandy Wilson. My own story judiciously edited from these notebooks would be subtler and more amusing.

June. Greece. 610 783 (Henry's telephone number; he is in Athens). It seemed strange after more than 30 years to be driving with him again. Heard cuckoo in Delphi. Sensational ride to Lamia through the mountains – pass of Thermopylae. As we get down into the straight road to Lamia after the slow grinding climbs and descents, the driver (who looks like a younger, benevolent Stalin) sounds his horn in triumphant paeans and the radio is blaring full blast. Lamia. Plastic doves are being sold in the square and on the back corner of the Hotel Achillia there is a stork's or pelican's nest with young. The conductor on the bus sniffs a red carnation, two elderly men sit at a table with a gardenia between them.

My dream about R. We are driving along somewhere in his car when I see he is obviously too drunk to drive so I say 'You shouldn't have let him get like this.' Then I pick R. up in my arms and he turns into a cat.

8 July. A disappointment for the Father at Farm Street? The voice of a lady telephoning to ask the time of the evening meal 'on behalf of Father Stefanizyn who is with me' [at the I.A.I.].

30 July. When I was out there arrived 12 beautiful deep pink roses from Constance Spry with a tender note. The roses were tight buds and have gradually unfolded till they are now enormous and flat, almost like peonies. Now he [Richard] has gone to Spain.

31 August. After a wet depressing day yesterday I have decided on a period of silence (by me at any rate) with a possible approach in September (to get Jumble).

15 September. After the Beardsley Exhibition at the V&A, walking along that endless tunnel to South Kensington station, I thought, why this is 'behaviour' – and I had said, perhaps even written: 'where does "behaviour" begin and end?'

23–25 September. Malvern [staying with Muriel Maby]. At the Writers' Circle Dinner. Margaret Drabble in a beautiful short flowered dress with long sleeves. Some in long glittering brocades. All with neat little 'evening bags' – only B.P. with her black leather day handbag.

To Bob Smith in Lagos   Brooksville Avenue

12 December 1966

Dearest Bob,

Anthony Powell's newest was a great comfort to me when I read it recently – a beautiful book! Poor Richard was very fond of Iris Murdoch's *Unicorn* which you couldn't finish. As for news of Richard, I fear it is all over now (it makes me sad to write this) – he did get in touch once but I think it was only because he and Maurice wanted to get rid of some jumble (which we were of course delighted to have, but still...?). Life has its farcical moments and perhaps my sense of humour is greater than his. Perhaps my sardonic tongue has sent him away or he has just lost interest, the latter probably.

How well I know that feeling of 'embarrassment' you speak of – racking one's brains for something to say!

Love,

Barbara

40 Brooksville Avenue

30 December 1966

Dearest Bob,

I'm so glad you liked *An Object For a Walk* and hope you will write and tell Jock so, as I'm sure he must be a little depressed by the meagre reviews and lack of enthusiasm for it. Naturally I could detect bits of myself in Flora and Hestha (strange spelling). Poor Henry [Harvey], what an inspiration he has been.

Richard gave me a nice lunch before Christmas at the eleventh hour, as it were, and we got on quite well. I don't imagine we shall see anything of him in 1967, but I might ask you and him to dinner in the summer. All I want now is peace to write my unpublished novels.

Love,

Barbara

To Philip Larkin   40 Brooksville Avenue

11 January 1967

Dear Philip,

Just a *note* to thank you for the kind message about my novels on your Christmas card (a very nice one, with foxes) – it did cheer me up. I doubt if I shall ever publish another now though I certainly am at work on something – perhaps the ideal state to be in, never finishing ('Bold lover, never, *never* canst thou kiss' etc). I did revise and improve the one you saw but still haven't managed to get any publisher to take, and at the moment it is lying on top of a cupboard in my room. Perhaps with the spring I may try it somewhere else.

I am surrounded by work, which is perhaps why I have broken off to write this. An excessive number of books on Africa coming out and the April number of the journal about to go to press... you will know about that cosily full in-tray.

With all good wishes for this year,

Yours ever,

Barbara

To Bob Smith in Lagos   40 Brooksville Avenue

16 February 1967

Dearest Bob,

A flat with a lift doesn't seem quite what I had imagined you living in. It was rather the large decaying old Brazilian-style mansion, though I don't think you ever said anything to suggest quite that. Bright yellow curtains in the bedroom(s) – how far from the anthropologist in the rest house in the twenties!

I met John Ballard [an anthropologist] once and I think he was rather shocked when I showed him a rather chaotic collection of Intelligence Reports we have at the I.A.I., and when he suggested mildly that it would be nice to have a list of them, I said roughly that there was certainly no hope of *that*. It might be a nice job to do on those long dusty August afternoons this year, perhaps, waiting for you to come to take me to tea at the Kardomah, but I have been so busy these last months and still am. All the same it has helped me overcome the depression that occasionally threatens when I think of nobody wanting to publish my novels, and my total 'failure' (if that's the word) with Richard. Trying to understand people and leaving them alone and being 'unselfish' and all *that* jazz has only the bleakest of rewards – precisely nothing! Now I am incapable of taking any action at all, which is just as well.

Much love,

Barbara

17 May. Hazel and I recalled Dryden living in Fetter Lane, perhaps writing *Absalom and Achitophel* in the place where our [I.A.I.] Library now stands.

28 May. Lying in bed with migraine or something like it. The best things – life, health, freedom from misery. Hilary was ill too, so after a light supper we welcomed Sir Francis Chichester back [from his round-the-world voyage] with brandy and dry biscuits.

7 June. A Corot birthday card from Skipper with affectionate message. Then the next day a long tortuous letter from Mollie Lightbourn explaining that it was late because she forgot to post it on the 1st, as Richard instructed her. I wrote a cool friendly p.c. back. A real B. Pym situation. Then *today* a card to us both from Richard in Elba. Perhaps one *could* be friendly again – yet I feel like a cat that's been offered a dish of plain Kit-e-Kat and wonders if it really wants *that*.

7 July. Oxford with Bob. Pusey House. Lunch at the Randolph. Pitt-Rivers Museum to look at cross-bows (all dusty and locked away). Blackwells. Writing p.c.s in the garden of Rhodes House then St Stephen's House (locked chapel and overgrown garden) tea in Henley on the way back. Then I let fly about Richard which rather spoiled things then and later in the evening, so that the thought of him has made my 'nervous indigestion' pain return. But only temporarily I hope.

'Top of the Pops'. 'A Whiter shade of Pale'. Sad Bach-like tune, but to see it is a kind of nightmare, the dark brooding youth playing the organ and the vocal sung by a man in full Chinese dress even to the pigtail. Decadent and horrible.

9 July. In the self-service, a monk doesn't manage his tray too well so the grey-haired woman table-clearer has to help him.

To Bob Smith in Lagos   40 Brooksville Avenue

9 August 1967

Dearest Bob,

These long lonely August afternoons are ideal for receiving visitors when one is dozing over proofs. The other day in a fit of boredom I nearly telephoned Richard for a bit of conversation but then I was afraid he might feel awkward and that I might not be able to think of anything to say, so I didn't. So *unflattering* to feel that a person really doesn't ever want to see you again – I don't think it's ever happened to me before *quite* like this! Now, alas, I am too old to change myself but shall just be more cautious in future – not allowing myself to get fond of anybody.

Much love,

Barbara

To Philip Larkin   40 Brooksville Avenue

7 December 1967

Dear Philip,

I hope you will have been having a good term and that your new Library extension has grown a few feet. I remember you mentioned it some time ago. There is something Ibsenish about it, or perhaps the idea of it, though I imagine you won't have to climb to the top or anything alarming like that. Lots of books to put in it, of course, and endlessly proliferating bibliographies. Our Institute is at this moment organising a biblio. conference in Nairobi – talk about 'Some Problems of…'!

Did you see in the chat about the Arts Council awards today that Edward Candy is a *woman*! I was rather disappointed, having pictured this rather nice sensitive amusing *man* – I think *Strokes of Havoc* is better than *Parents' Day* and agree that the influence of Ivy Compton-Burnett is too strong. Perhaps 'she' will grow out of it. In about ten years' time, perhaps somebody will be kind enough to discover *me*, living destitute in cat-ridden squalor, and recommend me for one of the grants, if there is still an Arts Council then.

The new book I mentioned [*The Sweet Dove Died*] really *is* new and I have finished the first draft. It will need some pruning and sharpening before I dare try it on a publisher, if I ever do. The friend who has read it thinks it almost a sinister and unpleasant book, which may be all to the good. I didn't try to make it so, but tended to leave out boring cosiness and concentrate on the darker side. (Now you will wonder what on earth it is about – in the main, the relationship of an older woman with a younger man.)

The Faustina novel I did prune and improve quite a lot but have now put aside – I may take it out again but I feel the subject and all those clergy could never be sympathetically considered by any publisher now. By the way *Some Tame Gazelle* and *Excellent Women* are to be modestly reissued by a reprint firm, Chivers of Bath, who do a lot for libraries, where there is apparently still some demand for these two. Next summer is when they should be available.

I haven't asked at all about *your* writing because you said you weren't – but I hope that was temporary?

Yours ever,

Barbara

To Bob Smith in Lagos   40 Brooksville Avenue

9 February 1968

Dearest Bob,

Are you beginning to experience 'Some problems of a review editor'? It makes one almost *hate* people when they don't send in reviews, I find, and I have my own private black list on which it is very terrible to be.

Hilary's book [*Songs of Greece: a companion for travellers,* publ. *Sunday Times*] is very pretty – you can't buy it except by ordering it through the *Sunday Times* – I should think she may send you a copy.

So clever of her to have done it – she is waiting anxiously for Jock's reaction. Francis King is very good, I think – *The Last of the Pleasure Gardens* very upsetting – Japanese ones fascinated me – *The Waves Behind the Boat*, excellent except for rather melodramatic ending. Jock says he has another coming, all about a prep. school and full of cruelty (I probably told you). I am still going on with something, trying to make it less cosy without actually putting in the kind of thing that would be beyond my range (keep *that* and quote it in my biography, young man from the University of Texas!).

Why you shouldn't get a job at an English university when your time in Lagos is up I can't imagine. Unless, of course, you intend to become a clergyman. You thought perhaps that I might have retained some idealised vision of the clergy and perhaps in a sense I still do, just as I still even now at my age tend to believe what people tell me – it's just a quality in oneself. But I am under no illusion about church people, on the whole, and the dullness and pettiness and dreariness of all the things a clergyman would have to do. Chaplain to a girls' school, perhaps? Probably the only kind that have such a thing now would be a fashionable Roman (of course) Catholic boarding school, where the Duke of Norfolk's daughters went, maybe.

I ripped this letter out of the typewriter because I thought I heard D.F. outside my door, but it was only the carpenter come to do some repairs! Still, the page was nearly finished anyway.

Much love,

Barbara

17 July. Dublin. In Molesworth St why should there be a notice to say 'Marmalade For Sale' in the window of the Hibernian Church Missionary Society?

The lone American lady drinking *crème de menthe* on the rocks to match her emerald ring and the other ladies so old and preserved enjoying exotic cocktails in the bar of the Great Southern Hotel Killarney.

To Philip Larkin   40 Brooksville Avenue

18 August 1968

Dear Philip,

Many thanks for your letter and the photograph of the new Library which I have studied with interest, noting particularly the opulent looking cars parked on the campus (or do they belong to the builders?). Also interesting is a shadowy figure in the foreground – ? the spirit of the Librarian?

I read about your sit-in. One wonders if all students would feel they *had* to have one. I of course saw it all in comfort on TV, which made it even more confused, especially when the foreign students used such phrases as (here I must consult my notebook) 'infiltration of negative elements in social unity'.

I wonder if you have been on holiday yet – I've had a pleasant few days in Ireland in May, with good weather – Dublin, Galway and Sligo – Yeats' grave and Lissadell – terribly sad decaying house where Constance Markiewicz was brought up and the Gore-Booths show one round. I urge everyone to go there because I feel they need the money, and it has a melancholy charm (and nowhere to have tea).

If you would really like to read my novel, of course I should be very pleased. My lending copy awaits you and I'll send it on receipt of a postcard or other intimation. I'm afraid it isn't going to get published easily, if at all. I sent it to Longmans, having an introduction to John Guest there who also read *An Unsuitable Attachment,* but last week he returned it...'fiction market increasingly difficult' etc. etc. Doesn't think anybody would buy it – only more elegantly expressed than that. Perhaps it isn't really sinister and unpleasant at all, and it does lack a central character with whom one can 'identify'. Maybe I have lost the knack of writing altogether – it's so hard to judge, and loyal friends have enjoyed it. I shall of course try a few more publishers – not Faber, I think, not wishing to embarrass poor Charles Monteith who was so kind (or you!).

I've written more about it than I meant to and left little space for an intelligent discussion on the Predicament of the Novelist in 1968. I haven't read *Melinda* or the new James Baldwin or the new Edna O'Brien but probably shall when I can get them from the *library,* out of curiosity and jealousy.

Yours,

Barbara

20 August. Philip Larkin sent me a photograph of his new Library extension. Was ever a stranger photo sent by a man to a woman (in a novel she might be disappointed).

To Philip Larkin   40 Brooksville Avenue

9 September 1968

Dear Philip,

I am sending *The Sweet Dove Died* (a thriller about the American Presidential Election?) for you to read and hope it may give you *some* amusement. Criticisms welcome, of course (one says bravely) or perhaps the whole thing is hopeless for this day and age. (At least it isn't in *dialect*). Chatto have it at the moment (3 weeks ago). I shall go on trying if they send it back.

Did any poem come to you in Sutherland? On the moors, or the rocky coast, or in the hotel lounge? I should like to think one did come.

Yours ever,

Barbara

40 Brooksville Avenue

20 October 1968

Dear Philip,

Many thanks for returning the MS of the *S.D.D.* and for your most interesting and helpful criticisms. Nobody has ever told me what was *really* wrong with the book and I felt there must be something. It suffered through starting off as one thing and ending up as another, the penalty of having so little free time and energy that continuity is lost and one's ideas change in the meantime. I started not at all in sympathy with Leonora, who began by being a minor character, but as the book progressed I got more interested in her and really enjoyed writing about her best in the end. I should really have scrapped Rose etc except as minor characters and concentrated on Leonora, James, Humphrey, and Ned (who came in as an afterthought). I wonder if I could do anything with it on the lines you suggest. I feel uncertain at the moment and have rather lost confidence in myself. It would be different if I had more time. As it is, I only write at weekends or on holiday. Yes, I do 'go in' every day and as one gets older one gets more tired, so that evenings are spent lazily watching the Telly rather than writing. What a mixed blessing that great invention is!

I really owe you two letters for I never thanked you for the brief, bitter, amusing one about your holiday and the horror of the single rooms. *On Thy Belly* would be a fine title for an autobiography. I could write *Dust Shalt Thou Eat*, which might be no more than a

247

guide to restaurants in the luncheon-voucher belt of E.C.4.

How good of you to speak to William Plomer like that! I saw him reading the lesson at Wren Howard's Memorial Service in September but I hurried away afterwards and didn't speak to anyone. I felt it was really in memory of the house of Cape as it used to be. All the same, if my two unpublished books really do have serious flaws in them perhaps the outlook is not so unpromising for me after all. I could do better in my old age, if I haven't given up by then.

I hope your students will be reasonably well behaved this year, though that is a lot to hope for. I think John Lennon so repellent-looking now – like a very plain middle-aged Victorian female novelist, with that long hair. I used to like the Beatles once and I still like their songs if I don't have to look at them.

Yes, I have two cats so their ways are known to me – one tortoiseshell and one black and white. We always had them at home, but couldn't in London till we got a house with a garden

I do hope you will get something better to read than unpublished, unpublishable novels! Let me thank you again for telling me (like D.H.L.) what my novel was really about, and apologise for this boring letter, but I felt I wanted to write soon.

With all good wishes,
Yours ever,

Barbara

40 Brooksville Avenue
7 February 1969

Dear Philip,

Your poem in *The Sunday Times* was powerful and haunting, the falling of those leaden words – I cut it out and put it in *The Whitsun Weddings*, though of course I hope I shall live to see another volume in which it will be printed.

I wish now I had thought of becoming a poet – and now I can see that I have let myself in for implying that a poem is less work than a novel. Please don't take it amiss! Anyway, if it comes not as naturally as the leaves to a tree . . . or whatever Keats said.

I am struggling to improve that Leonora novel but make slow progress. Anyway I like having something to think about and occasionally write a bit of. I have seen, or rather received, two copies of my Library Association reprint of *Excellent Women*. It looks rather nice, though I can't bring myself to *read* it. I get comfort from a re-reading of Anthony Powell and Charlotte Brontë (not *Jane Eyre*).

Very best wishes,

Barbara

15 May. At the Royal Society of Literature to hear a talk by Elizabeth Bowen on the novelist and his characters. Perhaps the most noteworthy thing that one, as it were, *brought away* was the idea of L.P. Hartley as a young man reviewing Elizabeth Bowen's first book for the *Spectator*, living in *Camden Road*. How different now in Rutland Gate! Perhaps I could have got up and protested, made a scene, have had to be 'removed' to everyone's embarrassment when Elizabeth Bowen seemed to praise Emily Brontë at the expense of Charlotte. 'Who was that woman who made a scene?' someone would ask. And nobody would know – only that I had been introduced by Philip Larkin, and that might have brought shame on *him*.

To Philip Larkin   40 Brooksville Avenue

27 May 1969

Dear Philip,

I did go to the Roy. Soc. Lit. (how do Librarians abbreviate it, when they have to?) and was most interested to set foot in there and hear Elizabeth Bowen give a very good and interesting talk, and see L.P. Hartley very much occupying the chair against a background of dusty dark blue velvet curtains. And who were all those ladies in beautiful hats, not all Fellows, I'm sure, though many of them looked as if they *ought* to have been. I was put in the second row (having arrived only just before it was due to start) so had little opportunity to look around me, but I found I was sitting just in front of Elizabeth Taylor, whom I know, who had come with her husband. Eliz. Bowen said that people never recognise themselves in novels (even if they have been 'put in') but I think one sometimes makes up a character and then he or she appears in the flesh, like a man now working in our Library, who is so like 'Mervyn' in my unpublished one, and even speaks of 'Mother'.

I went to the unveiling of the Byron memorial plaque in Westminster Abbey. There must have been lots of poets there but, apart from Day-Lewis, I recognised only politicians – Michael Foot and Bob Boothby! Afterwards, the friend I went with and I went to lunch at the Army and Navy Stores – perhaps not *quite* what one would have chosen as the perfect finish to a romantic and moving experience, but that area is not good for eating places.

We had a 'Festschrift' presentation to Daryll Forde a couple of weeks ago – he is retiring from University College London. A volume of essays had been contributed by his old students, called

Man in Africa, published by Tavistock. Of course these occasions are never quite as one would make them in fiction, except that one prominent linguist was seen surreptitiously refilling his glass when the presentation was being made. I was also struck by the number of academic women who appeared to have made really no effort at all – obviously none of that agonised 'But what shall I wear?' – really an enviable detachment and when will one ever reach it?

I've finished a very rough re-doing of that *Sweet Dove Died* novel about Leonora etc, but what reader would want to identify herself with Leonora? If only one could write about Margaret Drabble-like characters! But I suppose I couldn't have done, even when I was that age, so.... Perhaps the best thing to do now is to 'write' nothing but bibliographies.

All good wishes – Yours ever,

Barbara

31 July. Lunch at the Royal Commonwealth Society with Bob. In the restaurant all those clergymen helping themselves from the cold table, it seems endlessly. But you mustn't notice things like *that* if you're going to be a novelist in 1968–9 and the 70s. The posters on Oxford Circus station advertising Confidential Pregnancy Tests would be more suitable.

11 August. Visit to Jane Austen's house with Bob. I put my hand down on Jane's desk and bring it up covered with dust. Oh that some of her genius might rub off on me! One would have imagined the devoted female custodian going round with her duster at least every other day. Then to the site of Steventon Rectory the place of her birth – now a field overgrown with nettles and docks. We went into Steventon Church – very cool inside. Steventon Manor is deserted and overgrown, not beautiful but sad, almost romantic. Such enormous beech trees and that *silence* – a few miles away the road from Basingstoke to London and the traffic roaring by.

15 August. Longmans returned *The Sweet Dove* – 'well written' – but what's the use of that.

To Philip Larkin   40 Brooksville Avenue

19 September 1969

Dear Philip,

Thank you so much for *two* delightful holiday postcards – one from Norwich (bird with no lion above it) and the other from the

West of Ireland. I hope your room in Eire was more comfortable than Norwich seems to have been, though perhaps it's no use the single traveller expecting anything but the worst, as you seem to have found. I've twice been to Ireland, 1967 and 1968, and love it. Everyone is so *nice* to you and lots of cups of tea and Guinness, not to mention the beauty of scenery, fuschia hedges and arum lilies. I've not been to the North, but was glad to see that Queen's Univ. Belfast have had the discernment to give you a doctorate. Many congratulations! I cut the piece out of *The Telegraph* where it appeared in Peterborough but I haven't yet decided which of your poems it would go best in – I mean, as a resting-place, the Toad work rather than Faith Healing, perhaps?

My sister and I had a very good holiday in Greece, late May–early June. One felt a bit 'guilty' going there but Robert Liddell still lives in Athens and I've got to the age when I feel I must see friends rather than make protests. Robert wrote the *Times* obituary of Dame Ivy. Apparently she has left him part of her residuary estate which has touched and pleased him. He had a sentimental, un-Ivyish feeling about it. Yes, those obituaries, as you say! I was shocked at Pamela Hansford-J. turning up half an hour late for dinner and should have imagined that for somebody of *that* generation one would surely have been most careful to arrive punctually!

I'm glad to see your Jazz writings are to be collected, though I suppose I'd have preferred that Library novel or another volume of poems. I have nearly finished my revising and 'improving' of that novel I showed you about a year ago about Leonora. I have cut out a lot of the characters, ruthlessly suppressed (or tried to) all 'cosiness' and am now struggling with the last difficult chapters, which are new. Then I shall have to go through it all again to see what further improvements can be made. And after all that will there be any point in offering it to a publisher? One really does wonder! Still I suppose it's a nice 'hobby' for me, like knitting. Next I shall write a lighter academic one and perhaps after that one about the decay of the Anglican church. *Some Tame Gazelle* has just been done in the Portway Library Association reprints.

We continue to have trouble in staffing our Library at the Institute. A Ghanaian we had was *not* a success and spent a large part of his day conducting endless telephone calls in his native language (Fanti, I think). Hope you are all right in that respect!

With all good wishes,

Yours ever,

Barbara

40 Brooksville Avenue

10 December 1969

Dear Philip,

It was extremely kind of you to 'say a word' to James Wright of Macmillan about my book and I have just taken it along there. (I should explain that their new premises are so near to where I work that it is possible to walk along at lunch time with a manuscript in a shopping bag, thus avoiding the expense and frustration of the pre-Christmas post.) I am not very optimistic about the book's chances though it is improved, I think, and perfectly publishable if only somebody would have the courage to be unfashionable. I saw a most depressing TV programme on Saturday night about the dire state of fiction publishing. But I am not discouraged really, only fatalistic. I can now see how one might be led to have delusions of grandeur about one's work, or to develop persecution mania. You say that you are never 'seen' anywhere – and I can say that I write but don't get published!

Thank you very much for your last letter – written in October, when you had just got what sounds like a very splendid 'new' car – Vanden Plas Princess, indeed, with Rolls Engine! Hope she continues to please you.

Our work grows all the time. One of my tasks is to cope with review books sent for *Africa* and I have long discussions with Professor Forde who to send them to. Some of our academics might be surprised at the way they are judged when the criterion is whether they are quick and reliable reviewers. But perhaps what is to me in my narrow sphere a virtue, appears very dreary in the big world, like being 'a good husband and father' or 'a dutiful son'.

I hope nobody has asked you to act the part of Fr Christmas in your new Dr's robes. They do sound most reasonable at £35. What material are they made of? And is there a floppy hat to go with them? A pity you can't be photographed in them for your 1969 Christmas card – or perhaps you have been? People are too modest nowadays.

Yours ever,

Barbara

To Bob Smith in Lagos   40 Brooksville Avenue

11 December 1969

Dearest Bob,

The article ['How Pleasant to Know Miss Pym' by R. Smith] is most gratifying and soothing to my wounded ego, but providing suitable quotes is going to be difficult. Could you not give me a few clues, e.g. the bit where...and then I would cheerfully copy them out. Hazel may be able to help. I wasn't offended by anything – though curious to know just how many 'it so happened's' you found – and what you meant by woman's page or magazine style – making Wilmet say 'sweet' instead of 'agreeable'. The bits I might think most quoteable might not be your choice. But how nice of you to write it and it would be wonderful for both of us if Professor Jeffares would take it for *Ariel* magazine. Is he the man who edited the paperback selection of Yeats that I have? A far far cry....

Love,

Barbara

40 Brooksville Avenue

26 January 1970

Dearest Bob,

I fear Macmillan will not take *The Sweet Dove*, but only (they say) because it seems a risk commercially. I have never had a more flattering letter about my work (or even review) than the one James Wright wrote about it. He praised my 'perfection of taste' so you can see what is wrong, especially when you read the reviews in the Sundays any week. But how can one be different? Anyway I am going to send it round rather than let it lie at home. And I have even started my academic one about a provincial university [this novel never got beyond the first draft].

'Miss Austen' is wrong, of course, because Cassandra was the elder and Jane would be Miss Jane Austen. However, Miss Pym *is* correct for me if you are going in for that sort of thing.

St Lawrence's is in the red and numbers dropping all the time. But I hate the idea of 'meeting in people's houses' rather than going to church, as I have seen suggested. Just imagine Sung Mass at 40 Brooksville and Minerva jumping up on the altar and Tom sniffing the sacred vessels.

Much love,

Barbara

To Philip Larkin

40 Brooksville Avenue

1 February 1970

Dear Philip,

I was so delighted to get a copy of *All What Jazz* and I'm sure I shall gain much knowledge as well as pleasure from it. It's good of you to remember me! You look somehow different from the poet and novelist in the photograph on the jacket – something in the expression of the eyes or is that too far-fetched? How beautifully arranged the books are, presumably at 32 Pearson Park.

You have sent me so many books since we first, as it were, 'met' and I wish I could make some return. That is why I am sending you now this bound copy of *A Glass of Blessings* – perhaps you can regard it as a bibliographical curiosity, if nothing else, and it is the only such copy in existence.

James Wright couldn't have been nicer or more flattering about my rewritten version of *The Sweet Dove Died* but said Macmillan couldn't offer to publish as it seemed a risky commercial venture. Thank you *very* much for mentioning my name to him. At least I got a little confidence from his praise, i.e. it appears I can still write even if my type of book is no longer publishable. I have now sent the MS to a friend of mine, Dorothy Eden, an immensely successful writer of thrillers, 'gothic' and historical novels, and she is going to ask the advice of her agent, as she has also read and liked it. In the meantime Cape have got Portway Reprints to do *Jane and Prudence* and *Less Than Angels* in their Library reprints. They did *STG* and *Ex. Women* very nicely.

At the office I am surrounded by books about Africa, many of them 'marginal' to our field, and increasing numbers of bibliographies! Daryll Forde, who retired as Prof. of Anthropology at Univ. Coll. London this summer, now comes in to us *every* day (he is our Director) and makes lots more work, so that everyone has got rather fractious. We are hoping to get some Ford Foundation money to start an information and research center (I'm sure it should have American spelling) but we don't know yet if it will materialise.

Yours ever,

Barbara

40 Brooksville Avenue

21 March 1970

Dear Philip,

Easter is nearly here and I haven't yet bought any new clothes – all this anxiety about the skirt length – for people of my age it will be quite all right to wear things that seemed a little too long and are now the perfect mid-length. Did you see the picture of M. Drabble, Olivia M. and others in *The Sunday Times?* A pitiful group they looked – and what length were *they* wearing! Bringing culture to the North.

I hope you have been pleased with the reviews of *All What Jazz*. The ones I've seen have been good, though obviously you have shocked some reviewers deeply by your attitude! But of course I agree with you, though I wouldn't know about jazz. The introduction set me thinking back into my own girlhood – and that winding up of the portable gramophone – and the records – ours were mainly of the bands of the day – Jack Hylton and Jack Payne, and perhaps the odd Ellington – and my own favourite of Noel Coward and Gertrude Lawrence doing that scene from *Private Lives*. And of course we had ukuleles – *that* was surely before your time!

While on the nostalgic track – how wonderful to go to All Souls for six months – and may you have absolutely *no* worries, if such a state is possible. *The Oxford Book* [P.L. edited the *Oxford Book of 20th Century English Verse* (1973)] must be a bit nagging, though. How on earth do you decide what to put in? Perhaps it's a question of taking out poems that haven't stood 'the test of time' (sad, that) and substituting others or do you have to start again from scratch? Helen Gardner is your co-editor, I believe [H.G. edited the *New Oxford Book of English Verse* (1972)]. What happens if you disagree? As for revisiting places of one's youth and visiting places one never went to – perhaps the last is best. I wonder if Elliston's is now full of well dressed ladies having coffee mid-morning? I think the warm green-muffled Cumnor Hills were never as Arnold saw them. But Bagley Wood – ah... I think it belongs to St John's, doesn't it, and will have been preserved, bluebells and all.

Thank you for your sympathy about the *SDD*. Hodder were much of the opinion of James Wright at Macmillan – thought it very well written etc. in perfect taste (damning word?) but said that such books only sold in very small editions. Still, we will try it elsewhere. I certainly don't think it's worse than any of my others, but the main characters are perhaps not very sympathetic.

As for the reprinting – it is not Cape themselves who do this. They merely negotiated for me with Chivers of Bath who reprint (in very limited editions) for Libraries, the books not being on sale. The rights do revert to me when the books have been out of print a certain length of time, but what could I do with them myself if I hadn't got another publisher to do a new novel? It seemed best to let Chivers do them, so that at least they would be available in Libraries and the name of Barbara Pym not totally sunk in oblivion....

After that I must come to a different sort of end.

All good wishes,

Barbara

Easter Sunday. In St Lawrence's a fine polish on the bird (sprayed with Pledge by Hilary) especially on neck and claws. In the Hall a strong smell of tomcat, which is, after all, one of the smells of spring.

16 April. Sweet Dove rejected yet again (by Macdonald). Shall call it *Leonora* by Tom Crampton and send it out again.

29 April. What strikes one in going through the old I.A.I. Fellowship files – the difficulties over marriage – almost like entering a celibate priesthood. H. Beemer (1935) 'I think that the proper course for Miss Beemer would have been to raise the whole question with the Council before getting married. We have no precedent to guide us in a matter of this kind.'
The terrible illnesses – malaria, chiefly.
The low salary – £20 a month, £30 in the field.
Wife to live on £3 a week in England.
Frobenius 'behaved very badly' – *what* did he do?

3 July. Nellie's last day at the Kardomah. She got £5 a week part-time and had cleared the tables for 22 years. In the heat of June her remark to a man customer 'Oh, look at you perspiring'. The Kardomah closed July 3rd 1970.

Novel. Scene by scene. Write what researchers and biographers write of a person's life and then what really did happen (rather like *The Heroes of Clone* [by Margaret Kennedy]). Or first write the short biography, then write it again filled out and true. Beginning, perhaps, in 1939.

29 May [by bus to Athens]. Belgium, Germany, Austria, Yugoslavia. People in the coach: Young loving couple – he slightly Che Guevara; Irish couple – lady had too many changes of clothing and wore unbecoming beige slacks; elderly couple – tough know-all man; Katharine Wilkinson and her father – very nice; 'The wandering Scholar' – slightly odd, had diarrhoea; the Old Roué – military type, always at the bottle; Olde World Edwardian man about town; Australian couple (she of Greek origin) with little boy; Chris and Marie – Cockney couple.

3 June. Athens. Pension Penelope: It is a fine old house now somewhat in need of repair and redecoration. The inhabitants seem to be mostly elderly ladies, girl students and rather impoverished English tourists. A rather Katherine Mansfield sort of place – plastic bowls of washing soaking in the bathroom, eating in rooms, and every inhabitant has his or her own little corner of chaos. Our room has a stunning view of the Acropolis. A family of cats on the roof opposite.

4 June. In the evening we went to a taverna with Jock and Guido. Guido comes from Carrara and his family has a marble firm. Perhaps we could order our tombstones from him. When we got back to the Penelope I looked in my bag and saw that my passport wasn't there! Horror!

5 June. Went to the British Consulate about the passport. 'I'm afraid this is going to ruin your holiday,' said the man in a satisfied tone. I decided to go to places where I might have left it and finally ran it to earth in the American Express. Oh the relief!

Mycenae and Epidaurus. Found the Church of St Spyridon. There was an ikon of St Barbara (all silver) so I burned a candle to her as a thanks for finding my passport. Demoted she may be by Rome, perhaps, she is not by the Greek Orthodox.

To Philip Larkin   40 Brooksville Avenue

31 July 1970

Dear Philip,

Thank you for a beautiful card from the Hebrides – I dare say you are still there plodding through Scottish verse and Drinkwater. The latter reminds me so much of my schooldays in the twenties, though he was nothing like as popular as Rupert Brooke and Charles Hamilton Sorley.

Your going to All Souls [to work on *The Oxford Book*] suggests a plot for a novel though I doubt if I could write it. Middle-aged unmarried female don waits eagerly for the autumn when a friend of her Oxford days (the well-known poet, librarian and whatever else you like) is coming to spend a year at All Souls (doing some kind of research, perhaps). At first it is all delightful and they go for beautiful autumnal walks on Shotover (? can one still do this) but unknown to her he has been visiting a jazz club in the most squalid part of the town (where is that now?) and has fallen in love with a nineteen year old girl... the ending could be violent if necessary – or he could just go off with the girl, leaving the female don reading Hardy's poems. Perhaps it is a novel by Rachel Trickett, the first part, anyway?

I have no news of a publisher for *The Sweet Dove* and I don't think any one will *ever* publish it, though I go on sending it round. It is a wonder to me now that I ever published anything and I can hardly believe that I did! The article in *Ariel could* appear this autumn, but if it doesn't apparently it can't be till *next* autumn, I don't know why and neither does its author! Please don't feel guilty for not having written about me yourself – you have so often encouraged and cheered me, not to speak of amused, in countless ways, and that is better than anything.

My sister has bought a car and I am going to learn to drive. I wonder if I shall be able to do it? I *did* learn years ago but haven't kept it up and things are *very* different now, as people gleefully tell me. So I can but try, at the driving school which appears to be run by an Irishman – It would be a comfort if the car could be blessed at the Church of the Sacred Heart in Quex Road, Kilburn. I will let you know how I get on.

I suppose I ought to be grieved and shocked at your Library's withdrawal from SCOLMA, but I am not a bibliographer at heart so received the news without any emotion but a slight pleasure. The trouble with bibliographies about Africa is that they are getting so enormous that the quarterly one we publish in *Africa* is crowding out original work, such as articles and even book reviews. I long for the old innocent days when the bibliography was 8 or 10 pages instead of the 16–20 it now is!

I have had a week's holiday so far (in that good June weather) and hope to take some more in September. We picnicked just outside Iris Murdoch's village (Steeple Aston) but nothing sensational happened. Another time we got stuck in Woodstock and an L.P. Hartley-like chauffeur wearing dark glasses came to our aid.

Best wishes,
Yours ever,

Barbara

10 August. Had my third driving lesson from Peter – grinding round Willesden and Cricklewood in the rain in second gear.

20 August. If you were ever romantic, and, of course, you can't possibly be now, at your age, imagine lunching with somebody and him urging you to drink most of the wine because it makes him feel so sleepy. Tall Irish Murdoch waitress, perhaps a student doing a holiday job.

31 August. It seems unnatural not to be writing bits for novels in one's notebook. What sort of novel could I write now? A gothic novel – I thought of this as I made my daily visit to the nectarine tree, spread out against the south-facing wall at the top of the garden.

They seem old-fashioned fruit with their hard red cheeks, not soft and downy like a peach. Why shouldn't it be a *modern* gothic novel. What are the ingredients. A heroine, but much more of a heroine than Mildred or Wilmet. A setting. A hero. Mystery. A modern version of Jane Eyre?

6 September. Bob and I met at Green Park station to go to the Chapel Royal (11.15 Sung Eucharist), but when we got there found it was closed until October. '*And* you're too late for the Guards' Chapel,' said the man. So we made our way to St James Piccadilly where Matins had started. The rector (the Rev. William Pye Baddeley – brother of Hermione and Angela) was in the middle of reading the 2nd lesson in a modern version, where Mary Magdalen breaks the box of precious ointment over Jesus.... 'Here endeth that perfectly lovely lesson,' he declared. The congregation was mostly elderly and well dressed. We prayed for visitors to London, especially those from the USA and there were some dollar bills in the plate.... Then we had tea at the Ritz (which seemed to be the only place open round there) sage green and pink upholstery. But the reclining nymph at the fountain is golder and brassier than in Anthony Powell's *The Acceptance World* where she is bronze. Still the vaguely Latin-American looking people and the heat very fierce (central heating on a hot summer's day). But the waiter who brought our tea was Irish and it was hot and strong.

To Bob Smith in Lagos   40 Brooksville Avenue

6 November 1970

Dearest Bob,

I am feeling encouraged because *The Sweet Dove* was very nearly accepted by Peter Davies, and I sent it completely out of the blue with no indication that I had ever written anything else. One of the directors (Mark Barty-King) wrote me a long letter, quoting five readers' reports, some of which were very flattering. It was 'very accomplished' and 'a minor tour de force' but the general opinion was that it wasn't quite powerful enough or plotted enough to appeal to enough readers. I have had to write back and reveal my secret, but I don't suppose they can change their minds now. One of the less kind reports said that it was clever-clever and decadent – *that* made me feel about 30 years younger!

The Bishop's chaplain [Fr Jennings] has now materialised and it is all a bit like *A Glass of Blessings*. He hasn't moved into the house in

Kingswood Avenue yet because it is in a *filthy* condition and it needs to have £5,000 spent on it (*surely* it can't be 5,000, but that is what he said). He is going to have one of the front downstairs rooms made into a garage and is going to have ordinands living in the house. I gather he is director of the ordinands, if that is the correct title, as well as chaplain to Graham Willesden, who is no longer a Suffragan but Bishop of a new province which seems to include us and Hazel, far west in Ealing.

Love,

Barbara

9 November. I visit the Library at LSE. Waiting down below at the enquiry desk – the rough students with long hair and strange one-sex clothes make me feel old and vulnerable.

What is wrong with being obsessed with trivia? Some have criticised *The Sweet Dove* for this. What are the minds of my critics filled with? What *nobler* and more worthwhile things?

26 November. At the National Portrait Gallery with Hazel to hear the readings about Andrew Marvell. *Not* 'My love is of a birth so rare' – but, of course, 'Had we but world enough and time' – the audience of middle-aged and elderly ladies must surely have had the poem recited to them when young. I sat with bowed head as Robert Harris (himself a little too old) read it, but Hazel detected a triumphant smirk or two.

Reading Charlotte M. Yonge's *The Daisy Chain* and see the echoes or rather foreshadowings of Ivy Compton-Burnett in it. Ivy would have made Dr May marry Meta Rivers and she would then have had an affair with Norman. Some patches of Ivy dialogue too. Oh that some idea might come to *me*. It is enjoyable and very readable.

To Bob Smith in Lagos   40 Brooksville Avenue

31 December 1970

Dearest Bob,

There was no Christmas service at St Lawrence's which was rather sad, but of course there are plenty of nearby churches to go to. We went to St Anne's. A nice service and the church was really *warm*. Next Sunday Fr Jennings will be back and he does feel the cold so and certainly lets one know it. We fear he is rather pampered but certainly the object of interest and amusement. It never does to ask after his health or he will tell you. Work is going on on his house. It was burgled recently and some coffee tables were stolen, also an 'antique' clock which had been given to one of his ordinands. When commiserated with, however, he said the clock was really rather a hideous Victorian thing and not at all to *his own* taste, which Hilary and I thought rather mean of him. Little, of course, does he realise who is drinking it all in!

Much love,

Barbara

22 April 1971. It amuses me to read in a review of Malcolm Muggeridge's book about Mother Teresa that he describes Newman's 'Lead kindly light' as 'exquisite'. *Not* quite the word.

27 April. Morning at St Mary's Hospital, Paddington. O little lump – almost a subject for a metaphysical poem. Conveniently opposite are an ABC café and a pub. I choose the latter (Private Bar). Two elderly ladies with light ale, coughing and cackling, and an Irish Landlord. Andrew Cruickshank said that in the 18th century there was moss growing round the high altar of St Paul's cathedral. Can this be true?

To Bob Smith in Lagos   St Mary's Hospital
                                                          Harrow Road

                                                          1 May 1971

Dearest Bob,

I don't know how to prevent this letter being a shock to you, as it has been to me – because this time last week I never imagined I should be in hospital!

I discovered a lump on my left breast, immediately went to the doctor who got me in here for an examination next day, the day after I was taken into hospital, the next day they operated and now, two days later here I am writing to tell you about it.

Of course I couldn't have chosen a worse time, with Hilary away in Greece, but everyone has been *marvellous* and all those clichés about one's true friends are proved right. Hazel a tower of strength, Mrs P.C. coming round with grapes, my friends at the Institute rallying round.

You will have guessed that it was cancer and that was why they took away the left bosom. I can't make out whether the other ladies here are breastless (like Amazons?) or have other things the matter with them. Everyone is so kind – the black hands and the white hands, so cool and firm and comforting.

Don't worry about me, I am being well cared for.

Much love,

Barbara

To Philip Larkin   40 Brooksville Avenue

22 June 1971

Dear Philip,

Many thanks for your letter – also the note with your Christmas card – then came the postal strike and all those devious things we had to do (at the International African Institute) like giving letters to people to post in France and Belgium and various parts of Africa! I had imagined you having a lot of social life (the mantelpiece permanently dark with invitation cards) and wondered even if the plot of the novel I sketched out was coming true. You *do* seem to have worked hard – the (then) English Reading Room of the Bodleian has many sentimental memories for me – I can remember deliberately *not* going there for fear of seeing a certain person or to hope that my absence would be noticed. I do wonder which poems you will have chosen – how on earth do you know where to begin? I suppose that is settled beforehand.

I hope you won't think I am taking my revenge on you for not having written, but now you will have to hear all about my operation! In fact, at this moment (in time, as people say) I am sitting in the garden in a rare burst of sunshine and am on convalescent leave, probably returning (gently) to work the week after next. I was in hospital the first three weeks in May having been rushed in for a sudden operation. Since there are no longer hushed voices when one speaks of it I'll tell you that it was a breast cancer, luckily caught when very small so I hope there won't be any recurrence though I suppose one mustn't be over-optimistic. Now I am like the woman in that novel by Penelope Mortimer except that mine is the left side and hers was the right. Also, I'm about 25 years older which does make a difference – one minds much less about one's physical beauty and of course it doesn't show at all when one is dressed. It was my first visit to hospital and apart from the first few days of discomfort (and even that wasn't very bad) I rather enjoyed the experience. To have a lovely rest, to have flowers and grapes and books brought to you and to be a centre of interest is not at all unpleasant! I found I even didn't mind students looking at me. I had it done on the NHS but by luck I was put in a side ward which was as good as a private room – I used to mingle with people in the ward though and had a lot of talks – I discovered that all you need do is to make some enquiry and you will get a whole life story. I wonder if I could write a hospital novel, hardly a romance, I feel, nor yet *Doctor in the House.*

I cannot get anything published, though Peter Davies almost took the Leonora book. They thought they had discovered a new writer and, bearing that in mind, the readers' comments were rather funny. Rather to my surprise I find I have nearly finished the first draft of another novel about a provincial university [never revised, unpublished] told by the youngish wife of a lecturer. It was supposed to be a sort of Margaret Drabble effort but of course it hasn't turned out like that at all. The *Ariel* article is *supposed* to be coming out in October – I'll let you know when it does, *if* it does, but it has actually been in proof.

I was interested to hear of your meeting Iris Murdoch and wonder if we shall find a character like you in her next novel. Obviously a novelist should cross question people, like the anthropologist in the field, but I've never been able to do that very much myself though I love finding out things about people in my own way.

I have lately taken to reading Charlotte M. Yonge. I've found much enjoyment and richness especially in *The Pillars of the House*, which is a very churchy one. What a wonderful length books were allowed to be in those days before the telly and all that!

What do you think of *Maurice* in the *Sunday Times*? Hard to tell from the rather mangled extracts but I look forward to reading it in its proper form, I wonder what could possibly be regarded as too daring to publish nowadays?

I hope all went well at the Library when you were absent and everything wasn't left for you to decide (or perhaps you'd rather it was!). I am being quite gratifyingly missed at my work and the July *Africa* has come out 4 pages shorter than intended. Also the mystique of the advertisements has not been fathomed by anyone else trying to do my work. Yet I don't really want to become embroiled again. It is all too easy to pass the days pleasantly doing not very much, but I suppose that's convalescence.

With all good wishes,
    Yours ever,

                                                            Barbara

22 August. How splendid All Saints Margaret St is – close to 200 people there! I reckon when you compare it with the five to ten at St

Lawrence's it hardly seems to be the same religion. And yet, where two or three are gathered together....

Bob is taking Joan to Walsingham to give thanks for her recovery. I gave thanks for mine quietly in my bed at St Mary's Hospital, Harrow Road and at Brooksville Avenue, even in poor old St Lawrence's.

30 October. Cats Protection League Bazaar, held in Westminster Cathedral Hall. A few men, perhaps 2 or 3, but the rest women and me as dotty as any of them. Tea in pink or blue plastic cups, not very hot. A woman sitting by the door collecting money just 'for the cats'. She has a gentle face, wears slacks, voluminous coat and fine brown straw hat. Stuffed frog by her on table, but of no significance (at first I thought it was a raffle). This simple collecting was something, perhaps the only thing she could do.

To Bob Smith in Lagos   40 Brooksville Avenue

31 October 1971

Dearest Bob,

Thank you so much for having the copy of *Ariel* sent, it was lovely to see the article in print and I am so grateful to you for having written it and given me such pleasure. There are some rather good erudite articles about T.S. Eliot and 'that sort of thing'. One might contribute an obscure note on something: 'Mrs Widmerpool's bridge-coat', for example.

The event for us has been the closing of St Lawrence's. It closed at the end of September without ceremony, but last Wednesday the Bishop of Willesden came and gave us a Sung Mass and quite a lot of people came. Since the closing we have been to St Mary Magdalene's, Paddington. It has rather good music and quite an amusing vicar (dragging on a cigarette) and curate who live in a startlingly modern clergy house just opposite the church.

I have finished the first draft of a novel about a provincial university. The idea for it was inspired by that business of John Beattie and Rodney Needham in *Africa* [an academic wrangle] and the original version of Mrs Fisher's *Twilight Tales of the Black Baganda* – there are also two characters in it rather like Richard and his mother, exiles from the Caribbean. Perhaps my immediate circle of friends will like to read it.

Much love,

Barbara

To Philip Larkin   40 Brooksville Avenue

7 November 1971

Dear Philip,

I have made very good progress and when I went to hospital two weeks ago for a check-up they told me I needn't come back for a year – so unless anything unforeseen happens I am clear of *that*! I am working nearly full time.

The article Robert Smith wrote about me in *Ariel* has now come out in the October number. 'How Pleasant to Know Miss Pym', it is called. On reading it, I wonder if that is what I am really like or my books. If you see it, tell me what you think! Perhaps somebody in the University of Calgary would care to buy some of my old notebooks in a few years' time. (The Univ. of Calgary is connected with Leeds in the publishing of *Ariel*).

I still haven't passed my driving test! But am due to take it for the 4th time on 19th November at 12.15 (at Hendon). I don't know who the patron saint of such things is – possibly St Jude – or the demoted St Christopher? All middle-aged women fail their first test, my second was perhaps too soon after my being in hospital, my third I was not careful enough, but perhaps my fourth will be better if I am *very* careful. 'All he wants is a safe ride.' The examiners at Hendon are uniformly grey men; perhaps it is a breed, like customs officers.

I have no literary success to report. A reader at Barrie and Jenkins went so far as to admit that she had 'enjoyed' my book, but prospects of publication seem to get bleaker. In the meantime I will try to go on with the University one and maybe one day you may read it and advise me about it. But oh the effort of getting things finished. Did you see on the back of the *Sunday Times* today about the girl who is starting the Orlando Press, erotic books written by women for women? What can they possibly be like? (I shall look out for them with interest.)

I hope you are not feeling depressed (or won't be when you get this letter). I'm not sure that I agree about memories *always* being unhappy or uncomfortable ones. I find as I get older that I tend to steer clear of any kind of memories or push them away, unless I want to call them up for any special reason. But when I'm unhappy or depressed I do find myself remembering 'better times', those good reviews of my novels etc. but that doesn't make one any more cheerful – on the contrary, *Nessun maggior dolore*... and all *that* jazz! But now I want to pass my driving test and I want to publish another novel, and even to *write* another novel to my own satisfaction, so perhaps my mind is filled with all that, and I am lucky.

Our church has become 'redundant' and been closed! *There's* something I should like to write about. Now I can go around from church to church with no particular attachment. Neither my sister nor I really want to get involved anywhere at the moment, having had enough of all that to last a long time.

Yours ever,

Barbara

10 November. Mr C in the Library – he is having his lunch, eating a sandwich with a knife and fork, a glass of milk near at hand. Oh *why* can't I write about things like that any more – why is this kind of thing no longer acceptable? A failing novelist, but coming up to my 4th driving test on the 19th. Not that you won or lost but that you played the game. Only it doesn't seem to work out like that. Slow, careful and safe.... All the same I failed. I had Mr Bloomfield again. But afterwards he was quite nice and cosy, like talking over one's shortcomings with a priest after confession.

4 February 1972. Now that the possibility of being 'buried' in the country looms, one goes about one's bit of London taking it all in. But so much is being pulled down, especially between Fleet St and Aldwych (by King's College). And Gamage's is to be closed and pulled down. Oh unimaginable horror!

Lunch in the Kingsway Kardomah reading *The Church Times* (even that has gone off – no Answers to Correspondents). A tiny little elderly woman clears the tables – only about 5 ft high or less so that one nearly knocks her over with one's tray. Her little wrinkled claw-like hand comes towards me with a J-cloth to wipe the counter. Go away old crone, I want to say. The best place to sit is in the window, watching the cars come down Kingsway and stopping at the zebra crossings. The *only* places to have lunch now: Kingsway Kardomah, Holborn Kardomah (The Dutch House), Gay Fayre opposite the Prudential – very squashed but one could sit in the window there on a high stool and watch Gamage's being demolished. Then the Tea Centre in Lower Regent St is good too. 'You get a nice class of person there.'

6 March. Gamage's is having its final sale before being closed and demolished. A dreadful scene with empty counters and tumbled merchandise and people walking about like zombies. This is the year of change and decay, though presumably shoe-box buildings will spring up on the site of decay.

Being told that it is 'virtually impossible' for a novel like *The Sweet Dove* to be published now (by Constable). What is the future of my kind of writing? What can my notebooks contain except the normal kinds of bits and pieces that can never (?) now be worked into fiction. Perhaps in retirement, and even in the year before, a quieter, narrower kind of life can be worked out and adopted. Bounded by English literature and the Anglican Church and small pleasures like sewing and choosing dress material for this uncertain summer.

To Bob Smith in Lagos   I.A.I.
                                                       7 March 1972

Dear Bob,

At last we are moving the Institute to 210 High Holborn, then this building is to be demolished and so is Gamage's – a whole period of civilisation gone! Perhaps the rot set in with the closing of the Kardomah all those months ago. The new offices are nice but far less spacious than old St Dunstan's Chambers and we shall all be rather cramped. Hazel and I have a room rather like the one here but smaller. Of course the new place will be more convenient – nearer to the British Museum, SOAS, Bourne and Hollingsworth, Marks and Spencer and other desirable places.
     Much love,

                                                       Barbara

20 March. The ABC café in Fleet St, opposite the Law Courts – new but ever old. The new name (The Light Bite), the smart orange and olive green and beige and stripped pine decor, the hanging lamp shades, the new green crockery – but inside the food is the same, the little woman cooking, the West Indian lady serving the tea, the nice, bright efficient lady at the cash desk. You might quote Cavafy's poem about finding a new city, yet everything being the same, meaning oneself sitting there brooding.
     Have thought of an idea for a novel based on our office move – all old, crabby characters, petty and obsessive, bad tempered – how easily one of them could have a false breast! But I'd better not write it till I have time to concentrate on it (look what happened to the last).

3 April. Easter. At Buckland on Good Friday I had a migraine, oh the shame of it. As one gets older, the difficulties of being a guest, helping and not helping, doing and not doing.

19 April. In the new offices, the move successfully accomplished. Now I wander round Bloomsbury, scene of so many and distant past glories. Who can ever live here now?

The ageing white woman in the office. Beside the mysterious depths of the black girls she has nothing, no depths, no mystery, certainly no sexuality. She is all dried up by the mild British sun, in which she may sit in a deck chair, eyes closed against its ravages.

10 May. Sitting at lunch in the help-yourself in Bourne and Hollingsworth I think why, those women sitting round me are like lunatics in some colour supplement photographs of bad conditions in a mental home. Twitching or slumping or bending low over their food like an animal at a dish (especially if eating *spaghetti*).

To Philip Larkin   40 Brooksville Avenue

29 May 1972

Dear Philip,

What better time to reply to your letter than a cold windy cloudy Spring bank holiday, huddled in warm clothes, with a cup of coffee and a cat crouching on my desk? At least I shan't be tempted to go and sit in the garden and sleep in a deckchair.

One begins to wonder what is going to happen to us all, though mercifully one doesn't seriously worry yet. Kingsley Amis is 50, but I think you aren't yet or not quite? I am 59 this week and next year shall be an OAP or a senior citizen – special terms for hairdos if you go between 9 and 10 a.m. on a Monday or Tuesday and no doubt other privileges. The kiddies and the old people....I'm not sure that I like *that*.

Quite a lot of news since I last wrote! My sister and I have bought a cottage at Finstock (14 miles N.W. of Oxford) near Witney, Charlbury, Woodstock etc and hope to move into it later this summer, having sold this house. I shall still be working for another year anyway and shall try to find a room in London to live in during the week, as I wouldn't have the strength to commute from Oxford every day, though many people make even longer journeys. What a pity one can't still live in Bloomsbury for a pittance – that would suit me very well. I might advertise myself in the *Church Times* and now that I have definitely given up smoking I could say 'non-smoker', which would add to my desirability (gentlewoman, Anglican, quiet, 'business lady' etc) as a tenant. A pity one can't offer oneself to the advertisers who ask for '4th girl share super Chelsea flat'.

We have also moved our offices from Fetter Lane to High Holborn – not a very great distance, but very different in most respects. A smaller more modern building and we are all more squashed together and have less privacy. But nearer to shops, the British Museum, and many Italian restaurants, second-hand bookshops, Marks and Spencer. I long to write a novel about the office move and the strange passions aroused and the unpleasantness about who was to go where – perhaps when I have the time I will. My novel about Leonora is now with Chatto and Windus who wrote a kind letter saying that they would be glad to consider it, but I haven't very much hope. It's amazing though how many publishers there still are that I haven't tried, so I may go on with it. I have been too busy or too lazy or too discouraged to go on with my provincial university novel, though I much appreciated the local colour about the stink after the Sit-in!

Who will be the Poet-Laureate? It might well be you, but would you like it? Poor old Auden, coming to live in Oxford because he feels he might fall down or be taken ill and nobody would know, surely he isn't *that* old? Betjeman might be the best choice? I liked your article on him in the *Cornhill*, but I think women (I at any rate) do enter into what he describes more fully than you perhaps realise, even the business girls in Camden Town and even perhaps 'And now dear Lord I cannot wait, because I have a luncheon date!'

All good wishes,
Yours ever,

Barbara

19 June. The position of the unmarried woman – unless, of course, she is somebody's mistress, is of no interest whatsoever to the readers of modern fiction. The beginning of a novel?

22 June. Wilfred Whiteley's memorial service. The death of a younger colleague – that could be part of my novel about old people. Belief and non-belief. A rather bleak sort of service in a way.

6 July. Living at Finstock and with no permanent base in London now. A strange life and in the heat of Monday feeling quite ill at Paddington and having to be 'careful', then at lunchtime throat constricted and unable to eat. Most disconcerting. But gradually better. Saturday morning in Charlbury – the dead (dying) baby bat in the gutter with its chocolate brown fur.

Keats walking in the fields of Kilburn is what I should like to know more about.

Lovely walk on Sunday evening to Wilcote, St Peter's church with the little grassy graveyard and overlooking it the (apparently uninhabited but knowing Finstock probably not) back of a tall house, the windows overlooking the tombstones. It is left to me to find the dead bird, the dried up hedgehog body, the mangled rabbit.

2 October. Love between a middle-aged man and woman (i.e. Jane and Nicholas in *Jane and Prudence*) has softened into mild kindly looks and spectacles. Now consider how it might be in the unmarried middle-aged women in the office. Both have had affairs of some kind but now they can express love only through a tenderness and solicitude towards each other. 'Let me make you a cup of tea,' 'Shouldn't you go home.' These feelings that should have been directed towards husband or child.

The man in the office would bring his own lunch of course.

An older woman would say, 'Now what are your marriage arrangements?'

Could go back dispassionately naming earlier wives and mistresses.

What is a man's and what is a woman's work in an office?

Couldn't there be lots of acrimonious salary discussions and going into budgets? How do they spend their money. Who brings what for lunch. Smoked salmon, 2oz. Their director has no notion of what things cost – send him into Sainsbury's, an old man with a basket.

Someone has given John Middleton a folding umbrella – surely a *woman* – one could hardly envisage the exchange of such gifts between men.

To Philip Larkin   Barn Cottage   32 Balcombe Street
                         Finstock   London N.W.1.

24 October 1972

Dear Philip,

As you will see, I am now very well established in two places. I have been very lucky to find a nice little room in the house of friends of friends and I stay here Monday to Friday. Balcombe Street goes up from Dorset Square and is between Baker Street and Marylebone stations. Indeed as I lie in bed in the early morning I can sometimes hear the station announcer from Marylebone booming away about something. I have been here since August and now feel very much at home. I have 'use of kitchen' and make my own breakfast and evening meal ('dinner' is perhaps not quite the word for it). Then on Friday evening I go to Finstock (good train from Paddington) where I have a different sort of life. Rather strange and disorientating in a way but I feel I am getting the best of both worlds. Recently we had a monk staying – a cousin of my hostess.

We like Finstock very much and the people have been very friendly. It is not a beautiful village but so near all those lovely places like Minster Lovell, Burford, Swinbrook (grave of Unity Mitford in the churchyard), Westwell etc etc. Our house (cottage) is in the olde bit and was originally a 17th century barn, converted about six years ago. We have beams in every room, but modern comforts too. We have two bedrooms and a tiny spare room – sitting room and kitchen open plan – bathroom downstairs. A *double* garage! Excellent for storing all those odds and ends we still haven't been able to fit in. We had to dispose of quite a lot of furniture as our house in London was bigger. But this is much better – less work as one gets older! The cats love it and after a rather traumatic (for us) first night or two have settled down very well. Tom's idea of a 'happening' to amuse a party of ladies was to enter suddenly through the window with a not quite dead mouse in his mouth.

The church is not very high ('Series 2') but there is quite an enthusiastic congregation of people who have come fairly recently to the neighbourhood. Hilary and I are a bit jaded and cynical about things like bazaars but try not to show it. Like most country parishes the Vicar has 3 churches to cope with (*not* like the old palmy days of which I write in *Some Tame Gazelle* when every village had its own vicar or rector).

I haven't been doing any writing – my divided life hardly allows it – though I tinker with my provincial university novel sometimes. Next year when I'm due to retire I shall have more time. And I can't think whose biography to write as friends urge me to! There is another novelist in Finstock – Gilbert Phelps who wrote *The Winter People* (about South America). He is very nice.

I wonder how Betjeman will do as Poet Laureate, what he will write. If you had been P.L. what would *you* have written – much less predictable. I expect you are glad not to be? I enjoyed your 50th birthday tribute though nobody chose *all* my favourite Larkin poems – Roy Fuller chose one, I think.

Great staff dramas in our office – *that* set up suggests itself as fruitful novel material, but no time to go into that now.

Very best regards,

Barbara

31 October. How unsuitable to be reading Harold Acton's *Memoirs of an Aesthete* at lunch in Lyons (Jolyon) after a rather dire little service at St Alban's Holborn. Series *4* I should think. Oh pray for the Church of England!

5 November. Walking in Oxford on a Sunday afternoon – to look at the changed St Hilda's from the outside, though the gardens look the same. Then to Addison's Walk and deer and beech trees shedding their leaves. A good place to lie down waiting for death covered in leaves by the still streams.

8 December. The woman with the dogs very much in Baker St station these days. This morning the almost unbearable pathos of seeing the two of them curled up together asleep in a carrier bag.

A lonely person found dead with no food in the house (but what else would be there?). A cultured woman who has worked in an office, who realises that she is in danger but is too late to stop herself.

January 1973.
There could be talk in the office about elderly people being found dead with no food in the house.

'One might have a tin of soup but lack the strength to open it, or even to tear away the cellophane from a packet of biscuits.'

21 February. My novel has its umpteenth rejection (from Cassell). After lunch with Dirom at Oodles we go to Red Lion Square and I enter the portals of Cassell's to collect the nicely done-up MS. Where next? Up to Faber in Queen's Square?

27 February. Sometime in the early 1960s they had cleared away the undergrowth in the park and everyone said how much better it was. People couldn't throw things there or molest children (kiddies). But now the bushes were beginning to grow again and in places gave enough shelter for our heroine to conceal herself when the man came round at dusk blowing his whistle to get everyone out before shutting the park. I have fallen through the net of the Welfare State, she thought, picturing this more as a coarse serviceable hair net than a net to catch trapeze artists.

To Philip Larkin   32 Balcombe Street

13 March 1973

Dear Philip,

Now that Christmas is over, and winter almost, and spring really here (in the country) I begin to look forward to my retirement though it won't happen all at once when I reach 'the age' in June. I've already had papers to fill up and it's rather a comfort to think that somebody is prepared to pay me money for not working. Ironical to think that I used to look forward to retirement as the time when I would really be able to get down to *writing*! No doubt I shall try something and perhaps when I have more time I shall do it better – but to what end, if not publication?

We are in a confused and disturbed state at the place where I work – Professor Forde (now nearly 71) wishing to retire (or his wife wishing him to) but nobody suitable to take over – and what is the future anyway for Institutions like ours, founded in the twenties to help Africans to get school-books in their own languages? It is a rich subject for fiction if one can look at it with a novelist's cruelly dispassionate eye, as I fear I sometimes can. Added to all of which – should we register for VAT?! I was incensed to receive a communication from Cape asking if I proposed to register – the very small income I make from my books is much smaller because of their refusal to publish me any more!

Yesterday I was walking past a bookshop in Long Acre when I saw your face looking out from the cover of *All What Jazz*. Next to it were placed some Victorian photographs in those little folding cases of the period. There seemed no reason for the curious juxtaposition. It is a secondhand shop and everything is very expensive.

I suppose your Oxford Book is due out soon and I hope will be well received, though I suppose anthologies will always annoy as many as they please. I like Helen Gardner's very much but it is too big – in actual bulk – to read very comfortably.

With the best of wishes (and for the Oxford B.)

Barbara

To Bob Smith in Aberdeen   32 Balcombe Street
                                                13 April 1973

Dearest Bob,

I am really writing this at the I.A.I. where I am smothered in a mass of intractable French and English seminar papers which we are trying to make into a publishable volume. How nice it would be if the publication of such papers were to be forbidden by law!

No good news of writing, as far as I'm concerned. I've given up sending round the last one – 21 publishers is surely enough. Now I just jot things down in my notebooks, lacking the courage to start anything again though I suppose I will one day. Both Jock and I are longing for the sort of book which J. Guest in Longmans described as 'not the sort to which people are turning'. I've just read *The Golden Bowl* and the last 2 vols of Leon Edel's Henry James biography which I enjoyed very much. I got a bit muddled about Rye, though, thinking that it ought to be E.F. Benson dictating to the secretary when of course he came *after* H.J. He (H.J.) was worried in *1909* at the number of motor cars which seemed to be turning up in Rye. Happy, innocent days.

Have you any news of Richard? See how lightly I can write that now, as befits a woman on the threshold of sixty.

Much love,

Barbara

2 July. In the train. I can't have a Pepsi, she thought. A woman of my age and appearance would be expected to order coffee. Yet she longed for the dark icy liquid and the prickle of its bubbles.

Things you can do in London: Austerity meal (with wine) at St Alban's Holborn.

In order to cheat death or just to keep oblivion at bay their names had been given to Halls, lectures, memorial funds, prizes etc.

To Philip Larkin   32 Balcombe Street

11 July 1973

Dear Philip,

I hope the dust raised by the Oxford Book has now settled on the dark suit of the librarian – or perhaps he may be on holiday, having exchanged the dark suit for a T shirt – with an inscription like BIRD LIVES on the chest? It must be about this time that you take your car on holiday somewhere?

I am still at work, though I have just passed my 60th birthday, but various things have happened which make it difficult for me to retire immediately. To begin with our Director, Daryll Forde, suddenly died at the beginning of May – at work one day and dead that same evening. It was all very distressing and we have been rather like a rudderless ship, though things are beginning to settle down a bit now. We haven't really found a new Director yet but have two 'Acting Co-Directors'. I wonder how that will work out! There was a Memorial Service ('Thanksgiving Service' seems to be the term now) at the London University Church in Gordon Square. DF was *not* a believer so it wasn't very Christian though the Chaplain gave a kind of blessing at the end. It consisted of readings and music with an address by a colleague. Afterwards some of us were invited to have a drink in what was described as an 'anteroom' but really it was a kind of vestry with crucifixes and hymnbooks lying around and, on a hanger, a very beautiful *white* cassock or soutane, such as Roman priests in the tropics wear – that rather puzzled me. It was like something that I might have put into a novel, I fear. Anyway I am going on working for a bit but have told 'them' that I may feel like working at home in the country sometimes which I did rather successfully during June when my friends at Balcombe Street were away. I do rather agree with you about some of the difficulties of having *no* work, and *when* could one start drinking. Not before 12? Perhaps not *gin* and anything until 12? After all one doesn't want to develop what the Americans call 'a drinking problem' which I gather quite a few female American anthropologists have. One might do quite a good study on that – it might well be linked with other 'problems' (into which we need not go!).

The only good writing news I have is that Chivers of Bath have agreed to do *A G of B* and *No Fond Return* in their new Portway Reprint Series for Libraries. So that means that all my books have been done in this way and people can read them. I've really given up sending anything round at the moment, but still find myself trying to write. But about old people!

I hope you are well and that this year is being a good one for you. London gets even more dire though one still has some affection for it. All shops are now Travel or Photocopying or Employment Agencies, with the occasional Sandwich Bar. (I mean the small shops round here, when they fall vacant).

Very best wishes!

Barbara

6 August. Beautiful Tudor-style Old People's Home for sale.

Isak Dinesen (Karen Blixen) perhaps rather a tiresome person. Just imagine her with Truman Capote!

2 November. All Souls. If only, Letty thought, Christianity could have had a British, even an English origin! Palestine was so remote, violence on one's TV screen.

To Philip Larkin   Barn Cottage

16 October 1973

Dear Philip,

I hope all goes well with you. I still haven't quite retired, and love being in the country. Life is very full and the village is in many ways like *Some Tame Gazelle* or even T.F. Powys! 'Miss Hutt and the Paraclete' might be one chapter. (Our vicar does sometimes preach a little above the heads of his congregation).

I have written a letter to *The Author*, sparked off by Trevor Hoyle's account of publishing his own novel, about the difficulties even published novelists have now, so I hope it will be printed – rather more to the point, as far as I'm concerned, than this endless wrangling over Public Lending Rights, etc.

I am writing, quietly in bed in the early morning, a novel about four people in their sixties working in the same office. I don't know if I shall finish it or if I do whether it will be any good to try a publisher.

Excuse this egotistical letter – why does one get like this? Sad that Auden and William Plomer have gone

Very best wishes,

Barbara

28 November. They have pulled down Gamage's and so much in Fetter Lane including St Dunstan's Chambers where we worked for close on 20 years. The emotion that place saw will never be experienced in 210 High Holborn [new offices of the I.A.I.]. Now flat – nothing but rubble and a deep wide hole in the ground. Walked back through Lincoln's Inn Fields – so different from the summer – a *bitter* day, coldest for November since the beginning of the century.

12 January 1974. In Charlbury churchyard the older graves have sunk right into the turf – worn cherubs' heads just visible above the grass.

27 March. Balcombe St. Dark, dull and rather cold. Woke early. 'The Trout' on Radio 3 and reading *The Clever Woman of the Family* [by Charlotte M. Yonge] in bed. At Holborn station a notice on the blackboard explains a delay 'due to a person under the train' at Hammersmith.

Small strope [stroke]. [*This stroke caused a kind of partial dyslexia for a while, hence the spelling of this entry*]Investigation revealsed breask canser and exces of calcium thought to be from canser but bone trace did not conferm them. Dr Burke examineed me (+ studenns) and suscepts excess of parathroughoid [parathyroid] gland in the neck. More test may reveil that a small operation on the neck may be necessary, so tomorrow bariom meal, urine tests etc. On Tuesday examination by Mr Bron eye specialist to see if any calcium there. But hopefully home cerca Wednesday. Asphasia: stroke?

To Philip Larkin   Barn Cottage

3 June 1974

Dear Philip,

It was a marvellous surprise to get *High Windows* last week, especially as I didn't realise you had another book coming out. (I wish I could be more worthy of the very kind inscription you put in the book!) I am finding so much richness in it – I'm not sure that I agree with the *S. Times* reviewer's choice of favourite poems, or 'best' poems – 'Cut Grass', in this lovely early summer is immediately wonderful, but so is 'Friday Night in the Royal Station Hotel' – and what about 'The Old Fools' – horribly near the bone. The last rather appropriate as I have been ill for the last two months and am only now recovering. I have to be into hospital again tomorrow to have my parathyroid gland (or one of them!) removed. It was found that I had too much calcium in my blood – the doctors were certain that the cause of this was my cancer of 3 years ago but when I had a 'bone trace' it was found that there was nothing in my bones to confirm this diagnosis so they had to think again. I was an object of interest and had many doctors round me which was gratifying, of course. Apparently I have high blood pressure (which I never suspected) and have to take various pills of different colours. A subject for a poem might be 'pills'?

I must apologise for all this, but it is no more than the truth and it seems to have changed my life in a sense, bringing my retirement nearer, though I had intended to retire in October anyway. So I am no longer going to London every Monday morning but have had a long convalescence and much enjoyed being in the country. I was in the Radcliffe the whole of April, except for a few days at home for Easter. I didn't mind being in hospital and even found it quite interesting when I began to feel better. The food was quite good and I got to know a lot of people in the ward. The problem of being old is with one on such occasions, though. When I thought my days were numbered I did feel it was perhaps better to die in one's sixties. I feel that if I were disabled or incapacitated I wouldn't be able to bear it – wouldn't be 'splendid', as women are expected to be – men too, no doubt.

I haven't done any writing lately but think I will try again soon – at least to put words down on paper. Perhaps the only hope of getting published is a romantic or gothic novel?

Must stop now – I hope this letter hasn't too many mistakes in it. When I was first ill I had difficulty in reading and writing but this is now improving. Imagine the irony of *that*!

Once again very many thanks for the book. I shall take it into hospital. The Churchill this time, where they say you get bacon for breakfast!

All good wishes,
   Yours,

                                   Barbara

4 June. In the Churchill Hospital. The mixed ward. The pathos of men in pyjamas and dressing gowns. Philip Larkin type subjects. The complex of buildings like mission huts. In the morning birds picking about in the grass.

23 June. T.S. Eliot baptised on 29th June 1927 at Finstock. The Bishop of Oxford came and dedicated the T.S. Eliot memorial. Then followed a week of gloom and rain. I tried to write and make *An Unsuitable Attachment* into a romantic novel but I doubt if it's possible. On Friday I had been to the doctor who told me that I must retire and gave me a certificate for another four weeks.

To Philip Larkin   Barn Cottage
                                              19 July 1974

Dear Philip,

Yesterday my sister drove me to London and we collected my 'things' from 32 Balcombe Street, including my winter clothes and the manuscript of a novel I've started to write about older people working in an office. It's rather discouraging to go on writing with so little hope of publication but I try not to think about that. By the way, the letter I wrote to *The Author* about not getting published was never published, which seems to be the final accolade of failure.

Since I last wrote I've read more deeply in your new book and have learnt 'Jake Balokowsky' almost by heart – how well I remember that kind of (Assistant) Professor from my days of dealing with American anthropologists. 'The Building' is most moving and disturbing – it's a pity that so many of the people it could apply to will never read it, all the people sitting there.

I suppose you will be starting your holiday or 'leave' about now, though I suppose Librarians don't necessarily have to take August like school holidays. For the moment I find it enough to be in the country and able to visit stately homes and gardens open to the public in the summer afternoons. It is pretty good too to be able to read a novel *in the morning* though my conscience doesn't allow me to do that very often. Yet I can listen to the radio quite happily. I am doing some gardening and our garden is really rather pretty – mostly designed by my sister. She is now working part time in Oxford – I can't remember if I told you – cataloguing modern Greek books at the Taylorian [Institute]. So now our roles are reversed and *she* goes out and *I* stay at home.

I wonder what your neighbours are like in your new house. I hope not too much noise from kiddies or washing on a Sunday morning. Even the nicest young people err in this respect! Or perhaps you have elderly people next door to you. I'm sure anyway that your car will sit primly in its own little garage rather than outside on the pavement. This sounds as if I am mocking you but of course I don't mean to.

The sun is coming out again and I will turn to my novel. They say Graham Greene writes only 250 words a day, so I should be able to manage that!

With all good wishes,
    Yours ever,

Barbara

31 August. Our turn to do the flowers and brasses. If you forget and haven't quite enough flowers will it do to put some object (? a stuffed animal) on the pedestal usually adorned with a particularly splendid flower arrangement.

11 September. A full country day. Started off with a visit to Dr. My blood pressure is better ('super'). *Retirement:* I think – I am eating soup and jacket potato and drinking coffee in Oxford on a *Monday*. Letty would be doing this in a different place, probably in London among shopping women.

To Philip Larkin   Barn Cottage
                                                  1 December 1974

Dear Philip,

I hope you are really well settled in your new house so that you can hardly remember living anywhere else, though perhaps that doesn't happen with houses, only places. Although I have been to London twice since my illness it now seems completely alien, and of course one is rather glad not to be there, all things considered.

I had a checkup at the Radcliffe in October and the consultant was pleased with me. I go to my own doctor regularly – he is young and very conscientious. When I told him I was going to London for my retirement party he advised me not to get too emotionally excited. Luckily I didn't! The office gave me a nice lunch time party with wines and food and I was allowed to ask my favourite anthropologists and others. There weren't too many speeches and I was presented with a cheque and the promise of my 'present' the New Oxford Dictionary which (very suitably!) happened to be out of print or re-binding.

I find that I enjoy my retirement very much – I suppose having been ill means that it didn't happen in the way retirement usually does so the break didn't seem so violent. When I got back to the office I found such a lot of different things happening (there is a new young Director in place of Professor Forde) that I was rather glad to be out of it all! I am still doing a little mild work e.g. the African tribal index for the journal and the odd bibliography which I find quite a good discipline, so that I work for an hour or two in the morning. Did I tell you that I have agreed to act as one of the preliminary judges in the 1974 awards for the Romantic Novelists Association?! I have so far read about 10 novels. They are extremely varied in type – some historical, others more purely 'romantic' in a modern setting. The one thing they lack is humour or irony – and of course one does miss that. But in a way they do seem to reflect some aspects of life that may be valid for the fortunate ones! As much as Doris Lessing or Edna O'Brien, or even B. Pym.

Very best wishes,
Yours ever,

Barbara

25 *December.* A full Christmas Day in mild windy weather. Ginger wine with the Dores after church (duck in the oven), sherry with Vicki and Bob Redston (duck looked at and turned), punch with the Phelps (duck finally eaten).

2 *February 1975.* A day in Oxford 40 years on. Beginning in Duke Humfrey then a visit to the Ladies Cloakroom in the basement of the Radcliffe Camera (where smoking is forbidden), then in the local history department of the Central Library and after that lunch at

Selfridge's (beefburger, baked beans and chips). A wander round the various departments and then a visit to C & A and on a bus to the Radcliffe Infirmary where we get off and walk back to Little Clarendon St to Laura Ashley where I buy a bundle of patchwork pieces. Then a walk in the churchyard in Banbury Road, all almond and prunus in this early sun. Passing the Institute of Social Anthropology I saw they had blue curtains at the window and someone was cutting the grass.

To Philip Larkin   Barn Cottage

23 March 1975

Dear Philip,

For once it's a fine Sunday morning and the meat is in the oven so I have 'time' for a letter. It's funny how one harks back to one's childhood and schooldays, when Sunday was the letter-writing time. Today is Palm Sunday and we have a service in the evening with 'Prose, poetry and music'. I haven't helped to choose any of the readings on this occasion or I might have been tempted to put in the Arthur Symons Naples Palm Sunday poem which would hardly be suitable. My sister has just suggested that as so few people now go to church Palms might be distributed at garages on the appropriate Sunday morning.

I hope you are feeling more like writing and perhaps generally in better spirits with the coming of spring. I do feel like writing sometimes and am very gradually trying a novel, doing a bit every morning when I can. I have also been doing a little work for my old Institute, but I do find that I am *not* reading all those heavy works that people always say they will read in their retirement.

I have got Betjeman's new poems – not so very new now, but they went out of print. Not very good value for money (you get *more* with Larkin) but of course one is glad to have them. I lately read T.S. Mathews' biography of Eliot and apparently he often thought he would never write another line so it must be the sort of thing that all writers feel – but one does rather wonder if Shakespeare ever experienced it. But surely everyone must get the 'so little done' feeling as age creaks on? Here I am sixty-one (it looks worse spelled out in words) and only six novels published – no husband, no children. I do find though that people (especially at the hospital) now tend to call one 'Mrs' and it seems hardly worth the trouble to put them right. Anything is better than Ms. which American contributors to *Africa* were beginning to adopt before I left.

It would be so nice if you ever did 'find yourself' in Oxford and we could meet and have lunch – or even if we could give you lunch here if your car should ever find itself near Charlbury or Witney.

Best regards and wishes.

Barbara

29 March. A dire Good Friday service – the Bible (the gospel narrative) lamely paraphrased and meditations, so far from the old days when the preacher for the Three Hours Service would draw such a large congregation that extra chairs had to be brought in. A year now since my stroke and *Deo gratias* for my recovery.

To Philip Larkin   Barn Cottage

15 April 1975

Dear Philip,

Thank you very much for your letter. I should like very much to meet you for lunch on 23rd April (Wednesday) and, all things considered, I think it would be best to meet in Oxford. I'm always glad of an opportunity to go in and the country is so wet and depressing at the moment.

As for a meeting place, how would it be if we met at the Randolph? I should think at the entrance opposite the Ashmolean where people sit. I'm sure I should recognise you, but would *you* know *me*? I am tallish (5.8½ in the old measurements) with darkish brown hair cut short. I shall probably be wearing a beige tweed suit or a Welsh tweed cape if colder. I shall be looking rather anxious, I expect. About 12.30? Then if we don't fancy the Randolph we can go somewhere else.

Perhaps you are staying at the Randolph anyway or at St John's? Looking at your letter again I see it's a 'Feast' so we had better have an austere luncheon. Anyway, here's hoping to *meet* you anyway.

All good wishes,

Barbara

23 April. I had lunch with Philip Larkin at the Randolph sitting in the window looking out towards the Ashmolean and watching ambulances [echo of the Philip Larkin poem] driving up Beaumont St. What can I say? Wish *I* were a poet.

To Philip Larkin   Barn Cottage

24 April 1975

Dear Philip,

Just to thank you for lunch and to send you this 'artist's impression' of Barn Cottage (on the left, showing the front door) which was done as a 'notelet' for the Finstock History Society. I do hope you will one day come and see us there.

I also hope the 'Feast' went off well and that you were able to enjoy a good breakfast this morning with well cooked bacon.

I wonder if the man who got into conversation with us at the Randolph goes there every Wednesday (market day)? Perhaps I should stroll in there next week! After I left you I did a little shopping, then made my way to the station – having a few minutes to spare I went into the refreshment room and found myself sitting by a strange woman eating curry at 4 o'clock, a late lunch or an unusual tea.

Thank you again and also for the kind things you said about my novels. I will try and get on with something.

Very best wishes,

Barbara

12 May. Reading *Heaven on Earth* by Janice Elliot – a great 'tapestry' of a book in which I am now getting rather bogged down. Olive Wilson the 'heroine' might get together with Kate Brown of Doris Lessing's *The Summer Before the Dark* – they might have a cup of tea together somewhere. I must get on with *my* novel – austere and plain though it may be – and get a new small notebook.

28 June. When I wrote *Some Tame Gazelle* I didn't know *nearly* as much about village life as I do now.

28 July. Links' birthday. She would have been 88. Oh the mystery of it all – life, death and the passing of time.

31 August. 'Asphasia' at a drinks party on Sunday morning. When talking I couldn't remember the name of Dr Kissinger! That rendered me tongue-tied and speechless so that I couldn't speak at all. It didn't last long but must have been disconcerting for those involved. I wasn't offered another glass of sherry but perhaps that was just coincidence! Later a slight feeling of pins and needles in my right hand which seems to go with it. On Friday night after watching a terrible telly programme I was conscious of seeing jagged coloured shapes all the time when away from the TV, but that soon passed. Was that anything to do with what I am now calling The Kissinger Syndrome? Is that why I am now incapable of finishing this novel that is so near its end?

4 October. At the church to check the flowers. They are attending to the du Cros mausoleum [in Finstock churchyard], cutting the grass round it etc. Does a firm of undertakers do this sort of thing? There was a red Ford van parked outside.

8 October. There was a recital of baroque music in Ramsden church. A very dry and rarified programme – it makes one feel like eating sloes, I decided, that astringent feeling in the mouth. Now I am taking the stronger Propanalol (40mg 3× a day, 2 times as much as before). In the Library I read the effects it might have – so if you have nausea, diarrhoea, insomnia and generally feel a bit odd it's just the Propanalol!

20 November. General Franco died at last after being kept alive for so long and in *The Times* I saw that dear Elizabeth Taylor died yesterday.

To Bob Smith in Ibadan   Barn Cottage

11 January 1976

Dearest Bob,

Jock seems to have got over his eye operation very well but is still very upset about Elizabeth's death. Very little notice seems to have been taken of her but I am hoping that when her novel comes out there may be an appreciation in some of the TV book programmes. After all she was a friend of Kingsley Amis and Elizabeth Jane Howard who are well in with the 'media'. Still, what does it matter, really, such writers are caviar to the general, are they not, and fame is dust and ashes anyhow.

Having turned the potatoes (doing nicely) I can now go on to more mundane matters. And what could be more mundane than trying to type a novel which I shall finish, but that will be it, positively *no more.*

With love,

Barbara

17 February. Henry [Harvey] came to tea with a bad cold and bringing crumpets. Destroyed (in the fire, it being cold weather) some pages of a 1943 diary. The person who inspired the main reason for it [Gordon Glover] is now dead. Parts of it are worth keeping. Could one write a book (a sort of novel) based on one's diaries over about 30 years? I certainly have enough material.

23 February. Walked in the woods below Wilcote Manor and gathered wood (electricity bill of £77 arrived today). Now inspired to keep a daily diary as I'm reading *No Halt at Sunset* by Elizabeth Howland, a Norfolk housewife, published 1951 and reissued 1974. *But* she keeps pigs (3, with many piglets), has just got 1,000 chrysanthemum cuttings and is expecting bees. Nothing like that for me – lazy, doesn't like housework, unenterprising ('Barbara never initiates anything' Daryll used to say).

To Philip Larkin   Barn Cottage
                                                  8 March 1976

Dear Philip,

It's Monday morning and when I've finished writing to you I shall get on with a little novel typing. It is slowly progressing but I don't seem inclined to hurry as there seems so little chance of it getting published. Or perhaps I've just reverted to my natural indolence and anyway Professor Forde always used to say 'Barbara has no sense of urgency'. Of course he didn't mean it as a compliment.

I expect by now you'll have got the Humber Bridge poem (epic?) well behind you, even if you have to write another 20 lines to fill an extra 4 minutes. I thought of you specially the other day when I had to go to the Radcliffe for my six-monthly check-up, sitting reading a two-year old copy of *The Field* and wondering if my weight of 69 kgs. (fully clad) was anything like my normal $10\frac{1}{2}$ stone. Anyway the sweet young houseman seemed to think I was more or less all right and I've certainly felt quite well, take exercise, even saw wood.

I can't remember if I ever congratulated you on your honour [in November 1975, Philip Larkin was awarded the CBE] – perhaps it came at a time when I wasn't on the point of writing, so please accept these very belated felicitations. Was there any other interesting person being 'done' at the same time? It must be slightly nerve-racking, however homely!

How nice of Gwendoline Butler to like my books! I know of her but haven't actually read any of hers, though I did look for one in the library because I had heard it was a detective story set in Victorian Oxford, so I shall persevere.

Oxford is beginning to be nice and springlike, or was last week. I recently had my wallet stolen when I was shopping one day – not being in beastly old London I suppose one gets careless, and I was wandering about with my handbag on my arm and it was the kind that could be opened by a stealthy hand. Only the wallet was taken and it has since turned up in Debenham's (Elliston's of old!) and was traced by the Barclaycard inside. I found myself hoping that the person who took the money bought something nice, or that it was a really deserving person. A 'one-parent family' or a fellow pensioner, though the last would be rather shocking!

We have lost our dear old cat Tom, the black and white one, in his 16th year – peacefully at his home in West Oxfordshire at the end of January. He had been getting very fragile and thin (and very trying too!) but we didn't have to take him to the vet. He just quietly expired on a copy of *The Times* one Saturday morning. When he became cold the fleas left his body – I suppose that was how one knew he had really gone. I'd never seen that happen before. We still have Minerva, our brindled tortoiseshell.

Now I have finished reading another lot of 'Romantic' Novels and am able to read other things but don't find many novels I like – I suppose that must be a sign of old age but there do seem to be fewer good ones. Do you ever watch any of the 'Book' programmes on the telly? I enjoyed seeing Kingsley Amis getting annoyed with some fellow participants (I can't even remember now who they were).

Yours ever,

Barbara

To Henry Harvey in Willersey   Barn Cottage

6 April 1976

Dear Henry,

I thought of sending you a suitable postcard, but perhaps such a long letter deserves a letter in return, though there won't be a picture on this! The tap on the window, and its effect on us, seems to have remained in your memory and it did with us too because a few days after it there was a *murder* at Ramsden – apparently the poor woman surprised two burglars who had broken in and they killed her. So after that we became slightly nervous, not opening the door to strangers at night etc. So you see.... Anyway the feeling does wear off, and they seem to have caught the murderers.

I can tell you how to give the *impression of having a successful party* – lights on, of course, visible from the outside, clinking of washing up being done in the sink, Television on, giving the sound of voices and music. We seem to have done all that on that night you called.

But it's much more difficult to provide other kinds of advice – 'difficult' – impossible would be a better way of putting it. Novel writing is a kind of personal pleasure and satisfaction, even if nothing comes of it in worldly terms.

Hilary and I are making plans to go for a short holiday in Greece. All being well (as my mother used to say) we shall go in four weeks time about. We should have sown some vegetable seeds before then (? is gardening enough. No!)

Love,

Barbara

17 May. Greece has discovered Toyota (and other Japanese cars) also the plastic carrier bag – everyone carries one, even the priest in Nea Stira, an old, white-bearded man carrying a blue plastic bag. The sea and the beach (and indeed everywhere) are full of discarded plastic bags.

19 July. Anthony à Wood died at 63, my present age.
Better if I had followed an academic career rather than a novelist's – but it's certainly too late now!

28 July. Yesterday was the day of publication of the large print edition of *Some Tame Gazelle*.

30 July. Philip Larkin came to tea then walked up to the church to see the T.S. Eliot memorial. So two great poets and one minor novelist came for a brief moment (as it were) together. Philip took photos of us all with two cats outside the cottage. What is the point of saying (as if for posterity) what Philip is *like*. He is so utterly what he is in his letters and poems. In the best, like 'Faith Healing', 'Ambulances', and even Jake Balokowsky, my biographer. 'Life at graduate level' as he once said about my novel *No Fond Return*.

5 August. Yesterday we went to Spelsbury. Thought the church was locked (with new Yale lock) but in fact it wasn't. We had gone to the vicarage where the vicar and a large black retriever came with us to the church. A very fine Irish brogue and indeed he was at Trinity College Dublin. In the churchyard outside is the large square-oblong tomb where Carys are buried, but all tumbled on top and a scatter of bones, dry and grey-white, a plastic top of something modern – yoghurt or peanut butter.

6 August. A postcard of the Hardy statue from Philip Larkin. Shall I keep it as a marker in Hardy's poems or Larkin's?

12 September. In the morning Maurice Rogers called and brought us the left-over Ramsden jumble for the poor relation Finstock. We kept a copy of the Apocrypha and some old clothes.

21 September (staying with friends at Snape). On Thursday we went to Aldeburgh (full of refined-looking retired people) and spent some time at the 60–40 shop looking at second-hand clothes. Ploughman's lunch at the White Horse (exquisite Ladies Room).

24 September. Started back about 10 and stopped for lunch in Arkesden. Sad to think of Gordon dead after all those love affairs in that village.

25 September. Frugal lunch in the grounds of Middleton Park near the church. Went in and entered the Jersey Mausoleum, behind a gilded grille and heavy red curtains. Inside marble monuments and gloom, black and white floor and a storage heater (with instructions on how to maintain it).

18 November. Having failed with Hamish Hamilton I think I might try a lighter country novel, funny even, but something romantic for Collins or Hurst and Blackett – such as a woman going as a housekeeper to a large house in some village like Ramsden.

15 December. Writing to Pamela Hansford Johnson to tell her that Hamish Hamilton had already rejected my novel *(Four Point Turn)* [*Quartet*] when he had just written to her saying he was 'eager to read it'! The embarrassment of being an unpublished novelist knows no bounds and what price the memory of publishers!

10 January 1977. Yesterday a small congregation for the First Sunday after Epiphany – and ought not the Christmas decorations to have been taken down? A lapsed Catholic is no good to man or beast.

12 January. Have finished my 1976 read of Romantic Novels. I am reading Sylvia Plath's letters. All these years I seem to have misjudged her – the kind of person she seems to have been – dates with Amherst boys and at Cambridge that anthropological psychologist Mallory Wober. And liking clothes and hair-dos. Then alone in that bitter Winter of 1962–3 in a house in Fitzroy Rd – where Yeats lived – with two children, starting to write at 4 or 5 o'clock in the morning – deserted by Ted Hughes – that was how it was.

21 January. Yesterday we went to Delnevo's the woolshop – synthetics on the ground floor, wools on the first. Oh I have such a feeling for wool. It would be a great joy to work with wool.

Recognition

In January 1977 The Times Literary Supplement *published a list, chosen by eminent literary figures, of the most under-rated writers of the century. Barbara was the only living writer to be named by two people, Philip Larkin and Lord David Cecil, another long-time admirer of her novels. Partly because of the publicity, partly because the literary climate had gradually changed and partly because there had always been a strong band of faithful readers, her books were, virtually overnight, in demand again.*

Macmillan published Quartet in Autumn, *Cape reprinted the earlier novels, she was asked to write features and short stories, to broadcast in the series* Finding a Voice, *even achieving the final accolade of being a guest on the BBC's* Desert Island Discs. *In November 1977* Quartet *was shortlisted for the Booker Prize and the BBC made a television programme about her life and work.*

The Sweet Dove Died *was published by Macmillan in 1978 and was warmly received by the critics. She was also delighted by the success of her novels in America, where they were published by Dutton, and where she was building up a considerable reputation. 'I am being taught,' she recorded with surprise and gratification, 'in an American university!'*

She took this sudden fame and recognition as outwardly calmly as she had taken the years of hurt and failure. She knew that she had not many more years of life. A secondary cancer had manifested itself and, although it initially responded to treatment, it became apparent to her that she could not be cured.

She was very anxious to revise and 'improve' her final novel A Few Green Leaves. *She managed to complete a final draft just before she had to take to her bed, too weak to continue active life.*

She was concerned not to be a burden to Hilary, who had nursed her with such devotion, and arranged to go into Michael Sobell House, a hospice attached to the Churchill Hospital in Oxford. She was taken round it in a wheelchair and was, in a way, almost looking forward to going there ('so much rich material'). Early in January 1980 her condition worsened and she was admitted to the hospice, taking with her her final notebook. Henry Harvey, visiting her on January 8th, found her wit and her courage undiminished. It seemed, somehow, fitting that almost the last visitor Belinda had should be the Archdeacon. Within a week, on January 11th, she died.

Throughout her illness she had maintained a cheerful stoicism, very down-to-earth and practical, never self-pitying. She was sustained, certainly, by her strong faith and still able, as she had been throughout her life, to draw comfort from small pleasures and ironies, and this is, perhaps, the greatest gift she has bequeathed to all who read her.

H. H.

1977–1979

22 January. In the *Times Literary Supplement* of January 21st I was cited as 'an under-rated novelist' by Philip Larkin and Lord David Cecil. Paul Binding and Philip rang me up on Friday night to tell me. Then on Saturday it was referred to in *The Times* and my name appeared on the front page. Cape apparently said they 'might consider a reprint'. (*That*'ll be the frosty Friday!) Saturday afternoon at 5 o'clock Sarah Fuller from Radio Oxford came and I gave a little interview. During the week letters from kind friends but no agent or publisher approaching.

To Philip Larkin   Barn Cottage

                                                    30 January 1977

Dear Philip,

Thank you so much for sending me *The Times* cutting – I had already seen it as we take that paper (I had wanted the *Telegraph,* but now Hilary's choice is justified!) but I'm very glad to have another copy to send or give to people. Funny Cape's 'might consider...'. I can imagine some minion being phoned up on a Friday evening when everyone else had gone home! A pity they had already rejected *Four Point Turn.* Of course I haven't had a word from them.

I am struggling to get that novel into a fit state to send to Macmillan (as Pamela Hansford Johnson recommended) but I have no very high hopes. It is not the same person [James Wright] there that you once gave me an introduction to, who wrote very kindly about my work but thought it not a commercial proposition. I now rather regret having gone so far with this last one but perhaps we can't help ourselves. I am really better at making marmalade (very successful this week!) and doing patchwork.

A nice girl from Radio Oxford came and asked me a few questions and this was broadcast in the early morning programme on Monday. And somebody who had just been rereading *A Glass of Blessings*, heard this and wrote me a v. nice letter, so you and Lord David have certainly done a lot for my morale (if that's the right word).

Romantic novel reading is now finished so I can read what I like. I had the letters of Sylvia Plath from the Library. How is she regarded as a poet? I was amazed at what a simple ordinary sort of girl she seemed to be, writing about clothes and hair-dos and boy friends. I must say it put me against Ted Hughes but maybe there was something to be said for him. You probably know him? Then perhaps I shall reread that *not* overrated novelist A. Powell. Or perhaps not read at all, except for the odd Larkin poem, and *The Times* obituaries?

Excuse a short letter. I just wanted to thank you again.

Best regards,

Barbara

5 February. Tomorrow is Septuagesima. The question is do we have flowers in the church? Perhaps a few evergreens, but one would have thought not daffodils etc. Suppose somebody had given unsuitable flowers and hothouse plants? Some titled person.

7 February. The novel (*Last Quartet*) has arrived at Macmillan and the girl who acknowledges it addresses me as Mrs Pym. This puts me into a different category altogether.

To Bob Smith in Ibadan   Barn Cottage

8 February 1977

Dearest Bob,

I don't know whether you will have seen the *TLS* of 21st January in which various people were asked to list authors whose works they considered under- or over-rated. And Miss Pym was named twice as under-rated both by Philip Larkin and Lord David Cecil – and there was no collusion, as Philip afterwards told me!

Quite a lot of people rang up and wrote but of course Cape has been totally silent. Having just rejected my last novel what could they say, indeed? Anyway that same novel is now with Macmillan. I am not 'overly' hopeful but I did make it a bit longer as Hamish Hamilton had suggested. Difficult to pad things out, though. I made two more chapters – Edwin going to a memorial service and the three of them, with Father G, having lunch after Marcia's funeral at the crematorium. Then I added a few more 'bits', remembering that you had wanted more of Norman, I described his Christmas in more detail and the first morning of his holiday, though I did not dare penetrate too far into the bedsitter. (Didn't they say that Jane Austen never has two men talking alone together in her novels? I'm afraid I have been bolder than that). But don't let us forget that *you* were the first person to write an article about Miss Pym.

Life in 1977. Concorde, costing I don't know how many millions, flies over our heads, clearly visible from our cottage window, while the road outside is as full of potholes as in the 16th century.

Much love,

Barbara

'Rethink Motorways', 'Save Bath' (which I had read as 'Save Bathwater', referring to the drought last Summer). And now we see that there are some people who always have a Save Something sticker on their car. Save Me – a man might say, who wakes up in the watches of the night and thinks of death.

10 February. Letter from Tom Maschler!

14 February. No Valentines but during the morning as I sat at the sewing machine, Alan Maclean rang from Macmillan saying that they would *love* to publish the novel. Can hardly believe it can be true but he said he would confirm by letter (with 8½p stamp).

To Philip Larkin   Barn Cottage

21 February 1977

Dear Philip,

I haven't *dared* to write to anyone until I actually saw it in print, though Alan Maclean rang me up last week to tell me that Macmillan would like to publish *Last Quartet*! But now I have the letter before me, and it seems from this that you know (perhaps?), so this is just to say my inadequate thanks.... If it hadn't been for you, and sending it to Pamela H.J.... not to mention all those *years* of encouragement. What can I say that would be at all appropriate? I hope anyway (12.10) that you will be having a *good lunchtime drink*. We are about to have one – poor Hilary has a bad cold so hers will be whisky – mine sherry.

Alan Maclean said you had promised to send him your *TLS* piece – I do hope it hasn't been too grinding a chore – and that it or some of it might be used as a foreword if suitable. He says they will publish in October.

Of course the whole business of the *TLS* 'tribute' has meant that, for the first time ever, Tom Maschler of Cape has written to me! He says they intend to reissue some of the novels, though they haven't decided which ones, and he also enquired tentatively about *Four Point Turn* (as it was then called) which Cape rejected in July. I don't suppose for a moment that he has ever read anything of mine. I find it rather difficult to compose polite non-committal sort of letters to him, not of course revealing that I know about the rather unkind crack of the writer in that *Bookseller* article you sent me.

We have had practically continuous rain for the last few days, but spring is on the way with bulbs coming up in the garden and things beginning to sprout. And I have been spreading horse manure ('gift' from kind neighbour) over the place where we might grow some vegetables.

Last week we had a terrible meeting to decide what (if anything) Finstock is going to do for the jubilee. I suppose similar meetings have been taking place all over the country in dark village and parish halls, with the same jumble of ideas. I sometimes amuse myself by trying to guess what sort of poem (or hymn) *you* would have written if you had been Laureate instead of Betjeman! Jake Balokowsky, biographer – an impossible task for poor Betjeman because (presumably) you have to produce something that will be understood and appreciated by the great mass of loyal subjects who care nothing for literature – as well as being criticised in the quality papers.

Have you been following *The Times* correspondence about Keats and Claret? Rather pleasing, I thought. I suppose the beaded bubbles *might* have been something like Mateus rosé, unless it was just poetic fancy, and obviously a much darker-looking wine.

Thank you again!

Very best wishes,

Barbara

3 March. A lovely sunny day to go and see my new publishers, Macmillan. I was put to wait in the what-would-you-call-it, foyer, waiting room, reception – fresh daffodils and books and girls making lunch dates with each other. Alan Maclean is rather tall and elegant-looking, James Wright is smaller, with dark, curly hair (cut by his wife).

To Philip Larkin   Barn Cottage

4 March 1977

Dear Philip,

Thank you so much for your champagne-jumble letter. Isn't it splendid the way good news, when you're older, sends one to the drink of some kind – even if not M. et Ch. at least a glass of something extra! (When I was much younger unrequited love caused me to buy and eat halfpound slabs of Cadbury's coffee-milk chocolate. A good thing one's tastes change!)

Of course what I really wanted to know was, what *kind* of jumble. I dare say you'd have some old books from that Library of yours?

Yesterday I met and had lunch with my new publisher(s) – Alan Maclean and James Wright from Macmillans. They both seem to like my book and so of course I found them totally sympathetic and congenial! It was nice for me revisiting a part of London I know so well, having worked in that area from 1953 to 1972. After lunch I had a wander into Fetter Lane and gazed briefly at the spot where my old office stood, now occupied by a hideous office block advertising space to let in it. I even knew the restaurant at the bottom of Chancery Lane where we sat and discussed titles. *They* like *Quartet in Autumn* – a sort of compromise or mixture of various ideas – what do you think?

Of course the *TLS* article will be a pleasant surprise and I will see it however you prefer – certainly wouldn't want to see it in proof. Only let me know when it is coming out so that I can tell Hazel and others. Somebody did write and ask for a photograph but I don't know if they'll include one as I hadn't anything very suitable – two snapshots and another, with a rather worried but innocent expression. I suppose I ought to have some more taken when the book (*Q. in A.?*) comes out but I hate being done.

Caroline Moorehead from *The Times* has asked if she can come and see me. Hilary says we must clean the windows! Do you have a window cleaner in Hull?

I feel this letter is being rather incoherent, but I can still hardly believe it has all happened. One of the funniest things has been the reaction of Tom Maschler in Cape who has been writing me some quite cordial letters and I gather that he and Alan Maclean have spoken about me on the telephone. Hilary and I invented a Maschler pudding – a kind of milk jelly. Which brings me on to say that you would be most welcome to come here any time to lunch or whatever – perhaps a choice of puddings ought to be provided –

nothing milky for a librarian. And why was/is there that delay in getting cards into the catalogue? Did you solve the problem?

Very best wishes,
Yours ever,

Barbara

18 March. Went to see Dr S today. He is kind and efficient but so brisk that one wonders if one had a psychological problem how much time he would be able to give it. In this connection – the doctor's surgery is crowded but the vicar's study is empty. And there could be a sort of rivalry between them when it comes to dealing with life's difficulties.

To Philip Larkin   Barn Cottage

14 April 1977

Dear Philip,

No proofs yet or other news at the moment though James Wright says they hope to get finished copies at end of July and to publish in September. Now, having no complete copy of the book with me I feel I could have made it much better – will it seem very thin and meagre in print? Anyway, not to worry, as they say. Did you notice, by the way, that there was a little tiny Larkin quote at one point, where Marcia is in the ambulance ['Unreachable inside a room']? I never asked the author's permission! I felt in some superstitious way it might bring me luck, as indeed it did. Thank you again!

As that was intended to be the last thing I ever wrote I hadn't got anything else in mind, though I have always wanted to write something vaguely about this place and its environs and I have now started to think and make a few notes and bits. There is so much rich material, of course, if only I could do it! Now Macmillan want to see the one about Leonora and James which James Wright saw and liked in 1970 (by coincidence) so perhaps they will take that.

Hilary and I sat up late one evening (bathed and in our nightwear) hoping to see C. Isherwood on *Tonight* but all we got was the Stetchford by-election. I suppose it served us right. One gets very tired of all this publicity by the 'media' when a book comes out. I have *not* watched *Roots* either, only seen cruel, horrible trailers.

Do be careful that when you go to the Hull Jazz Record Soc. Eamonn Andrews doesn't pop up and get you for *This is Your Life*! But we shall see you before that date so can give more practical advice and warning. I look forward very much to seeing you.

All good wishes,

Barbara

15 April. Went into Witney on the bus – excessive exuberance of daffodils in Ramsden. Who is that woman sitting on the concrete wall outside Barclay's Bank reading the *TV Times?* That is Miss Pym the novelist.

23 April. Philip Larkin to lunch. We had sherry and then the wine (burgundy) Bob gave me for Christmas (was this rather insensitive to Bob?). We ate kipper paté, then veal done with peppers and tomatoes, pommes Anna and celery & cheese (he didn't eat any Brie and we thought perhaps he only likes plain food). He's shy but very responsive and jokey. Hilary took our photo together and he left about 3.30 in his large Rover car (pale tobacco brown).

24 April. 'Dialogue service' in church with Mr M. (from Ramsden) explaining the service to the children (of which there weren't all that many). He looked like a driving examiner with his clipboard. Said we were invited to a 'meal' and we had a picture of sliced loaves and fish fingers. He did quite well apart from that.

To Philip Larkin   Barn Cottage

5 May 1977

Dear Philip,

Many thanks for your nice (All Souls) letter. We did enjoy seeing you and I only wish it could happen more often. Perhaps it can now that you know the way from Oxford. (Or do you? I very much hope you didn't really get lost – it is a pretty tortuous way but the one we always go. Then it occurred to me that you might be a motorway man – or your car might be!)

I had meant to write sooner but I have been expecting those photographs every day but they still haven't come, so I feel that if I write and post a letter to you they will arrive the day after. I called in the last time I was in Oxford but didn't like to bully the nice middle-aged ladies. I can't suddenly start developing a sense of urgency in my old age!

My proofs have come and I have corrected them and sent them back yesterday – those rather nasty greyish computer-set sheets which took me back to I.A.I. days, when latterly we had our books done like that. The novel reads quite well in parts – rather short, and of course it could have been so much better – Hilary was enthusiastic as she was reading it for the first time and helped me with the proofs. Then this morning James Wright rang and apparently both he and Alan Maclean like *The Sweet Dove Died* so it looks as if that will be published too. I don't remember if you saw it in its final form – perhaps you will now!

I meant to ask you about Samuel Beckett but of course I don't suppose you saw the plays that Sunday night on the telly. I fell asleep in one which made me ask myself if these Irishmen aren't making fools of us!

I've been reading the diaries of Evelyn Waugh – what a lot he drank, though he often felt ill after it or was even sick. The book is too big to read in bed which is a pity. As for fiction (usually of a size to read in bed) I haven't found anything very good lately. Seeing all the reviews of these sexy American female novelists it makes me wonder if anyone will review mine! I suppose I can't expect that Lorna Sage or Jacky Gillott will notice it – I suppose it rather depends what else is available at the time. I don't really mind, though of course one would hope for one good review in one quality paper.

All good wishes,
Yours ever,

Barbara

10 May. The contract for *The Sweet Dove Died* came from Macmillan and James Wright and I are James and Barbara to each other. Ghastly PCC meeting in the evening. I must have an organist in my next novel, being paid in bottles of sherry left at his back door. 'The opportunity to play a remarkably fine instrument'.

18 May. Dorset. Stopped for tea in Sturminster Newton and went into the church. We admired all the hassocks and kneeling cushions, hand-embroidered with flower motifs in tapestry. A woman with a slight foreign accent (perhaps the vicar's wife, met all that time ago on a walking tour in Switzerland?) showed us round and explained about the embroideries but did not comment on any other aspect of the church.

19 May. Tea with Lord David Cecil. A comfortable, agreeable room with green walls and some nice portraits. They are so easy to talk to, the time flew. We had Lapsang tea, brown toast, redcurrant jelly and ginger cake. He told me he had been inspired to write after reading Lytton Strachey's *Eminent Victorians* (just as I had been inspired by *Crome Yellow*). He said that Anthony Powell and I were the only novelists he would buy without reading first. A.P. was his fag at Eton. Lord D. said he thought comedy in the novel was out of fashion now – not well thought of – we agreed on this.

20 May. Seeing a handsome Dorset woman at a petrol pump I thought a Hardy heroine of today might well follow such an occupation. Tess for instance.

To Philip Larkin   Barn Cottage

22 May 1977

Dear Philip,

Now that I'm back from Dorset I can answer your letter properly.

We did go to tea with Lord David on Thursday last and thoroughly enjoyed it. Of course we talked a lot about 'writing' – did you know that Anthony Powell was Lord David's fag at Eton? He also told me that John Bayley was his star pupil, which brings me to the letter you so kindly sent me – of course I was thrilled and astonished. Another nice thing was that he appreciated your *TLS* article in a way that I feel it ought to be, though perhaps I can hardly do it myself being the subject of it. And yet why not? Perhaps in the distant future people will think it much better than the novels it celebrates!

As for the Booker prize – did you say that each publisher can send in four? I suppose Macmillan may well have already made their choice but anyway here are the details of mine. Now called *Quartet in Autumn* and due to be published in September. James Wright told me they hoped to have some copies by the end of July. I suppose they would have something available before then, though, as I think I told you, the proofs were rather nasty looking and grey (perhaps like the book) computer set and not in a nice little book like proofs used to be. Anyway, I'm sure James Wright would be the person to approach. Both he and Alan Maclean like *The Sweet Dove Died* and will publish it next year – marvellous, as it went to about twenty publishers in one form or another!

I'm sure that under your benign reign [as Chairman of the selection committee for the Booker Prize] all will be sweetness and light – one had certainly heard of 'difficulties' in the past. I'm sure Robin Ray won't give any trouble!

I was interested in what you said about Kingsley and Jane. Everyone now seems to go to Weidenfeld – the publisher who told me that their fiction list was full up for the next two years! Robert Liddell tells me that Olivia Manning has left Heinemann for Weidenfeld. (There's literary talk for you!)

I'm finishing this letter in bed with a cat on my knee, just before getting up, and with luck I shall catch the morning post. Tomorrow a girl is coming from BBC 2 to talk to me – she is a 'researcher', I suppose, who will case the joint to see if a short film could be made for the *Book Programme*. Miss Pym in bed with her cat or watering the lettuces in her dried-up garden? Or just sitting. As for the photograph, I don't think I had Tom Maschler in mind when it was taken. I was recovering from a cold but felt I mustn't smile too much. I would really like to achieve a dark brooding expression but don't think I ever could.

The car went splendidly in Dorset and Hilary is very pleased with it. I kept wondering if Hardy ever had a car. I could imagine Florence driving but not, of course, Emma Lavinia. Do you know if he did?

All best wishes,
    Yours ever,

Barbara

26 May. Why nothing to read in the outpatients at the Radcliffe? Must we be content with our thoughts?

To Bob Smith in Ibadan   Barn Cottage

Jubilee + 18 June 1977

Dearest Bob,

Macmillan have taken (and are publishing early next year) an earlier novel which I had been trying to get published and which I feel is one of the best I have ever done. About an older woman and a younger man – I hope 'sentiments to which every bosom returns an echo'. I don't think I have anything else that I would like published without a great deal of alteration, though several of my unpublished works have bits in them that might be used. I feel it's probably better to write something new after these two have come out.

Much love,

Barbara

To Philip Larkin   Barn Cottage

9 July 1977

Dear Philip,

By now you will be back at work. 'Oh, I thought you were coming back *next* week' is another office reaction I remember, making one feel subtly unwelcome.

Yes, it has certainly been all go on the Pym front lately and I'm sure people will now get as sick of me as I used to get of various over-exposed novelists in the days when *I* couldn't get anything published! But it's rather nice to bask in it for a change.

The BBC 2 thing [a *Book Programme* film about her life and work] was very enjoyable – they were all so nice, though unfortunately Robert Robinson himself couldn't come as he had 'flu. There were two cameramen, a lighting man, a sound man, Will Wyatt, the Producer, and Jennifer McKay the 'researcher' (whom I'd already met). They made me walk out of the cottage, up the hill, then we all went into the churchyard where I again had to walk about and answer questions against a background of the church door. (I seem to remember that you were taken in a churchyard – it makes a good background for all shades of belief, and after all it's what we all come to!) Then we broke for lunch – they went off to a pub, and Hilary and I had a drink quietly here. In the afternoon Lord David appeared driven in a large BBC hired car (black and a chauffeur wearing dark glasses), much too big to park comfortably in our country road and there were fantastic traffic jams. We all had tea in the garden – Lord D., Hilary, Jennifer and myself, and Minerva was rather troublesome, leaping up on to the tea tray and trying to put her paw into the milk jug. Lord D. and I chatted and we agreed that the whole thing might easily have lapsed into farce, rather like the Mad Hatter's tea party. All was finished at about 5.30. I enjoyed it all very much, my only fear being that I may have said rather foolish things or not said anything I meant to say – e.g. I couldn't remember what I read, who were my favourite authors etc. I did at least save myself once when a question about my treatment of men characters suggested that I had a low opinion of the sex. My instinctive reply sprang to my lips 'Oh, but I *love* men', but luckily I realised how ridiculous it would sound, so said something feeble, but can't remember what. They are going to invite me to a preview which will reveal the worst.

Sunday

It would be interesting to meet John Bayley some time – a bit alarming to think of Iris [Murdoch], though everyone says how nice she is, I'd love to know how she actually *does* her writing because she seems able to produce such a lot. No philosophical stuff, just real nitty gritty, which brings me to you getting up at 6 to add a few lines to your poem about DEATH. How many lines might you expect to add? I have been re-reading Larkin very much this summer – in the garden among the roses – but the later poems rather than the earlier ones. 'The Building' is 'remarkably fine', as an old Oxford friend of mine used to say about many things, and makes one long for DEATH. Hurry up with it.

I had a very cordial conversation with Helen Gardner in Oxford when I went to lunch at St Hilda's recently – we spoke 'warmly' of you. I wandered about the College, trying to find bits I remembered among all the new buildings.

Best wishes,

Barbara

17 August. The wettest day of the year, or ever – thunder at 7 a.m., flooding etc. We went to Bristol where I did a talk for Pamela Howe to be broadcast in *Woman's Hour.* And in the end got her umbrella and she got mine, not discovered until we were miles apart! This could well provide a ridiculous episode for a novel. Emma meeting Claudia and then annoyed at getting C's inferior umbrella.

To Philip Larkin Barn Cottage

21 August 1977

Dear Philip,

August is a funny time (not necessarily a wicked month?), holidays and all that, though I always used to like it in the old days in London – summer dresses in the office and visiting American anthropologists and slipping out for tea at the old Kardomah in Fleet Street.

But the weather makes no difference to the great joy of receiving the advance copy of *Q. in A.*, looking so *much* better than the terrible grey proofs. And yesterday a huge parcel from Cape with copies of the re-issues in beautiful brilliant colours with my name in enormous letters! Publication date for all three has been fixed for 15th September. I suspect that Cape's contribution has been ready first but like to think that Tom Maschler is behaving in a gentlemanly way – about time too! What a good thing you got that handsome tax rebate, otherwise you'd surely be asking for a rake off on my royalties because of the use of Larkin quotes on the jacket. (Perhaps you will anyway). Where shall I send the copies I'm going to send you – to the Library or your private address?

I don't think *The Times* is going to do me as I haven't heard anything more from Caroline Moorehead but someone from *The Guardian* is coming on Sept. 1st and I have done a chat with Pamela

Howe in Bristol, going out in *Woman's Hour*, and *Harpers/Queen* in September, due out the end of next week. What a lot of film is wasted on taking photographs now – still it's nice to think one is providing work for nice young photographers. I sat in the chilly garden recently while somebody else snapped me. I see Miss Drabble is out soon – glad she doesn't clash with me – I wonder who will?!

Later

We went into Oxford and into the Ashmolean. Correspondence displayed led Hilary to say that if you keep things long enough you can have an exhibition of absolutely anything!

Cat purring on my knee, making it difficult to write!

Best of wishes,

Barbara

27 August. Tullia Blundo the Italian girl who is writing a thesis on my novels came. She is a small dark Sicilian (living in Pisa) wearing mauve-tinted glasses – lively and interested in everything. Her word is 'tremendous'.

4 September. Kew. Staying with Bob. Getting off the bus we walked past Sanders the Funeral Directors – a notice 'Driver Wanted'. Church of St John the Divine – as we were going in a young man in black jacket and crash helmet who turned out to be the MC. Rather trendy clergy and American or Canadian curate preached.

To Philip Larkin   Barn Cottage

Publication Day + 1 (16.9.77)

Dear Philip,

Just a line to thank you for the *wonderful* publication day card, which arrived on the dot yesterday morning. Now I know what those enormous cards are really for! What impressed Hilary was your skill in portraying the vanquished Maschler (a hidden talent?).

I had a marvellous day – lovely weather and plenty of drink and even a telegram from James Wright in Macmillan. And of course the day before, articles in *Times* and *Guardian* by those clever young women. Caroline Moorehead told me how hard it was to find writers to write about these days so perhaps I have been a godsend to somebody! Actually the *Guardian* article is even better, I think. And surely those photographs show that slightly mad jolly fun face (that I don't much like)? Two good reviews so far.

I have been making plum jam and shall soon make (green) tomato chutney, though a few of the latter have started to ripen. [She was stirring and consequently 'distant', when James Wright rang to congratulate her on *The Times* and *Guardian* articles.] And blackberries in the hedgerows of course. Season of M. and M. etc.

All good wishes,

Barbara

26 September. Met the Grottanellis for lunch at the Randolph on an unnaturally warm September day. The Italian who shops in London for long woollen underpants, doesn't care for children so won't see his grandchild. Tells me of his old father who died recently in his 90s. All right to have a mistress in your 40s but *not* in your 80s. The great house and estate in Tuscany now fallen into decay.

29 September. Leapt into a taxi at Paddington and drove on a bright morning (St Michael and All Angels) to the *Daily Express* building where Will Wyatt and the photographer were waiting [to do the London sequences for the television film]. Walked in Fleet St and Fetter Lane past the grey office building that stands on the site of St Dunstan's Chambers. Sat in Oodles, where we drank coffee, looked in the windows of the Protestant Truth Society, stood by the drinking fountain at St Dunstan's, was photographed in the bus queue. Then Will and I had lunch in a pub in Essex St and from the window I could see the Macmillan building. Then bus to Trafalgar Sq (7p) and underground to Paddington (35p).

1 October. We took two sisters from the village to visit their other sister 'terminally' ill in the Churchill. Driving in the car, the smell of poverty. They are still that old-fashioned category 'the poor', harking back to the old days when they were in service at a North Oxford vicarage and things were so much better. Not for them the glories and advantages of the welfare state. Looking at one of them with her hairy chin and general air of greyness one couldn't help thinking that this was as much a woman as a glamorous perfumed model.

8 October. She knew that she dared not pray for humility, to be granted the grace of humility, it being such a precious thing, but when others were decorating the church for Harvest Festival she chose a humble, even humiliating task, emptying the cat's tray, bundling the soiled Katlitta into a newspaper. Yet had she even chosen it – it was just something that had to be done. Whatever thy hand findeth to do, do it with all thy might.

306

To Bob Smith in Venice   Barn Cottage
                                            9 October 1977

Dearest Bob,

Things go well, still, with more good reviews of *Quartet*. The only less favourable ones have been in the *Sunday Telegraph* – not bad but the woman obviously didn't like BP type novels – and the *New Statesman* – again not bad, but the reviewer thought my novels must have had mainly Oxbridge readers (and what's wrong with *that* as Philip Larkin said to me when we were having lunch in Oxford some days ago). *TLS* has been very favourable, also (surprisingly) *Financial Times*. And a very nice thing – I had a letter from the Editor of the *Church Times* saying that although they didn't now normally have space for novel reviews he was going to review mine in November (the new one and the reprints) if only because I had given so many splendid free commercials for the *Church Times*.

I have had quite a lot of letters from various people, including several from people who say they have always liked my novels and thought I was dead! A very nice, generous letter from Jock in Athens, who thinks *Quartet* very fine, even if 'darker' than my others.

Hilary and I went to see Beatrice Wyatt, former Secretary of the I.A.I. We talked of the old days at the I.A.I. but she had obviously forgotten my connection with it so one couldn't have much coherent conversation. Really one feels that poor Marcia in *Quartet* was the best off, seeing Mr Strong smile at her in her last moments. Luckily one doesn't brood too much about one's declining years, being blessed with an optimistic temperament and realising that there is nothing you can do about it. Also I have faith that I would somehow be sustained – I felt that very much when I was in hospital and couldn't read or write properly.

Oh dear, I hadn't meant to write all this – that is the worst of doing it on a typewriter. I should never dare to write about *really* old people, only those in their sixties, and my next is ('hopefully') going to be about village life in the 1970s. I had already started it when all this excitement of publication and endless letter-writing came upon me. But now it seems to be changing course. 'Do you find that the characters, etc? ...'

I have already had proofs of *The Sweet Dove Died* (from the Keats quotation) which should come out in March or April next year. It is totally different from *Quartet* and there are no clergy in it, so goodness knows what people will think of it. Yet it is a chunk of my life, in a sense!

Love,

                                            Barbara

Letty and Marjorie could come to live in the village [in *A Few Green Leaves*] Marjorie not wishing to live in the village where she had been jilted and having sold her cottage nearer London for a vast sum.

The novel could begin with the woman coming to the village and her first social occasion, as it were a set piece. And what more suitable or more full of set pieces than a flower festival in the church.

Setpieces – a series of them. Why not? Write them first then weave a plot round them.

21 October. My BBC 2 programme. Quite pleasing and not too embarrassing. Finstock looked better than it really does in various shots.

22 October. To Paul Binding's. Iris Murdoch and John Bayley called in for a drink. She is much smaller than I had imagined. Fairish short hair, a rather dumpy woman wearing trousers and a sort of ethnic tunic. Very nice face and pleasant to talk to. Told me she had to write things many times over – nothing comes out absolutely first time. John Bayley is just as I had imagined. Very pleasant and, of course, knowing what he feels about my books made him even nicer to talk to.

In church thinking of Heaven. There seated on one side of the Almighty would be her headmistress, eyes gleaming (but kindly) behind her pince nez.

27 October. Went to lunch with Henry at Willersey. Beautiful day and drive. In front of us two women driving, pensioners no doubt, saying how nice it is to be driving in the Cotswolds on a Wednesday *morning*. Lunch with Henry in his nice cottage. Three pensioners.

28 October. James had rung to say that *Quartet* is on the Booker shortlist. Caroline Blackwood, Paul Bailey, Jennifer Johnston, Penelope Lively, BP and Paul Scott.

1 November. Went to London with Poopa to have lunch with Will Wyatt at the TV Centre in Wood Lane. A beautiful glittering palace, all glass windows and long shining corridors – almost like a hospital. Saw the film again then lunch, joined by Robert Robinson who is most pleasant. Bottles of wine and the bright glass walled room and a bird getting in (which they apparently often do). Afterwards a taxi (paid for by the BBC!) took us to Oxford Circus where we surged round John Lewis. Cup of tea and scone in the Tournament Bar at Paddington, all squashed up in wooden booths. What you think is a mirror turns out to be another person sitting beside you. A real *Norman* [*Quartet*] place.

2 November. It is All Souls and I think of the people who have died – Links, Dor, Ack, Nellie, other aunts and uncles, Rupert Gleadow, Gordon Glover, Elizabeth Taylor, etc.

4 November. A power cut for about 2½ hours, 6.30–9 p.m. Supper was gin and tonic and boiled eggs and toast done on the fire. The old cope better than the young on these occasions, especially in a village.

To Philip Larkin   Barn Cottage

9 November 1977

Dear Philip.

Many thanks for your letter. Don't apologise for not writing sooner – you have far more reason not to write than I have, in my retirement, when you are in the full flower of your active Librarianhood. I hope you have managed to 'do' Marvell by now – you really are having a year, beginning with having to write about me in the *TLS*. Not to mention Booker!

I have had my invitation to the dinner though I haven't accepted yet, but I expect I shall go – a once-in-a-lifetime opportunity to mingle in the Literary World, perhaps even to catch a glimpse of Maschler! I imagine you will be there? Anyway, Booker (Ballroom entrance, you note), here we come! Poor Paul Scott – one hears he is seriously ill. I hope he wins. Then Paul Bailey. Then B. Pym. I don't know enough about the other women to pass judgement, but I'm not antifeminist.

Talking of Bailey – we met John Bayley and Iris at drinks with a young friend some weeks ago. I thought they were extremely nice and we had some agreeable conversation, enlivened by John suddenly dropping his glass which seemed to go off with a loud explosion and there we were all scrabbling on the floor picking up bits of glass! Iris was much smaller than I had imagined – I'd always thought of her as tall, but I seemed to tower above her (though only in height, of course).

I didn't hear all of *Jill* but the bits I did hear seemed funny and moving and I really could hardly bear the attempts to cut thin bread and butter and in the end her not coming to the tea party. I hope this never happened to you – well, perhaps the bread and butter part did.

So glad you saw the TV programme and didn't think it too bad. Hilary and I were invited to see it again and have lunch with the Producer and R. Robinson and others at the TV Centre last week! It was a bright day and all that glittering glass seemed like a temple of Mammon or the House of Pride, which I suppose it is in a way. They are all so nice though and I was presented with a book containing all the photographs etc. There have been various repercussions in the form of letters from people who haven't seen me for 30, 40 or (in one case) even 50 years. 'Yes, I am that Barbara Pym....' I let them go through our photograph albums because I like seeing things like that myself, but one friend who saw the programme didn't like that aspect of it so you can't win. Looking at those early photographs makes one wonder about the pattern of life and what the point of it all is – but luckily one doesn't brood about it over much.

Quartet in A. has been accepted in Sweden! My ambition would be to have Liv Ullmann read it on the equivalent of Swedish *Woman's Hour*! I think it might appeal to the Scandinavians. James Wright told me they are reprinting but what that means in sales figures I'm not sure as they probably wouldn't print more than 3,000 to start with? Like Blackwell's being 'sold out' (of 3 copies!!). Anyway I am so happy just to be in print again that nothing else matters.

Yours ever,

Barbara

Remembrance Sunday
Romans 8:35-39

Firemen on strike. 'They didn't want people to die' said a firemen's spokesman and the public have 'avoided a fire situation'.
Success: cooking in sunflower oil a dry, unripe avocado.

18 November. Thoroughly cleaned sitting room, washed kitchen floor, did stairs with Hoover (flea preventative). Made scones. James W. rang up to say that an American publisher (Dutton) had taken *Quartet*. 'Only' 5,000 dollars! Henry rang.

23 November. Booker Prize. James and Alan drove me to Claridge's. Very spacious inside, white and gold and a roaring coal fire in a sort of hall. In the ballroom a group had already assembled. I had a gin and tonic and was introduced to Lettice Cooper, Penelope Lively and her husband, various literary editors etc. and Tom Maschler. Francis King was sitting opposite when we arranged ourselves for dinner. I was next to Ion Trewin (Literary Editor of *The Times*). Philip spoke on what they had looked for in the novels. Could I read it? Did I believe it? Did it move me? Then he mentioned two of the near misses, mine and Caroline Blackwood's, before coming to the winner, Paul Scott. His daughter Carol received it and made a short speech, then each of the runners up went up to receive a leather bound copy of their book. P. Bailey – not there. C. Blackwood – greyish, rather too-long hair, 2-colour long-sleeved dress. Jennifer Johnston – blonde, longish hair, dark-rimmed glasses, black dress. Penelope Lively – rather tall, glasses, flowered long sleeved dress. BP in her 65th year. Tall, short hair, long black pleated skirt, black blouse, Indian with painted flowers (C & A £4.90) and green beads.

To Philip Larkin   Barn Cottage

24 November 1977

Dear Philip,

What a marvellous evening it was – I did so enjoy it. Words are beginning to fail me ... but you must know what a real deep pleasure the whole thing was – even to the meeting with Tom Maschler! (charming, of course). I thought your speech was splendid.

Alan talks of more reprints, perhaps he and 'Tom' can fight it out between them! Dutton in U.S.A. have taken *Q. in A.*

It was fascinating to me seeing the other short-listed authors – Penelope Lively seems to live not so very far from us – I now want to read her book. Also Caroline Blackwood's. Hilary bought Paul Scott's before she left for India and read and much enjoyed it, so I am looking forward to reading it myself.

Don't bother to answer this – I don't expect or wish it. It's only just a heartfelt expression of thanks from the most over-estimated novelist of 1977.

Barbara

25 November. Took a condolence card to the Miss Hutts, popped it through their letter box and ran away. Bought two in Woodstock. The kind of thing you would always have by you.

30 December. Young Chinese American Ping Dai called after tea. Wanted assistance with 'creative writing', being disappointed in the facilities offered him at Oxford – St Clare's Hall. This would make a short story for him – calling round West Oxford villages on a dank December evening in search of novelists.

1978

'Winter Break' with Henry to Ross-on-Wye. Drove to Cheltenham where we had a drink at the Pump Room – salty, healthy-tasting water. Huge deserted ladies cloakroom – except for a lady traffic warden – one could imagine scenes from the past. Drank coffee and cream in a nice trendy café. Then to Deerhurst and visited Odda's Chapel where a beautiful black and white cat rolled and accompanied us. In this area one sees mistletoe and black and white houses. Then to the forest of Dean where we had a pub lunch at the Speech House Hotel and walked in the forest. Arrived at Ross about 3.30. Henry made tea in his room – then a walk. Piped music everywhere and at dinner 'Ain't Misbehavin' in a bouncy electronic way (Emma would know the tune – Graham wouldn't).

To Philip Larkin   Barn Cottage

29 January 1978

Dear Philip,

I regret that I didn't see a *TLS* with the death poem – will I have to wait till another collected poems? Perhaps one ought to have the *TLS* regularly, 1977 having been such a good year. If you have a copy of the poem I'd love to have it. (Can one ask for such things, a poem taking a bit less paper than a novel?)

Since I last wrote I've been busy coping on my own here, with Hilary in India but expected back next week. People have been very kind to me and I had a lot of invitations for Christmas and hardly needed to cook at all. I haven't done as much writing as I'd hoped (of course) but a little and have been asked to do a talk in a radio series on 'The Novelist's Voice', how I found my voice as a novelist etc. so I've been trying to write that and will be going to record it in February.

I have had some correspondence with Maschler ('Dear Tom' now) about reissuing the other books which he intends to do. And if he doesn't Macmillan will! I had the proofs of *The Sweet Dove Died* some time ago, apparently done in India but rather fewer mistakes than the proofs of *Quartet*! I think it will be published in April. I wonder what people will think of it – so many people have not liked *Quartet* as much as my earlier books. Not reviewers, but friends and people who have written to me. But I have to point out that I wrote it entirely for my own satisfaction with (at that time) very little hope of publication!

Later

I started this letter in the morning, then broke off to get lunch and now how nice it was to hear *you* talking about the photocopying business on the radio, over my rice pudding. I used to spend happy minutes in the office copying letters in the old innocent days when the thing was first invented (early sixties?). That wonderful light that used to glow, quite inspirational.

This weekend, cold and sleety, has been busy with the Local History Society Jumble Sale at which I assisted. Then on Tuesday we have the collection of clothes for Help the Aged, at which I shall also assist. Then cleaning the cottage to prepare for Hilary's return! I've just made marmalade, quite successfully – the lure of the Seville Orange is not be resisted, and you can cut them up while watching the telly.

All the very best wishes,
Yours ever,

Barbara

To Bob Smith in Ibadan   Barn Cottage

10 February 1978

Dearest Bob,

The Sweet Dove will be published late April or early May (*Some Tame Gazelle* was published 1st May 1950). I expect people will find the *SD* totally different from *Quartet* and I daresay it will not be liked, but you can't win, really, because quite a lot of people don't like *Quartet at all* because it isn't light and funny like some of my earlier ones. But the whole thing makes one wonder about the 'literary scene'! Are there not other good writers in the wilderness who deserve the sort of treatment I'm now getting?

Much love,

Barbara

To Philip Larkin   Barn Cottage

5 March 1978

Dear Philip,

Thank you so much for sending the poem which fits very well into the blank page at the end of *High Windows*. I have read it many times, with, I was going to say, increasing pleasure and enjoyment – words which may seem inappropriate but that's the feeling it gives me. I know it will be among the ones I like best – 'Faith Healing',

'Ambulances', 'The Building' and of course 'Jake Balokowsky'. But when I wake in the small hours I don't think of death, I always try to switch my thoughts to something frivolous like clothes or planning a scene in a novel. And it's not so much death that would worry me as an incapacitating illness or something like that.... And as of now, as they say, I can worry about a talk I am going to give to the Romantic Novelists' Association on Wednesday next! Still, I'm sure they'll be friendly and at least they're all novelists, and I've been reading their works for the past four years.

Talking of 'Jake Balokowsky' reminds me that I have had a letter from Rota, the antiquarian bookseller, acting on behalf of an American University (he doesn't say which) wanting to buy some or any of my manuscripts or typescripts of my immortal novels! This immediately reminded me of a correspondence (or was it an article?) from you in *The Author* some years ago about this sort of thing but I don't think I've still got it. Ought one to bequeath one's MSS to some English University (much to their dismay)? I imagine you must always be having requests for the scraps of paper you keep by your bed to write down things. What do you do about it?

It was so sad to learn that Paul Scott did die – I had hoped he wasn't so ill after all. I had just finished reading *Staying On* which made me weep as well as laugh a lot. It must have been far and away the best of the six! Now I'm reading Penelope Lively's which is most enjoyable and *readable*.

Occasionally I dip into *Quartet in Autumn* – open a page at random and marvel about the whole thing! James Wright tells me that they have reprinted it again, so that's twice, and Blackwell's now have a respectable number of copies! *The SDD* comes out end of May. You will of course be getting a copy when it appears. Which brings me to comment on your economy drive! At least you need not buy *books*. I don't think one needs to buy much in the way of clothes either, though perhaps women ought to. Yet it isn't done to wear furs now which in my youth I always longed for. But Earl Grey tea has gone *down* from 46p to 44p a quarter! Drink one needs, but luckily I don't like whisky and am just a small steady drinker of wine and sherry with the occasional gin. But *you* of course seem to go to so many functions – your letter was full of a variety of social occasions and when you mentioned having to chair a lecture by William Empson I was taken back to 1943–4 in the Wrens in Naples where I used to ponder over that poem of his which begins 'Not locus if you will but envelope'...with whom did I ponder? Can't remember now!

Did you see my piece in *The Times*? – Caroline Moorehead asked me to do whatever I felt like so I produced a half-joke half-serious defence of the poor novel. I was very pleased to be published *there.*I've also done a radio talk in the *Finding a Voice* series which Beryl Bainbridge started last week. Mine comes on 4th April. I rather dread hearing it as I don't like my voice but maybe I'll get used to it. Such is 'Fame', as you must know!

Yes, I did see the *Book Programme* about Susan Hill having given up novel writing. Exactly how one often feels oneself don't you think!

All good wishes,
Yours ever,

Barbara

Barn Cottage

16 March 1978

Dear Philip,

Yesterday I went into the garage and delved in the packing case or tea chest, where the MS remains of Miss Pym are deposited and I came up with what you see on the attached list! I suppose 'draft' is more appropriate than 'version' but the way I wrote, and still do, was to work straight on to a typewriter with a hand written draft or a few notes or even nothing. If whole chapters exist in handwriting it is because I didn't have a typewriter available at the time, was away or ill in bed (the first version of *Quartet* was written in bed with my breakfast in Balcombe Street – 1973-4).

(Do *you* have the MSS drafts of *A Girl in Winter* and *Jill?*)

Of course with moving at various times I have destroyed a lot that I might otherwise have kept, though I still have a lot of unpublished stuff, novels and short stories. Perhaps the prize is my first novel written in 1929! [*Young Men in Fancy Dress,* unpublished] But I haven't included these on the list. When I am gone, perhaps? What I personally value most are nearly 40 small notebooks (of a size to go in the handbag) in which I have since 1948 or thereabouts kept a kind of diary, not only of events and emotions but also of bits and ideas for novels. But these I couldn't let go, while still alive!

I had written a noncommittal letter to Rota when I wrote to you, saying I would look and see if I had anything suitable though I hadn't kept much. I honestly don't care about the *money* – after all it would be money for nothing as it were – and wouldn't like any of my MS handwritten material to go to USA to be pored over by earnest Americans (not even Jake Balokowsky). I wouldn't mind letting them have a typescript but perhaps they would want more than that, though Rota did say typescript, and even proof copies; but proof copies I have mostly given away. Anyway since the Americans never published any of my novels (except *Less Than Angels* which sold 1 copy a year till Cape got the rights back!) their Eng. Lit. students might not be all that interested. Now of course Dutton has taken *Quartet* and also *Excellent Women,* but even so....

As you see, my remains are by no means complete, and if there was any chance of a British Library or University being interested I would gladly leave the whole lot to them, even without getting money. I suppose Rota acts mainly for USA (Texas or others?). I would really like to have something at Amherst, where a very nice American anthropologist I knew told me that certain 'pornographic' type books were kept in what was known as 'The Treasure Room' in the Amherst library. Surely New England for me, if anything?

The post brought a letter from my publisher to say that *Woman's Hour* is to do a serial reading of *Quartet*! Rather unsuitable I would have thought, but a lot depends on the adaptation. Perhaps they will leave out the exact nature of Marcia's operation ('major surgery' would be enough), otherwise listeners will think me horribly unfeeling and lacking in sympathy, hardly realising that I know all about hospitals and operations from practical experience!

With best wishes and renewed thanks,
    Yours ever,

Barbara

18 February. Long walk through churchyard and woodland paths and by fields full of frozen cabbages. (Graham and Emma. He just wanted someone to bully and criticise when they were together. In small domestic matters at first).

26 February. People have now become familiar with the words and liturgy of the burial service through hearing them so often in TV plays. 'For as much as it has pleased almighty God....'

To Philip Larkin   Barn Cottage

6 April 1978

Dear Philip,

Thank you very much for your most helpful letter, suggesting all the things I might do with my remains. I have decided, for the moment, on 1. (Do nothing). After all it had not occurred to me to do *anything* until Rota suggested it and now that I realise what the possibilities are I can consider things more carefully. So I wrote to

Rota to this effect and haven't heard anything more. And now my literary remains are all in a large cardboard box in my bedroom – more like a novel by J.I.M. Stewart than *The Aspern Papers*! As well as your letter, other things have inspired me to hang on to my MSS for the moment – one was going to an exhibition of Oxford writers in the Bodleian (a copy of *Jill* corrected for the re-issue among them), and another was reading a book about L.V. Woolf and seeing that various papers of his illustrated were stamped 'University of Sussex'.

You say you will be in Oxford 19th–20th April – is that by any chance for the Rawlinson dinner at St John's on the 19th? Because if it is, we may catch a glimpse of each other ('across a crowded room', of course) as I have been invited to this as a guest by an anthropologist I used to know in London who is now in Oxford (Edwin Ardener). I thought I had better warn you, though in a novel one would prefer the man to be taken by surprise and even dismayed!

This letter seems to be full of coincidental meetings and possibilities for turns of plot, which sound improbable, so I had better turn to Finstock news. Uproar at the annual church meeting, mostly over finance. The trouble is that the village of Ramsden (we share a vicar) does better than we do, but then they have more wealthy residents. I think if I had my time over again I would keep aloof from all this and, as it is, I never say much.

The S.D.D. comes out in June, I'm told. Prepublication sales have been quite good and Cape are reissuing *STG* and *Less Than Angels*. I don't think I shall ever be liable for VAT but I have bought a new account book (as advised in the last no. of *The Author* – I expect sales have shot up!). But the main thing is to feel that I am now regarded as a novelist, a good feeling after all those years of 'This is well written, *but....*'

Yours ever,

Barbara

7 April. Friday. Nasty turn (faint, heart attack, stroke) in Abingdon on our way out to lunch [with Hilary]. Came to to find myself in the hospital there – then taken by ambulance to the Radcliffe. Conscious by now. Doctors all round me but no food all day. Next day Prof. Sleight and his boys came round. Home after lunch. On Tuesday went to the Radcliffe again and had an ambulatory electro-cardiogram attached to me for 24 hours. Took it off and returned it on Wednesday but have heard nothing. Am taking it easy and have written nothing for over a week.

28 April. To Dr S. He told me about a pacemaker that could be fitted to the heart but which must be removed at death as it is liable to explode in the crematorium. (He said I could use it in a book.)

13 June. I wrote all morning but feel depressed about it. The copies of *The Sweet Dove* have come. Marvellous bits on the back – what the critics said about *Quartet.* Can one ever do it again? Or even if one does will the critics allow it?

6 July. Sweet Dove published at last. Marvellous press – *Times, Guardian, Telegraph, Financial Times.* In the evening we drank a bottle of Castilio la Torre (Spanish champagne!).

14 July. On the way back from Malvern [to visit Muriel Maby] we stopped at Willersey for dinner with Henry and the Barnicots. Forty years and more I have known them, I thought as we sat there talking.

19 July. Went to London to record *Desert Island Discs* [for BBC Radio 4] with Roy Plomley. Lunch (cold salmon) with him at the Lansdown Club. A vast spacious room. Then listened to records, a cup of tea, then did recording. Ate with Poopa in the Viking Bar at Paddington Hotel and back on the 8.15 train. Relief to be home and in the country again.

To Philip Larkin   Barn Cottage

                                                    27 July 1978

Dear Philip,

I don't seem to have thanked you properly for your nice letter (of 17th June!) in which you sent me the valuable and interesting Sycamore Broadsheet with the early Larkin 'Femmes Damnées'. A fascinating curiosity. I was a bit reminded of the work of Arthur Symons. I shall treasure it. Which reminds me, I have chosen you reading one of your poems ['An Arundel Tomb'] for my *Desert Island Discs* which is going out this Saturday (29th)! The other discs (records, I call them) are mostly rather romantic music, and the book Henry James *The Golden Bowl* (which I have already stumbled through once). I went to London last week for the day to record it – Roy Plomley is so nice and easy to get on with, I found, didn't you? It must be a kind of silly season for the programme if they are having a *novelist!*

Thank you so much for the kind things you said about *The Sweet Dove*. It has been gratifyingly well received, enough balm to soothe and heal all those wounds when only you and a few kind friends thought anything of my works. Francis King has written beautifully in *Books and Bookmen*. It's interesting that some people definitely like *SDD* better than *Quartet* – Francis King, notably. But Lord David and Robert Liddell prefer *Quartet* and the earlier ones. My next, if it ever gets finished, will probably be a let down for everyone – a dull village novel, with no bi- or homo-sexuality.

I have recently met, or rather he has visited us, Fr Gerard Irvine who seems to know Charles Monteith (and indeed everyone worth knowing!) – perhaps you know him too? Very amusing, talks nonstop and has invited me to sample the hospitality of the Clergy House when I'm next in London. That might be worth trying! He has complimented me on my accuracy in church matters in my novels.

I hope your various troubles have sorted themselves out – the sofa, immersion heater, the bookcase, the car.... Today we see that a huge branch has blown down off the elderberry tree in the back (the branch where we hang one end of the clothes line) so that has to be dealt with. A great deal of jam has been made, strawberry and raspberry – jam-making seems to be associated with the publication of novels.

Must stop and go to the hairdresser (in the village) but *shan't* have that fashionable frizzy style that the young seem to be adopting.

Yours ever,

Barbara

23 September. Hooray! *The Sweet Dove* is no. 3 in the *Sunday Times* Best Sellers List. Whatever the significance (or lack of it) it's nice to see it in print.

17–19 August. Spent at Willersey staying with Henry. Elsie [Henry's first wife] was there too. Strange situation dating back over 40 years. A long walk up the hill in lovely country. Three elderly people walking – not together but in a long line separately, Elsie stopping to pick flowers.

The things people say:
I never read novels
I never watch television
I never eat jam
I never have tea

To Philip Larkin   Barn Cottage

20 October 1978

Dear Philip,

I suppose you are back at 'work' now. Yesterday at the dentist, the young dentist asked me 'Are you working today?' – for a moment I couldn't think what he meant, then my thoughts went back to how I used to arrange my dental appointments in those old days – not a *whole* day off, unless you were having a tooth out, but you could wangle most of the afternoon for a simpler operation and perhaps tea afterwards in Wigmore Street.

I was amused by the cutting of the Larkin–Pym engagement ['Mr R.G. Larkin to Miss E.A. Pym']. No relation of mine either, as far as I know. Do you think we'll get an invitation to the wedding? (Comforting to know that young people *do* still announce their engagement in this formal way, isn't it.)

I was also highly amused by your description of being installed as a C.Lit. Had the Duke written the speech himself, and did all those ladies know who Satchmo was? You once gave me a card to go and hear Elizabeth Bowen talking there. And now, as I may have told you on my postcard, even I have been made a Fellow. I always used to envy novelists who were, little thinking that I should ever achieve it. I don't know when I shall be able to go and sign the book or whatever one does. Robert Liddell told me he had never been (as he is in Athens, anyway) but they didn't seem to mind.

You have been a good deal in my thoughts lately as two people here have had to 'do' you for their Open University Exams! So I have been lending volumes of Larkin and adding a few discreet reminiscences. I don't know whether the fact that you have actually been in this cottage adds to one's ability to interpret the more obscure poems. But I have been very cautious. Who can say what anyone, let alone a poet, *might* have meant when he wrote that particular line?

Since I last wrote I've been to another 'feast', this time at Univ. The Feast of St Simon and St Jude, though that day doesn't really come till 28th Oct. I suppose they have to have it before term starts. It was all most enjoyable, not only because Harold Wilson and Stephen Spender were among the other guests. I didn't get to speak to them, only glimpsed them in the distance. I had said I would like to stay the night in college and, remembering what you had told me about it, didn't know what to expect, but I and another female guest were to stay with the master, Lord Goodman. So it was all very comfortable, almost excessively warm as the central heating was on!

Lots of bedside lamps and a bottle of Malvern water by the bed. Breakfast next morning with the Master and Mrs Brigstocke (High Mistress of St Paul's, but young and attractive as they seem to be nowadays). Luckily I was able to face bacon and eggs and a certain amount of civilised conversation. Lord G's solicitor's offices are in the same building as Macmillans which gives us a curious unexpected link. Afterwards Mrs Brigstocke drove me to the station in her *Daimler* – an elegant woman in a beautiful car. All the same I had hoped I would sample the kind of rude undergraduate accommodation I'd heard about and perhaps even meet Harold Wilson at breakfast. (Could one have stood that?)

Well, that seems to finish this letter on a rather misleading social note. Life otherwise goes on as usual. I have been invited by the editor of *The Church Times* to write them a story. I wonder if I can!

Best of wishes,

Yours,

Barbara

To Bob Smith in Ibadan   Barn Cottage

25 October 1978

Dearest Bob,

Of course Richard *did* write when he had read the book [*The Sweet Dove*] – the card was only to say it had arrived and I've also had an affectionate card from him from Indonesia, of all places. What did he say about the book? Well, rather wisely he didn't make much comment except to say how much he had enjoyed it. It was all such a long time ago anyway....Little did I think that anything as profitable as this novel would come out of it.

I am struggling to write another novel but nothing good seems to come from me at the moment and having been so successful with the last two I am a bit apprehensive about the next one. Yet who really cares! I really think all those years of not being published have made me as hard as teak, or whatever is a hard wood. I wrote my little piece in the *New Review* symposium – if you haven't seen it I can tell you briefly that I said I had been too much occupied in trying to get published again to reflect overmuch on 'the state of the novel' during the last ten years or so! There is one misprint or rather word left out in what I wrote which makes it appear that I regard romantic and historical novels as the most prestigious kind!

I have been made a FRSL [Fellow of the Royal Society of Literature], rather to my surprise and pleasure. I never thought I should make it. I haven't yet been able to go up and sign the book (and have my hand held by the president at my inauguration) but I *have* paid my subscription and that surely must be the main point. Robert is one and Elizabeth Taylor was – it's interesting to study the list. Philip Larkin is a Companion of Lit. of which there are only 10 at one time.

Much love,

Barbara

9 November. Haven't written in this notebook for ages, not since I was asked to write a short story for *The Church Times.* Today Iain Finlayson came to interview me for *Cosmopolitan* – a discussion of Cyril Connolly's *Enemies of Promise* and what the enemies of promise are now. I had to point out that sloth and sex are less potent temptations for a writer in her sixties than for a younger writer.

18 November. Rather chaotic Bring and Buy coffee morning in aid of the CPRE. Held at Mrs C's house. It is surely better, one feels, not to see how one's doctor lives, to discover the secrets of his life, that he has fine Waterford glass and exquisite Persian rugs.

8 January 1979. Went to Dr S. to consult him about my increasing bulk, which seems unnatural. He did tests and told me several things it might be. Naturally I seized on the most gloomy (if it would be gloomy to die at 66 or 67?). He gave me a letter to Mr Webster, a consultant surgeon in Oxford. I went to 23 Banbury Rd where the consultants live. Mr Webster thinks it is fluid in my abdomen (dropsy, but he had a grander name for it) and thinks I should go into the Churchill, perhaps next week. Great relief at getting all this over, even euphoric, though no doubt unjustified.

13 January. In the Churchill. Lunchtime – purple jelly with a dab of synthetic cream and 'All right dear?'

An Indian gentleman sitting at the bedside across the way stretches out his long fingers and takes a grape.

Opposite two women wait for their operations. Almost like Henry Moore figures.

The analysis of the fluid from my abdomen shows that there is something (malignant) though the X-rays didn't indicate what. It could be something in the ovaries or secondaries from the breast cancer – which could be treated either by an operation or drugs or radiotherapy.

Immoderate laughter of the evening visitors.

A thought. We pray at Finstock church for Mr Cashman – is this because, strictly speaking, he lives in Finstock – or do we pray for Ramsden people when they're sick or vice versa.

In hospital one has to fight very hard to keep one's independence and most of the time it isn't worth it.

How did people die in the old days (not the 19th century but really old days like the 17th century). What did they do about cancer? If I'd been born in 1613 I would have died in 1671 (of breast cancer). I'd certainly have been dead in 1674.

20 January. Mr Webster said it is probably 'an ovarian problem'. He says the drug will work – it is a poison and may make me feel sick. It is a long-drawn-out treatment, may last months – injections every three weeks.

5 February. Home again. Went to see Dr S. Very kind and practical. Asked me to consider now how I wanted my end to be, whether at home, in hospital or hospice, or private nursing home.

14 February. My first visit to the radiotherapy clinic at the Churchill for my second injection. Waited in the dreary Out Patients waiting room with others and only one doctor coping. Waited nearly half an hour in a cubicle, sitting on a bed (shoes off) or lying gazing up at the ceiling. If you think wouldn't it be better if I were just left to die you remember the fluid and how impossible it made things.

In the afternoon I finished my novel in its first, very imperfect draft. May I be spared to retype and revise it, loading every rift with ore!

All humanity is in the Out Patients, those whom we as Christians must love.

4 March. Henry came to lunch and we planned to go to Derbyshire for a 'Winter Break'.

To Bob Smith in Ibadan   Barn Cottage

25 February 1979

Dearest Bob,

I have had to go into hospital (the Churchill) but am happily much better. I developed fluid in my abdomen which is apparently the result of an ovarian tumour, but fortunately they didn't make me have an operation but are treating it with drugs which are supposed to 'kill' it, so that with luck I shall have a few more years of good life. I have to go to the outpatients' radiotherapy clinic every three weeks – a rather dire place, but luckily I manage to get some amusement and 'material' out of hospital visits, as you know. Of course, having had the fashionable breast cancer op. in 1971 I suppose I have been lucky to have had nearly eight years without anything further!

Much love,

Barbara

5 March. Today the vet came and helped Nana [Minerva] out of this life. He took the body away. All very quick – a powerful injection and it was all over in a second. She was slumped in the green metal box he had brought, a little limp bag of bones. She would have been 18 in June.

To Philip Larkin   Barn Cottage
15 March 1979

Dear Philip,

We are both well now, though I had to go into hospital (the Churchill) in January and stayed a week during which time they did various tests and told me I had a malignant tumour somewhere inside, but they are treating it with drugs and seem hopeful of success, whatever that may be! After all, I have lived eight years since my breast cancer operation in 1971 so I suppose you could say that I *have* survived. And now I feel so much better again and don't seem to have any ill effects from the drugs so far. Of course 'they' won't tell you how long you've got – it may be several years yet and as I don't want to live to be very old (what one says in middle age anyway!) it is really not so bad. Hard to know what to tell people really, but what with all these programmes about cancer on TV one feels it's best to be honest. But in some ways you feel a bit foolish, looking and seeming quite well. (What, you *still* here?)

Otherwise some rather good news (if that is bad). Penguin are going to do *Excellent Women* and *A Glass of Blessings*, Cape tell me, though not till next April or thereabouts. This is an enormous pleasure to me. I have had super American reviews for *E. W.* and *Quartet in Autumn* including a long one in the *New Yorker* from John Updike (did you ever read *Couples?*). *The Sweet Dove* comes out there this month. The advance copy has a springlike or greenery yallery cover with a design of doves (Miss Pym, the ornithologist). I daresay the Americans won't like that book, perhaps Leonora could only be credible in England? (I'll send you a copy shortly).

324

But this letter mustn't be only medical and literary. We've had quite a full time in the village with the usual events – Hilary gave a talk to the W.I. on her experiences in India. The church is organising a clothes sale – the history society has its monthly meetings, etc. etc. Our old cat has gone to her rest, assisted by the vet who came here to do it. So very quick, with an injection (I suppose you'd say a 'massive' injection, to use the in-word!). Sad to be without her but she was nearly 18 and had got to be a mere bag of bones and impossible to keep warm except by continual hot water bottles in her basket. But a new little tabby has adopted us and *she* is pregnant, so new life is springing up. If she has a black kitten we may keep it, but after this birth she will have to be 'done'.

The garden still looks terrible but I suppose we must prune the roses soon. A few snowdrops have appeared and Iris Stylosa in the front but I'm reminded of that song we used to sing in the war. 'Spring will be a little late this year!' But I have finished the first draft of another novel, pretty poor so far and it is so strange to have 'my publisher' asking for it and saying he's longing to see it. I fear he will be disappointed, and anyway I can't suddenly turn into the sort of writer who can produce something quickly. Don't you think one gets slower as one gets older – 'stands to reason' as Norman *[Quartet]* might say!

Gilbert Phelps (the other Finstock author) and I have recently been judging entries for the Southern Arts Association Prize – open to people living in Oxfordshire, Hampshire, Isle of Wight etc. We gave the prize to Penelope Lively for her book of short stories [*Nothing Missing but the Samovar*] and we had a little gathering at Chipping Norton to meet her, drank champagne, ate canapés and had 'literary talk'. Do you remember *The Road to Lichfield* her novel for Booker? She went to the dinner this year but said A.J. Ayer wasn't nearly as good as you! She has a nice husband who teaches at Warwick University. I have also been reading some romantic novels, as one of the final judges this time, so only 8 books to read. One all about the mistresses of Louis XIV that I'm learning a lot from – I am so ignorant of French history!

A horrible wintry sleety day! I hope tomorrow is better as a young woman is coming to lunch who is writing a book about Elizabeth Taylor (the novelist, of course). I am to delve back into my memories of the fifties when we sometimes went to PEN together.

Very best wishes,

Barbara

23 March. 'Weekend Break' with Henry in Derbyshire. Large dinner at hotel in Grindlewood Bridge and a bottle of Orvieto. I didn't drink much – no ill effects. Couldn't make the bathwater run or fill my hot water bottle. Good breakfast! Drove to Eyam, the plague village, then to Bakewell. Beautifully situated church, warm and fragrant (but not incense, perhaps furniture polish). Saturday evening was hectic in the hotel, large parties dining, masses of people in the bar and, in the Rutland Lounge, even a private showing of somebody's holiday slides – a group sitting in the darkened room with their coffee and drinks. I fled though Henry would have stayed. Was awakened at midnight by hotel staff asking if it was O.K. for me to be called at 8.30 instead of 7.30 as it was Sunday!

Sunday: on the way back we stopped at Hassop where there is a Catholic church (early 19th century classical style) and Hassop Hall Hotel, formerly the home of the Eyre family – now a rather superior hotel and restaurant. We walked round the front and saw many tables laid for lunch. Inside a very nice hall with a coal fire, silver in a glass-fronted cabinet and fresh flowers. Then as we left cars began to arrive – Derbyshire Catholics to a good Sunday lunch? – quite a stream of them.

Then we tried to find Newstead Abbey and Byron. (Had to find a public loo.) After landing in a street of miners' houses we asked the way and were directed through the colliery. Then on to the motorway and stopped to have tea and sandwiches in a motorway café. A whole new civilisation. 'The cold, dark wine in Derbyshire' [*No Fond Return of Love*] – Henry on Friday demands that the Orvieto shall not be *too* cold.

28 March. Hatchard's Authors of the Year Party. Young man from Hatchard's introduced Hilary and me to Patience Strong (and her agent) first – all in green, small, difficult to talk to because sitting rather low down. Then we went over and spoke to Steve Race, Iris Murdoch (red dress and black stockings) and the Vicar of St James Piccadilly (Rev. W. Baddeley). Then to Olivia Manning who was a bit peeved because her books were not displayed. (One of mine – *Less Than Angels* – was next to Diana Dors' autobiography.) The Hatchard's men came and spoke very kindly and were flattering about my books. We spoke to Jilly Cooper before leaving.

To Philip Larkin   Barn Cottage
                                                          1 April 1979

Dear Philip,

Thank you so much for your letter and sympathetic words –

actually I'm feeling fine at the moment – went to London last week to Hatchard's Authors of the Year Party. Diana Dors was holding court at a large round table, but I did have a word with Iris Murdoch. The Duke of Edinburgh was there but I don't think he reads my books.

No kittens as yet though she is spherical – she herself is a very pretty tabby, greyish, not exactly silver.

This is only a scrappy note to send with the book, not a proper answer to your letter. I am trying to finish and improve a country novel, a new one 'based' on life here (but of course nothing like it, really?). The University one I have done nothing about – I feel it would be out of date now and I hardly know about such life after all this time.

Yours ever,

Barbara

A fine Easter, sunshine and things burgeoning. I live still!

26 April. Romantic Novelists' lunch at the Park Lane Hotel, Piccadilly – a curiously deserted hotel, vast ladies' cloakroom in the basement with marble basins and pink velvet sofas. After, bus to Paddington and had a quiet calm of mind all passion spent tea in the refreshment room on platform 1 before getting the five o'clock train home.

1 May. Typing the new novel slowly – have only done 63 pages. some people may be disappointed in it – others will like it.

To Philip Larkin   Barn Cottage

1 May 1979

Dear Philip,

Just a brief letter to tell you that four lovely kittens were born on 11th April – all Toms! We think we've found homes for all and shall keep one ourselves, a black one. The others are two very prettily marked tabby and white and third is dark smoky grey. They are a great pleasure and interest and we have quite a stream of visitors, especially children, wanting to see them. As a result of the birth, watching them with their mother when they were feeding while still very young, I thought of a splendid title for a novel *Blind Mouths at the Nipple*.

I hadn't really expected you to come last week – in fact I went to London for a day on Wednesday to attend the luncheon of The

327

Romantic Novelists' Association – quite an enjoyable occasion – at the Park Lane Hotel in Piccadilly. It didn't seem the kind of hotel where you could imagine people *staying* – perhaps it only exists to have 'gatherings' of this kind?

As a result of showing you the American reviews I spent Easter sorting them out and have now stuck them into a book! And I had such a nice letter from the Boston man who wanted my literary remains that I felt almost sorry to have refused him. And I've just had the proofs of the story I did for the *New Yorker* [*Across a Crowded Room*]. *And* a large cheque (for me) from Macmillan and quite a respectable one from Cape. Cape are also going to reprint *Jane and Prudence* and *No Fond Return* now – cordial letter from Maschler. So I wish all neglected novelists could have the good friends and luck that I've had.

Greetings and best wishes,

Barbara

2 May. To the radiotherapy unit at the Churchill. It is Thiotepa, the drug they put into me. Afterwards a large lunch at The Gate of India in Oxford.

10 May. Heard the cuckoo for the first time this year, on a damp May evening, wet and green.

18 May. Summer at last! (What one has stayed alive for?!)

26 May. In the early morning I woke having dreamed of finding a splendid title for a novel (the one about the two women, starting off with their Oxford days) which has been simmering in my mind. The Keats poem:

> In a drear-nighted December
> Too happy, happy tree
> Thy branches ne'er remember
> Their green felicity

2 June. I am now in my 67th year – shall I make 70?

3 June. Went to 11 o'clock Mattins at Spelsbury. Welcomed by the vicar (Irish charm) who invited us to sit anywhere we liked in the empty church. Whit Sunday, but of course they had had their 'family communion' service at 9.30. At the service I felt I could enrich my novel by giving more about Tom's church, which was probably like this one. The enrichment of my own novels may be suggested by my reading of the two latest Margaret Drabble novels

(*The Ice Age* and *The Realms of Gold*). She gives one almost *too* much – but I give too little – laziness and unwillingness to do 'research', which doesn't seem to fit my kind of novels.

16 June. Adam Prince at the end of the holiday – a short section or vignette. He experiences not only a motorway café but a motel (or 'Posthouse') – the impersonality of it all. No human face, no charming elderly ladies crocheting in the lounge, no discussion (even if/albeit ill-informed) about modern art or women priests. Plastic continental breakfast – and *how un*continental such a breakfast was! No '*Buongiorno Signore*' from a smiling young waiter bearing a tray on his shoulder. On the motorway 'Oh Central Reservation', like a line from a hymn.

17 June. Went to Snape – three lovely days. Sat on the beach at Aldeburgh collecting stones and drinking coffee. On the way back called in at the Priory, Horton-cum-Studley, now a hotel. Asked for tea. There was a conference going on; perhaps salesmen from Birmingham. Youngish men, rather too fat. Tea very expensive (£1.40). Chateaubriand Steak on the à la carte menu was £11.50! It would be a good setting for a romance, an unexpected meeting, or a short story about a conference or seminar.

24 June. In this new novel [never written] there will be two women, starting with their college lives (not earlier). One from a privileged background, the other from a more ordinary one (but not working class) and the subsequent course of their lives. This would be a chance to bring in World War II.

The great house where one lives becomes a hotel for conferences etc (like Studley Priory).

A hymn writer in the family or a woman like Charlotte Elliott or Frances Ridley Havergal.

When she comes to stay with her friend she hopes to 'get to know her husband better' – with unexpected results.

Rev. and Hon. or is it Hon. and Rev. A great-uncle. Always this tradition of service in the family.

The nice 'girls lunch' – could a husband or other intrusive man walk in at this time.

Victorian vicar who enlarges a church and puts (perhaps) a spire in memory of his first wife or mother.

An ancestor was a missionary in East Africa. On leave (furlough) he happened to be in Trafalgar Square when the lions were brought there (?1867).

She ought to have some fine old Victorian Christian name –

Maud, Violet, Edith, Ethel, Florence. But, of course the fashion for such names had not come back, though Hannah, Emily, Emma and Harriet were beginning to be in vogue. So what was her name? One of the 30s – Joan, Gillian, Barbara, Mary, Margaret, Edna, Hilda, Nancy, Ruth.

To Philip Larkin   Barn Cottage

2 July 1979

Dear Philip,

I had such a nice letter from the USA asking me to 'lecture', but won't go. It is Carlisle, Pennsylvania, and the man who wrote had got on to my novels because of his interest in *your* work! A nice thought.

Two days of beautiful weather and I'm sitting in the garden. Went to the doctor this morning and all seems well at the moment. He had been on holiday but stayed at home during the time except for a visit to a conference in Liverpool – and he still hasn't got a new car (still K registration). Now, I ask myself, ought I to be worried about him? Perhaps he has heavy family commitments – two girls to educate, I believe. Perhaps I ought to be a private patient.

I went to lunch at St Hilda's on Saturday and had the usual consolation of not looking as old (or as fat) as some of my contemporaries! They were having a Gaudy but I didn't stay for it. I usually have a word with Helen Gardner but didn't manage to this time, though she was there.

The kitten we've kept is called Justin – I'm not quite sure how the name came about – the others were Oscar, Felix and Julius, mostly named by the people who took them.

How interesting about losing your taste for drink! I only lose it when I'm ill or in hospital, but it always comes back – though I don't drink all that much, don't like whisky which is the mark of a *real* drinker.

Shall I be embarrassed if we have lunch together, wondering if you're going to offer me a drink? I'll be prepared – do hope we manage to meet.

All good wishes,
    Yours ever,

Barbara

19 July. A pathetic sight in Waitrose: the elderly woman, very old, leaning against a frozen food cabinet while her friend (also ancient) went round with her basket. And, in the doorway, a clergyman stands, contemplating the scene.

4 August. Mark Gerson came to photograph me – a nice, easy to get on with person. Luckily it took my mind off my poor physical state. Very blown out and feeling disinclined to eat and rather sick. I wore my loose black cotton dress and a red scarf.

5 August. I feel awful on waking but a bit better now sitting in the sun writing this, also trying to finish off my novel. Shall I write more in this notebook?

Perhaps what one fears about dying won't be the actual moment – one hopes – but what you have to go through beforehand – in my case this uncomfortable swollen body and feeling sick and no interest in food or drink.

9 August. Woke up in the Churchill, Ward 7 (Radiotherapy) this time, having had the fluid removed yesterday and so feeling better. It is now 7.10 a.m. Men at one end of the ward and women at the other, but you don't mix except in the dayroom, where I can't go as I'm imprisoned in bed.

29 August. I went to the clinic and they have decided to take me off the thiotepa. Presumably the blood count has shown them something but I don't know what. Has it worked? I asked the doctor but he gave me a somewhat non-committal answer. So I am to come off it for 6 weeks and come back to the clinic again. They have lots of other things they can try, he said. We had lunch at Quills in Oxford in the rather hushed, net curtained atmosphere (the restaurant used to be the Kemp Hall Cafeteria, scotch eggs, etc).

1 October. As I am not feeling well at the moment (more fluid) I find myself reflecting on the mystery of life and death and the way we all pass through this world in a kind of procession. The whole business as inexplicable and mysterious as the John Le Carré TV serial, *Tinker, Tailor, Soldier, Spy*, which we are all finding so baffling.

To Bob Smith in London   Barn Cottage

18 October 1979

Dearest Bob,

I've now heard from the hospital at last – in fact I rang them up to find out something (how useful to have a tongue in one's head). Apparently they are not going to take off any more fluid at this stage but will try some new tablets which I am to get from the doctor. He is coming to see me today as I didn't feel well enough to go to the surgery – my appetite has been even more miserable the last few days and I've been feeling sick, so not getting much nourishment. A few nips of brandy, Lucozade, weak tea, toast – hardly enough to sustain me.

Later. The doctor has just been and cheered me up as he thinks he may be able to give me something to combat the nausea. Also he says that champagne is better than Lucozade.

A simply lovely day here – sun so powerful that I had to draw the curtains in my bedroom. Hazel has brought Tom [her son] to Wadham (I suppose young people are all brought to Oxford by car these days). So he is embarking on what should be the happiest days of his life.

Much love,

Barbara

To Philip Larkin   Barn Cottage
28 October 1979

Dear Philip,

Many thanks for your letter – also a nice postcard in the earlier part of this curious late summer (now, with the clocks back, turning into winter!).

I sent you copies of the reissue of the last two books (*Jane and Prudence* and *No Fond Return*) to the Library and hope they will arrive safely. The whole six really look quite handsome in their bright jackets and looking at them perhaps I can quote St Hilda's motto – *Non frustra vixi* – though I still wonder if any of this would have happened if it hadn't been for you and Lord D. And the dear *TLS*!

I'm afraid I'm writing this in bed as I haven't been well during the last week or two. It is, I fear, the inexorable progress of this 'tumour' I've been having drug therapy for since January. I was very well the earlier part of the year but haven't been so good the last month – now they are trying a new drug. They don't seem to operate these days as they used to. I go to the Churchill regularly and feel I'm getting the best cancer treatment there is. At the moment though I've lost my appetite and don't even like *drink* which is a bore.

I thought I'd keep you up to date with all this as you are such a good friend and I'd want you to know – of course I don't know quite what the future will be – who does, come to that! – and I'm quite cheerful and active in my brain, even if physically weaker. (Better that way round.)

I've finished my country novel except for a few finishing touches, so that is something, even if it isn't all that brilliant. Glad you liked the story [in the *New Yorker*]. I think it was mostly based on St John's – especially the pineapple neatly cut up and the lovely box of crystallised fruits. Univ. could furnish material for 'Breakfast with Lord Goodman', I suppose, but I have no plans for writing that!

It must be a blow losing your deputy, but how distinguished and splendid is her new job – almost like being Mrs Thatcher – perhaps even more so with all the esoteric expertise she will bring to it. Perhaps it will be rather like the bit in my new novel where the rector's sister suddenly goes off – I hope people will rally round. Meals and drinks and other comforts.

Wedding presents. Do brides (if the term is still appropriate?) still present you with a 'list', usually from Harrods or Peter Jones, of presents they would like to receive? I know they used to, a very ungracious custom, I thought. Babies are easier – something silver?

What did you think of *Booker*? Not what it was, except for the money? I read Penelope Fitzgerald's *The Book Shop,* shortlisted in 1978, and liked it but thought she should have given us a bit more – filled it out a bit. I'm not much attracted by her winner this year. I've read a few romantic novels, in the course of duty, and lately much enjoyed Penelope Lively's new one *The Treasures of Time.* I waded through A.S. Byatt's long novel *The Virgin in the Garden* but that was published last year, I think.

No more space – a lovely sunny day, but the windows need cleaning.

Hilary is well, looks after me very well, and sends greetings. And of course all these from me.

Barbara

31 October. In the Churchill hoping for relief from my fluid. Conversation in the bed opposite:
'There's some nice music tonight.'
'I'm not a great lover of music.'
'No – it just passes the time.'
'That's right.'

21 November. Churchill. Ward 7. A cold, raw typical November day, but we got here and I've just eaten a kind of supper – vegetable soup, baked beans and sausage. After the removal of four pints of fluid. The curious mixed or unisex ward is surely Donne's

> Difference of sex no more we know
> Than our guardian angels do.

December 1979. Christmas card to Philip Larkin

WITH BEST WISHES FOR CHRISTMAS AND THE NEW YEAR

(Still struggling on – perhaps a little better!) Another visit to hospital (brief) on 2nd Jan.

Barbara

She died on 11 January 1980

A Publishing History
&
Index/Glossary

A Publishing History

	Written	Hardcover Publication	
		UK	US
Some Tame Gazelle	1935–50	Cape, 1950 Reissued, 1978	Dutton, 1983
Excellent Women	1949–51	Cape, 1952 Reissued, 1978	Dutton, 1978
Jane and Prudence	1950–2	Cape, 1953 Reissued, 1978	Dutton, 1981
Less than Angels	1953–4	Cape, 1955 Reissued, 1978	Dutton, 1980
A Glass of Blessings	1955–6	Cape, 1958 Reissued, 1977	Dutton, 1980
No Fond Return of Love	1957–60	Cape, 1961 Reissued, 1979	Dutton, 1982
An Unsuitable Attachment (Revised for publication by Hazel Holt in 1981)	1960–5	Macmillan, 1982	Dutton, 1982
The Sweet Dove Died (Revised for publication by Barbara Pym in 1977)	1963–9	Macmillan, 1978	Dutton, 1979
Quartet in Autumn	1973–6	Macmillan, 1977	Dutton, 1978
A Few Green Leaves	1977–9	Macmillan, 1980	Dutton, 1980

Index/Glossary